BIRDS TO WATCH

The ICBP World Checklist of Threatened Birds

by
N. J. COLLAR and P. ANDREW
with contributions from
L. P. Gonzaga, R. F. Grimmett,
T. H. Johnson, A. J. Stattersfield
and S. N. Stuart

ICBP Technical Publication No. 8
Smithsonian Institution Press
Washington, D.C.

Copyright © 1988 International Council for Bird Preservation,
32 Cambridge Road, Girton, Cambridge CB3 0PJ, England.
All rights reserved.

Library of Congress Cataloging-in-Publication Data

Collar, Nigel J.
Birds to watch; The ICBP World Checklist of
Threatened Birds
Bibliography: p
Includes index
88-42876
ISBN 0-87474-301-X

Camera-ready text prepared for publication by
Tim Johnson, using facilities provided by
the Nature Conservation Bureau, Thatcham, Berkshire, England.
Printed and bound by Page Bros. (Norwich) Ltd, Norfolk, England.

SMITHSONIAN INSTITUTION

The Smithsonian Institution has long been involved in the protection of wild birds and their habitats. Smithsonian scientists have ranged over the world, from the United States to New Guinea, in their efforts to gather data that have been useful in designing and implementing conservation efforts. The Smithsonian Press has participated in the Institution's larger mission to support "the increase and diffusion of knowledge" by acting as an agent for the dissemination of important research. One aspect of that effort has been our cooperation with the International Council for Bird Preservation. In 1981 we worked with the ICBP to reprint and distribute in North America the *Bird Red Data Book*, a compilation of encapsulated information pertinent to the conservation of threatened species and subspecies of bird the world over. In 1980 we published the American edition of a volume on *The Conservation of New World Parrots*, based on an ICBP symposium. With the publication of the present volume on birds of threatened status we continue our cooperative efforts to bring before the public information on vital conservation issues.

INTERNATIONAL COUNCIL FOR BIRD PRESERVATION

ICBP is the longest-established worldwide conservation organization. It is devoted entirely to the protection of wild birds and their habitats. Founded in 1922, it is a federation of 330 member organizations in 100 countries. These organizations represent a total of over ten million members all over the world.

Central to the successful execution of ICBP's mission is its global network of scientists and conservationists specializing in bird protection. Its ability to gather and disseminate information, identify and enact priority projects, and promote and implement conservation measures is unparalleled. Today, ICBP's Conservation Programme includes some 100 projects throughout the world.

Birds are important indicators of a country's environmental health. ICBP provides expert advice to governments on bird conservation matters, management of nature, and such issues as the control of trade in endangered species. Through interventions to governments on behalf of conservation issues ICBP can mobilize and bring to bear the force of international scientific opinion at the highest levels. Conferences and symposia by its specialist groups also attract worldwide attention to the plight of endangered birds.

Publications include the Bird Red Data Books. ICBP maintains a comprehensive databank concerning the status of all the world's threatened birds and their habitats, and from this the Red Data Book is prepared. The most recent edition, Threatened Birds of Africa, was published in 1985. A series of Technical Publications (of which the present volume is the eighth) gives up-to-date and in-depth treatment to major bird conservation issues.

CONTENTS

FOREWORD

by Christoph Imboden, Director,
International Council for Bird Preservation

In my foreword to *Threatened Birds of Africa*, published by ICBP and IUCN in 1985, I referred to the fact that some conservationists are questioning the concept of the species-orientated Red Data Books which, in their eyes, are giving too much attention to the fate of individual species and diverting us from the task of conserving habitats and ecosystems. However, now as then, I remain convinced that a focus on species - ecosystems are after all assemblages of interdependent species - remains crucial for achieving and promoting conservation. Complex and abstract arguments are not a good means of creating widespread awareness among the public and decision makers; the well-presented plight of an individual flagship species - birds are particularly suitable - are still one of the best ways of concentrating public attention on broader environmental problems.

A rehabilitation of the role of species in the conservation debate might, however, be under way. The conservation of biological (or genetic) diversity has been emerging in the past few years as a top global conservation priority. It is recognised that, in order to maximise our efforts to save biological diversity, we need a much broader knowledge than hitherto about the distribution, abundance and conservation needs of individual species of plants and animals. Many projects have been initiated by national and international organisations all over the world to provide better and more up-to-date information about the status of species.

Birds can make a special contribution to this debate. Despite many gaps in our knowledge about some of the world's 9,000 species they are generally still better researched than any other group of animals and plants and hence offer the best all-round picture. The aim of this book, therefore, is to provide a new global overview of the status of this conspicuous and versatile group of animals.

The result must surely be highly disturbing to everyone. One thousand bird species, over 11% of all species, are to varying degrees at risk from global extinction! Since the destruction, modification and fragmentation of habitats are by far the most common types of threat, there is no reason to assume that other life forms - plants, insects and lower animals - that share the habitats of these threatened birds are any better off. The birds are in fact just the tip of the iceberg, concealing thousands of other species we know nothing or little about, many of them still undiscovered by science, and facing the same fate as the birds. This adds up to a most serious threat to the overall genetic diversity of our globe.

In view of these alarming figures, the task of conservationists seems to grow more daunting all the time. However, for the bird expert and anyone else, the concern should by no means end with these 1,000 threatened species listed here. They are the ones already visibly in danger, emitting a red warning light and calling for fire brigade action to save them and we must also look ahead to identify all those others whose problems are not yet so directly obvious to us: the candidates of tomorrow's Red Data Books. In order to get an even truer picture of the problem at hand we might have to change our approach. Instead of defining criteria that render a species threatened we ought to define which species are 'safe', ie. not decreasing in abundance or with contracting distribution ranges, and likely to remain so in the near future despite further predictable man-induced environmental changes. The species passing this test could be included in a 'green list' of resilient and adaptable species or species inhabiting areas and habitats not significantly affected by man. The green lists' main value for conservation would be for what is does *not* contain. All the species excluded from it are the ones we should worry about. (A global assessment of the world's birds in this manner is unfortunately too ambitious a task at this stage. It would require lots of information about ecological requirements of species and sound predictions about their possible reaction to further environmental changes.)

Looking, for example, at the extent of the threats to the world's tropical lowland forests, with 1,500-2,000 species dependent on it, or at the rate of change in agricultural practices all over the world, rendering these areas less and less favourable for wildlife, I believe the results of such a study could come as an even greater shock than this new checklist of threatened birds. The potentially threatened species could out-number the Red Data Book entries by a factor of three or four. If anything, the conservation problems implicitly summarised in this book are an understatement of the true global situation. The message behind these thousand threatened birds has to be taken extremely seriously, not only by ornithologists and conservationists, but by every responsible citizen of our small earth.

INTRODUCTION

The stimulus for the production of this checklist came at the ICBP World Conference in Kingston, Ontario, Canada, in June 1986. W. B. King, compiler of the second edition of the international bird Red Data Book, observed that the more detailed treatment of species in the current, geographically organized third edition meant that a perceived function of the work, that of rapid transmission of updated information for the benefit and response of the conservation community, was being lost. He made the plea that ICBP should seek to publish an interim volume, regularly updated, summarizing the latest data on the world's threatened birds. This would mean that the world was kept more closely informed of the newest developments, and that the chance to act on behalf of certain species need not be forfeited simply through the delays that detailed species analysis inevitably entails. In his co-authored review (*Auk* 104 [1987]: 586-587) of *Threatened birds of Africa and related islands* (Collar and Stuart 1985), the first of four planned volumes that are to comprise the third edition, this appeal was repeated.

Collar and Stuart (1985: xvi) did, however, make it clear that unpublished information requiring action would not be information left unacted upon; in the past seven years, with the establishment of an international secretariat expressly to promote bird conservation throughout the world, new data on threatened species have repeatedly prompted ICBP projects, interventions and advice (for example, 13 of the 27 ICBP Study Reports published since the series began in 1982 stem from projects identified through the Red Data Book programme). Moreover, the development of our newsletter, *World Birdwatch*, has allowed us to keep the conservation community informed of recent developments with many short news items and a regular "Red Data Bird" column. Neverthless, King's proposal is original and important, and the credit for this book's inception is his.

With only limited resources to finance the evaluation and documentation of species at risk, there is inevitable tension between the urgency imposed by their plight and the responsibility of making the analyses as thorough and hence as truthful as possible. Work on the first edition of the Red Data Book began and was published in loose-leaf form in 1964, and proceeded piecemeal over eight years (Vincent 1964-1971). Work on the second edition was undertaken from around 1974 on a part-time basis, resulting in the publication of two taxonomically non-sequential parts, still in loose-leaf form (King 1978-1979), though subsequently as a book. Recent indications of the incompleteness of this edition (Diamond 1987), resulting in such unwelcome commentary as "the publication of Red Data Books may be guilty of engendering a degree of complacency" *(Kukila* 3 [1988]: 77), imply judgement seriously at variance with one that sees speed of output as a principal value of the work; the two positions strain authorial responsibilities in diametrically opposite directions. *Birds to watch* ought to remove some of the stress.

The introduction to Collar and Stuart (1985) established certain principles which are followed here. Subspecies are excluded from consideration, for reasons of practicality, although specific rank is allowed in certain cases where the status of a form as a species or subspecies is uncertain. Sequence and nomenclature follow Morony *et al*. (1975) plus Bock and Farrand (1980), with exceptions, adjustments and additions: White and Bruce (1986) provide the basis for Wallacea, Pratt *et al*. (1987) for Hawaii and the tropical Pacific, Dickinson *et al*. (in press) for the Philippines, though even here there are points of divergence; at family level, the "List of avian families" in King (1978-1979: Preamble 4) is followed. All statements are attributed to source, in chronological order of publication and alphabetical order of personal communication (either verbal or written, and indicated by initials and name only). Place names conform as much as possible to those in *The Times atlas of the world*, comprehensive (seventh) edition with revisions, 1986 (London: Times Books). Institutions indicated by their initials beyond this point are: AMNH, American Museum of Natural History; BMNH, British Museum of Natural History; CSIRO, Commonwealth Scientific and Industrial Research Organisation (Australia); CVRD, Companhia Vale do Rio Doce (Brazil); IUCN, International Union for Conservation of Nature and Natural Resources; MNRJ, Museo Nacional (Rio de Janeiro); RAOU, Royal Australasian Ornithologists' Union; RSPB, Royal Society for the Protection of Birds; WWF, World Wide Fund for Nature (World Wildlife Fund). We apologise that it has not been possible to introduce accents on the final version of this text.

We have sought to treat species accounts in a standardized manner, but have fount it impractical always to mention the racial variants of the species listed. Readers may find the compulsive repetition of certain things, notably the indication of ownership of well-known islands, a cause of impatience, but the intention is partly to remain entirely even-handed and partly to emphasize where ultimate responsibility lies. We have, however, sought to avoid too pedantic a treatment of Borneo, an island consisting of four geopolitical units and three nations: we have not sought intensively to confirm whether or not a species occurs in Brunei.

We have endeavoured to cover the literature as thoroughly as possible within the time constraints on the project, but will have missed many sources; moreover, we have inevitably needed to select general, summarizing sources of information, even though their authorship and titles may not indicate the principal student(s) of the species. We are aware that there are several new species soon to be described, but have not sought to complicate matters by mentioning them here; but many of them must immediately be considered threatened.

Persistent uncertainty has attended the identification of species to treat in this book. The fundamental criterion is that they are at risk of global extinction. IUCN has provided guidelines for the categorization of life-forms in such plight ("threatened" being a general term for anything at risk, "endangered", "vulnerable", "rare", "indeterminate" and "insufficiently known" being particular ranks of threat, here in diminishing intensity), but these categories have not been applied, since it is only really practicable to decide the degree of threat when a much more thorough analysis of a species's situation has been concluded. However, the definitions of "rare" and "insufficiently known" have been useful in deciding whether a species is "threatened" or not. "Rare" allows for small or highly restricted world populations that need not be declining but merely run the risk of extinction as a function of their small range, while "insufficiently known", a category introduced after King (1978-1979), provides for species suspected but not definitely known to be threatened. The annotations to the species listed give data on range (always with countries involved), numbers if possible, habitat and food where helpful, and in certain cases threats: where these last are not mentioned it can be inferred that the definitions of "rare" and "insufficiently known" are in play.

Everything given full treatment in Collar and Stuart (1985), with the exception of the Seychelles Kestrel *Falco araea* ("out of danger"), is included here; so also is every species treated in King (1978-1979), except those already discounted by Collar and Stuart (1985) plus Peregrine Falcon *Falco peregrinus*, a global species that can never have been at global risk of extinction. A very small number of species treated in King (1978-1979) have now been judged or proved secure, but as a matter of information and simplicity they are retained on this list. A few species treated in King (1978-1979), Marianas Mallard *Anas "oustaleti"*, Kleinschmidt's Falcon *Falco kreyenborgi*, Orange-fronted Parakeet *Cyanoramphus malherbi*, Klabin Farm Long-tailed Hermit *Phaethornis margarettae*, Black-billed Hermit *Phaethornis nigrirostris* and Black Barbthroat *Threnetes grzimeki*, have been subject to taxonomic revision and so discounted, the authority for such judgements to be identified in subsequent editions of the ICBP/IUCN Red Data Book. The evaluation of New World species has been in progress since 1985, as preparation for the forthcoming *Threatened birds of the Americas*, the second part of the current third edition of the Red Data Book: several candidate lists for this volume have already been circulated, and it is the most recent of these that forms the basis for the New World species listed here.

Greatest difficulty was experienced with the Oriental region, notably in areas where outdated taxonomy combined with absence of recent information (whether about the species or even merely their habitat). Our budget allowed for six months to compile the non-African, non-American material, and this inevitably meant that the pursuit of information could not lead too far into particular cases and problems. The technique was adopted of drawing up candidate lists for discrete areas (Indian subcontinent, China, South-East Asia, Greater Sundas, Wallacea, Philippines, Papuasia, and so on) and mailing them as widely as prudently possible for commentary; but with each list taking time to research, so later evaluations had less time to benefit from written dialogue. In some cases the selection and rejection of species became necessarily speculative, though certainly never arbitrary.

To lay down rigid criteria by which to judge whether a species is threatened or not is ultimately self-defeating. Variation in the quantity and quality of information is so great as to clog and smother with incertitude any system neatly designed for the mechanical selection of priorities. There is the actual situation of a species; there is knowledge of that situation, held in many different places and forms, never complete except perhaps in the case of tiny island populations; and there is the endeavour to assemble and interpret that knowledge. In other words the desk-bound researcher views his unstill subject through a whole array of distorting lenses and semi-opaque fragments, and his best hope must be that the most reliable image is that composed from the widest degree of scrutiny, the fullest use of sources. The major requisite is to remain sensitive to the limitations not only of the evidence but also of its interpretability. The judgements in this book are not always confident, and the decisions it takes are by no means infallible.

For this reason we provide in Appendix 2 a list of species (and their range states) that were strong candidates for treatment in the main body of the book. The list, which includes those ("near-threatened") species treated in Appendix C of Collar and Stuart (1985) (except for five that have been treated here as threatened), consists chiefly of genuine borderline cases, although to some extent it accommodates species we are satisfied are not at risk but which were strongly promoted as such by certain contacts or published sources. This then gives public acknowledgement of our awareness of these species and people's concern for them, and it indicates the species beyond the main list to which ornithologists and conservationists might devote some supplementary endeavour. Even here, however, we cannot pretend comprehensiveness or full authority; but such a list at least serves to indicate that there is no easy dividing line between being threatened with extinction and not.

Perhaps too much of this hedging, intended to inspire confidence in authorial humility and scruple, only serves to erode confidence in authorial ability and purpose. It needs, then, to be stressed that the 1,029 species listed here as threatened are all unquestionably birds to watch, birds to seek out, survey, monitor and conserve. Whether they precisely fit IUCN's or anyone else's definition of courting extinction matters rather less than that the world is aware of their need for our concern and vigilance. Further analysis will show the most appropriate courses of action and the priorities to pursue, but here at least is concrete evidence of the scale of the responsibilities we - the world - must assume.

That the scale is so great should come as no surprise. Although King (1978-1979) treated only some 275 full species in his review of the global situation (roughly 290 when we add in the fifteen or so of his subspecies that appear here as full species, on the principle established in the fourth paragraph above), Collar and Stuart (1985) already treated 172 as at risk merely for one continent, and their introduction identified five causes of this increase: (1) the establishment in 1980 of the "insufficiently known" category, (2) the description of new species of restricted range, (3) more exhaustive analysis, (4) a broader interpretation of the IUCN definitions of threat, and (5) the continuing deterioration of the environment. There are, according at least to Bock and Farrand (1980), something over 9,000 species of bird, so for over a thousand of them to be at risk of extinction

means that roughly 11% of the world's avifauna is at stake. Such a statistic is one
we should all find alarming, but one we would be wise not to dismiss out of hand
as alarmist.

To facilitate the perception of where the most critical areas are and where
ultimate responsibility at the national level lies, Appendix 1 identifies the
threatened species by country and geopolitical unit. Accidental or irregular
occurrence in a country has been discounted, and for certain Palearctic migrants
not all (and in one case none of the) countries in which they winter are given. If
the species occurs in more than one country, the total number of countries it
occurs in (according to this list) is given in parentheses after its name. All these
data are subject to further analysis and discussion in due course.

It needs to be noted that two other publications with which ICBP has been
closely associated, the *1988 IUCN red list of threatened animals* (IUCN Conservation Monitoring Centre 1988) and the *Collins/ICBP guide to rare birds of the
world* (Mountfort in press) contain lists of threatened birds not wholly consistent
with the list in this book. The IUCN list made use of our working candidate list
as it was in December 1987. The Collins guide, although a more popular work
that had developed its identity and content over several years, likewise accom-
modated material from ICBP up to December 1987. These two lists therefore
almost entirely coincide, and are a good but not the most recent reflection of our
judgement.

Comments, corrections, and details of observations new or old of any of the
species listed in this book are most welcome, and should be mailed to the senior
author at ICBP, The Mount, 32 Cambridge Road, Girton, Cambridgeshire CB3
0PJ, U.K.

ACKNOWLEDGEMENTS

Hundreds of people have helped this book into existence, and thanking them all
presents difficulties. As noted above, credit for its inception lies with W. B. King,
and we thank him for the stimulus. All those who assisted with Collar and Stuart
(1985) were gratefully acknowledged there, but new contributions of information have come from P. Alden, P. D. Alexander-Marrack, J. S. Ash, E. Brewer,
T. M. Butynski, C. Balchin, I. Bullock, P. Chapman, S. Cook, J. Cooper, D.
Dekker, S. D. Eccles, J. Hart, T. Hart, C. G. Jones, P. J. Jones, J. Komdeur, M.
Komdeur, V. Laboudallon, O. Langrand, B. Lenormand, G. Lewis, A. Martin,
R. Massoli-Novelli, D. V. Merton, M. E. Nicoll, B. Reed, D. Rockingham-Gill,
P. B. Taylor, C. G. Violani and L. Wilme; we thank them warmly. S. N. Stuart
added many additional pieces of information obtained since 1985.

All those - the figure runs well beyond 200 - who have assisted or are assisting
with the forthcoming *Threatened birds of the Americas*, and who have thereby
helped in considerable degree here, will receive proper recognition of their
kindness in the introduction to that volume, and here we merely offer collective

thanks for their generous and enthusiastic support; we trust they will accept the deferment of expression of our individual obligations (those named in the text as a source of information represent only a fraction of the number of helpers involved, and only one aspect of the valuable information received: the list is also the product of "negative" evidence, i.e. information allowing us to discount species from further consideration). It is, however, necessary to name J. Fjeldsa, T. A. Parker III, R. S. Ridgely and D. A. Scott as the principal sources of guidance and information for the Neotropical element, each of them devoting several days of work to help ICBP's development of a clear perspective on the realm's threatened avifauna.

For the non-African, non-American component of the book we have been helped enormously by extensive notes from B. M. Beehler (Papuasia), B. D. Bell (New Zealand), K. D. Bishop (Papuasia, Wallacea), M. A. Brazil (Japan), J. P. Croxall (seabirds, Greater Sundas, Papuasia), J. M. Diamond (Papuasia), S. C. B. Harrap and N. J. Redman (Indian subcontinent, South-East Asia), S. A. Hussain (Indian subcontinent), T. P. Inskipp (Indian subcontinent), R. S. Kennedy (Philippines), B. F. King (India, China, Greater Sundas, Philippines, South-East Asia), C. R. Robson (Indian subcontinent, China, South-East Asia), F. G. Rozendaal (Wallacea), D. A. Scott (Asia in general, based on data gathered for Scott in prep.), J.-C. Thibault (French Polynesia), M. G. Wilson (U.S.S.R.) and D. Yong (Wallacea, South-East Asia). For Australia, D. Baker-Gabb, S. Bennett, J. Brouwer, K. Fitzherbert (RAOU), R. Schodde (CSIRO), M. Fleming and J. Woinarski (Northern Territory Conservation Commission) and R. Buckingham (ICBP-Australia) worked in concert to provide judgement. In addition, help, sometimes very substantial, was provided by P. Alstrom, J. H. Andrews, G. Baines, B. van Balen, M. van Balgooy, M. A. S. Beaman, G. A. Bertrand, B. Bhushan, C. J. Bibby, J. Bowler, M. D. Bruce, R. W. Campbell, C. R. Cox, Lord Cranbrook, A. Davis, G. W. H. Davison, S. R. Derrickson, G. Duke, P. Dukes, D. S. Farrow, T. H. Fisher, W. C. Gagne, A. J. Gaston, J. P. Gee, D. Gibbs, A. Goodwin, P. D. Goriup, R. F. Grimmett, T. Gullick, He Fen-qi, P. Heath, B. van Helvoort, D. A. Holmes, T. W. Hoffman, J. Hornskov, J. Howes, Hsu Weishu, C. Inskipp, S. Jensen, P. Jepson, E. de Juana, Z. J. Karpowicz, M. Kasparek, M. Kavanagh, A. C. Kemp, P. R. Kennerley, S. Kotagama, G. R. Kula, F. R. Lambert, R. Lansdown, M. LeCroy, Li Guiyan, N. Lindsay, R. D. Mackay, P. Magsalay, S. Manan, J. McKean, J. McNeely, D. S. Melville, D. V. Merton, G. R. Milton, J. F. Monk, G. E. Morris, G. Mountfort, Nguyen Thi Man, T. Norman, V. Olsson, R. H. Pickering, M. K. Poulsen, I. S. Robertson, J. G. Robertson, P. D. Round, J. Scharringa, E. Schmutz, C. Schouten, D. A. Scott, L. L. Severinghaus, R. Sison, L. S. Stepanyan, B. Stewart Cox, J. B. Taylor, D. Thorns, W. J. M. Verheugt, J. D. R. Vernon, C. Viney, V. Vinogradov, Vo Quy, K. H. Voous, P. Walton, A. Wassink, D. R. Wells, T. Weselowski, Martin D. Williams. If there are any omissions from this list we offer our sincere apologies and will rectify the matter in any subsequent editions or in the appropriate full volume of the Red Data Book.

At the ICBP international secretariat in Cambridge, U.K., A. C. Dunn and H. G. Main very ably and speedily wordprocessed the document, M. R. W.

Rands, Director of Programme, added information on current ICBP projects. Our thanks extend further, and in greater measure still, to four colleagues at ICBP, three who wrote parts of the text, namely L. P. Gonzaga (based in Rio de Janeiro), who provided detailed notes on Brazilian species as part of his co-authorship of *Threatened birds of the Americas;* R. F. Grimmett, who drafted the entire Palearctic material while involved with his Important Bird Areas in Europe documentation on behalf of the European Continental Section of ICBP, funded by the RSPB; A. J. Stattersfield, our steadfast assistant and ICBP librarian, who wrote all the entries for the New Zealand species, almost all the seabirds, and many incidental extras, besides helping in innumerable ways with the provision of references, wordprocessing, proof-reading, cross-checking, and general mastery of all panic situations; and the fourth colleague, T. H. Johnson, Islands/Data Officer, who sacrificed many hours to its production, particularly to develop the database, which facilitated the listing of species by geopolitical unit in Appendix 1 (and which now enables us to produce species accounts for countries and regions); S. N. Stuart, now with IUCN, is named on the title-page in recognition of his part-authorship of the African material.

This book is a contribution from the ICBP/IUCN Red Data Book programme, and ICBP is greatly indebted to IUCN for its major long-term financial support, and to CVRD for its major financial support for L. P. Gonzaga. Work on *Threatened birds of the Americas,* on which part of this book is based, has been generously supported by Elizabeth Jones, Mr and Mrs J. D. Mitchell and Ing. A. M. Sada, and we offer them our warmest thanks.

29 April 1988   N. J. Collar, P. Andrew

REFERENCES

Collar, N.J. and Stuart, S. N. (1985) *Threatened birds of Africa and related islands: the ICBP/IUCN Red Data Book, part 1.* Third edition. Cambridge, U.K.: International Council for Bird Preservation and International Union for Conservation of Nature and Natural Resources.

Bock, W. J. and Farrand, J. (1980) The number of species and genera of recent birds: a contribution to comparative systematics. *Amer. Mus. Novit.* 2703.

Diamond, J. M. (1987) Extant unless proven extinct? Or, extinct unless proven extant? *Conserv. Biol.* 1: 77-79.

Dickinson, E. C., Kennedy, R. S. and Parkes, K. C. (in press) *Check-list of the birds of the Philippines.* London: British Ornithologists' Union.

King, W. B. (1978-1979) *Red data book, 2: Aves.* Second edition. Morges,

Switzerland: International Union for Conservation of Nature and Natural Resources.

King, W. B. (1981) *Endangered birds of the world: the ICBP bird red data book.* Washington, D.C.: Smithsonian Institution Press in cooperation with the International Council for Bird Preservation.

Morony, J. J., Bock, W. J. and Farrand, J. (1975) *Reference list of the birds of the world.* New York: American Museum of Natural History (Department of Ornithology).

Pratt, H. D., Bruner P. L. and Berrett, D. G. (1987) *A field guide to the birds of Hawaii and the tropical Pacific.* Princeton: Princeton University Press.

Scott, D. A. (in prep.) *A directory of Asian wetlands.*

Vincent, J. (1964-1971) *Red data book, 2: Aves.* Morges, Switzerland: International Union for Conservation of Nature and Natural Resources.

White, C. M. N. and Bruce, M. D. (1986) *The birds of Wallacea (Sulawesi, the Moluccas and Lesser Sunda Islands, Indonesia): an annotated check-list.* London: British Ornithologists' Union (Check-list no. 7).

WORLD CHECKLIST OF THREATENED SPECIES

Order APTERYGIFORMES

Family Apterygidae
Kiwis

Little Spotted Kiwi *Apteryx owenii* is confined to forest and scrub on Kapiti Island off the south-west coast of South Island, **New Zealand**, where the population was estimated at 500-600 birds, all descended from a few birds released this century (Williams and Given 1981). Productivity appears to be low, perhaps owing to population pressure and predation by Wekas *Gallirallus australis*, and the species is also threatened by the high fire risk in summer (B. D. Bell). There is an urgent need to establish colonies on other islands (Bell 1986).

Order TINAMIFORMES

Family Tinamidae
Tinamous

Solitary Tinamou *Tinamus solitarius* of Atlantic forest in eastern **Brazil**, **Paraguay** and **Argentina** has declined seriously as a result of both habitat destruction and very intensive hunting, although there are still places where it can be found with some ease (Sick and Teixeira 1979, M. A. Andrade, J. C. Chebez).

Black Tinamou *Tinamus osgoodi* is known only from humid forest in Huila, southern **Colombia**, where it is very rare (Hilty and Brown 1986), and south-eastern **Peru**, where it is also rare (D. A. Scott), although within the latter country in its very limited range it was evidently once common (see Traylor 1952).

Yellow-legged Tinamou *Crypturellus noctivagus* of caatinga (thorn scrub) and humid forest in eastern **Brazil** is suffering from both habitat destruction and hunting, and has declined seriously mainly in the Atlantic portion of its range (Sick 1969, 1972, 1985, Sick and Teixeira 1979), where it has been recorded recently from a very few places (Willis and Oniki 1981, Scott and Brooke 1985, A. Brandt, M. A. da Re, F. C. Straube); it is also apparently rare now in parts of the north-east (M. A. Andrade, A. G. Coelho, R. Otoch).

Magdalena Tinamou *Crypturellus saltuarius* is known from a single specimen from the middle Magdalena Valley at the western base of the Eastern Andes near La Mata, north-central **Colombia** (King 1978-1979), but is now provisionally lumped with Red-legged Tinamou *C. erythropus* (Blake 1977, Hilty and Brown 1986).

Taczanowski's Tinamou *Nothoprocta taczanowskii* is confined to high temperate-zone grasslands (or probably woodlands - J. Fjeldsa) in central and southeastern **Peru** (Blake 1977). It is nowhere common, its range is small and cultivation threatens to transform its habitat (J. Fjeldsa, J. P. O'Neill, F. Vuilleumier).

Kalinowski's Tinamou *Nothoprocta kalinowskii* is a high temperate-zone grassland species recorded in just two areas of **Peru**, in the north-west and south-east (Blake 1977) and its habitat is threatened by cultivation (J. P. O'Neill).

Lesser Nothura *Nothura minor* of central **Brazil** is an insufficiently known and possibly much overlooked campo species (D. M. Teixeira) which is locally common (J. Vielliard) but threatened by habitat loss (T. A. Parker) through large-scale agricultural development with eucalyptus, pines, sugarcane and soybeans (de Magalhaes 1978, E. O. Willis).

Dwarf Tinamou *Taoniscus nanus* of central **Brazil** and **Argentina** (two skins from Rio Bermejo in BMNH: L. A. P. Gonzaga) is considered a threatened campo species (Sick and Teixeira 1979, T. A. Parker) owing to habitat loss through large-scale agricultural development with eucalyptus, pines, sugarcane and soybeans (E. O. Willis). There are no recent records from Minas Gerais where it was formerly common (M. A. Andrade), although elsewhere it may possibly be much overlooked and commoner than generally thought (Teixeira and Negret 1984, D. M. Teixeira).

Order SPHENISCIFORMES

Family Spheniscidae
Penguins

Yellow-eyed Penguin *Megadyptes antipodes* occurs on South and Stewart Islands, **New Zealand**, **Auckland Islands (to New Zealand)** and **Campbell Island (to New Zealand)**, and is vulnerable to farm development, human disturbance and predation at its nesting sites (Robertson and Bell 1984). The total population is estimated at 1,200 to 1,800 pairs (Darby 1985).

Jackass Penguin *Spheniscus demersus*, although still plentiful and breeding only in **Namibia** and **South Africa**, suffered a drastic population decline in the nineteenth century and earlier this century from egg-harvesting and guano-scraping, and is now subject to further decline from competition for food with the pelagic fishing industry, from harbour developments near breeding islands, and from oil pollution (Collar and Stuart 1985). New data bearing on the species's conservation are in Brooke (1984), Nagy *et al*. (1984), Broni (1985), Cooper (1985), Wilson (1985a,b), La Cock (1986), Randall and Randall (1986), Duffy *et al*. (1987) and La Cock *et al*. (1987).

Peruvian Penguin *Spheniscus humboldti* has been seriously declining in numbers on the coast of **Peru** since the mid-1800s, but the El Nino phenomenon of 1982-1983 caused a 65 per cent depletion to between 2,100 and 3,000 birds (Hays 1984, 1986); there appear to be no recent figures on the status of the species in **Chile**, where surveys in the early 1980s (before El Nino) suggested 10,000-12,000 birds to be present (Araya Modinger 1983).

Order PODICIPEDIFORMES

Family Podicipedidae
Grebes

Madagascar Little Grebe *Tachybaptus pelzelnii*, endemic to **Madagascar** where in the recent past it was common and widespread on lakes, pools and rivers, has suffered a considerable decline in certain areas and faces threats from reduction of habitat, introduction of exotic fish, and competition and hybridization with the Little Grebe *T. ruficollis* (Collar and Stuart 1985; also Dee 1986). It is, however, recorded from six protected areas (O. Langrand, M. E. Nicoll).

Alaotra Grebe *Tachybaptus rufolavatus*, endemic to **Madagascar** and known chiefly from Lake Alaotra, is in the irreversible process of disappearing through hybridization with the Little Grebe *T. ruficollis* (Collar and Stuart 1985). It is, moreover, threatened by poaching and hunting (O. Langrand).

Atitlan Grebe *Podilymbus gigas*, estimated to have a population of 210 in 1973 (King 1978-1979), is apparently now extinct on Lake Atitlan, **Guatemala**, owing probably to either replacement by or hybridization with the Common Pied-billed Grebe *P. podiceps* (Hunter in press; see also *World Birdwatch* 9,4 [1987]: 3).

Colombian Grebe *Podiceps andinus*, last seen in 1977 (King 1978-1979), is probably extinct, having been searched for carefully without success throughout its limited range in the lakes of the Bogota savanna, **Colombia**, in 1981 (Fjeldsa 1984) and 1982 (Varty *et al.* 1986).

Junin Grebe *Podiceps taczanowskii* is confined to Lake Junin in **Peru**, where its population is falling rapidly towards extinction, with only roughly 100 birds left in 1987, in response to pollution and water-level changes induced by man (King 1978-1979, Fjeldsa 1981, J. Fjeldsa).

Hooded Grebe *Podiceps gallardoi*, although originally thought to be confined to one lake with a dwindling population (King 1978-1979), is now known to occur more widely on many scattered basaltic lakes in Santa Cruz, **Argentina**, with a total estimated population of 5,000 or more (Fjeldsa 1986).

Order PROCELLARIIFORMES

Family Diomedeidae
Albatrosses

Amsterdam Albatross *Diomedea amsterdamensis* is confined as a breeding bird to **Amsterdam Island (to France)**, southern Indian Ocean, where an average of merely five pairs breed per year (Collar and Stuart 1985).

Short-tailed Albatross *Diomedea albatrus* has a very restricted breeding range on islands south of Japan, with the volcanic ash slopes on **Torishima (to Japan)** the only confirmed breeding locality; feather-hunting at the turn of the century and volcanic eruptions in 1902 and 1939 nearly caused extinction (King 1978-1979). The population is slowly recovering (Hasegawa 1982) with 146 adults and 77 fledglings observed on Torishima in 1986; breeding success has improved with grass transplantation to stabilise the nesting areas (H. Hasegawa).

Family Procellariidae
Petrels, shearwaters

Mascarene Black Petrel *Pterodroma aterrima* is known only from **Reunion (to France)** by four specimens collected in the nineteenth century and three birds found dead in the 1970s, and by subfossil remains on Rodrigues (Mauritius), in the Indian Ocean (Collar and Stuart 1985).

Black-capped Petrel *Pterodroma hasitata* is known as a breeding bird from **Haiti** in the south-east mountains (in the 1970s the only known site: King 1978-1979) and now also at one site in the west (P. E. Paryski, C. A. Woods), and from the **Dominican Republic** in the Sierra de Bahoruco (Stockton de Dod 1987) and **Cuba** at an inaccessible site in the southern coastal slopes of Sierra Maestra (Garrido 1985). At sea its distribution largely follows the Gulf Stream off the eastern United States (Haney 1987).

Cahow *Pterodroma cahow* breeds in very low numbers on some small islets in Castle Harbour, **Bermuda (to U.K.)** (King 1978-1979), but intensive conservation work has sought to optimize the situation (Wingate 1985); 35 pairs fledged 21 young in 1985 (D. B. Wingate).

Beck's Petrel *Pterodroma becki* is known from two specimens taken at sea in 1928, one east of New Ireland and north of Buka, **Papua New Guinea**, the other north- east of Rendova Island, **Solomon Islands**; it is sometimes regarded as a subspecies of *P. rostrata* (King 1978-1979, Jouanin and Mougin 1979).

Magenta Petrel *Pterodroma magentae* is a recently rediscovered species from the **Chatham Islands (to New Zealand)**; two birds were located in 1978, 111 years after the unique type-specimen was collected at sea in the southern Pacific Ocean (King 1978-1979, Crockett 1979, Williams and Given 1981). Twenty-nine individuals have since been identified, and on the basis of capture/recapture figures a population of 50-100 birds has been postulated (Crockett 1986). In 1987 the first breeding site was found on a small stack off the south-west coast of the main Chatham Island (M. Imber; see also Muller 1988), and burrows may be scattered over the south-west corner of the main Chatham Island too (B. D. Bell).

Gon-gon *Pterodroma feae* breeds on four islands in the **Cape Verde Islands** and on Bugio in the Desertas off **Madeira (Portugal)**, but the most recent reports suggest the total population may now stand at several hundred pairs; the species suffers considerable human exploitation (Collar and Stuart 1985).

Freira *Pterodroma madeira* is known only from a few localities in the mountains of **Madeira (Portugal)**; the most encouraging reports on its population indicates perhaps only 50 pairs (Collar and Stuart 1985). Only one breeding site is known, at which no successful activity occurred in 1985 or 1986, almost certainly owing to rat predation, but three pairs bred in 1987; other breeding sites may exist, and the latest population estimate is 20 pairs (F. Zino and M. Biscoito *per* R. F. Grimmett).

Dark-rumped Petrel *Pterodroma phaeopygia* is declining seriously at both its breeding stations, in **Galapagos Islands (to Ecuador)** (nominate *phaeopygia*), and in Hawaii, **Hawaiian Islands (to U.S.A.)** (race *sandwichensis*) (King 1978-1979). The species breeds on at least four islands in the Galapagos, but suffers there from predation and habitat loss produced by rats, cats, dogs, pigs, burros and cattle; these problems are now subject to rectification (Coulter 1984, Coulter *et al.* 1985, Cruz and Cruz 1987). In Hawaii, some 430 pairs nest largely in Haleakala National Park and are at risk from a variety of introduced mammals (Simons 1985, Stone *et al.* 1988).

Cook's Petrel *Pterodroma cooki* is a **New Zealand** breeding species found on Little Barrier Island (10,000-50,000 pairs, Robertson and Bell 1984), with small colonies on Great Barrier Island (less than 20 pairs, Robertson 1985) and on Codfish Island (about 100 pairs, Robertson 1985); introduced predators on its breeding islands are the main threats (King 1978-1979). Eradication programmes have removed cats from Little Barrier Island (Veitch 1985) and Wekas *Gallirallus australis* from Codfish Island (M. J. Imber *per* B. D. Bell), and the species is recovering (B. D. Bell).

Chatham Island Petrel *Pterodroma axillaris* breeds on Rangatira Island in the **Chatham Islands (to New Zealand)**; the island has been managed as a reserve since 1954, resulting in the recovery of vegetation, but the total population has remained very small (King 1978-1979), estimated at less than 500 birds (Williams and Given 1981). It is thought that the species is being overwhelmed by the vigorous Broad-billed Prion *Pachyptila vittata* which takes over the breeding burrows (M. J. Imber *per* B. D. Bell).

Defilippe's Petrel *Pterodroma defilippiana* of the **Juan Fernandez Islands (to Chile)** and **Desventuradas Islands (to Chile)**, is restricted to a few colonies that all appear to suffer from cat predation: the population on Isla Robinson Crusoe (Juan Fernandez) is in the hundreds, possibly thousands (Brooke 1987), that on the Desventuradas is around 400 (Schlatter 1984).

Pycroft's Petrel *Pterodroma pycrofti* breeds on the Poor Knights Islands and a few others off the north-east coast of **New Zealand**, and has an estimated population of less than 1,000 breeding pairs (Robertson and Bell 1984). Introduced mammals and environmental damage must be significant threats (Williams and Given 1981), although eradication programmes have been implemented (Robertson and Bell 1984).

Fiji Petrel *Pterodroma macgillivrayi* was formerly known from one specimen collected on Gau Island, **Fiji**, in 1855 (King 1978-1979). However in 1984 an adult was captured on Gau and released (Watling and Lewanavanua 1985) and in 1985 a fledgling (which later died) was found there (D. Watling). Although nests have not been located, breeding conditions appear favourable with sufficient undisturbed mature forest, but feral cat predation is a potential threat (Watling 1986).

Black Petrel *Procellaria parkinsoni* breeds on Little and Great Barrier Islands, **New Zealand**, where the population is estimated at fewer than 1,000 breeding pairs (Robertson and Bell 1984). Predation by cats appears to have been the biggest threat, with 100 per cent of fledglings killed on Little Barrier Island in 1974 and 1975 (King 1978-1979). Eradication programmes on Little Barrier Island have been successfully implemented (Veitch 1985) and chicks have been translocated, but predation is still a threat on Great Barrier Island (B. D. Bell; but see Imber 1987).

Westland Black Petrel *Procellaria westlandica* breeds in one small mountain range on South Island, **New Zealand**, where it is subject to predation by introduced mammals (King 1978-1979) and vulnerable to timber-milling (Robertson and Bell 1984). In 1982 the population was estimated at 1,000-5,000 breeding pairs, representing an increase in numbers attributable to adaptation to scavenging from the commercial fisheries within its feeding range (Robertson and Bell 1984).

Pink-footed Shearwater *Puffinus creatopus* breeds only on Mocha Island, **Chile**, and on the **Juan Fernandez Islands (to Chile)** where it is decreasing: there are a few thousand pairs each on Islas Robinson Crusoe and Santa Clara (Juan Fernandez) (Brooke 1987) and an unknown number on Mocha which, however, requires protection to conserve the species there (Schlatter 1984).

Heinroth's Shearwater *Puffinus heinrothi* is known only from a handful of specimens from the northern coast of New Britain, **Papua New Guinea**, (King 1978- 1979). The breeding site has not been found, but the recent discovery of two individuals on eastern Bougainville suggests that the species could breed there (Hadden 1981), this being supported by several further records from the island (K. D. Bishop).

Newell's Shearwater *Puffinus newelli* has a much reduced breeding range on forested slopes on Kauai, **Hawaiian Islands (to U.S.A.)** (King 1978-1979) where it has suffered from predation, destruction of some colonies by fire and mortality of fledglings attracted to street lights; from 1969-1984 a programme to recover disorientated fledglings recorded 10,000 young birds (Harrison *et al.* 1984).

Townsend's Shearwater *Puffinus auricularis*, as determined taxonomically by Jehl (1982), is confined as a breeding bird to the **Revillagigedos Islands (to Mexico)** (nominate *auricularis*), where it has suffered considerable nest destruction by pigs and predation by cats (S. N. G. Howell, J. R. Jehl), and in the race *newelli* on the **Hawaiian Islands (to U.S.A.)** (Kauai, Molokai and Hawaii), where it is threatened by the introduced mongoose *Herpestes auropunctatus* (King 1978-1979, Pratt *et al.* 1987).

Family Hydrobatidae
Storm-petrels

Guadalupe Storm-petrel *Oceanodroma macrodactyla* is presumed extinct on

Guadalupe Islands (Mexico) (King 1978-1979), but no thorough survey of the breeding grounds has been made at the appropriate season since 1906, and despite the presence of cats the species may still survive (Jehl 1972, Jehl and Everett 1985).

Markham's Storm-petrel *Oceanodroma markhami* occurs in waters off western South and Central America, notably **Peru** and **Chile**, also **Galapagos Islands (to Ecuador)**, **Clipperton Island (to France)**, **Cocos Island (to Costa Rica)**, but its breeding grounds were unknown (Blake 1977, Duffy *et al.* 1984, Schlatter 1984) until a nesting area was found in August 1987 on Paracas Peninsula in the Reserva Nacional Paracas (by P. Donahue).

Ringed Storm-petrel *Oceanodroma hornbyi* occurs in waters off western South America (**Ecuador, Peru, Chile**) but its breeding grounds are unknown (Blake 1977, Duffy *et al.* 1984, Schlatter 1984).

Family Pelecanoididae
Diving-petrels

Peruvian Diving-petrel *Pelecanoides garnoti* is declining seriously and perhaps the seabird of most concern in **Peru**, along with the Peruvian Penguin *Spheniscus humboldti*, but it is still considered common though decreasing in **Chile** (Duffy *et al.* 1984, Schlatter 1984).

Order PELECANIFORMES

Family Pelecanidae
Pelicans

Spot-billed Pelican *Pelecanus philippensis*, once widespread in Asia, is currently confined to south-eastern **India** (fewer than 400 pairs in four colonies) and **Sri Lanka** (approximately 900 pairs in 23 colonies, thought to be a stable population; T. W. Hoffman); the species has suffered a considerable decline in the past few decades, probably owing to the combination of human disturbance, destruction of nesting and roosting-loafing areas, declines in fish availability and increased pesticide usage; its status in Burma and China is unknown (Crivelli and Shreiber 1984).

Dalmatian Pelican *Pelecanus crispus* breeds from **Yugoslavia** east to **China**, generally wintering south to **Greece, Turkey, Iran, Iraq, Pakistan, India** and **China** (King 1978-1979, Crivelli and Vizi 1981, Ali and Ripley 1984, Crivelli 1987). It has declined dramatically since the last century and the total world population has been estimated at 514-1,368 pairs at 19 sites in **Albania,** **Yugoslavia, Bulgaria,** Greece, **Romania,** Turkey, Iran, U.S.S.R., **Mongolia** and **China** (Crivelli 1987), although the population in China is not known and Kolosov (1983) estimated a breeding population of 1,500-2,000 pairs in the U.S.S.R.

Family Sulidae
Boobies, gannets

Abbott's Booby *Sula abbotti* (considered distinctive enough for its own genus *Papasula*: Olson and Warheit 1988) breeds on **Christmas Island (to Australia)** in the Indian Ocean (having become extinct on Assumption or Gloriosa and probably other islands in the western Indian Ocean: Nelson 1974, Bourne 1976, Stoddart 1981), with a population estimated at a maximum of 2,000 breeding pairs (Reville *et al.* 1987). An egg-production rate of 1.27 per pair per two years has been recorded, and the birds nest at the top of forest trees on the island plateau, not colonizing hitherto unoccupied areas (Nelson and Powell 1986): thus the breeding performance of a substantial and increasing proportion of the population has been adversely affected by the stripping of forest for phosphate mining (*World Birdwatch* 7,4 [1985]: 1-2). A national park encompasses about 30 per cent of the nest sites but the long-term effects of a reduced breeding population on the species are not known (Stokes 1988; also King 1978-1979); non- breeding birds disperse north to Java, **Indonesia** (Becking 1976, P. Andrew). A relict population conceivably occurs on Cocos Island (to Costa Rica) in the eastern Pacific (Nelson 1974).

Family Phalacrocoracidae
Cormorants

New Zealand King Cormorant *Phalacrocorax carunculatus* is endemic to **New Zealand** where it occurs as three allopatric subspecies which are sometimes regarded as distinct species: nominate *carunculatus* is restricted to Cook Strait with a total population of fewer than 1,000 pairs (formerly collected in excessive numbers for the feather trade, King 1978-1979), *P. c. chalconotus* occurs on southern South Island and Stewart Island with a population of less than 5,000 pairs and *P. c. onslowi* on the **Chatham Islands (to New Zealand)** with a population of less than 1,000 pairs (Robertson and Bell 1984). Numbers in colonies fluctuate considerably (B. D. Bell).

Pygmy Cormorant *Halietor pygmeus* is confined to the Palearctic west of the Aral Sea, breeding only in **Albania, Yugoslavia, Bulgaria, Romania, Greece, Turkey, Iraq, Iran** and **U.S.S.R.**, and its range is believed to be steadily contracting mainly because of drainage (Cramp and Simmons 1977). Outside the U.S.S.R., the main breeding colonies are at Lake Shkodra (Albania), c. 2,000 pairs; Lake Kerkini (Greece), Danube Delta (Romania), c. 12,000 pairs; and the marshes of the Euphrates (Iraq) (Cramp and Simmons 1977, Grimmett and Jones in prep.); in the U.S.S.R. it breeds mostly in Azerbaydzhan (Caspian Sea) and it is considered threatened with only 3,200 - 6,600 pairs (Kolosov 1983).

Galapagos Flightless Cormorant *Nannopterum harrisi* is a rare and permanently vulnerable seabird confined to the **Galapagos Islands (to Ecuador)** (King 1978- 1979), but its numbers recovered rapidly after the 1982-1983 El Nino phenomenon to around 800-1,000 (Rosenberg and Harcourt 1987). Data on population dynamics are in Harris (1979).

Family Fregatidae
Frigatebirds

Ascension Frigatebird *Fregata aquila* has its entire breeding population confined to the 3 ha Boatswainbird Islet, 250 m off the north-east coast of **Ascension Island (to U.K.)** in the Atlantic Ocean, and since 1982 has been at considerably increased risk of serious disturbance (Collar and Stuart 1985).

Christmas Frigatebird *Fregata andrewsi* is known to breed on **Christmas Island (to Australia)** in the Indian Ocean, and suspected (on little evidence) to breed on the Anambas Islands, Indonesia (King 1978-1979); the current population is estimated at less than 1,600 pairs and none of the three colonies in which it is known to breed is protected (Stokes 1988). Non-breeding birds disperse north to Borneo (**Indonesia** and **Malaysia** (White and Bruce 1986) and the Phi-Phi Islands, **Thailand** (P. D. Round), east as far as Timor, Indonesia (McKean 1987) and west as far as the coast of Kenya (Mann 1986).

Order CICONIIFORMES

Family Ardeidae
Herons, egrets, bitterns

Zigzag Heron *Zebrilus undulatus* is a little-recorded species apparently ranging from eastern Colombia, through Venezuela, into Guyana, Suriname and French Guiana, and from Ecuador and north-eastern Peru into the Amazon basin of Brazil, the southern limit of its range reaching the borders of Bolivia (Hancock and Kushlan 1984). In Venezuela the species is vulnerable to uncontrolled hunting by natives (S. Coats).

Japanese Night-heron *Gorsagius goisagi* breeds at very low densities along watercourses in broadleaf evergreeen forests in mountain foothills from Honshu south to Kyushu, Japan, wintering south to the Kazan-retto i.e. Volcano Islands (to to Japan), Taiwan, China, the Philippines and Palau (to U.S.A.) (Sonobe 1982, Hancock and Kushlan 1984, M. A. Brazil). Virtually nothing is known about the distribution, status and biology of the species, but in Japan its habitat is being converted to plantations (M. A. Brazil).

White-eared Night-heron *Gorsachius magnificus* breeds only on Hainan, China, but after breeding wanders north in south-east mainland China and has occurred as a vagrant to northern Viet Nam (Vo Quy 1975); it lives in dense hill forest and is rare and local (Meyer de Schauensee 1984); and has not been recorded in recent years (Hsu Weishu).

Slaty Egret *Egretta vinaceigula* occurs in the Okavango Delta in northern Botswana (whence come the only breeding records), the Caprivi Strip in Namibia, and the Kafue Flats, Liuwa Plain and Bangweulu Swamp in Zambia, but it is nowhere common: flood regulation has caused it to disappear from one part of the Kafue Flats and there are plans that may seriously affect the ecology of the Okavango Delta (Collar and Stuart 1985). Further breeding data are in Fry *et al.* (1986).

Chinese Egret *Egretta eulophotes* formerly bred along the coast of China from Hainan north to North Korea and on islands in the Yellow Sea, and has been recorded in winter and on passage north to Japan, coastal U.S.S.R. and the Aleutian Islands, and south to Singapore, Malaysia, Indonesia, Taiwan and the Philippines, but was almost eradicated by the trade in plumes at the end of the last century (King 1978-1979). Today it is known to breed on islands on the west coast of North Korea where there are an estimated 250 pairs (K. Sonobe *per* R. Lansdown; map in Sonobe and Izawa 1987), and on islands off Shanghai, China, where there is a colony of 20 pairs (Cheng Zhao-quing *per* R. Lansdown). It apparently winters mainly in the Philippines where 108 were recorded on Palawan in 1986 (B. F. King, D. Yong) and 73 noted at eight coastal sites on other islands in spring 1987 (J. Howes; also Gast and King 1985). It is a scarce migrant in Hong Kong (to U.K.), but may still breed on rocky islets offshore (P. R. Kennerley) and has been recorded on passage in Taiwan (L. L. Severinghaus).

Madagascar Heron *Ardea humbloti*, a large but very little-known waterbird breeding only in Madagascar but recorded also on the Comoro Islands and

Mayotte (to France), was reported in 1973 to have declined alarmingly and to be facing extinction unless completely protected, although it appears to be safe in parts of the west coast of Madagascar (Collar and Stuart 1985; also Dee 1986) and is recorded from four protected areas (O. Langrand, M. E. Nicoll). It possibly breeds in the Comoros (Draulans 1986).

White-bellied Heron *Ardea imperialis* was formerly a local resident along the eastern Himalayan foothills from Nepal, through **Bhutan** to **Burma** (Ripley 1982), and south-east Xizang Zizhiqu, **China** (Meyer de Schauensee 1984), but it has not been recorded in Nepal this century (Inskipp and Inskipp 1986) and is rare in north-east **India** and **Bangladesh** (Ali and Ripley 1984). Smythies (1953) describes it as not uncommon in northern Burma but its current status there is not known.

Family Balaenicipitidae
Shoebill

Shoebill *Balaeniceps rex* is widely but very locally distributed in swamps throughout **Sudan, Uganda,** parts of **Zaire** and **Zambia,** with populations in **Central African Republic, Ethiopia, Rwanda** and **Tanzania,** where it subsists on fish and other aquatic vertebrates; in most of its range it is threatened in the medium or long term by the development and disturbance of its habitat, but it is apparently not yet in serious danger of extinction (Collar and Stuart 1985). However, more recent comment on its status in Sudan, its stronghold, is that the species is "very much endangered by destruction of papyrus swamps by cattle and fire" (Nikolaus 1987).

Family Ciconiidae
Storks

Milky Stork *Mycteria cinerea* occurs in southern **Viet Nam** and **Kampuchea,** peninsular **Malaysia,** Sumatra, Java and Sulawesi, **Indonesia** (King 1978-1979), but breeding is confined to a few colonies; it has not been proved in Malaysia since 1935, on Java the known population is around 30 pairs, breeding is not confirmed in Sulawesi, and the species's status in Kampuchea and Viet Nam is unclear (Verheugt 1987). The population on the east coast of Sumatra was estimated to be 6,000 in 1984 (Silvius *et al.* 1986, Silvius 1988), though more recently 5,000 (Verheugt 1987). Principal threats are habitat destruction by tidal rice cultivation and fish-farming, timber exploitation and, recently, direct exploitation by man for food (Verheugt 1987).

Storm's Stork *Ciconia stormi* is resident in Borneo and Sumatra, **Indonesia,** and either a rare resident or irregular visitor to peninsular **Malaysia** (King 1978-1979). It is scarce but probably widespread in south-east Sumatra, north to at least central Jambi (Holmes 1977, J. P. Gee), and through Central and East Kalimantan (Holmes and Burton 1987). There are few recent records from Malaysia and a breeding record from **Thailand** (Luthin 1987, Nakhasathien 1987).

Oriental White Stork *Ciconia boyciana* breeds in south-east Siberia, **U.S.S.R.,** and north-east **China,** and in winter disperses widely into south and south-east China (Meyer de Schauensee 1984). It used to breed in Japan but was shot out by the turn of the century (King 1978-1979), the only post-war breeding record in **South Korea** was in 1971 (Gore and Won 1971), and in **North Korea** it is a winter visitor in very small numbers (Sonobe and Izawa 1987). An estimated 400-500 pairs breed in the U.S.S.R. and aerial surveys in Heilongjiang in 1984-1985 located 123 birds (*per* D. A. Scott; also Luthin 1987). There are no population estimates from Jilin or Nei Mongol Zizhiqu where it also breeds but 2,729 birds, the bulk of the known population, were recorded on migration at Beidaihe, Hopei province, in autumn 1986 (Williams 1986).

Lesser Adjutant *Leptoptilos javanicus* has suffered a serious decline throughout its range, attributable to poaching, human disturbance and forest clearance (Luthin 1987). Recent reports are from **Sri Lanka** (about 100 breeding pairs), **India** (Madhya Pradesh, Assam and Sundarbans), **Nepal** (an occasional resident), **Bangladesh** (widespread but fast disappearing), **Burma** (nine birds in 1982-1983), **Thailand** (rare and almost certainly no longer breeding), **Viet Nam** (one breeding colony), **Malaysia** (two colonies totalling about 140 birds), Sumatra, **Indonesia** (579, 1,095 and 686 birds in 1984, 1985 and 1986), Sarawak, Sabah and Bali (various sightings); no information is available from **Laos** or **Kampuchea** (Luthin 1987).

Greater Adjutant *Leptoptilos dubius* formerly ranged widely in northern **India,** Assam, **Bangladesh,** southern **Burma, Thailand,** southern **Laos, Kampuchea** and **Viet Nam** (Ali and Ripley 1984), once breeding in large colonies in Burma (Smythies 1986). It has suffered catastrophic decline everywhere, probably no longer occurring in Burma or Thailand, not recently recorded from Viet Nam, extinct in Bangladesh, and extremely rare in India where the only breeding records (and the only recent ones anywhere) are from Assam (Luthin 1987).

Family Threskiornithidae
Ibises, spoonbills

White-shouldered Ibis *Pseudibis davisoni* was formerly widespread in **Burma, Thailand, Kampuchea,** southern **Laos** and southern **Viet Nam** (King 1978-

1979), and is known from Borneo (**Malaysia** and **Indonesia**) (Smythies 1981) and south-west Yunnan, **China** (Meyer de Schauensee 1984). It is only recently known from the Dong Thap Muoi lowlands of southern Viet Nam (C. S. Luthin) and Kalimantan, **Indonesia** (Holmes and Burton 1987).

Giant Ibis *Pseudibis gigantea* formerly occurred in south-east **Thailand**, central and northern **Kampuchea**, southern **Laos** and southern **Viet Nam** (King 1978-1979). It is almost certainly extinct in Thailand and its status is not known in Laos or Kampuchea; the only recent records are from southern Viet Nam, where small numbers are reported from the Dong Thap Muoi, an inland delta of the Mekong (C. S. Luthin).

Northern Bald Ibis *Geronticus eremita* has a tiny relict breeding population at Birecik, **Turkey**, supported by a local captive breeding operation, the wild birds migrating to **Ethiopia** and (presumably) **North Yemen**, and it survives at a handful of dwindling colonies in **Morocco** (one, possibly now extinct, in **Algeria**), where hope for its long-term conservation rests with the population protected in the Oued Massa National Park; it breeds well in captivity (Collar and Stuart 1985; parallel review in Kumerloeve 1984). In 1985 and 1986 the free-flying Birecik population was 32 and 35 birds, 11 and nine of which (respectively) were migratory (Akcakaya and Akcakaya 1986); this conforms reasonably with the observation of 12 adults and two juveniles in autumn 1985 in North Yemen, with 11 last seen there in February 1986, although the adults were claimed to have been present "throughout the summer" of 1985 (Brooks *et al*. 1987). In Birecik on 1 May 1987 six nests of free-flying birds held 10 juveniles while the content of a seventh was not determined (T. Norman). A bird was seen in Sinai, **Egypt**, in 1962 (Kyllingstad 1986) and in **Senegal** in March 1985 (P. Alden, E. Brewer), and the species was historically present in Greece (Desfayes 1987).

Southern Bald Ibis *Geronticus calvus* has a population of 5,000 to 8,000 birds restricted to the highlands of **South Africa**, **Lesotho** and **Swaziland**, where it requires safe, undisturbed nesting cliffs and areas of short-grazed and recently burnt grassland (Collar and Stuart 1985; also Brooke l984, Manry 1985a,b).

Crested Ibis *Nipponia nippon* formerly bred in south-east Siberia, U.S.S.R., in north-east China, from Zhejiang and south Shaanxi north to North Korea, and in Japan (King 1978-1979). A population survives at the edge of its former range, in the Qinling Shan in south Shaanxi, **China**, and the wild population was estimated to be around 40 birds in 1987 (Luthin 1987). A survey is being undertaken to document and investigate recent reports of the species in the Soviet Far East (Shibaev 1987a).

Dwarf Olive Ibis *Bostrychia bocagei* is (or was) confined to (probably only) primary forest on Sao Tome, **Sao Tome e Principe**, where it has not been seen this century other than one collected in the south-west in November 1928 (Collar and Stuart 1985, Jones and Tye 1988).

Black-faced Spoonbill *Platalea minor* is presumed to breed in east **China**, from Heilongjiang south to Fujian, and **North Korea**, on a few islands (30 birds in total) off the north-west coast (Sonobe and Izawa 1987). Non-breeding birds have been recorded south and east to **Japan, Taiwan,** the **Philippines** and **Viet Nam** (with up to 62 at the mouth of the Hong River) (Meyer de Schauensee 1984), and in **Hong Kong (to U.K.**), where up to 30 birds regularly winter (M. D. Williams). It was identified amongst parties of European Spoonbill *P. leucorodia* from photographs taken at Lake Poyang, Jiangxi, in 1986 (Kennerley 1987) but no other wintering sites are known, and there are no estimates of population.

Family Phoenicopteridae
Flamingos

Andean Flamingo *Phoenicoparrus andinus* of high mountain lakes in **Peru, Chile, Bolivia** and **Argentina** (Blake 1977) appears to be the least common of the South American flamingos, with fewest regular haunts, very low reproductive success and only one or two regular breeding sites (J. Fjeldsa, D. A. Scott). Egg-collecting and habitat loss through the diversion of streams for human utilization are suspected of affecting the species adversely (S. H. Hurlbert).

Puna Flamingo *Phoenicoparrus jamesi* is restricted to a small number of lakes in the puna zone of the Andes, including southernmost **Peru**, northern **Chile**, western **Bolivia** and north-west **Argentina** (Blake 1977), and should be monitored (T. A. Parker). Egg-collecting and habitat loss and deterioration through pollution and the diversion of streams for human utilization are suspected of affecting the species adversely (S. H. Hurlbert).

Order ANSERIFORMES

Family Anhimidae
Screamers

Northern Screamer *Chauna chavaria* is restricted to lowland marshes in northern **Colombia** and north-western **Venezuela** (Blake 1977), and although it remains common in some localities it is suffering from loss of habitat in others (Hilty and Brown 1985, J. Botero).

Family Anatidae
Ducks, geese, swans

West Indian Whistling Duck *Dendrocygna arborea*, from the **Bahama Islands, Cuba, Haiti, Dominican Republic, Jamaica, Cayman Islands** (to **U.K.**), **Puerto Rico** (to **U.S.A.**), **Virgin Islands** (to **U.S.A.**), **Leeward Islands** (to **U.K.**), has been declining markedly throughout its Caribbean range (King 1978-1979). However, in **Cuba** the species is now fully protected and is found locally in good numbers in swamps, along coasts and even on keys (Garrido 1986); on **Barbuda** a "large population" has been found (Faaborg and Arendt 1985); and there has been a minor recovery in numbers on the east coast of **Puerto Rico** (H. Raffaele, J. W. Wiley).

Lesser White-fronted Goose *Anser erythropus* breeds south of the Arctic Ocean in northern **Norway, Sweden, Finland** and **U.S.S.R.**, wintering sparsely in **Yugoslavia, Romania, Bulgaria, Greece, Turkey, Iraq, Iran**, southern U.S.S.R. (25,000+ birds), **China, Pakistan, India** and **Japan** (Cramp and Simmons 1977, Ali and Ripley 1984, Skokova and Vinogradov 1986). In Fennoscandia the species is believed to have declined by 95 per cent to about 60-90 pairs (Norderhaug and Norderhaug 1984). In the U.S.S.R., breeding is possibly concentrated in the Yamal and lower Ob region (6,000-10,000 birds) (V. Vinogradov) and it has become rarer in the north-east in recent years (Kolosov 1983). Numbers occurring on passage and in winter in central and southern Europe are considerably reduced, and large numbers no longer stop over in autumn in Hungary: 80,000-120,000 birds before 1950, reduced to just a few thousand birds in recent years (Sterbetz 1982). In China it was once described as the most numerous wintering goose along the Yangtse River (La Touche 1925-1934) but there are no recent reports of large numbers.

Hawaiian Goose *Branta sandvicensis* occurs on the flanks of Mauna Loa and Hualalai on Hawaii, and in the Haleakala National Park on Maui, in the **Hawaiian Islands** (to **U.S.A.**) (Pratt *et al.* 1987). It breeds on sparsely vegetated lava slopes between 1,500 and 2,400 m, but it is not known whether the wild population can survive predation from introduced rats, cats, dogs and mongooses; the species declined from an estimated 25,000 birds at the end of the last century to a low of perhaps 30 by 1952, and only the release of over 1,400 captive-bred birds has maintained it in the wild (King 1978-1979).

Red-breasted Goose *Branta ruficollis* breeds only in the Taymyr, Gydan and Yamal regions of the **U.S.S.R.** (although there is a remarkable breeding record from Ercek Golu in **Turkey**), with a total population of about 27,500 birds (Bannikov 1978, Kasparek and van der Ven 1983, Borodin 1984). Large numbers formerly wintered at Kirov Bay (Caspian Sea), but because of adverse land-use changes (cereal crops to vineyards) the majority now winter along the western shore of the Black Sea in the Dobrogea region of **Romania** and northern

Bulgaria (Cramp and Simmons 1977, Skokova and Vinogradov 1986). Wintering birds also irregularly occur in Greece, Turkey and Iran (Beaman 1975, Cramp and Simmons 1977, D. A Scott).

Freckled Duck *Stictonetta naevosa* ranges widely across **Australia**, but breeding records are clustered in the south-west of Western Australia and the Murray-Darling drainage in New South Wales; it inhabits open lakes and swamps and gathers in a few refuge areas when the wetlands of the interior dry up (Blakers *et al.* 1984). A census in 1983 grossed 8,000 (Cowling and Davies 1983) though not all wetlands were visited and it was projected that the total population in eastern Australia was not more than 19,000 birds (Martindale 1986). The species is threatened by changes to the flooding patterns of inland swamps (Hermes 1980) and illegal shooting (Martindale 1986).

Ruddy-headed Goose *Chloephaga rubidiceps* breeds in the grasslands of northern Tierra del Fuego, **Chile** and **Argentina**, migrating to southern Argentina, with a second population resident on the **Falkland Islands (to U.K.)**; the southern South American population has declined markedly, probably as a result of the introduction of foxes, and the Falklands/Malvinas birds are treated as an agricultural pest (King 1978-1979). However, there are some tens of thousands on the islands and their mobility makes attempts to reduce numbers ineffective (Summers 1985, Summers *et al.* 1985).

Crested Shelduck *Tadorna cristata* (regarded as extinct in King 1978-1979) is known by three specimens only, a female collected near Vladivostok, **U.S.S.R.**, in 1877, and a male and a female from **South Korea**, collected between 1913 and 1916: records of small flocks in 1964 and 1971 suggest that the species still survives in very small numbers, breeding in easternmost U.S.S.R., north-east **China** and/or northern **North Korea**, wintering along the coasts of South Korea, eastern China and/or southern **Japan** (Nowak 1983, 1984a,b, O myong Sok 1984).

White-winged Duck *Cairina scutulata* is known by one undated specimen from **Malaysia** and is extinct on Java, but survives in north-eastern **India**, **Bangladesh** and probably **Burma**, where numbers are thought to be small (King 1978-1979). It has been recorded recently at the proposed Umphang Wildlife Sanctuary, Thung Yai and Hua Kha Khang in south-west **Thailand** (P. D. Pound, C. R. Robson), and the capture of three individuals in south-eastern Thailand or **Kampuchea** (Grimmett 1986) suggests an unknown population in the region. The most substantial populations are likely to be in Sumatra, **Indonesia,** where it is found in fresh- water and peat-swamp forest north to at least central Jambi, but apart from two protected areas suitable habitat is being converted to settlements and agricultural projects (Nash and Nash 1986, J. P. Gee). Since the 1970s all records in Bangladesh refer to a small population in the Hill Tracts North Forest Division, where the causes of decline seem to be forest clearance, hunting, entanglement in gill-nets and disturbance by settlers (Khan 1986).

Baykal Teal *Anas formosa* breeds within the forest zone of north and north-east Siberia, U.S.S.R., wintering in **Japan** and east and south-east **China**, occurring on spring passage in **North Korea** and **South Korea** and more widely as a vagrant (Cramp and Simmons 1977). There appears to have been a dramatic decline in recent years (Brazil 1987) with no large concentrations recorded anywhere except in South Korea (c. 19,000 in 1987/1988 on a small reservoir near Pusan) (D. A. Scott).

Madagascar Teal *Anas bernieri* is a little-known and much persecuted freshwater duck, endemic to **Madagascar**, apparently confined to a few sites along the west coast with a low total population (Collar and Stuart 1985; also Dee 1986). It is recorded from two protected areas (O. Langrand, M. E. Nicoll).

New Zealand Brown Teal *Anas aucklandica* is endemic to **New Zealand** and has suffered from drainage, introduction of predators, excessive shooting and possibly poultry disease: *A. a. chlorotis* is distributed widely but only in small relict populations remote from humans; nominate *aucklandica* occurs on several of the **Auckland Islands (to New Zealand)**; and *A. a. nesiotis* is confined to Dent Island, an offshore islet of **Campbell Island (to New Zealand)** (King 1978-1979). A captive-breeding programme for *aucklandica* and *chlorotis* has been successful, but a suitable predator-free island for release has not been found (B. D. Bell). The overall population is estimated at about 500 individuals for *aucklandica* (Williams 1986), 1,000 for *chlorotis* and unknown for *nesiotis* (King 1978-1979).

Hawaiian Duck *Anas wyvilliana*, once an inhabitant of all the **Hawaiian Islands (to U.S.A.)**, but now restricted to Kauai and reintroduced on Oahu and Hawaii, suffers from loss of its wetland habitat and predation to mongooses, rats, cats and dogs; in 1967 the population was estimated at 3,000 (King 1978-1979, Pratt *et al.* 1987).

Laysan Duck *Anas laysanensis*, having declined to near extinction owing to denudation of the vegetation of Laysan Island, **Hawaiian Islands (to U.S.A.)**, by introduced rabbits and then recovered following elimination of the rabbits, had declined again to less than 40 birds by 1973 (King 1978-1979). The population is now considered stable at about 500 birds (Pratt *et al.* 1987), which must be the maximum that the island can support; the possibility of establishing it on other islands is also being considered (Madge and Burn 1988).

Marbled Teal *Marmaronetta angustirostris* has a fragmented distribution, probably breeding in **Spain, Morocco, Algeria, Tunisia, Egypt, Turkey, Israel, Iraq, Iran, U.S.S.R., Pakistan** and possibly China (Cramp and Simmons 1977, Ali and Ripley 1984, Harvey 1986). The main breeding populations are possibly now in Morocco, Iraq and Iran (Cramp and Simmons 1977, Carp 1980, Scott and Carp 1982). In the U.S.S.R. it is currently known to breed at only three lakes in Azerbaydzhan (M. G. Wilson). Post-breeding dispersion and migration are poorly understood with the largest wintering concentrations recorded in Morocco, Turkey, Iran and Pakistan, with wintering birds also recorded in Egypt, **Senegal, Mali, Chad** and **India** (Cramp and Simmons 1977, Ali and Ripley 1984, Roberts 1985; also *Brit. Birds* 78 [1985]: 639).

Pink-headed Duck *Rhodonessa caryophyllacea* is regarded as extinct (King 1978-1979) but was formerly a local species found on wet ground and pools in the forests and grass jungles of north-east **India** (Ripley 1982), recorded in central **Nepal** last century, and last sighted at Bihar, India in June 1935 (Ali and Ripley 1984, Inskipp and Inskipp 1985). The possibility that a small population survives in a remote region was raised (Greenway 1958) and dropped (Greenway 1967), but rumours persist.

Baer's Pochard *Aythya baeri* breeds in eastern **U.S.S.R.**, north-east **China** and apparently **North Korea**, and winters south of the Chang Jiang in China, **South Korea**, north-east **India, Bangladesh, Burma, Thailand** and north **Viet Nam** (Kolosov 1983, Meyer de Schauensee 1984), **Nepal** (Inskipp and Inskipp 1985a), with one or two reaching **Japan** each year (M.A. Brazil). Despite this wide range the species appears to be rare, and the only significant counts known in recent years are of 40 near Hanoi, Viet Nam, March 1988 (D.A. Scott), 50 at Pearl River estuary, China (C.R. Robson) and around 600, most at Bung Boraphet, Thailand (P.D. Round). There has been a sharp decline in U.S.S.R. in recent years linked with drainage for rice cultivation and increased disturbance (Kolosov 1983).

Madagascar Pochard *Aythya innotata* is a freshwater diving duck, endemic to **Madagascar**, apparently confined to lakes and pools in the northern central plateau, where it has become increasingly rare this century and has not been seen since 1970 (Collar and Stuart 1985), despite four years of vigilance to date (O. Langrand).

Brazilian Merganser *Mergus octosetaceus* occurs on small rivers in central **Brazil**, eastern **Paraguay** and northern **Argentina**, and is everywhere rare (King 1978-1979). The main Argentinian population is threatened in Misiones (where rediscovered after 30 years in 1984) by hydroelectric development and other habitat disturbance (Johnson and Chebez 1985). Another breeding population is known from the Serra da Canastra National Park, one of the best protected parks in Brazil (J. M. Dietz), and the species has recently been recorded also in the Chapada dos Veadeiros National Park, central Goias (C. Yamashita), on the upper rio Paranaiba, Minas Gerais (G. T. Mattos), in eastern Paraguay (N. E. Lopez) and in other parts of Misiones (Johnson and Chebez 1985, M. Nores and D. Yzurieta).

Scaly-sided Merganser *Mergus squamatus* inhabits rivers and lakes in the Sikhote Alin ranges of south-east Siberia, **U.S.S.R.**, and in the mountains of north Heilongjiang in north-east **China** (King 1978-1979). In the winter it disperses south to south-east China and occasionally to north **Viet Nam** (King *et al.* 1975), but the bulk of the population stays within the breeding range (King 1978-1979);

it also breeds at Lake Chon-ji and Lake Sarnjiyan, **North Korea** (*per* D. A. Scott), these presumably being in the Mayang Chosuji area identified for the species in Sonobe and Izawa (1987).

White-headed Duck *Oxyura leucocephala* has a fragmented and much reduced distribution, breeding only in **Spain, Algeria, Tunisia, Romania, Turkey, Iran** and U.S.S.R., having become extinct in Hungary, Yugoslavia, France, Italy and Greece in the last twenty years (Cramp and Simmons 1977, Carp 1980). The world population has been estimated at 15,000 birds with the majority thought to breed in Kazakhstan, U.S.S.R. (Matthews and Evans 1974), although Borodin (1984) gives only 700-900 pairs for the U.S.S.R.. Grozdev (1978) gives several examples of decline or disappearance at sites in Kazakhstan. The species is migratory and partially migratory (some perhaps resident), wintering sparsely in North Africa, south-east Europe east across Asia Minor to north-west **China** (Cramp and Simmons 1987; also Meyer de Schauensee 1984); the largest wintering concentrations are in Turkey and **Pakistan** (Beaman 1975, Ahmad in prep.).

Order FALCONIFORMES

Family Cathartidae
New World vultures

California Condor *Gymnogyps californianus* from the foothills of the Coast Range and Sierra Nevada of California, **U.S.A.**, has declined owing to shooting, trapping, poisoning, disturbance, egg-collecting and low reproductive potential (King 1978-1979), and the enigmatic frequent use of poor-quality nesting sites (Snyder *et al.* 1986). Poisoning from lead-shot fragments in game carcasses left in the field seems to have been an important source of mortality (Pattee 1987). The last wild bird was captured in 1987 to join 26 others held for captive breeding in San Diego Wild Animal Park and Los Angeles Zoo, and in March 1988 the first egg from a captive pair was laid; condors have been previously hatched in captivity but only from eggs taken from the wild (*New Scientist* 117,1603 [1988]: 23). A captive-breeding and release programme developed by the New York Zoological Society for the Andean Condor *Vultur gryphus* may provide a model for the Californian Condor (Bruning 1983).

Family Accipitridae
Hawks, eagles, harriers, Old World vultures

Black Honey-buzzard *Henicopernis infuscata* is a rare and little-known endemic of **New Britain**, **Papua New Guinea**, where it occurs in forest to 1,000 m (Schodde 1978), but there are few recent records of the species: Bishop (1983) observed it only twice in nearly two years of fieldwork in West New Britain and reports two other sightings in the previous decade; it occurs at very low density in lowland forest that is increasingly logged and cleared for oil-palm (K. D. Bishop).

Red Kite *Milvus milvus* is confined to the western Palearctic, where there has been a marked decrease in range and numbers in many areas, with a total breeding population estimated at 5,500-15,000 pairs spanning **Belgium, Czechoslovakia, Denmark, France, West Germany, East Germany, Hungary, Italy, Luxembourg, Netherlands, Poland, Portugal, Romania, Spain, Sweden, Switzerland, U.K., U.S.S.R.** and **Yugoslavia** (Cramp and Simmons 1980, Gensbol 1986). In the U.S.S.R., it breeds in Belorussia, Ukraine, Moldavia and perhaps the Caucasus with a population of approximately 100 pairs only (Borodin 1984). The species is migratory in north and central Europe, wintering in the Mediterranean basin, resident and dispersive further south (Cramp and Simmons 1980).

Solomons Sea Eagle *Haliaeetus sanfordi* is endemic to the **Solomon Islands** where it was reported common along coasts and in lowland forest (Brown and Amadon 1968). However, coastal forests are now rapidly disappearing, the species requires a large territory, and appears to have become uncommon (K. D. Bishop).

Madagascar Fish Eagle *Haliaeetus vociferoides* is confined to the rivers, shorelines and offshore islands of the west coast of **Madagascar** north of Morondava (Collar and Stuart 1985). Forty-eight occupied sites were recorded, 1982-1986, comprising 96 individuals and including 40 pairs plus 10 adults; at least two protected areas are needed to secure the majority of these birds (Langrand 1987).

Pallas's Fish Eagle *Haliaeetus leucoryphus* occurs from Kazakhstan, **U.S.S.R.**, east through **Mongolia** to **China**, south to northern **India, Nepal** (chiefly a winter visitor), **Pakistan** and **Burma**, northern breeders normally wintering south to **Iran** and probably the Indian subcontinent, birds breeding in the subcontinent dispersing perhaps north to the plateau lakes of western Xizang Zizhiqu (Cramp and Simmons 1980, Inskipp and Inskipp 1985a). In the U.S.S.R. the species has bred this century only in Kazakhstan and it may no longer do so with a total population of only 100 birds (Bannikov 1978, Borodin 1984). In India it is described as more or less common where it occurs (Ali and Ripley 1984), although recent observers have found it to be thinly distributed (R. F. Grimmett); it is rapidly declining in Bangladesh (Sarker and Iqbal 1985) and occurs throughout Burma but with no information on its recent status (Smythies 1986), whilst its situation in Mongolia and China is very poorly known (e.g. Piechocki *et al.* 1981, Mauersberger *et al.* 1982).

White-tailed Eagle *Haliaeetus albicilla* is widely but sparsely distributed from west **Greenland (to Denmark)**, east to Kamchatka, **U.S.S.R.** and north-west **China,** breeding in **Austria, Bulgaria, Czechoslovakia, Finland, West Germany, East Germany, Greece,** Greenland, **Hungary, Iceland, Iran, Japan, Mongolia, Norway, Poland, Romania, Sweden, Turkey,** U.K. (introduced population), U.S.S.R. and **Yugoslavia** and possibly Albania, with migratory populations wintering south of this, in the Middle East, Indian subcontinent, China and Japan (King 1978-1979, Cramp and Simmons 1980, Piechocki *et al.* 1981, Ali and Ripley 1984, Meyer de Schauensee 1984, Gensbol 1986). In Europe, the species has declined in most parts of its range because of human persecution, habitat destruction and pollution, and breeding populations are mainly in East Germany, Norway, Poland, Sweden and Yugoslavia (Gensbol 1984). In the U.S.S.R. it is declining across much of the country with 2,000 or more pairs (Kolosov 1983, Borodin 1984). Recent studies in Sweden include Helander (1980, 1983), Helander *et al.* (1982), and in Norway Folkestad (1984) and Willgohs (1984), and an important general account is by Love (1983).

Steller's Sea Eagle *Haliaeetus pelagicus* breeds only in the U.S.S.R., along the coast of the Bering Sea, Okhotsk Sea and Sakhalin Island, wintering south to **Japan** and Korea (presumed **North Korea** and **South Korea**) (Flint *et al.* 1984, Brazil 1986). The breeding population is estimated to be 2,200 pairs (Lobkov and Neufeldt 1986), with very large numbers gathering in winter on Shiretoko Peninsula, Hokkaido (Japan) (Brazil 1986). A survey in winter 1985/1986 indicated around 4,000 birds in Kamchatka Peninsula (the main and almost only Russian wintering area) and just over 2,000 in Japan, giving a total population estimate of 6,000-7,000 (Fujimaki 1987, Shibaev 1987b).

Cape Vulture *Gyps coprotheres* breeds in **Botswana, Lesotho, Mozambique, Namibia, South Africa, Swaziland** and formerly **Zimbabwe,** with a world population in 1983 of 10,000 birds facing a multitude of threats and steadily declining (Collar and Stuart 1985; also Brooke 1984). New data bearing on the species's conservation are in Boshoff and Robertson (1985), Brown (1985), Borello (1985, 1986), Piper and Ruddle (1986), Robertson (1986), Robertson and Boshoff (1986), Robertson and February (1986), Vernon and Piper (1986), Borello and Borello (1987) and Boshoff and Vernon (1987).

Black Vulture *Aegypius monachus* has an extensive breeding range from **Spain** east to **China**, but has disappeared from most of Europe. It breeds in **Spain, Greece, Turkey,** U.S.S.R.**, Iran, Afghanistan, Pakistan, India, Mongolia** and China, possibly also Morocco, Portugal, Yugoslavia, Albania, Bulgaria, Cyprus and Nepal (where it is mainly an uncommon winter visitor) (Meyburg and Meyburg 1983, Ali and Ripley 1984, Inskipp and Inskipp 1985a). In Europe, only Spain has a sizeable population (365 pairs) (E. de Juana), in Turkey the population is estimated to be over 100 pairs, in U.S.S.R. it breeds mainly in the Caucasus and Central Asia, and it is described as common in Mongolia, but there are no recent data from Iran, Afghanistan, Pakistan or China (Meyburg and Meyburg 1983).

Kinabalu Serpent-eagle *Spilornis kinabaluensis* is known only from Kinabalu and Trus Madi in Sabah, and Gn Mulu and Gn Murad in Sarawak, **Malaysia** (Smythies 1981). A large raptor with such a localised distribution and a small population is presumed sensitive to minor degradation of its habitat, particularly as in some areas it might be sympatric with the Crested Serpent-eagle *S. cheela* (S. C. B. Harrap, N. J. Redman; see Amadon 1974).

Dark Serpent-eagle *Spilornis elgini* is a low-density endemic resident of the **Andaman Islands (to India)** (Ripley 1982). It is little known but apparently favours clearings in the interior forests whilst the local race of the Crested Serpent-eagle *S. cheela davisoni* occurs more commonly in coastal forest and mangroves (Brown and Amadon 1968, Amadon 1974).

Madagascar Serpent-eagle *Eutriorchis astur* is a very rare inhabitant of primary rainforest in **Madagascar** where, apart from unconfirmed reports of its presence in Marojejy Reserve in the 1960s and 1970s, it has not been recorded since 1930 despite persistent recent searches (Collar and Stuart 1985, O. Langrand). A ninth specimen is in Dresden (Eck 1986) and two more are in Boston (N. J. Collar), but none provides data extending the range of the species.

Red Goshawk *Accipiter radiatus* is still known from much of its historical range in northern and eastern **Australia**, from Kimberley in Western Australia to northern New South Wales, but is sparsely distributed (Blakers *et al.* 1984) and its breeding range has apparently shrunk by approximately 25 per cent (D. J. Baker-Gabb). It affects woodland and repeated burning for grazing may be causing the species's decline; a three year study funded by the WWF and RAOU has started (D. J. Baker-Gabb).

Small Sparrowhawk *Accipiter nanus* is endemic to Sulawesi, **Indonesia**, and is believed to be a rare resident of mountain forest, usually between 900 and 2,000 m (White and Bruce 1986). It is not readily separable from the widespread Vinous-breasted Sparrowhawk *A. rhodogaster* (White and Bruce 1986) and consequently its status is uncertain.

New Britain Sparrowhawk *Accipiter brachyurus* is confined to New Britain, **Papua New Guinea**, where it occurs at very low density in forest and forest edge to 1,000 m (Schodde 1978). Records are extremely sparse: Diamond (1971) collected one in 1969 and one was observed at forest edge on the north coast of western New Britain in 1980 (K. D. Bishop) and its status is uncertain.

Imitator Sparrowhawk *Accipiter imitator* is known from Bougainville, **Papua New Guinea**, and Choiseul and Santa Isabel, **Solomon Islands**, where it is rare (Hadden 1981, K. D. Bishop, J. M. Diamond). All adult specimens are female, and the male remains undescribed (Brown and Amadon 1968).

Semicollared Sparrowhawk *Accipiter collaris* is a rare bird of humid or wet forest (there is apparently no evidence of its use of forest edge, *contra* Blake 1977) with a very restricted range (recorded from a very few localities) in **Colombia** and **Ecuador**, with one record each from **Venezuela** and **Peru** (Blake 1977, Collar 1986, Hilty and Brown 1986).

Gundlach's Hawk *Accipiter gundlachii* frequents forest borders, swamps, wooded coasts and mountains below 800 m on **Cuba** where, despite reports of it being extremely rare, it appears to be widely recorded, very secretive, and possibly at no risk (Garrido 1985, Collar 1986); however, Wotzkow (1985) identifies only three main areas for the species and considers it has suffered seriously from deforestation and persecution. Ecological data are in Wotzkow (1986).

Grey-bellied Hawk *Accipiter poliogaster*, although widely distributed with records in **Suriname** (Haverschmidt 1972), **Guyana, Venezuela, Colombia, Ecuador, Peru, Brazil, Bolivia, Paraguay** and **Argentina**, appears to be rare throughout its range, where it has been found in humid lowland forest, riparian forest borders and patches of dense woodland (Hilty and Brown 1986, D. A. Scott); all Colombian records are from the austral winter, suggesting it is a migrant from the south (Hilty and Brown 1986).

Plumbeous Hawk *Leucopternis plumbea* has a fairly restricted range and is apparently rare in **Panama** (rare or extinct in the west), western **Colombia** (a few scattered localities), western **Ecuador** and extreme north-west **Peru** (Blake 1977, Hilty and Brown 1986, J. R. Karr). However, much of its habitat remains intact (R. S. Ridgely).

White-necked Hawk *Leucopternis lacernulata* is endemic to mainly lowland forest in the Atlantic region of **Brazil** (Sick 1985), where it is almost wholly sympatric with its threatened (but somewhat more widespread, higher-level) congener the Mantled Hawk *L. polionota*, and must be at risk from habitat loss (Collar 1986, Meyburg 1986). In southern Brazil the only recent records are from sectors of dense forest in the Serra do Mar, Parana (Albuquerque 1986).

Grey-backed Hawk *Leucopternis occidentalis* is restricted to western **Ecuador**, where it is known to have declined seriously with forest destruction (King 1978-1979), and adjacent north-west **Peru** (Parker *et al.* 1982, Wiedenfeld *et al.* 1985).

Mantled Hawk *Leucopternis polionota* inhabits primary forest in south-east **Brazil**, eastern **Paraguay** and northern **Argentina** and is known to have become extremely scarce (King 1978-1979), although it may be (regionally at least) commoner than its congener the White-necked Hawk *L. lacernulata* (E. O. Willis, F. C. Straube, J. F. Pacheco).

Solitary Eagle *Harpyhaliaetus solitarius*, although widely distributed in the forested foothills and uplands of **Mexico, Guatemala, Honduras, Costa Rica, Panama, Venezuela, Colombia, Ecuador** and **Peru** (Blake 1977), now also **French Guiana** (Thiollay 1985), is nonetheless very rare and local, and hence vulnerable to montane forest destruction (S. L. Hilty, D. A. Scott).

Crowned Eagle *Harpyhaliaetus coronatus* of open country and cerrado (woodland savanna) in **Brazil, Paraguay**, possibly Uruguay, **Bolivia** and **Argentina** is very local and suffering seriously from habitat modification and hunting (Albuquerque 1986, W. Belton, J. C. Chebez, T. A. Parker, R. S. Ridgely, E. O. Willis, C. Yamashita). The population in Argentina may only comprise two or three pairs (Olrog 1985).

Ridgway's Hawk *Buteo ridgwayi* is confined to **Haiti** and **Dominican Republic** and surrounding islands, where it was formerly common but has now suffered from extensive and continuing forest clearance, such that there is now concern for its future (Wiley and Wiley 1981, Wiley 1986); it may already be extinct in (mainland) Haiti (M. McDonald).

Galapagos Hawk *Buteo galapagoensis* is endemic to the **Galapagos Islands (to Ecuador)**, where it has declined seriously and on five islands become extinct (King 1978-1979), or nearly so (Faaborg 1984). However, it remains quite common on seven islands with a total population of around 130 pairs or groups, "cooperative polyandry" being a notable feature in the species's biology (see Faaborg 1983, 1985), and restocking of certain islands has been proposed (Faaborg 1984) and counselled against (de Vries 1984).

Hawaiian Hawk *Buteo solitarius* breeds on Hawaii in the **Hawaiian Islands (to U.S.A.)** (King 1978-1979). It has wandered to Maui and Oahu, and is thinly but widely distributed on Hawaii; recent surveys suggest it is now quite common (Pratt *et al.* 1987) although this is questioned (W. C. Gagne).

Rufous-tailed Hawk *Buteo ventralis* inhabits the Andean region of central **Chile** and adjacent **Argentina** south to Tierra del Fuego, and is everywhere rare (Clark 1986, F. Vuilleumier), although there have been some recent sightings generally suggesting it may not be at risk (J. Fjeldsa, R. S. Ridgely).

Crested Eagle *Morphnus guianensis* occupies humid lowland forest in the tropical and lower subtropical zones in **Guatemala, Honduras,** presumably Nicaragua but no records, **Costa Rica, Panama, Colombia, Venezuela, Guyana, Suriname, French Guiana, Brazil, Ecuador, Peru, Bolivia, Paraguay** and northernmost **Argentina** (Blake 1977, AOU 1983, Olrog 1985), south throughout such habitat primarily east of the Andes (AOU 1983). In much of its range it is accounted rare (e.g. Blake 1977, Parker *et al.* 1982) and is "nowhere numerous" (Friedman 1950); because of this, its wide territorial needs and its dependence on primary rainforest, it was treated as threatened by King (1978-1979). Two recent observers, however, consider it probably better able to withstand a small degree of human pressure than the Harpy Eagle *Harpia harpyja* (Thiollay 1984, D. A. Scott). Nevertheless, in some areas (e.g. Central America, Venezuela, Suriname) it seems much rarer than the Harpy (see Phelps and Phelps 1958, Haverschmidt 1968, Blake 1977). Breeding biology data are in Bierregaard (1984).

Harpy Eagle *Harpia harpyja* occurs over an enormous range in the lowland rainforests of Central and South America (southern **Mexico, Guatemala, Belize, Honduras, Nicaragua, Costa Rica, Panama, Colombia, Venezuela, Guyana, Suriname, French Guiana, Ecuador, Peru, Bolivia, Brazil, Paraguay,** northern **Argentina**) but is everywhere rare (King 1978-1979). Extensive areas of pristine habitat remain in the Amazon basin, but this species, the most powerful of raptors, will only survive in the long term if the exponential rate of forest destruction in the region (see Malingreau and Tucker 1988) is brought under control and a network of inviolate reserves established.

New Guinea Harpy-eagle *Harpyopsis novaeguineae* is widely distributed at low density on mainland New Guinea (Irian Jaya, **Indonesia,** and **Papua New Guinea**), in undisturbed forest, in the lowlands and to 3,000 m; it is hunted for its tail and primary feathers and this pressure on a naturally small population, combined with habitat destruction, is thought to threaten the species, particularly in Papua New Guinea where firearms are prevalent (Beehler 1985, K. D. Bishop, J. M. Diamond, G. R. Kula).

Philippine Eagle *Pithecophaga jefferyi* still occurs throughout its historical range on Luzon, Leyte, Samar and Mindanao in the **Philippines** in forest from the lowlands to 2,000 m, but the population is now estimated at fewer than 200 birds in the wild (R. S. Kennedy). In the past hunting and trapping contributed to the species's decline (King 1978-1979), but deforestation is now the main cause of breeding failure and numerical decrease: the forests of the Sierra Madre mountains in Luzon represent the largest single stronghold for the species (Lewis 1986), but it is thought that deforestation at its present rate will lead to its extinction in the near future (R. S. Kennedy), although Samar is well forested and may hold a sizeable population (N. Lindsay).

Spanish Imperial Eagle *Aquila adalberti* is endemic to the Iberian Peninsula where it is resident but confined almost entirely to **Spain**, formerly breeding in north-east Algeria and northern Morocco (King 1978-1979). In **Portugal**, there were still 15-20 pairs prior to 1974-1975 but there are now probably only 1-2 pairs, although about 104 pairs remain in central, west and south-west Spain (Palma 1985, Gonzalez *et al.* 1986, E. de Juana). Important recent studies include Delibes (1978), Meyburg (1982, 1987) and Heredia *et al.* (1985).

Imperial Eagle *Aquila heliaca* is sparsely distributed from central and south-east Europe east to Lake Baykal in the **U.S.S.R.** and west Sinkiang, **China** (Cramp and Simmons 1980, Meyer de Schauensee 1984). In Europe, there are very small breeding populations in **Bulgaria, Cyprus, Czechoslovakia, Greece, Hungary, Romania, Yugoslavia** and possibly Albania (Gensbol 1986). In **Turkey** the species is thinly distributed in the northern half of the country and the population is estimated as 50-150 pairs (Beaman and Porter 1985, Gensbol 1986). In **Israel** it is rare and breeds only irregularly (Cramp and Simmons 1980). In **Iran** its status is apparently not known, whilst in the U.S.S.R. (which comprises the bulk of its distributional range) there are less than 500-1,000 pairs and its range has retreated southwards (Cramp and Simmons 1980, Borodin 1984). It is partially migratory, wintering sparsely in north-east Africa, Pakistan, India and east to Japan (Cramp and Simmons 1980, Ali and Ripley 1984).

Javan Hawk-eagle *Spizaetus bartelsi* is endemic to the forests of Java, **Indonesia**, where it is known from the lowlands to 2,000 m, but favours forest on the lower slopes between 200 and 1,200 m (Kuroda 1936), a habitat now much reduced (P. Andrew). It is largely confined to forest reserves, and is rare below 1,000 m in western Java though more widespread in the east; small numbers still appear in bird markets, but the principal threat is deforestation and the further fragmentation of the population (P. Andrew; see Andrew 1985).

Wallace's Hawk-eagle *Spizaetus nanus* occurs in south Tenasserim, **Burma**, peninsular **Thailand** and **Malaysia**, Borneo and Sumatra, **Indonesia** (King *et al.* 1975). It is an extreme lowland forest specialist (Wells 1985); continuing fragmentation of lowland forest may threaten an already rare and thinly distributed species (F. R. Lambert).

Family Falconidae
Falcons, caracaras

Plumbeous Forest-falcon *Micrastur plumbeus* is a rare bird restricted to southwest **Colombia** (foothills and lower slopes in wet forest, 600-900 m) and northwest **Ecuador** (Blake 1977, Hilty and Brown 1986). Despite its rarity, much habitat remains (R. S. Ridgely).

Traylor's Forest-falcon *Micrastur buckleyi* is a rare forest bird in Amazonian **Ecuador** and north-east **Peru** (Blake 1977). Despite its rarity, much habitat remains within its range (R. S. Ridgely).

Lesser Kestrel *Falco naumanni* breeds widely in the Palearctic with a dramatic decline in many areas in recent years due probably to pesticides, modern agricultural methods and climatic conditions (Cramp 1980, Gensbol 1986). The species breeds in **Portugal** (decreasing), **Spain** (decreasing markedly), **Gibraltar (to U.K.**), **France, Italy** (decreasing), **Austria, Yugoslavia, Albania, Greece** (most colonies reduced to two or three pairs each in 1987), **Bulgaria** (rare) **Romania** (rare), **U.S.S.R.** (common in Ukraine, Crimea and Caucasus in 1951), **Turkey** (locally common), **Cyprus, Syria** (decreasing), **Lebanon** (decreasing), **Israel** (considerable decrease), **Tunisia** (200+ pairs in 1982) **Algeria** (rare), **Morocco** (1,000+ pairs), **Egypt** (rare), **Iran, Mongolia** and **China**; it is now extinct or breeds only irregularly in Poland, Czechoslovakia, Switzerland, and Hungary (Cramp 1980, Piechocki *et al.* 1981, Gensbol 1986, Meyer de Schauensee 1984, HOS 1987, Hollom *et al.* 1988). On migration it is widely recorded throughout the Indian subcontinent, Middle East and Africa (some birds staying to winter), wintering mainly in southern Africa, notably **Botswana, Namibia** and **South Africa** (Cramp 1980, Ripley 1982).

Mauritius Kestrel *Falco punctatus* is restricted to the remaining forest of southwest **Mauritius**, where in 1974 its known population was only six birds although a decade later six pairs were estimated present and 10 additional birds were in captivity (Collar and Stuart 1985; see also Jones 1987). Fourteen young were reared in captivity, 1985-1986, when the wild population was 19-25 birds (Cheke 1987d). This was still the situation in the wild at the start of the 1987-1988 breeding season, when eight pairs bred or attempted to breed, and 21 birds were released into the wild (10 of them having been reared from wild-laid eggs), 12 of them into the Bambous Mountains where currently no wild birds are present (C. G. Jones).

Grey Falcon *Falco hypoleucos* is widely but very sparsely distributed across **Australia**, and outside its main island range reports are incidental and years apart (Blakers *et al.* 1984; also Cade 1982). It affects acacia scrub, spinifex and tussock grassland and is sensitive to the agricultural development of timbered plains (Hermes 1980). Breeding records indicate that the species's range has shrunk in recent years and is now largely confined to areas within the 250 mm annual rainfall zone (Olsen and Olsen 1986).

Orange-breasted Falcon *Falco deiroleucus* occurs over an enormous range in Central and South America (southern **Mexico, Guatemala, Honduras, Nicaragua, Costa Rica, Panama, Colombia, Venezuela, Trinidad and Tobago, Guyana, Suriname, Ecuador, Peru, Brazil, Paraguay**, northern **Argentina**, eastern **Bolivia**) but is everywhere rare and patchily distributed (Blake 1977,

Remsen and Traylor 1983). The species requires level lowland forest over which to hunt, but only appears to be found where higher ground provides nest-sites and vantage-points and where concentrations of avian aerial feeders (a common prey) occur (Jenny and Cade 1986, Jenny and Burnham 1987, J. P. Jenny). In Argentina it survives in three and possibly six provinces, and occupies savanna woodland (Olrog 1985). In certain areas it may be affected by the use of insecticides in agriculture (P. Roth).

Order GALLIFORMES

Family Megapodiidae
Megapodes

Nicobar Scrubfowl *Megapodius nicobariensis* is endemic to the **Nicobar Islands (to India)** (Ali and Ripley 1984). It occurs in forest undergrowth and lays in a mound of sand and vegetable matter built within a few metres of the high water mark; it is still believed to be common (Ali and Ripley 1984) but is vulnerable to predation and egg harvesting, particularly as development of the islands proceeds (S. A Hussein).

Sula Scrubfowl *Megapodius bernsteinii* is found on the Banggai and Sula Islands, **Indonesia**, but is unknown in the wild and has not been recorded since 1938 (White and Bruce 1986); commercial logging is believed extensive on the islands (K. D. Bishop).

Micronesian Megapode *Megapodius laperouse* is restricted to **Palau (to U.S.A.)** and the **Northern Marianas Islands (to U.S.A.)** (King 1978-1979, Pratt *et al.* 1987). In Palau it is locally common on the limestone islands and on outlying islands such as Kayangel, but it is rare on the larger volcanic islands; in the Marianas a small population remains on Saipan and it is known from nine of the ten small, mostly uninhabited islands to the north (Engbring and Pratt 1985), but the species remains vulnerable to egg harvesting and the introduction of predators (Hay 1986).

Niuafo'ou Megapode *Megapodius pritchardii* is confined to the remote island of Niuafo'ou, **Tonga**, where it uses hot volcanic ash to incubate its eggs, a habit which concentrates its nesting sites to areas of loose soil close to vents, either in forest or in open ash; population estimates in the last decade have varied considerably but between 200 and 400 birds are thought to inhabit the island; the major threat to the species is from predation by feral cats and egg harvesting

(Todd 1983, Hay 1986). Although the species is protected by law, there is no enforcement and more than 100 eggs can be collected at each breeding site in one year (Rinke 1986).

Moluccan Scrubfowl *Megapodius wallacei* is known from some of the larger islands of the Moluccas, **Indonesia**, where it inhabits hill and mountain forest but lays on coastal beaches (White and Bruce 1986) and hence is vulnerable to egg harvesting (K. D. Bishop). It is still common on Buru (M. van Balgooy *per* F. G. Rozendaal), and has been observed in undisturbed forest on Seram where it does not tolerate disturbance as readily as Orange-footed Scrubfowl *M. reinwardt* (J. Bowler, J. B. Taylor).

Malleefowl *Leipoa ocellata* was formerly widespread in the mallee forests in Western **Australia** through South Australia, south-west Northern Territory, to north-west Victoria and west New South Wales (Blakers *et al.* 1984). It has disappeared or is now rare through 80 per cent of its range, continues to decline in New South Wales and is probably extinct in Northern Territory; except in South Australia and Victoria, reserve pockets of mallee are proving too small to support a viable population (J. Brouwer; see also Booth 1987).

Waigeo Brush-turkey *Aepypodius bruijnii* is an apparently rare inhabitant of Waigeo Island, Irian Jaya, **Indonesia**, where it inhabits evergreen forest in the interior of the island, an inaccessible and secure habitat; it is known only from specimens obtained by native collectors in the last century and by one specimen collected in 1939 (Rand and Gilliard 1967). It has been reported by natives on Waigeo and probably sighted on Batanta in 1986 (K. D. Bishop, J. M. Diamond,), but the only other record is a report of two nest mounds on an unnamed islet in 1973 (G. Mountfort).

Maleo *Macrocephalon maleo* is endemic to Sulawesi, **Indonesia**, and found chiefly in the northern peninsula (White and Bruce 1986). It lays communally on coastal beaches and in sandy-bottomed forest clearings where geothermal activity maintains a suitable substrate temperature; the eggs are harvested by local villagers (Dekker 1987). In northern Sulawesi there were an estimated 3,000 adult birds in 13 known colonies (King 1978-1979), but despite conservation measures, which included the artificial incubation of clutches, unprotected nest sites remain vulnerable to over-exploitation and predation by village dogs (Dekker and Wattel 1987; see also MacKinnon 1983, Watling 1983b, van den Berg and Bosman 1986).

Family Cracidae
Curassows, guans, chachalacas

Rufous-headed Chachalaca *Ortalis erythroptera* occurs in thickets and deciduous forests in western **Ecuador** and extreme north-west **Peru** (Blake 1977, Wiedenfeld *et al.* 1985), and is now seriously at risk from habitat destruction that has fragmented its already small range (J. P. O'Neill, T. A. Parker, R. S. Ridgely, F. Vuilleumier).

Bearded Guan *Penelope barbata* occurs only in forest in southern **Ecuador** and north-west **Peru** (Blake 1977), and is now very rare in the former (R. S. Ridgely) and declining owing to hunting and habitat destruction in the latter (see, e.g., Parker *et al.* 1985).

Red-faced Guan *Penelope dabbenei* occupies a restricted range in montane forest (1,500-2,000 m) on the eastern slopes of the Andes from southern **Bolivia** to north-west **Argentina** (Blake 1977), where it is apparently rare and local (T. A. Parker, D. A. Scott) and suffering from habitat loss in Bolivia (J. V. Remsen), although it receives some protection from Calilegua National Park in Argentina (M. Rumboll).

White-winged Guan *Penelope albipennis* survives in scattered small areas of dry forest on lower slopes in north-west **Peru**, and perhaps now numbers no more than a hundred individuals (King 1978-1979, O'Neill *et al.* 1981, Ortiz Tejada and Purisaca Puicon 1981, Eley 1982).

Cauca Guan *Penelope perspicax* has suffered severe loss of its humid forest habitat on the slopes of the middle Cauca Valley, **Colombia**, and the absence of recent records had suggested its impending extinction (King 1978-1979, Hilty and Brown 1986). However, a *Penelope*, presumably this species, was glimpsed in early 1988 in the Bosque de Yotoco (E. Velasco), a locality identified in King (1978-1979) as possibly important for its survival, and there are still several well-forested but unvisited sites within its range, notably in the south, that merit investigation (J. Hernandez Camacho).

White-browed Guan *Penelope jacucaca* occupies dry areas of stunted forest in the interior of north-east **Brazil** (Blake 1977) and occurs in some densely populated areas (T. A. Parker): it is not yet rare but under great pressure from habitat loss and hunting (L. P. Gonzaga; also Estudillo Lopez 1983).

Chestnut-bellied Guan *Penelope ochrogaster* is a bird of wooded areas in central **Brazil** (Blake 1977): there has been much habitat destruction within its range (R. S. Ridgely), and it is now notably uncommon (L. P. Gonzaga, T. A. Parker, C. Yamashita).

Black-fronted Piping Guan *Pipile jacutinga* is restricted to small patches of forest in south-east **Brazil**, northern **Argentina** and south-east **Paraguay** (King 1978-1979). It is now known with certainty from fewer than 10 highly disjunct localities (Collar and Gonzaga in press).

Highland Guan *Penelopina nigra* is resident in cloud forest, chiefly at 1,000- 2,600 m, in the mountains of **Mexico** (south-eastern Oaxaca and northern Chiapas), **Guatemala, El Salvador** (at least formerly), **Honduras** and north-central **Nicaragua** (Blake 1977), and is severely at risk throughout is range from hunting and deforestation (Estudillo Lopez 1983, S. N. G. Howell, S. D. Strahl).

Horned Guan *Oreophasis derbianus* has a highly restricted distribution in cloud-forest, chiefly at 1,600-3,000 m, in the mountain regions of southernmost **Mexico** and western **Guatemala** (King 1978-1979). The only protected area in Mexico where the species occurs is the El Triunfo Reserve covering about 10,000 ha (M. A. Ramos), but there remain many sites in both countries where the species is likely to survive and others where it has yet to be sought (Collar and Gonzaga in press). Biological data are in Gonzalez Garcia (1984).

Alagoas Curassow *Mitu mitu* (here separated as a full species from the Razor-billed Curassow *Mitu tuberosa*) is or was restricted to a tiny region of remnant forest in north-east **Brazil** (King 1978-1979), but now chiefly or only survives in a single private collection in Rio de Janeiro (Estudillo Lopez 1983, L. P. Gonzaga).

Northern Helmeted Curassow *Pauxi pauxi* has a restricted range in cool humid forest in north-east **Colombia** (race *gilliardi*) and eastern Colombia through the mountains of northern **Venezuela** (nominate *pauxi*) (Blake 1977, Hilty and Brown 1986), where it lives at low density in declining numbers owing to hunting pressure and habitat loss (J. L. Silva, S. D. Strahl).

Southern Helmeted Curassow *Pauxi unicornis* is evidently extremely rare, being known from two specimens from central **Peru** and two from east-central **Bolivia** (Blake 1977). It is highly vulnerable, forest in its elevational zone being rapidly cleared (J. V. Remsen, J. W. Terborgh). In October 1987 a study of the species began in Amboro National Park, Bolivia, and rapidly located at least six birds in one locality (R. O. Clarke, G. G. Cox).

Blue-billed Curassow *Crax alberti* occurs in humid lowland, foothill and lower montane forest (up to 1,200 m) in discrete areas of northern **Colombia**, and suffers from habitat destruction and heavy hunting (King 1978-1979, Hilty and Brown 1986). It may now survive in only a very few localities (Collar and Gonzaga in press, J. Hernandez Camacho).

Wattled Curassow *Crax globulosa* of **Colombia, Ecuador, Peru, Brazil** and **Bolivia** (Blake 1977) inhabits river islands and riverine forest and is threatened by habitat loss and hunting pressure throughout much of its range (T. A. Parker, J. V. Remsen, R. S. Ridgely), although it has been found commonly in remote areas of northern Bolivia (J. Estudillo Lopez) and eastern Peru (F. Lehmann).

Red-billed Curassow *Crax blumenbachii* is restricted to primary forest in south-east **Brazil** (King 1978-1979), where it is currently known from only five forest patches: Sooretama Biological Reserve and the adjacent Linhares Forest Reserve in Espirito Santo, Monte Pascoal National Park and Una Biological Reserve in Bahia, and Rio Doce State Park in Minas Gerais (Collar *et al*. 1987, Gonzaga *et al*. 1987, Collar and Gonzaga in press).

Family Phasianidae
Pheasants, francolins, quails, peafowl

Bearded Wood-partridge *Dendrortyx barbatus* is a very rare forest species of the mountains of eastern **Mexico**, in a region where deforestation is rampant and hunting uncontrolled (S. N. G. Howell, D. A. Scott).

Chestnut Wood-quail *Odontophorus hyperythrus* occurs in humid montane forest in the Western and Central Andes of **Colombia**, where it is uncommon and local (Hilty and Brown 1986), and threatened by continuing deforestation (S. L. Hilty, R. S. Ridgely).

Gorgeted Wood-quail *Odontophorus strophium* was known only from four specimens (up to 1915), two from "Bogota", two from Subia (Cundinamarca), and a possible 1972 specimen near Betulia (Santander), all from the Eastern Andes of **Colombia** (King 1978-1979). These data have been corrected and extended, the species being recorded from four localities, although apparently only at the most recent, near Virolin (Santander), does any extensive habitat survive (see Romero-Zambrano 1984): this area is of enormous biological richness (M. A. Andrade, J. Hernandez Camacho) and a survey in March 1988 confirmed good numbers there of the wood-quail (M. de L. Brooke).

Djibouti Francolin *Francolinus ochropectus*, a ground-dwelling gamebird endemic to **Djibouti**, faces extinction as its juniper forest habitat in the Foret du Day National Park is destroyed by overgrazing, clearance, firewood-gathering, army manoeuvres and other developments (Collar and Stuart 1985). The report of a population of 5,000 in 1984 was provided in error: in 1978 it was 5,600 falling by 1985 to 1,500, 200 of which had that year been located in a second (relict) forest at Mablas (Blot 1985). However, even these figures are open to question, and the species may have had a lower but relatively stable population all along (Welch and Welch 1986, Welch *et al*. 1986; see also Urban *et al*. 1986).

Mount Cameroon Francolin *Francolinus camerunensis* inhabits dense forest undergrowth and clearings above 850 m on Mount Cameroon, **Cameroon**, where hunting appears to pose the only (and still relatively insignificant) threat to the species (Collar and Stuart 1985, Stuart and Jensen 1986, Urban *et al*. 1986).

Swierstra's Francolin *Francolinus swierstrai* has been found in forest and forest edge in a few montane areas in western **Angola**, principally in the Bailundu Highlands where hunting may represent a serious problem (Collar and Stuart 1985) and where even in the early 1970s the patches of surviving forest were already only a few hectares each (Collar and Stuart 1988).

Nahan's Francolin *Francolinus nahani* is a rare gamebird known only from a few localities in lowland forest in eastern **Zaire** and central and western **Uganda**, where the paucity of records and lack of recent contact (no records from Zaire since 1960 or from Uganda since 1970) render its status obscure (Collar and Stuart 1985; see also Urban *et al.* 1986).

Swamp Partridge *Francolinus gularis* is a resident of the Ganges and Brahmaputra river basins from western **Nepal** and Uttar Pradesh east through northern Bihar, **Bangladesh**, and Assam in north-east **India** (Ripley 1982). It is a bird of grass jungle and swamps, and is threatened by the drainage and agricultural development of this habitat (Ali and Ripley 1984). In Nepal it is found in Kosi Tapu (T. P. Inskipp) and Sukla Phanta (Inskipp and Inskipp 1985a).

Manipur Bush Quail *Perdicula manipurensis* affects wet grassland and sometimes swamps in the hills of north-east **India** and **Bangladesh**, where it is believed to be getting scarcer as its habitat is drained (Ali and Ripley 1984).

Sichuan Hill-partridge *Arborophila rufipectus* is endemic to southern Sichuan, **China**, and restricted to broadleaf forest between 1,000 and 2,000 m elevation, where its known range is only 9,600 sq km in Mapien, Ebian, Ganluo and Ping Shan counties; it is fairly common in the 800 ha Huang Nian Shan forest but all the remaining forest in the species's range is scheduled for logging in the next 15 years, and it is unlikely to survive in the plantations of conifers that are replacing the indigenous forest (B. F. King and Li Guiyan).

Rickett's Hill-partridge *Arborophila gingica* is resident in south-east **China**, in the low wooded hills of Fujian, north Guangdong, and in the Yao Shan in Guangxi (Meyer de Schauensee 1984). Its status in this largely deforested region is unknown: it was noted at Kuatan, north-west Fujian, in June 1986 (C. Viney *per* C. R. Robson), is known from reserves in south Zhejiang and is fairly common in several areas of Guangdong (B. F. King).

Orange-necked Partridge *Arborophila davidi* remains known from one specimen collected at Phurieng, 250m, some 60 km east of Ho Chi Minh City, **Viet Nam**, (Delacour 1927, Vo Quy 1975).

Chestnut-headed Partridge *Arborophila cambodiana* is known from the mountains of south-east **Thailand** (one specimen from 1930) and adjacent south-west **Kampuchea** (King *et al.* 1975, F. G. Rozendaal); however, it is probably common at Khao Soi Dao in south-east Thailand, where captive birds have been photographed (F. G. Rozendaal).

White-eared Hill-partridge *Arborophila ardens* is endemic to the hills of the island of Hainan, **China** (Meyer de Schauensee 1984). Its status is unknown; it must be seriously at risk from habitat destruction but probably exists in one or two reserves (B. F. King).

Chestnut-necklaced Partridge *Arborophila charltonii* occurs in peninsular **Thailand** and **Malaysia**, Borneo and Sumatra, **Indonesia**, where it is found in forested lowlands to about 200 m (Davison 1982), but has not recently been recorded in Thailand (C. R. Robson), is patchily distributed in peninsular Malaysia (D. Yong) and Sumatra (van Marle and Voous 1988) and known only from Sabah on Borneo, where it is locally common, at least in the Danum Valley (D. Yong; for taxonomic treatment see Davison 1982).

Himalayan Quail *Ophrysia superciliosa* was an endemic of the western Himalayas in **India**, occurring in long grass and scrub on steep hillsides between 1,600 m and 2,100 m; the last specimen was collected near Naini Tal, Uttar Pradesh, in 1876, and the species is presumed extinct (King 1978-1979, Ali and Ripley 1984), yet perhaps survives.

Western Tragopan *Tragopan melanocephalus* is considered to be threatened in the western Himalayas, in **Pakistan**, **India** and south-west Xizang Zizhiqu, **China** (Meyer de Schauensee 1984), and is seriously reduced in distribution and abundance (King 1978-1979). Gaston (*et al.* 1981, 1983) identified two main blocks of occupied habitat: the Neelum Valley, India and Pakistan (see Islam and Crawford 1985, 1986), and the Chenab Valley east through the Ravi and Beas catchments to the eastern side of the Sutlej Valley, India. More recently a third block of occupied habitat has been located in the valleys adjoining the Indus River in north-west Pakistan (G. Duke, R. F. Grimmett, P. Walton).

Blyth's Tragopan *Tragopan blythii* is known from **Bhutan**, north-east **India**, **Burma**, and adjacent south-east Xizang Zizhiqu (Meyer de Schauensee 1984) and western Yunnan, **China** (C. R. Robson). It was, at least formerly, locally common in Burma (King 1978-1979) but its current status anywhere within its historical range is unknown.

Cabot's Tragopan *Tragopan caboti* is recorded from Fujian, Guangdong, Guangxi and Hunan provinces, southern Jiangxi (He Fen-qi) and southern Zhejiang, **China** (Meyer de Schauensee 1984). It affects evergreen broadleaf and coniferous forest between 1,200 and 1,400 m, descending to 800 to 1,000 m in winter (Zheng Guangmei *et al.* 1985, 1986). Forest destruction and human persecution have reduced the population and it is now local (King 1978-1979) though there are recent observations from the Wu Yi Shan (Fujian), Ba Bao Shan (Guangdong), and Wuyanling (Zhejiang), with a further population reported from a reserve in Jiangxi (King 1987c).

Sclater's Monal *Lophophorus sclateri* is found in the eastern Himalayas, in north-east **India**, northern **Burma** and in south-west **China**, including Yunnan and south-east Xizang Zizhiqu, but is rare over much of its range (King 1978-1979) and recent information on status is lacking (A. J. Gaston, C. R. Robson).

Chinese Monal *Lophophorus lhuysii* is resident in the mountains of north-central **China**, in northern Sichuan, eastern Qinghai and southern Gansu, where it affects meadows and scrub above 3,000 m, but hunting rather than habitat destruction is believed responsible for its being local, although it may not be uncommon in protected areas (King 1978-1979). It is fairly common at Wolong and Baihe, Sichuan (King 1986) and occurs in three other Giant Panda reserves in Sichuan (B. F. King; see also Lu Tai-chun *et al.* 1986).

Imperial Pheasant *Lophura imperialis* is known only from the provinces of Dong Hoi and Quangtri in **Viet Nam**, and adjoining parts of **Laos**, in dense forest of rough limestone mountains (King 1978-1979). It is considered rare in Viet Nam (Vo Quy 1975).

Vo Quy's Pheasant *Lophura hatinhensis* is a recently discovered species from northernmost central **Viet Nam**, only known from a small area south of Vinh in several adjacent valleys on the eastern slopes of the mountains, preferring lower altitudes than Edwards's Pheasant *L. edwardsi* (Vo Quy 1975, Robson 1987).

Edwards's Pheasant *Lophura edwardsi* is endemic to central **Viet Nam** where it is found in rugged limestone hills covered by damp forest with thick underbrush (King 1978-1979) and is considered a rare species (Vo Quy 1975). It was reportedly common at one locality during the last decade, but its current status is largely unknown (B. F. King).

Swinhoe's Pheasant *Lophura swinhoii* is widespread in breadleaf mountain forest on **Taiwan**, occurring down to sea level though usually in the hills to 2,000 m, but has declined to several thousand in number owing to the clearance of hardwood from gentler slopes and to its intolerance of modified habitats (King 1978-1979, Severinghaus 1978, 1986).

Salvadori's Pheasant *Lophura inornata* is endemic to Sumatra, **Indonesia**, where it is not well known but apparently affects forest between 600 and 2,200 m, particularly on the flatter ground around peaks (Delacour 1951). It was last collected in 1937 (Chasen and Hoogerwerf 1941) and the only recent record is of a pair at 2,000 m on Gn Kerinchi, West Sumatra (F. R. Lambert).

Crested Fireback *Lophura ignita* is a resident of south Tenasserim, **Burma**, peninsular **Thailand** and **Malaysia**, Borneo and Sumatra, **Indonesia** (King *et al.* 1975). It is confined to level lowland forest, particularly along river terraces, a habitat that has a high commercial timber content, is easily logged and is becoming increasingly rare (G. W. H. Davison; also, e.g., Wells 1985). It is locally common in Borneo (Smythies 1981) but has disappeared from parts of Sumatra where rubber plantations have replaced forests, and is known there since 1950 by one record (K. H. Voous).

Siamese Fireback *Lophura diardi* is found in north-west, north-east and south-east **Thailand, Laos, Kampuchea** and all but extreme northern **Viet Nam** (King *et al*. 1975; centre of Central Viet Nam in Vo Quy 1975). It does not appear to coexist with the Silver Pheasant *L. nycthemera*, and consequently is restricted to the narrow altitudinal zone between lowland cultivation and approximately 750 m (Round in press).

Bulwer's Pheasant *Lophura bulweri* is endemic to Borneo (**Malaysia** and **Indonesia**) and found in primary forest between 300 and 750 m and occasionally to 1,500 m altitude, being not uncommon (Smythies 1981) but patchily distributed with no recent records from Kalimantan (King 1978-1979). The species occurs in the Lanjak-Entimau Orang-utan Sanctuary, Sarawak, and is well-known to natives in the south who do not regard it as rare (M. Kavanagh).

White Eared-pheasant *Crossoptilon crossoptilon* is distributed through the mountains of north-east **India, Burma** and western **China,** where it was once considered relatively abundant but was later judged possibly vulnerable (King 1978-1979). It is now found to be a tolerant high-altitude species (C. R. Robson), locally common in parts of western Sichuan (B. F. King).

Brown Eared-pheasant *Crossoptilon mantchuricum* inhabits forest in the mountains of northern **China,** in north Shanxi and formerly in north Hebei, and declined with the deforestation of the mountains (King 1978-1979). It is now only known to survive in three reserves, in one of which - the Pangquanguo Nature Reserve in the Luliang Shan in west central Shanxi - it is fairly common (King 1987a).

Cheer Pheasant *Catreus wallichii* occurs in the western Himalayas, from northern **Pakistan** and **India,** south-east along the foothills to central **Nepal;** it is considered threatened by habitat destruction and hunting (King 1978-1979). The species was deemed extinct in Pakistan but small populations still survive in the Neelum Valley (R. F. Grimmett). Since 1978 a reintroduction programme in the Margalla Hills, Pakistan, has been attempted without success (Young *et al*. 1986). A population of 40 pairs was estimated for the Chail Wildlife Sanctuary, Himachal Pradesh, India (Gaston and Singh 1980), with viable populations in several other areas in the state, suggesting a total population there of more than a thousand pairs (Gaston *et al*. 1981). However, results obtained for Chail in 1983 suggested there could have been a 50 per cent decline, with poaching, grass harvesting, disease and breeding failure possible causes (Garson 1983). Observations in Nepal are very limited (Lelliot 1981, Inskipp and Inskipp 1985a). Census techniques are discussed in Young *et al.* (1987).

Elliot's Pheasant *Syrmaticus ellioti* is recorded south of the Chang Jiang, from northern Guangdong, Fujian, Jiangxi, Zhejiang, Guangxi and southern Anhwei, in eastern **China** (Knoder 1983, Meyer de Schauensee 1984). It frequents forest and ravines in the hills, and is becoming increasingly scarce as forest is removed and its habitat becomes accessible to hunters and trappers (King 1978-1979). It is still to be found in the Yi Shan, north-west Jiangxi, but the forests are not protected and the species could be extinct in the province within a decade (King 1987b), and it is uncommon at Wuyanling in southern Zhejiang (B. F. King).

Hume's Pheasant *Syrmaticus humiae* is found in north-east **India**, northern and eastern **Burma** and adjacent hill country in southern Yunnan, **China**, and north-west **Thailand**, and although not believed to be immediately threatened it is rare (King 1978-1979). It is found at 1,500 m in eastern Burma on oak-dotted slopes cut by evergreen forested valleys and ravines (King 1985). There are few recent records.

Mikado Pheasant *Syrmaticus mikado* mainly occupies coniferous and mixed coniferous and broadleaf forest on the steeper slopes of mountain forest on **Taiwan**, although it is adapting to secondary habitats (King 1978-1979). While its status could well change with the construction of new roads (Severinghaus 1978), it is still regarded as relatively secure (Severinghaus 1986).

Reeves's Pheasant *Syrmaticus reevesii* is recorded from the hills of central and northern **China** (Meyer de Schauensee 1984), primarily between 350 and 1,000 m but up to 2,000 m in Guizhou where the population is put at around 500 (Wu Zhi-kang and Hsu Wei-shu 1986). It is said to be extirpated in Shanxi (King 1987a); its predilection for lower-altitude deciduous forest, of which there is little remaining, seriously threatens the species in the wild (B. F. King). Introduction to Hawaii and various parts of Europe (Cramp and Simmons 1980, Lever 1987) has led to its firm establishment at least in **Czechoslovakia** (Pokorny and Pikula 1987).

Germain's Peacock-pheasant *Polyplectron germaini* is a resident of southern **Viet Nam**, usually in damp forest up to 1,200 m, and was, at least formerly, common (Delacour 1951); it is also reported from the Boloven Plateau in **Laos** (J. McNeely). Its current status is unknown, but in 1986/1987 it was reported in Nam Cat Tien National Park in southern Viet Nam (Morris 1987).

Malaysian Peacock-pheasant *Polyplectron malacense* is known from south Tenasserim, **Burma**, peninsular **Thailand** and **Malaysia**, and **Borneo** (King *et al.* 1975). It favours level lowland forest, especially river terraces, and is consequently threatened by the logging of such commercially valuable forest (G. W. H. Davison; also, e.g., Wells 1985) although it is still locally common in peninsular Malaysia (D. Yong). The Bornean race *schleiermacheri* is sometimes treated as a separate species (see Johnsgard 1986) and is apparently rare, being known by a handful of specimens collected over half a century ago (Smythies 1981) and a single record from West Kalimantan in 1981 (Holmes and Burton 1987). The species is listed by Chasen (1935), but its occurrence in Sumatra is not supported (van Marle and Voous 1988).

Palawan Peacock-pheasant *Polyplectron emphanum* is endemic to Palawan in the **Philippines**, where it affects lowland and hill forest (King 1978-1979). The highest densities are found in forest edge and undisturbed forest but it also occurs in logged forest (Caleda *et al.* 1986). It is still widespread on the island and common in St Paul's National Park (B. F. King, J. Scharringa), but is heavily shot and trapped, and is extirpated from the vicinity of towns (T. H. Fisher).

Crested Argus *Rheinartia ocellata* is found in distinct populations, nominate *ocellata* in central **Viet Nam** and central **Laos**, and the race *nigrescens* in central peninsular **Malaysia**; the status of the former population is unknown though it was considered common within its restricted range in 1924 (King 1978- 1979, Vo Quy 1975). In Malaysia it favours forest in the 800 to 1,050 m altitudinal range, and is locally distributed in the mountains of north Pahang and south Kelantan; almost the entire population is contained in Taman Negara National Park (G. W. H. Davison).

Green Peafowl *Pavo muticus* is described in three races: *spicifer* in north-east **India** and the hill tracts of Bangladesh where it is probably extinct, and western **Burma** where its status is unknown; *imperator* in eastern Burma, **Thailand**, southern Yunnan, **China**, **Laos**, **Kampuchea** and **Viet Nam**, where it is locally and patchily distributed; and nominate *muticus* in peninsular Malaysia where it is probably extinct, and Java, **Indonesia** (King 1978-1979, Hillgarth *et al.* 1986). The species is locally common in Burma but despite official protection it is still hunted (Salter 1983), and still occurs (estimated maximum of 200 birds) at Huai Kha Khaeng in south-west Thailand (P. D. Round) and in Nam Cat Thien in southern Viet Nam (G. E. Morris *per* C. R. Robson; see *Garrulax* 5 in press). In Indonesia it is essentially restricted to the island of Peucang in the Sunda Straits, and to the reserves of Ujong Kulon and Leuweng Sancang (B. van Balen) in western Java and Baluran in eastern Java (P. D. Round, B. Stewart Cox).

Congo Peacock *Afropavo congensis* is a shy, ground-haunting pheasant (the only species native to Africa) known from a wide area of equatorial rainforest in eastern **Zaire**, where it appears to be uncommon but secure (Collar and Stuart 1985; see also Urban *et al.* 1986).

Family Numididae
Guineafowl

White-breasted Guineafowl *Agelastes meleagrides*, endemic to the Upper Guinea forest zone of West Africa but possibly already extinct in **Ghana**, requires primary or mature secondary forest and freedom from persecution to survive, and is consequently becoming isolated and depleted in the ever-diminishing pockets of such habitat in **Ivory Coast** and **Liberia** (Collar and Stuart 1985; also Urban *et al.* 1986), although it is now known to persist in Gola Forest, **Sierra Leone** (Davies 1987). In Tai Forest (Ivory Coast), four adults with a small chick were observed in late December 1987 (C. Balchin, S. Cook, B. Reed).

Family Meleagridae
Turkeys

Ocellated Turkey *Agriocharis ocellata* is restricted to lowland forest of the Yucatan Peninsula, **Mexico**, north-east **Guatemala** and north-west **Belize** (Blake 1977; for biology see Steadman *et al.* 1979). Although some reports indicate that certain populations (mostly those in protected areas) appear secure, there has been a serious decline in Belize in the past five years, possibly caused by disease (D. Weyer).

Order GRUIFORMES

Family Mesitornithidae
Mesites

White-breasted Mesite *Mesitornis variegata* is an inconspicuous, rail-like ground-dweller of deciduous forest in north and west **Madagascar**, where until recently all records in the past half-century had come from Ankarafantsika Reserve (Collar and Stuart 1985). The species has now been found in several localities in the west (Appert 1985; also Hamsch 1987) and has been located and relocated respectively at Analamera Special Reserve (O. Langrand, M. E. Nicoll) and Ankarana cliffs (P. Chapman; see *BBC Wildlife* 4 [1986]: 622-623), both in the north.

Brown Mesite *Mesitornis unicolor* is a cryptic and retiring rail-like ground-dweller of eastern rainforest in **Madagascar**, known for certain as far north as

Antongil Bay and almost as far south as Fort Dauphin (Collar and Stuart 1985) where it was recently relocated (Appert 1985). It has been found breeding in forest at Ranomafana (O. Langrand; see Dee 1986, Collar and Stuart 1988), and there are very recent records from Marojejy Reserve (O. Langrand, M. E. Nicoll) and the Masoala Peninsula (L. Wilme per O. Langrand), both to the north of the species's previously known range.

Subdesert Mesite *Monias benschi* is an apparently group-territorial grounddweller of subdesert scrub in south-west **Madagascar**, where like the threatened Long-tailed Ground-roller *Uratelornis chimaera* it is restricted to a 70 km wide coastal strip between the Mangoky and Fiherenana rivers and subject to predation by dogs and trappers and to habitat destruction (Collar and Stuart 1985). It occurs in no protected area and tree removal for charcoal production is increasing (O. Langrand).

Family Turnicidae
Button-quails

Sumba Button-quail *Turnix everetti* is known from Sumba, **Indonesia**, by three specimens, a female collected in 1896 and a juvenile pair collected in 1949 (White and Bruce 1986, K. D. Bishop). It presumably inhabits grassland, much of which is burnt regularly, but competition with the widespread Red-backed Button-quail *T. maculosa* may be important (P. Andrew).

Worcester's Button-quail *Turnix worcesteri*, from north and central Luzon in the **Philippines**, was described in 1904 from four birds bought in the Quinta Market in Manila, but remains virtually unknown: it was trapped in the late 1960s using floodlights at Dalton Pass (Cordillera Central) but there appear to be no field observations (R. S. Kennedy).

Black-breasted Button-quail *Turnix melanogaster* has declined drastically this century and is now largely restricted to remnant patches of forest in south-east Queensland (Blakers *et al.* 1984) and northern New South Wales, **Australia** (Hermes 1980). It is local and still rare but recent observations of the species in introduced *lantana* and hoop-pine plantations indicate that it may be adapting to a modified environment and increasing in numbers (Blakers *et al.* 1984).

Buff-breasted Button-quail *Turnix olivei* is known from Cape York in northern Queensland, **Australia**, where it inhabits grass clearings in forest, woodland and swamps, and has been observed on only a few occasions since its discovery in 1894 (Blakers *et al.* 1984). Its status is unknown.

Family Pedionomidae
Plains-wanderer

Plains-wanderer *Pedionomus torquatus* (to be reclassified in the Charadriiformes: D. J. Baker-Gabb) was formerly widespread in inland New South Wales, southern Queensland, western Victoria and eastern South **Australia**, but its range has shrunk markedly this century, particularly from the coast (Blakers *et al.* 1984, Burbidge and Jenkins 1984). It requires extensive areas of natural pasture with a varied community of grasses and herbs, and is locally common where intensive farming practices have not been introduced; it is effectively managed in core areas of grassland that are fenced from sheep (D. J. Baker-Gabb).

Family Gruidae
Cranes

Black-necked Crane *Grus nigricollis* breeds in small numbers in **China** and Ladakh, **India**, and winters in China, **Bhutan** and, at least formerly, in northern **Burma** and northern **Viet Nam** (King 1978-1979). The species's total population is estimated at between 1,400 and 1,500; the main breeding area is probably Chang Tang, Xizang Zizhiqu, but counts are not available, and the known wintering populations include an estimated total of 800 in China, excluding Lhasa, Xizang Zizhiqu, where a further 140 winter (*per* D. A. Scott; see also Robson 1986), and between 500 and 600 in Bhutan (Clements and Bradbear 1986). In Ladakh there are two or three breeding pairs but no birds winter (see five papers on the species in Archibald and Pasquier 1987).

Hooded Crane *Grus monacha* is known to breed in two areas of central Siberia, **U.S.S.R.** (Potapov and Flint 1987), and winters south to **Japan**, **North Korea**, **South Korea** and **China** (King 1978-1979). Winter counts of 5,484 at Izumi, Japan, in 1983-1984, of between 200 and 350 in South Korea each year since 1984 (over 1,000 according to Sonobe and Izawa 1987), and of 400 to 600 in China in 1987, indicate a total population of 6,100 to 6,500 birds (*per* D. A. Scott; see also four papers in Archibald and Pasquier 1987). In 1985, 309 were recorded at Beidaihe, Hebei province in China (Williams *et al.* 1986).

Red-crowned Crane *Grus japonensis* breeds in **Japan**, where it is resident and the population numbered 384 birds in 1985, in the **U.S.S.R.** (150-200 birds including 30-45 breeding pairs: Potapov and Flint 1987), and in northern **China** where aerial surveys in 1981, 1984 and 1986 revealed a breeding population of 620 birds (*per* D. A. Scott; see also King 1978-1979). It winters in China (224 counted on passage at Beidaihe, Hebei, in 1985: Williams *et al.* 1986), principally at Yancheng (608 in 1987), **North Korea** (290 in 1982) and **South Korea** (130 in 1987), and the species's total population is put at approximately 1,450 birds (*per*

D. A. Scott; see also four papers in Archibald and Pasquier 1987). The Japanese population is increasing slowly, but breeding success is not improving, and the breeding grounds are being lost through drainage; much of the increase may be due to the provision of winter food, which helps immature birds survive (M. A. Brazil).

Whooping Crane *Grus americana* breeds in the Northwest Territories, **Canada**, and winters south to Texas, U.S.A., with a second population created in Idaho in 1975 (by using Sandhill Cranes *G. canadensis* as foster-parents) and now wintering in New Mexico; hunting and extensive disturbance or destruction of wetlands has contributed to the species's decline (King 1978-1979; see also three papers in Archibald and Pasquier 1987). In 1987 there were 134 Whooping Cranes including 24 chicks wintering in Texas, about 20 young birds successfully fostered in Idaho (although no two of the latter have yet mated) and 41 captive at the Patuxent Wildlife Research Center, Maryland (Archibald 1988).

White-naped Crane *Grus vipio* breeds in the U.S.S.R. and adjacent regions of **Mongolia** and **China**, and winters south-east to China, **North Korea**, **South Korea**, and **Japan** (King 1978-1979, Ostapenko and Zewenmjadag 1983). A maximum of 18 pairs is known to breed in three areas in the U.S.S.R. (Potapov and Flint 1987) and breeding information from China is scant; wintering populations have recently been estimated at 2,100 in China, between 600 and 1,200 in Japan and between 200 and 250 in South Korea (but up to 1,500 according to Sonobe and Izawa 1987), indicating a total population of 3,000 to 3,500 birds (*per* D. A. Scott). The remarkable passage of up to 2,300 on the Han River in South Korea a decade ago no longer occurs (*per* D. A. Scott).

Siberian Crane *Grus leucogeranus* breeds in Siberia, **U.S.S.R.**, in two discrete areas, the tiny western population (nests not found till 1981 and only eight territorial pairs recorded) wintering at Bharatpur, **India**, whence it arrives via **Afghanistan**, and at two locations in **Iran**, the much larger eastern population wintering south to **China**, where 652 were recorded on passage at Beidaihe, Hebei, in 1985 and 1,784 were counted in 1987 at Lake Poyang, Jiangxi and 30 at Lake Dongting, Hunan (King 1978-1979, Williams *et al.* 1986, Kennerley 1987, Massey Stuart 1987, Potapov and Flint 1987, G. Archibald, D. A. Scott; see also eight papers in Archibald and Pasquier 1987).

Wattled Crane *Bugeranus carunculatus*, a large, shy, mainly vegetarian crane requiring very large territories and achieving very low reproductive success, occurs in marshes and floodplains in **Angola**, **Botswana**, **Ethiopia**, **Malawi**, **Mozambique**, **Namibia**, **South Africa**, **Tanzania**, **Zaire**, **Zambia** and **Zimbabwe**, and has declined locally in response to habitat loss and disturbance, and other factors (Collar and Stuart 1985; also Urban *et al.* 1986). An aerial survey of the Caprivi Strip in Namibia, 1986, produced only two birds and an estimated total of 11 (Williams 1987). A case of territorial overlap was recently documented (Masterson 1986).

Family Rallidae
Rails, crakes, coots

Okinawa Rail *Rallus okinawae* is a newly described flightless species restricted to dense evergreen hill forest in Yambaru, the northern third of **Okinawa (to Japan)**, with a population estimated at more than 1,500 birds but threatened by substantial and continuing deforestation (Yamashina and Mano 1981, Thiede 1982, Brazil 1984a,b, 1985a,b, Collar 1987).

Plain-flanked Rail *Rallus wetmorei* is restricted to mangrove swamps and shallow saltwater lagoons along a restricted part of the coast of **Venezuela** in the provinces of Falcon, Carabobo and Aragua (Meyer de Schauensee and Phelps 1978). Its current status is unknown (Scott and Carbonell 1986).

Austral Rail *Rallus antarcticus* is apparently now a very rare bird of southern **Chile** and **Argentina**, with no records in the latter since 1959 (M. Nores and D. Yzurieta). Conversion of its wet grassland habitat appears to be responsible for its decline and possible extinction (J. Fjeldsa).

Bogota Rail *Rallus semiplumbeus* is restricted to the Bogota savanna of **Colombia** (King 1978-1979) where it survives in generally low numbers in lakeside marshes and reedbeds (Hilty and Brown 1986, Varty *et al.* 1986).

Brown-banded Rail *Rallus mirificus* is known only from two localities in the western foothills of the southern half of the Sierra Madre, Luzon, **Philippines** (Ripley 1977). There appear to be no recent records and its current status is unknown.

Guam Rail *Rallus owstoni* is flightless and endemic to **Guam (to U.S.A.)**, where it was widely distributed in forest, scrub and agricultural areas until 1968 when, along with most other indigenous species, it entered a decade of decline owing to the spread through the island of the accidentally introduced Brown Tree Snake *Boiga irregularis*, and by 1981 the population was put at approximately 2,000; the most recent estimate was made in 1983 when the population was reckoned at fewer than 100 and the species only hope of survival is thought to be in captive breeding (King 1978-1979, Engbring and Pratt 1985, S. R. Derrickson).

Inaccessible Rail *Atlantisia rogersi*, the smallest flightless bird in the world, is confined to 16 sq km on Inaccessible Island in the **Tristan da Cunha group (to U.K.)**, South Atlantic Ocean: an estimated 10,000 birds live amidst the dense vegetation of the island, but there is a permanent risk that the island will be colonized by mammalian predators, particularly rats (Collar and Stuart 1985).

New Caledonian Rail *Tricholimnas lafresnayanus* is known from the island of **New Caledonia (to France)** and is treated as extinct by King (1978-1979). It has not been recorded by ornithologists this century, but local reports suggest that it survives in small numbers (Stokes 1979). There was an unsubstantiated sighting in the north of the island in 1984 (Hannecart in press).

Lord Howe Island Woodhen *Tricholimnas sylvestris* is endemic to **Lord Howe Island (Australia)**, and was formerly abundant and distributed throughout; it is now restricted to the remnant forest on the summits of Mt Lidgbird and Mt Gower where feral pigs are relatively uncommon (Fullagar and Disney 1975, King 1978- 1979). There is little suitable habitat left on the island and, although captive breeding has increased the population from 50 birds in 1981 to 150 birds in 1984, the success of reintroduction into alternative sites is not assured (Burbidge and Jenkins 1984).

Zapata Rail *Cyanolimnas cerverai* is endemic to the Zapata Swamp, **Cuba** (King 1978-1979), but over a larger area than had previously been believed, such that, barring disastrous fires or droughts, it should be in no danger (Garrido 1985).

Snoring Rail *Aramidopsis plateni* is an elusive and flightless rail of Sulawesi, **Indonesia** (Ripley 1977), known from eleven specimens, all but one collected over 40 years ago (White and Bruce 1986), although in some areas it is said to be well-known to local villagers (Watling 1983a). Recent field records are from dense vegetation, notably rattan thickets, in pristine forest (F. R. Lambert, K. D. Bishop): it is certainly rarely observed, probably local and possibly vulnerable to village dogs (K. D. Bishop).

Barred-wing Rail *Nesoclopeus poeciloptera* is known from 12 specimens collected on the islands of Viti Levu and Ovalau, **Fiji,**in the last century; there is a recent (1973) but unconfirmed record from the Nadrau Plateau on Viti Levu but if the species does survive it is probably close to extinction; a number of other ground-dwelling species, including the Banded Rail *Rallus philippensis* and the Purple Gallinule *P. porphyrio*, have disappeared from Viti Levu as a result of mongoose predation (King 1978-1979, Hay 1986).

Woodford's Rail *Nesoclopeus woodfordi* is known from Bougainville, **Papua New Guinea**, Santa Isabel, Guadalcanal and possibly Choiseul, **Solomon Islands** (J. M. Diamond). It was last collected in 1936 (Diamond 1987) but, at least formerly, occurred in lowland forest, occasionally to 1,000 m, and was probably flightless. It has been included with the Barred-wing Rail *N. poeciloptera* of **Fiji** (Ripley 1977): both forms may be extinct (Watling 1983a, J. M. Diamond).

Bald-faced Rail *Gymnocrex rosenbergii* is known from north and central Sulawesi and by three specimens from Peleng, **Indonesia**, where it appears to be a rare bird of primary forest (White and Bruce 1986). Specimens have been obtained from dense second-growth in abandoned cultivation (Ripley 1977) but recent records are from undisturbed forest (F. R. Lambert, F. G. Rozendaal).

Invisible Rail *Habroptila wallacii* is a shy flightless rail found in dense impenetrable swampy thickets, particularly those of heavy sago swamp, on Halmahera, **Indonesia** (White and Bruce 1986). It was described as fairly common (Ripley 1977) and specimens were collected between 1980 and 1983 (A. Messer) but there are no recent field records.

Corncrake *Crex crex* is widely distributed in the Palearctic, wintering mainly in Africa south of the Sahara: it breeds (or is thought to breed) in **Albania, Austria, Belgium, Bulgaria, China** (west Sinkiang), **Czechoslovakia, Denmark, Finland, France, East Germany, West Germany, Greece, Hungary, Ireland, Italy, Liechtenstein, Luxembourg, Netherlands, Norway, Poland, Romania, Sweden, Switzerland, U.K., U.S.S.R.** and **Yugoslavia** (Cramp and Simmons 1980, van der Ven 1984, Jacob *et al*. 1985). There is clear evidence of a long-term decline (including from the U.S.S.R.), owing to advanced farming machinery and early mowing (Cramp and Simmons 1980, Andrusaitis 1985, Potapov and Flint 1987). The species has been recorded throughout Africa in non-breeding season with the main distribution in southern **Zaire**, southern **Tanzania, Zambia, Malawi, Mozambique**, eastern **Zimbabwe** and eastern **South Africa** (Urban *et al*. 1986).

Dot-winged Crake *Porzana spiloptera* is known from **Uruguay** and central **Argentina** (Blake 1977) but its status is "completely unknown at present" (Ripley 1977). However, there were records from Cordoba and Buenos Aires provinces of Argentina in the 1970s, although there may have been a marked decline in numbers since the 1930s (M. Nores and D. Yzurieta). A specimen was collected in Uruguay in 1973 (Escalante 1980).

Henderson Rail *Nesophylax ater* is endemic to Henderson Island in the **Pitcairn Islands (to U.K.)**, a small uninhabited raised-reef island in the central Pacific Ocean, whose biological fragility was exposed in 1982-1983 when a millionaire sought to make it his home (Bourne and David 1983, Fosberg *et al*. 1983, Serpell *et al*. 1983). The bird is tame and flightless, and would be at considerable risk from introduced predators (Hay 1986).

Junin Rail *Laterallus tuerosi* is only known from the south-western shores of Lake Junin, **Peru**, although it may occur throughout the Junin altiplane (Fjeldsa 1983). Pollution and water-level changes at the lake may be affecting it adversely (J. Fjeldsa). Although described as a race of the Black Rail *L. jamaicensis*, it is so distinctive that specific rank appears permissible (J. Fjeldsa).

Rufous-faced Crake *Laterallus xenopterus* is known from three localities in eastern **Paraguay** and one in Brasilia National Park, central **Brazil**, occupies dense, tussock-like habitat in marshes, and may prove commoner than records have suggested (Myers and Hansen 1980, Storer 1981).

Rusty-flanked Crake *Laterallus levraudi* occurs in lagoons and marshes in north-central **Venezuela** (Blake 1977) where, however, it has recently been found at only a single lake which in January 1986 had receded so much that the birds could not be found (A. Alltman, K. Alltman, C. Parrish, B. Swift).

Asian Yellow Rail *Coturnicops exquisitus* is a very rare bird of wet meadows and short grass marshes breeding in Transbaykalia and the southern regions of the Soviet Far East, U.S.S.R., and Heilongjiang, **China**, wintering south and east through the Korean Peninsula (**North Korea** and **South Korea**) to **Japan** (including the Nansei Shoto) and eastern China (Sonobe 1982, Flint *et al*. 1984, Meyer de Schauensee 1984).

White-winged Flufftail *Sarothrura ayresi*, a tiny enigmatic rail, probably nomadic in pursuit of suitable marshland conditions, occurs in **South Africa**, where records are from 1877 to 1901 and from 1955 to 1983, **Ethiopia**, where records are from 1905 to 1957, and **Zambia** (two records) and **Zimbabwe** (three records) (Collar and Stuart 1985, Urban *et al*. 1986; also Hopkinson and Masterson 1984). A single bird in flight was seen at Sululta, an established site for the species in Ethiopia, on 26 August 1984 (R. Massoli-Novelli).

Slender-billed Flufftail *Sarothrura watersi*, a tiny marsh rail, was known up to 1987 from only four well-separated areas in central and east **Madagascar**; one of these areas was the Antananarivo district, and if doubts about the validity of the records from this area are accepted, then the species was thought perhaps to have a distribution related to the distribution of rainforest, although not recorded since 1930 (Collar and Stuart 1985). In November 1987 birds were found at a small marsh in rainforest at Ranomafana (O. Langrand, L. Wilme).

Sakalava Rail *Amaurornis olivieri* is a marsh-dwelling rail known from just three widely separated areas in the Sakalava country of western **Madagascar**, and is rare and localized, with extremely few records (Collar and Stuart 1985). Searches in the past four years have proved fruitless (O. Langrand).

San Cristobal Mountain Rail *Gallinula sylvestris* is known from the type-specimen, collected at 600 m in the central ranges of San Cristobal, **Solomon Islands**, in 1929 (Ripley 1977). It inhabits dense forest on precipitous terrain but, despite repeated attempts to secure further specimens, the only subsequent observation is of one in 1953 (King 1978-1979). It was reported by local people in 1974 and the habitat is secure (J. M. Diamond).

Gough Moorhen *Gallinula comeri*, a flightless relative of the Common Moorhen *G. chloropus*, is endemic to Gough Island and introduced to Tristan da Cunha, **Tristan da Cunha group (to U.K.)**, South Atlantic Ocean; there may be up to 3,000 pairs on Gough and around 250 pairs on Tristan, but there is a permanent risk of mammalian predators becoming established on the islands (Collar and Stuart 1985, Watkins and Furness 1986). It continues to breed so well in Amsterdam Zoo that other zoos are urgently needed to take excess stock (D. Dekker).

Takahe *Notornis mantelli* is confined to the alpine tussock grasslands of the Murchison Mountains on South Island, **New Zealand**; competition from deer for food and predation by introduced mammals have contributed to its decline (King 1978- 1979, Williams and Given 1981, Lavers and Mills 1984), as well as the spread of forest in the post-glacial Holocene (Mills *et al*. 1984). Deer management has resulted in a recovery of vegetation but the population has declined to about 180 birds; captive breeding has been successful and has led to the establishment of a population on Maud Island (B. D. Bell).

Horned Coot *Fulica cornuta* is confined to a few high-altitude Andean lakes in **Chile, Bolivia** and **Argentina** (King 1978-1979), and suffers from several factors, chiefly loss of habitat owing to the piping of water to lower-level cities (J. C. Torres-Mura).

Family Heliornithidae
Finfoots, sun-grebes

Masked Finfoot *Heliopais personata* is a secretive bird of dense forest pools and streams, and in winter, of mangroves, at best local and uncommon, breeding in **Bangladesh**, east Assam and probably north-east Manipur, **India** (Ali and Ripley 1984), and **Burma** (Smythies 1986), and dispersing to peninsular **Thailand** and **Malaysia**, Sumatra and Java, **Indonesia** (Milton 1985). The species faces habitat loss in both its breeding range and winter quarters (F. R. Lambert).

Family Rhynochetidae
Kagu

Kagu *Rhynochetos jubatus* is endemic to **New Caledonia (to France)** where it was once widespread in undisturbed forest, but has become localized in those valleys of the central mountain range least accessible to man (King 1978-1979). The population is estimated at between 500 and 1,000 individuals; the species is caught by hunting dogs, and other introduced predators and pigs probably take eggs or compete for food, although the greatest threat is deforestation (Hay 1986). More recently, dogs have been branded the chief threat to the species (Bregulla 1987, Hannecart in press). Biological data are in Bregulla (1987).

Family Otididae
Bustards

Great Bustard *Otis tarda* is declining throughout its broad but increasingly disjunct Palearctic range on undeveloped farmland and steppe in the following countries (population in brackets): **Morocco** (100), **Portugal** (1,015), **Spain** (5,000 to 8,000), **Austria** (151), **East Germany** (560), **Czechoslovakia** (315), **Poland** (16), **Hungary** (3,442), **Yugoslavia** (30-40), **Bulgaria** (practically extinct), **Romania** (300-350), **Turkey** (145-4,000), **Syria** (probably extinct), **Iraq** (few if any), **Iran** (100-200), **U.S.S.R.** (2,980-4,000) **Mongolia** (at least 1,000), **China** (probably at least 1,500) (Collar 1985, Williams *et al*. 1986, Potapov and Flint 1987).

Little Bustard *Tetrax tetrax* is declining steeply throughout its disjunct Palearctic range on undeveloped farmland and steppe in **Morocco, Portugal, Spain, France, Italy** (chiefly Sardinia), **Turkey, Iran** and the **U.S.S.R.**, the species being extinct as a breeding bird (or apparently so) in Algeria, Tunisia, Greece, Austria, Czechoslovakia, Hungary, Yugoslavia, Romania and Bulgaria (Schulz 1985, Potapov and Flint 1987).

Great Indian Bustard *Ardeotis nigriceps* is confined to grassland areas of western **India** where it occurs at low densities (King 1978-1979, plus 37 papers in Goriup and Vardhan 1983, five in *Bustard Studies* 3[1985]), although recent efforts to conserve the species appear to have stabilized the remaining populations (Rahmani 1987).

Houbara Bustard *Chlamydotis undulata* ranges widely but patchily and in seriously declining numbers (owing to hunting and habitat disturbance) through the semi- desert regions of the Palearctic, from the eastern **Canary Islands (to Spain)** (Collar and Goriup 1983, Osborne 1986), Western Sahara, **Morocco, Algeria, Tunisia, Libya, Egypt, Israel, Jordan, Syria, Iraq, Kuwait, Saudi Arabia, Bahrain, Qatar, United Arab Emirates, Oman, Iran, Afghanistan, Pakistan, India, China, Mongolia** and **U.S.S.R.** (Collar 1979, Goriup 1983, Mian 1986, Urban *et al*. 1986, Potapov and Flint 1987; also 14 papers in *Bustard Studies* 3[1985]).

Bengal Florican *Houbaropsis bengalensis* is seriously at risk from the loss of its wet grassland habitat on the **Nepal/India** border and in north-east India, with a wholly unknown population in **Kampuchea** and north-west Cochinchina, **Viet Nam** (Inskipp and Inskipp 1983, 1985b, Inskipp and Collar 1984).

Lesser Florican *Sypheotides indica* is restricted as a breeding bird to primary grassland patches in western **India** (Ali and Ripley 1984, Goriup and Karpowicz 1985, Magrath *et al*. 1985, Saxena and Meena 1985, Sankaran 1987; also three papers in Goriup and Vardhan 1983) and probably **Nepal** (T. P. Inskipp) where its population is now very low following the massive loss of its habitat (Ali *et al*. 1986). Its non-breeding distribution in India is not properly known (Goriup and Karpowicz 1985, Sankaran and Rahmani 1986).

Order CHARADRIIFORMES

Family Haematopodidae
Oystercatchers

Canarian Black Oystercatcher *Haematopus meadewaldoi* may be extinct, having always been uncommon and known with certainty only from the eastern **Canary Islands (to Spain)**; repeated recent searches have drawn blank, although there have been four apparently genuine records of black oystercatchers (two on Tenerife, two on the West African coast) since 1968, and it is just conceivable that a population remains undetected in the western Canaries (Collar and Stuart 1985). Surveys of the eastern islands in 1985 and 1986 drew blank, but the former assembled evidence that the species's disappearance is ultimately related to habitat loss, strongly compounded by competition from man for the intertidal invertebrates on which both once depended (Hockey 1986, 1987, Piersma 1986).

Chatham Island Oystercatcher *Haematopus chathamensis* occurs on Chatham, Pitt, Rangatira and Mangere islands in the **Chatham Islands (to New Zealand)**; introduced predators are a threat to its survival with only Rangatira and Mangere islands predator-free (King 1978-1979, Williams and Given 1981). A proposal to remove predators from Pitt Island is under consideration but the species's low productivity may also be related to human disturbance, so on Rangatira access to a section of coast has been prohibited (B. D. Bell). The total population is about 80 individuals (A. Davis *per* B. D. Bell).

Family Charadriidae
Plovers

Sociable Plover *Chettusia gregaria* breeds only in the **U.S.S.R.** from the Volga east to Zaysan (Bannikov 1978). It is considered threatened in the U.S.S.R. where there has been a rapid decline and range contraction owing to the cultivation of steppe areas though with a population still estimated at several tens of thousands of birds (Bannikov 1978, Cramp and Simmons 1980, Borodin 1984). The species winters in **Pakistan**, north-west **India** (with a flock of 25 at Bharatpur in 1988), **Iraq** (widespread in small numbers), **Saudi Arabia**, **North Yemen**, **Oman**, **Ethiopia** (scarce), **Sudan** (scarce) and **Egypt** (no recent reports) (Cramp and Simmons 1980, P. Jepson).

Javanese Wattled Lapwing *Vanellus macropterus* is known from Java, **Indonesia** and doubtfully from Sumatra and Timor (King 1978-1979). It was regularly reported from the marshes of north-west Java until 1930 and survived in the river deltas on the south coast of east Java until at least 1940 (Kooiman 1940), but the conversion of this habitat to agricultural land and the persecution of all large birds on Java means it is by now almost certainly extinct (P. Andrew).

Piping Plover *Charadrius melodus* breeds locally on sandy beaches in southern and eastern **Canada**, and in northern and eastern **U.S.A.**, and winters primarily on the Atlantic-Gulf coast including **Mexico** and, less commonly, in the Greater Antilles, [**Bahama Islands, Barbados, Bermuda (to U.K.), Haiti, Dominican Republic, Cuba, Puerto Rico (to U.S.A.), Virgin Islands (to U.K.) and Virgin Islands (to U.S.A.)**] (AOU 1983). Uncontrolled hunting in the early 1900s brought the species close to extinction, and today expanding recreational use of beaches, increases in water levels, and development of winter habitat are causing numbers to plunge again; a population census, 1977-1984, indicated 3,535 to 4,147 birds in breeding areas (Haig and Oring 1985). Protection of breeding areas, creation of new habitat, closure of beaches during the nesting season, fencing to reduce predation pressure, and public education will all aid the species's recovery (McNicoll 1985).

Madagascar Plover *Charadrius thoracicus* is now apparently restricted to coastal grassy areas of south-west **Madagascar**, where it is greatly outnumbered and possibly outcompeted by Kittlitz's Plover *C. pecuarius* (Collar and Stuart 1985; also Dee 1986). However, it is locally abundant at Lake Tsimanampetsotsa and is recorded from two other protected areas (O. Langrand, M. E. Nicoll).

St Helena Plover *Charadrius sanctaehelenae* occurs only in the northern, flatter parts of the interior of **St Helena (to U.K.)**, southern Atlantic Ocean, where several hundred pairs may still survive (Collar and Stuart 1985). A study in 1984 produced a minimum of 126 birds, estimated 200-300 in total, and supplied evidence of competition from and nest-predation by the introduced Indian Myna *Acridotheres tristis* (Alexander 1985).

Hooded Plover *Charadrius rubricollis* has a contracting range on the coast and around salt-lakes in southern Western **Australia** and on coastal beaches and dune systems in Victoria, South Australia, New South Wales and Tasmania, and a population estimated at 1,800; the small population in Western Australia is probably secure but the species is easily disturbed, and in eastern Australia the increasing human use of beaches has probably contributed to its decline (Lane 1987).

New Zealand Shore Plover *Thinornis novaeseelandiae* is highly vulnerable to predation and is now confined to Rangatira Island in the Chatham Islands group, **New Zealand**; reintroduction to Mangere Island has been attempted, but unsuccessfully owing to the birds' strong homing instinct (King 1978-1879). The population is estimated at about 120 birds (Williams and Given 1981), and appears stable, but Rangatira is in the centre of a lucrative lobster fishery and illegal landings pose a threat (B. D. Bell).

Family Recurvirostridae
Avocets, stilts

Black Stilt *Himantopus novaezealandiae* is restricted during its breeding season to the upper Waitaki Valley on South Island, **New Zealand**, where hybridization with the Pied Stilt *H. h. leucocephalus* occurs (King 1978-1979). It suffers from heavy predation and nest areas have been destroyed by drainage and hydroelectric development (Williams and Given 1981). The predation risk is sharply increased by its nesting preference for dry banks which are also favoured hunting habitat of cats and ferrets (Pierce 1986). The population, estimated at under 70 birds, is being maintained by predator-trapping and artificial incubation of eggs (B. D. Bell).

Family Glareolidae
Coursers, practincoles

Jerdon's Courser *Cursorius bitorquatus* is a nocturnal bird of scrub country in central-eastern **India**, and had been assumed extinct (King 1978-1979) until its rediscovery in January 1986 (Bhushan 1986a,b). Since January 1986 there have been seven sightings of a single bird in a 10 sq km area (B. Bhushan).

Family Scolopacidae
Snipes, woodcocks, sandpipers

Eskimo Curlew *Numenius borealis* formerly bred in enormous numbers in northern **Canada** and **Alaska** (**U.S.A.**), migrating south through **Guyana, French Guiana, Suriname, Brazil**, and **Paraguay**, wintering in **Uruguay**, probably **Chile** and chiefly **Argentina** (King 1978-1979, Gollop *et al.* 1986). Hunting, habitat and possibly climatic changes have combined to bring the species to the brink of extinction (King 1978-1979). The most encouraging recent evidence of its survival are reports of a flock of 23 in May 1981, Texas, U.S.A., an adult and one young in August 1983, Alaska, and six birds in the Mackenzie Delta, Northwest Territories, Canada, in July 1985 (Gollop *et al.* 1986). There were at least four reliable reports of the species in 1987 (*World Birdwatch* 10,1 [1988]: 3).

Bristle-thighed Curlew *Numenius tahitiensis* inhabits montane tundra during the breeding season in western **Alaska (U.S.A.)**, and grassy fields, tidal mudflats and beaches in its wintering range in the **Hawaiian Islands (to U.S.A.), Marshall Islands (to U.S.A.), Fiji, Tonga, Western Samoa, Samoa (to U.S.A.), Marquesas Islands (to France)** and **Tuamotu Archipelago (to France)** (AOU 1983). The species is usually seen in flocks of a few to over 100 individuals, and is often wary, probably because it is hunted on some islands (Pratt *et al.* 1987). Its low numbers and restricted breeding range are a source of concern (J. Sheppard).

Slender-billed Curlew *Numenius tenuirostris* breeds only in the **U.S.S.R.**, although breeding localities are not known (but are presumed to be the southern belt of the Taiga between the Urals and the Ob Valley) and there are no positive breeding records for the last 50-60 years (Kosolov 1983, Prater and Scott in prep.). Since 1900, the species has undergone a dramatic decline and the total population is now estimated to be less than 1,000 birds (Prater and Scott in prep.). The species has been recorded widely in the western Palearctic on migration and in winter mainly in **Turkey, Romania, Greece, Hungary, Yugoslavia, Italy, Tunisia** and **Morocco** (where the largest wintering concentrations have been recorded) (Prater and Scott in prep., M. R. W. Rands, A. B. van den Berg).

Spotted Greenshank *Tringa guttifer* breeds only in the **U.S.S.R.** on southern Sakhalin Island and possibly also in Kamchatka, the Bering Islands and along the Gulf of Okhotsk (King 1978-1979). Only one Sakhalin area is known, where there were 14 pairs in 1976 (Borodin 1984), this presumably being the same as the 3-4 connected localities named by Howes (1988). The species has been recorded widely as a migrant and winter visitor in **Bangladesh, Burma, China, Hong Kong (to U.K.), Japan, South Korea, Malaysia, Singapore, Taiwan** and **Thailand** (King 1978-1979), but numbers are always very small (suggesting a total world population of under 1,000), with almost all records since 1973 stemming from Japan, Hong Kong and peninsular Thailand (Howes and Lambert 1987, Kennerley and Bakewell 1987). A flock of 14 was seen in Hong Kong in April 1988 (*per* D. A. Scott).

Tuamotu Sandpiper *Prosobonia cancellatus* is extinct on Kiritimati (Christmas Island), Kiribati, where the type-specimen was collected, but survives on certain atolls in the **Tuamotu Archipelago (to France)** (King 1987-1979). It was formerly widespread in the archipelago, occurring at least as far north-west as Kauehi, but the introduction of rats and cats has probably eliminated the species from all but the most infrequently visited islands (Hay 1986). The current situation is that there are recent records from three localities, Marutea Sud (1965), Maturei Vavao (1970) and Tenararo (1986), and there are a further three where it has not been found in recent searches (Puka-Puka, iles Gambier, Raraka), 12 localities identified before 1925 not subsequently visited, and 24 atolls in the Tuamotus, some apparently suitable, which have never been surveyed for birds (Thibault in press; details in Holyoak and Thibault 1984; see also Hay 1984).

Sulawesi Woodcock *Scolopax celebensis* is found in mountain forest in north, central and south-east Sulawesi, **Indonesia**, between 1,100 and 2,300 m (White and Bruce 1986). It is little known and there appear to have been no records in the past decade (Whitten *et al.* 1987).

Obi Woodcock *Scolopax rochussenii* is known from Obi and by one specimen of doubtful provenance, from Bacan, **Indonesia** (White and Bruce 1986). It is probably a bird of hill forest but prior to 1980, when two specimens were taken, it was known only by five specimens collected before 1903 and one taken in 1953, and nothing has been recorded of the species's habits or habitat; much of Obi is under logging concession, though patches of forest are likely to survive in the rugged interior (F. G. Rozendaal).

New Zealand Snipe *Coenocorypha aucklandica* has four subspecies, each confined to New Zealand's oceanic islands, while a fifth became extinct in the last decade: *aucklandica* occurs in the **Auckland Islands (to New Zealand)**, *huegeli* is known only from **Snares Island (New Zealand)**, *meinertzhagenae* occurs in the **Antipodes Islands (to New Zealand)**, *pusilla* occurs on Rangatira in the **Chatham Islands (to New Zealand)** and *iredalei*, now extinct, was known from islands off Stewart Island (King 1978-1979). Two of the subspecies have good numbers and are relatively secure (B. D. Bell) and the species is not listed by Williams and Given (1981).

Wood Snipe *Gallinago nemoricola* is believed to breed in wooded habitats between 1,200 m and 4,000 m in the Himalayas, from Kulu, Himachal Pradesh east through **Nepal** and **Bhutan** to Arunachal Pradesh in north-east **India** (Marchant *et al.* 1986) and was recently found, probably breeding, in central-western Sichuan in central **China** (B. F. King). Outside the breeding season it occurs at lower altitudes in the Himalayas and is dispersed sparingly through the hill ranges of most of India and **Pakistan** (Marchant *et al.* 1986). There appear to have been few recent records.

Asian Dowitcher *Limnodromus semipalmatus* breeds in several small, widely scattered areas in **U.S.S.R.**, **Mongolia** and **China**, nesting in colonies of 10 to 20 pairs (King 1978-1979); breeding behaviour and habitat are reported in Yurlov (1981), Liedel (1982), Mauersberger *et al.* (1982), Fiebig and Jander (1985). The species has been recorded on passage and in winter in **Japan**, China, **Hong Kong (to U.K.)**, **Thailand** (400 recorded in 1984: Round 1985), **Philippines**, **Malaysia**, **Singapore**, **Burma**, **India** and **Australia** (King 1978-1979, Melville and Round 1982, Lane 1987) with the largest wintering concentrations (1,460) recorded in Sumatra, **Indonesia**, in 1984 (Silvius *et al.* 1986) and 3,800 (estimated maximum of 4,000) in 1986 (Silvius 1988, Verheugt 1988). The species has suffered owing to fragmentation of its breeding habitat, disturbance during breeding and trapping of waders in Thailand and Indonesia (W. J. M. Verheugt).

Cox's Sandpiper *Calidris paramelanotos* has only been recorded outside the breeding season (presumably breeding in the northern U.S.S.R.), having first been described in 1982 (Hayman *et al.* 1986). Nearly all records are from **Australia**, mainly Victoria (Howes 1986), with recent records of a passage bird from Massachusetts, U.S.A. (G. A. Bertrand).

Spoon-billed Sandpiper *Eurynorhynchus pygmeus* breeds only in north-east **U.S.S.R.** from Chukotka south to Kamchatka with a breeding population estimated at 2,000- 2,800 pairs (Kolosov 1983). It has been recorded on passage or in winter in **China, Hong Kong (to U.K.)**, **India, Japan,** Korea (presumably both **North Korea** and **South Korea**), **Thailand** and **Singapore** but only in small numbers and no regular wintering site is known (Hayman *et al.* 1986).

Family Laridae
Gulls, terns

Olrog's Gull *Larus atlanticus* is known to breed only on islands near the mouth of Rio Colorado, Buenos Aires province, **Argentina**; 310 birds were counted on two of these islands, and the total population is estimated to be very small and vulnerable to tourism, an increase in fishing traffic, egging and petroleum exploitation (Devillers 1977).

White-eyed Gull *Larus leucophthalmus* is confined to the Gulf of Aden and the Red Sea, breeding in **North Yemen, Saudi Arabia, Egypt** and possibly South Yemen (Gallagher *et al.* 1984). The largest known breeding concentration is on islands at the mouth of the Gulf of Suez where between 1,500-2,000 pairs are thought to breed (or at least 30 per cent of the world population) (Jennings *et al.* 1985). It is permanently at risk from floating and beached oil (Jennings *et al.* 1985).

Audouin's Gull *Larus audouinii* is confined as a breeding species to the Mediterranean, with colonies in **Cyprus, France** (Corsica), **Italy, Greece, Turkey, Tunisia, Algeria** and **Spain** (including several Spanish islands) (King 1978-1979, James 1984) and a total population estimated to be 5,500-6,000 pairs (Evans 1986), the largest colonies being in the Ebro Delta and on the Chafarinas Islands (de Juana 1984, Hoogendoorn and Mackrill 1987). In 1986, 1,930 nests on the Chafarinas almost totally failed, and consequently a cull of the islands' increasing population of Yellow-legged Herring Gulls *Larus argentatus michahellis* took place; in 1987, 2,845 nests fledged an estimated 1,027 young (de Juana and Varela 1987). In winter the species occurs in some numbers along the coast of **Libya**, Tunisia, Algeria, **Morocco** and probably Western Sahara and possibly further south in Mauritania and Senegal (Hoogendoorn and Mackrill 1987).

Relict Gull *Larus relictus* breeds only at Lake Alakul in Kazakhstan and Torey lakes in Transbaykalia, **U.S.S.R.** and Tatsain Tsagaan Nuur in **Mongolia** (King 1978-1979, Kitson 1980, Fisher 1985), with up to 2,000 pairs in the U.S.S.R. (Borodin 1984). The nesting sites in the U.S.S.R. are unstable owing to fluctuating water-levels (Bannikov 1978). During the non-breeding season, the species has also been recorded in **China** and **Viet Nam** (Kitson 1980). Ecological and other data are in Zubakin and Flint (1980).

Saunders's Gull *Larus saundersi* was believed to breed on inland lakes in Mongolia and north-east **China** (Meyer de Schauensee 1984); but breeding colonies are now known from a lake in Heilongjiang and coastal Jiangsu (Shi *et al.* in press; *BBC Wildlife* 6 [1988]: 118-119). It has been collected in winter on estuaries along the south and east coasts of China, from the mouth of the Chang Jiang south to Hainan, but most recent records are from: **Hong Kong (to U.K.)**, where up to 60 birds are regularly recorded; Lake Poyang, Jiangxi; the Dadu River, **Taiwan**, where between 10 and 20 birds may be be present (D. S. Melville), and mouth of the Hong River, **Viet Nam**, where over 200 were seen in March 1988 (D. A. Scott); it occasionally reaches **Korea** and **Japan** (regular in Okinawa and Kyushu) and has occurred north to Vladivostok, **U.S.S.R.** (M. A. Brazil, D. S. Melville).

Kerguelen Tern *Sterna virgata* breeds in the southern Indian Ocean on **Prince Edward Island (to South Africa)** (50 pairs: Williams 1984), **Crozet Islands (to France)** (over 148 pairs) and **Kerguelen Islands (to France)** (population not known, but small and scattered); introduction of salmonid fish into rivers on Kerguelen has provided a new source of food, but the large population of feral cats remains a major threat (Jouventin *et al.* 1984).

Black-fronted Tern *Sterna albostriata* is confined to South Island, **New Zealand**, where it breeds along dried river-beds and lake shores; the population is estimated to be 1,000-5,000 pairs, but the major breeding sites are threatened by hydroelectric development (Robertson and Bell 1984). Breeding sites in the tundra zone have been observed and these may have been established following the loss of lower riverbed habitat (Child 1986).

Damara Tern *Sterna balaenarum* breeds in low-density colonies on beaches in **Namibia** and **South Africa** (where it incurs reproductive failure through disturbance) and possibly Angola, wintering north to **Gabon, Cameroon, Nigeria** and **Ghana**; an estimated world population of around 4,000 birds may be too low (Collar and Stuart 1985; also Urban *et al.* 1986). In Gabon the species has been found to be a common migrant, with 2,000 southward-moving birds counted over three days in October 1986, suggesting that the population wintering in the Gulf of Guinea, May to October, may be larger than previously judged (P. D. Alexander-Marrack).

Chinese Crested Tern *Sterna bernsteini* is believed to breed on islands off Shandong, China, where 21 were collected in 1937, and disperses south in winter; there are specimens from Halmahera, **Indonesia**, Borneo, (Indonesia and **Malaysia**), the coast of **Thailand** (King 1978-1979) and the **Philippines** (Dickinson and Eck 1984). Recent unconfirmed sight records from are Hebeh, China, in 1978 and Thailand in 1980 (Melville 1984, Boswall 1986).

Family Alcidae
Auks, murres, puffins

Japanese Murrelet *Synthliboramphus wumizusume* breeds on the **Izu Islands (to Japan)** and in southern **Japan** and and disperses to mainland coasts from Sakhalin, **U.S.S.R.** to Korea (presumably **North Korea** and **South Korea** (Harrison 1983). The population is estimated at 1,650 birds; nest sites are threatened by the increase in sport-fishing which destroys coastal habitat and disturbs the breeding activities (Hasegawa 1984).

Order COLUMBIFORMES

Family Columbidae
Pigeons, doves

Somali Pigeon *Columba oliviae* is an extremely poorly known ground-feeding, rock- dwelling species endemic to the arid coastal regions of north-east **Somalia**, not known to be declining but in need of survey to establish its status and needs (Collar and Stuart 1985; see also Urban *et al.* 1986).

Madeira Laurel Pigeon *Columba trocaz* is confined to dense forest in the northern part of **Madeira (Portugal)**, where it numbers something over 500 but is subject to continuing hunting pressure (Collar and Stuart 1985; see also Cramp 1985). From further study and analysis, the population is probably in excess of 1,000 (Zino and Zino 1986).

Dark-tailed Laurel Pigeon *Columba bollii* occurs in laurel forest on Tenerife, La Palma and Gomera in the **Canary Islands (to Spain)**, where it is moderately common and well conserved by recent measures (Collar and Stuart 1985; see also

Cramp 1985, Emmerson *et al.* 1986, Martin 1987). It is now known also from Hierro (Martin 1985).

White-tailed Laurel Pigeon *Columba junoniae* occurs in laurel forest on Tenerife, La Palma and Gomera in the **Canary Islands (to Spain)**, being relatively common only in parts of La Palma, but is well conserved by recent measures (Collar and Stuart 1985; also Huizinga 1984, Cramp 1985, Martin 1987).

Maroon Pigeon *Columba thomensis* occurs in low numbers in the upland mist-forest of Sao Tome, **Sao Tome e Principe**, where it suffers from hunting (Collar and Stuart 1985, Urban *et al.* 1986, Jones and Tye 1988).

Nilgiri Woodpigeon *Columba elphinstonii* occurs in evergreen forest on the hills of the Western Ghats, **India**, including the Anaimalais, Nilgiris, and Palnis, apparently ranging widely in search of fruit (Ali and Ripley 1984), and now local and perhaps declining (N. J. Redman, A. J. Gaston, R. F. Grimmett, S. Harrap).

Sri Lanka Woodpigeon *Columba torringtoni* is endemic to **Sri Lanka** and confined to forest above 1,000 m (Henry 1955). It has declined markedly and has disappeared from some areas, probably as a result of the continued loss of natural forests; monocultures of *Eucalyptus* and *Pinus* do not support the species (Hoffmann 1984).

Pale-capped Pigeon *Columba punicea* has been recorded from north-east **India**, **Bhutan**, **Burma**, **Thailand**, south Xizang Zizhiqu in the Chumbi valley and Hainan, **China** (Meyer de Schauensee 1984), southern **Laos** and southern **Viet Nam** (King *et al.* 1975). The few recent records are from Thailand, where it is occasionally observed in the spring, suggesting the species is at least partially migratory (C. R. Robson), although despite its wide range it seems to be very poorly known.

Grey Woodpigeon *Columba argentina* is an island species, formerly known from the Mentawi Islands and Simeulue, off the west coast of Sumatra, the Karimata, Natuna, and Anamba islands in the South China Sea, in the Riau and Lingga Archipelagos (all **Indonesia**), and Burong Island, **Malaysia** (Goodwin 1983, van Marle and Voous 1988), but currently is of unknown status on any of the islands except Burong where it is extinct (Smythies 1981). Some of these islands are still forested (P. Andrew) but there appear to be no recent reliable records.

Yellow-legged Pigeon *Columba pallidiceps* occurs on islands in the Bismarck Archipelago, **Papua New Guinea** and **Solomon Islands** (Goodwin 1983). It is an apparently rare inhabitant of lowland forest and has not been recorded in the Solomon Islands since 1928 (Diamond 1987); a specimen was obtained on New Britain in 1959, when the species appeared uncommon (Gilliard and LeCroy

1967) but there appear to be no other recent confirmed records. It is possibly a ground dwelling species victim to introduced predators (K. D. Bishop, J. M. Diamond).

Ring-tailed Pigeon *Columba caribaea* is restricted to forested hills in **Jamaica** (Bond 1975) where it is very scarce (T. A. Parker); it may have a mutualistic relationship with the endemic tree *Nectandra antillana* (Davis *et al.* 1985).

Pink Pigeon *Nesoenas mayeri* survives in very low numbers (about 20) in the upland areas of native forest in south-west **Mauritius**, where all breeding takes place in a single small unprotected grove of *Crytomeria* trees; however, the species is well established in captivity (Collar and Stuart 1985; see also Jones 1987). An attempt in 1984-1985 to introduce it to the botanic gardens in Pamplemousses failed through vandalism (Cheke 1987d). In January 1988 five or six pairs were present in the *Cryptomeria* grove, but the one breeding attempt watched failed through egg-predation (C. G. Jones).

Socorro Dove *Zenaida graysoni* is extinct on Socorro Island, in the **Revillagigedos Islands (to Mexico)**, probably owing to the introduction of feral cats with the establishment of a military garrison in 1958, and survives only in captivity (Jehl and Parkes 1982, 1983, Jehl 1983, 1984). Captive birds number at least several hundreds and reintroduction is being contemplated (Parrott-Holden 1987).

Blue-eyed Ground-dove *Columbina cyanopis* of central **Brazil** is extremely rare, known from eight specimens collected in southern Mato Grosso, southern Goias and western Sao Paulo in and before 1941 (Pinto 1937, 1945), until it was recently rediscovered in the Serra das Araras Ecological Station, Mato Grosso (J. M. C. da Silva). Its range is under great agricultural pressure (P. T. Z. Antas).

Purple-winged Ground-dove *Claravis godefrida* is restricted to south-east **Brazil**, eastern **Paraguay** and north-eastern **Argentina**, and is in serious decline (King 1978-1979), being a bamboo-flower follower (Sick 1972) and consequently in trouble even with moderate deforestation (E. O. Willis). Flocks of 50 to 100 once occurred on the coast of south-east Brazil (Sick 1972) but the species has never been seen by one long-term field-worker in Sao Paulo (E. O. Willis) and only single individuals or pairs have been recorded recently from Rio de Janeiro, Espirito Santo (Scott and Brooke 1985, C. E. Carvalho) and Misiones (M. Nores and D. Yzurieta), though birds are regularly seen in Iguazu National Park (M. Rumboll).

Grenada Dove *Leptotila wellsi* is thought to be very rare and local in the xerophytic scrubland of the south-west coast of **Grenada** (King 1978-1979), and this was confirmed by fieldwork in July 1987, when 105 birds were estimated to survive in 500 ha in the south-east corner of the south-west peninsula (Blockstein

1987). Habitat destruction and possible predation by the introduced mongoose *Herpestes auropunctatus* threaten the species, which appears fully distinct from the Grey-fronted Dove *L. rufaxilla* (Blockstein 1987).

Ochre-bellied Dove *Leptotila ochraceiventris* is confined to south-west **Ecuador** and northern **Peru** (Meyer de Schauensee 1982), and as an inhabitant of the much- threatened decidous forest in these countries is gravely at risk (R. S. Ridgely).

Tolima Dove *Leptotila conoveri* is very locally distributed in humid forest and bushy forest borders, 1,800-2,500 m, on the east slope of the Central Andes from near Ibaque (Tolima) south to the head of the Magdalena Valley (Huila) in **Colombia**, an area where forest destruction has been severe (King 1978-1979, Hilty and Brown 1986).

Grey-headed Quail-dove *Geotrygon caniceps* occurs on **Cuba**, where it is much the rarest of the country's pigeons and moving towards extinction (Garrido 1986), and in the **Dominican Republic**, where it is (or was) confined to three mountain ranges but has been reduced to near-extinction in two of them by habitat destruction, and is now overall very rare (Stockton de Dod 1987, A. Stockton de Dod).

Blue-headed Quail-dove *Starnoenas cyanocephala* inhabits **Cuba** including Isla de la Juventud (Isle of Pines), and although not considered in a review of Cuba's threatened birds by Garrido (1985) it is described by the same author as "in grave danger of extinction" owing to habitat loss throughout its range (Garrido 1986).

Nicobar Pigeon *Caloenas nicobarica* occurs on the **Nicobar Islands (to India)** and **Andaman Islands (to India)** and islands east through **Indonesia**, the **Philippines** to **Papua New Guinea** and the **Solomon Islands**, where it is found on small wooded islands and was, at least formerly, locally abundant (Ali and Ripley 1984). Its status is hard to assess as its habitat is infrequently visited and it is known to wander amongst groups of islands, but it is known to have declined markedly in parts of its range: there do not appear to be any recent records from Indonesia (K. D. Bishop), it is being extirpated by hunters in Papua New Guinea and the Solomon Islands (J. M. Diamond) and the clearing of small islands for coconut plantations threatens all small-island species in the Philippines (R. S. Kennedy). The isolated race *pelewensis* on **Palau (to U.S.A.)** (King 1978-1979) may still number up to 1,000 birds (Engbring and Pratt 1985).

Mindoro Bleeding-heart *Gallicolumba platenae* is endemic to Mindoro in the **Philippines**, where it inhabits forest (Goodwin 1983). There have been no observations in recent years, despite considerable ornithological coverage of the island, and its status is unknown (R. S. Kennedy).

Negros Bleeding-heart *Gallicolumba keayi* is endemic to Negros in the **Philip-**

pines, where it inhabits forest and woodland, and is now rare although common in the last century (Goodwin 1983). There have been no observations in recent years, despite considerable ornithological coverage of the island, and its status is unknown (R. S. Kennedy). Only fragments of lowland forest remain on the island (T. H. Fisher, C. R. Cox).

Sulu Bleeding-heart *Gallicolumba menagei* is endemic to Tawi Tawi in the Sulu Archipelago in the southern **Philippines** (Goodwin 1983). Its status is unknown but it is assumed to be rare (R. S. Kennedy).

Society Islands Ground-dove *Gallicolumba erythroptera* was formerly distributed on Tahiti and Moorea in the **Society Islands (to France)** and throughout the **Tuamotu Archipelago (to France)** (King 1978-1979). Its ground dwelling habits have apparently resulted in its extirpation by rats and cats over much of its range and it is only known to survive on Maturei Vavao (King 1978-1979, Hay 1986). Two races are at stake, nominate *erythroptera*, known from eight islands (extinct on three, four unvisited since 1922, and Maturei Vavao where seen in 1968), and *pectoralis*, also known from eight islands (extinct on six, two unvisited since 1923), but 24 atolls in the Tuamotus, some apparently suitable, have never been surveyed for birds (Holyoak and Thibault 1984, Thibault in press).

Santa Cruz Ground-dove *Gallicolumba sanctaecrucis* is known from Tinakula and Utupua, **Solomon Islands** and Espiritu Santo, **Vanuatu**, (Mayr 1946) where it is a rarely seen species inhabiting mountain rainforest to about 1,000 m (Bregulla in press).

Thick-billed Ground-dove *Gallicolumba salamonis* is confined to the islands of San Cristobal and Malaita in the **Solomon Islands** (Goodwin 1983). It was collected in lowland forest to an altitude of 300 m but has not been recorded since 1927 (Diamond 1987).

Marquesas Ground-dove *Gallicolumba rubescens* is restricted to two uninhabited islets, Hatuta'a (18 sq km) and Fatu Huku (1 sq km) in the **Marquesas Islands (to France)** but probably formerly occurred on Nuku Hiva where the type-specimen is reputed to have been collected; the population on Hatuta'a, estimated at around 225 birds in 1975, remained stable in 1987 (King 1978-1979, Holyoak and Thibault 1984, Thibault in press).

Wetar Ground-dove *Gallicolumba hoedtii* is known from Wetar and by two records from Timor, **Indonesia** (White and Bruce 1986). It is certainly rare on Timor, and has not been relocated at Camplong where it was collected in 1939 (P. Andrew, K. D. Bishop, J. McKean). Its status on Wetar is unknown: the island has not been visited by ornithologists for seventy years (White and Bruce 1986).

Solomon Island Crowned-pigeon *Microgoura meeki* is known from Choiseul, **Solomon Islands**, where it was discovered and last reliably recorded in 1904

(Diamond 1987). Suitable habitat is not lacking but native-owned dogs and feral cats have preyed on the species (Schodde 1978) and it is probably extinct (King 1978-1979); information from local villagers on Choiseul tend to confirm this (J. M. Diamond).

Western Crowned-pigeon *Goura cristata* occurs in north-west Irian Jaya, and on the West Papuan Islands of Misool, Waigeo, Salawati and Batanta, **Indonesia** (Beehler 1986 *et al.*). It is a common inhabitant of wet lowland forest on the mainland (Rand and Gilliard 1967), but is rapidly being extirpated by hunting in the vicinity of villages (K. D. Bishop). The three members of the New Guinea genus *Goura* are hunted for food and plumes (Beehler 1985), but pressure is less on this species as shotguns are not readily available in Irian Jaya (J. M. Diamond).

Southern Crowned-pigeon *Goura scheepmakeri* occurs in lowland forest along the southern side of Irian Jaya, **Indonesia**, from Etna Bay to Milne Bay in furthest east **Papua New Guinea** (Beehler *et al.* 1986). It is a colonial species and is a prized, large and easy target for hunters (Rand and Gilliard 1967), and has already been hunted to extinction throughout much of its range in the south-east (Schodde 1978, G, R, Kula). It is still common in undisturbed forest on the Bian River, south-east Irian Jaya, but shot indiscriminately by the police and military, and young are taken for pets (K. D. Bishop).

Victoria Crowned-pigeon *Goura victoria* is found on Biak and Yapen Islands, and on the northern side of New Guinea from Geelvink Bay, Irian Jaya, **Indonesia**, to Milne Bay in furthest east **Papua New Guinea** (Beehler *et al.* 1986). It is prized by hunters and threatened in areas accessible to man (Rand and Gilliard 1967). It is fairly common in the hills of Supiori, adjacent to Biak (K. D. Bishop).

Tooth-billed Pigeon *Didunculus strigirostris* is restricted to the islands of Savai'i and 'Upolu, **Western Samoa**, where it is locally distributed in forest between 300 and 1,400 m, but is apparently unable to adapt to areas that have been logged or replanted with exotic species (King 1978-1979). On 'Upolu, where demographic pressure is heavy, it is hunted avidly and already restricted to the higher valleys, and on Savai'i, where it is more widely distributed, it is threatened by commercial deforestation (Hay 1986). Recent studies have shown that it is a tree-living species, feeding on the fruits of the *Dysoxylum* genus; the population is estimated at 4,800 to 7,200 birds (Beichle 1987; also 1982)

Sumba Green-pigeon *Treron teysmanni* is found in the lowlands of Sumba, **Indonesia**, to 500 m (White and Bruce 1986). It is confined to pockets of forest and still locally common at fruiting figs, with at least 12 seen at one fig-tree in 1987 (B. F. King, J. McKean, D. Yong), but despite the fact that an endemic disease is reducing human population pressure in Sumba, lowland forest is still being removed (P. Andrew).

Timor Green-pigeon *Treron psittacea* is found in lowland forest on Timor and the satellite islands of Roti and Semau, **Indonesia** (White and Bruce 1986). It is evidently uncommon, and restricted to the few remaining pockets of deciduous forest in West Timor (P. Andrew) though more widespread in East Timor (J. McKean). If the cessation of the hostilities that followed the Indonesian annexation of East Timor is followed by the widespread acquisition of guns, a combination of hunting and a severely depleted habitat could eliminate the species (P. Andrew).

Large Green-pigeon *Treron capellei* occurs in Tenasserim, **Burma**, peninsular **Thailand** and **Malaysia**, Borneo, Sumatra and Java, **Indonesia** (Goodwin 1983). It is a scarce but widespread resident and is largely restricted to lowland forest although it has been recorded to 1,200 m in both peninsular Malaysia (Medway and Wells 1976) and Sumatra (Voous 1988), where it is dependent on large-fruited fig-trees that strangle the large and commercially logged tree species (F. R. Lambert). There are no recent records from Java and it is thought to be threatened in Thailand (Round in press).

Red-naped Fruit-dove *Ptilinopus dohertyi* is endemic to Sumba, **Indonesia** (White and Bruce 1986). It has been collected at 500 m (Mayr 1944) but, being an allospecies of the White-headed Fruit-dove *P. cinctus* (White and Bruce 1986), it presumably also occurs in mountain forest. It remains locally common (B. F. King, T. McKean, D. Yong) but further deforestation of an already bare island would seriously threaten the species (P. Andrew).

Marianas Fruit-dove *Ptilinopus roseicapilla* occurs on **Guam (to U.S.A.)**, where it is now very rare (disappeared from about 90 per cent of its former range: Jenkins 1983), and on Saipan, Tinian, Rota and Aguijan in the **Northern Marianas Islands (to U.S.A.)**, where it is still common (Pratt *et al.* 1987). Forest clearance and excessive hunting have probably contributed to the species's overall decline (King 1978-1979).

Rapa Fruit-dove *Ptilinopus huttoni* is endemic to Rapa in the **Tubuai Islands (to France)**, where it is becoming increasingly restricted in range as forest continues to be degraded and destroyed by goats, cattle, fire and felling (Thibault in press). The population was estimated at about 125 pairs (200-300 birds) in 1974 (King 1978-1979, Holyoak and Thibault 1984) but reckoned at only 30 individuals in 1984 (Pratt *et al.* 1987).

Marquesas Fruit-dove *Ptilinopus mercierii* is almost certainly extinct, as listed by King (1978-1979). It is known from Hiva Oa and Nuku Hiva in the **Marquesas Islands (to France)** and was apparently extinct on Nuku Hiva by 1922 (Holyoak and Thibault 1984). It was reported on Hiva Oa in 1980 (Hay 1986), but not in 1985 (Pratt *et al.* 1987), and there is some doubt over the 1980 record given the observers' failure to record Hiva Oa's common fruit-dove and previous observers' failure to find the species in the 1970s, when the cause of its extinction was speculated to be the introduction of the Great Horned Owl *Bubo virginianus* (Holyoak and Thibault 1984, Thibault in press).

Carunculated Fruit-dove *Ptilinopus granulifrons* is endemic to Obi, **Indonesia** (White and Bruce 1986). Nine were collected in 1982 and it is probably locally common (F. G. Rozendaal); there is no information regarding habitat requirements, but as an allospecies of the Grey-headed Fruit-dove *P. hyogaster* it is probably found in both forest and secondary vegetation; the island is scheduled to be logged (F. G. Rozendaal).

Negros Fruit-dove *Ptilinopus arcanus* remains known only from the type-specimen collected at 1,200 m on Mt Canlaon on Negros in the **Philippines** and described in 1955 (Goodwin 1983).

Cloven-feathered Dove *Drepanoptila holosericea* is locally distributed on **New Caledonia (to France)** and was formerly found on the Ile des Pins (Isle of Pines) (King 1978-1979). It is still fairly common in the forested hills on the eastern side of the island, but as areas are opened up by logging or by prospecting for or mining of nickel the species is hunted and trapped (Stokes 1980, Hannecart in press).

Mindoro Imperial-pigeon *Ducula mindorensis* is endemic to Mindoro in the **Philippines,** where it affects montane forest above 1,500 m (Delacour and Mayr 1946) and was common on Mt Halcon in 1983 (B. F. King). It is also recorded from the lowlands of north-east Mindoro (R. Sison *per* R. S. Kennedy), but the island is extensively deforested (Cox 1988).

Society Islands Imperial-pigeon *Ducula aurorae* is known from Tahiti (only 10 estimated left in 1972) in the **Society Islands (to France)** and Makatea (around 500 in 1972) in the **Tuamotu Archipelago (to France)** (King 1978-1979). The population on Tahiti may now be very close to extinction (no birds could be found in 1984: M. K. Poulsen); that on Makatea appears stable, but is now less precisely judged to lie between 100 and 1,000 birds (Thibault and Guyot in press). The species (probably a race of Pacific Imperial-pigeon *D. pacifica*) apparently once inhabited Moorea and possibly certain other islands where its extinction may have been the consequence of the spread through Polynesia of the Swamp Harrier *Circus approximans* (Holyoak and Thibault 1984, Thibault in press).

Marquesas Imperial-pigeon *Ducula galeata* is endemic to Nuku Hiva in the **Marquesas Islands (to France)**; it is now restricted to valleys at the western end of the island, where the population was estimated at between 75 and 105 in 1972 (Hay 1986) but between 200 and 400 in 1975 (Holyoak and Thibault 1984). The grazing of cattle, pigs and goats has degraded the habitat and despite a local ban on the hunting of all birds it is still occasionally shot (King 1978- 1979, Thibault in press). (Re-)introduction to Henderson Island in the Pitcairn Islands (to

U.K.) has been put forward for consideration (Steadman and Olson 1985).

Christmas Imperial-pigeon *Ducula whartoni* is endemic to **Christmas Island (to Australia)** in the Indian Ocean, where the population appears to fluctuate; in 1887 it was considered to be abundant, in 1940 it was thought to be approaching extinction, and in 1977 it was found to widespread and increasingly common (King 1978-1979). The species's future would probably be assured if hunting were eliminated and the maximum amount of forest were retained (Stokes 1988). Breeding data are in Hicks and Yorkston (1982).

Grey Imperial-pigeon *Ducula pickeringii* is known from small islands off the north coast of Borneo and in the southern **Philippines**, and some of the Kepualaun Islands, **Indonesia** (Goodwin 1983, White and Bruce 1986). It is regularly recorded on the coast of Sabah, **Malaysia** (Smythies 1981) but its status on the islands is unknown.

Giant Imperial-pigeon *Ducula goliath* is restricted to indigenous forest in the mountains and remote valleys of **New Caledonia (to France)**; it is known from Ile des Pins (Isle of Pines) but has not been recorded there recently (King 1978-1979). It is still quite common in the more inaccesible areas, but as these are opened up it is hunted to extinction despite an eleven-month closed season (Hay 1986).

Order PSITTACIFORMES

Family Psittacidae
Parrots, cockatoos, lories, macaws

Biak Red Lory *Eos cyanogenia* is known from Biak, Numfor, Manim and Meos Num Islands in Geelvink Bay, Irian Jaya, **Indonesia** (Beehler *et al.* 1986). On Biak in 1982 it was found to feed in inland forest and roost in coastal coconut plantations, and was uncommon but abundant in forest on adjacent Supiori (K. D. Bishop). Its status on the other islands is unknown.

Blue-streaked Lory *Eos reticulata* is endemic to the Tanimbar Islands, **Indonesia** (White and Bruce 1986). It was described as locally abundant, particularly along the coast (Smiet 1985), but trade in this species has increased: licenced exports for 1984, 1985 and 1986 were 2,451, 1,720 and 6,085 respectively (S. Manan *per* C. Schouten).

Red-and-blue Lory *Eos histrio* is known from the Talaud and Sangihe Islands, **Indonesia** (White and Bruce 1986). It occurs in small numbers in open country, and more commonly in forest, on Karakelang in the Talaud Islands, but has not recently been recorded on Sangihe (F. G. Rozendaal).

Purple-naped Lory *Lorius domicellus* is an uncommon endemic of Seram and Ambon, **Indonesia**, and is found in hill forest from 400 to 900 m (White and Bruce 1986). Although it is not exported from Seram, it is a popular cage-bird on the island and any external demand could seriously threaten it (J. Bowler, J. B. Taylor).

Scarlet-breasted Lorikeet *Vini kuhlii* is restricted to Rimitara in the **Tubuai Islands (to France)**, and to Teraina (Washington), Tabueran (Fanning) and Kiritimati (Christmas Island), all in **Kiribati**, to which it appears to have been introduced (Forshaw and Cooper 1981, Holyoak and Thibault 1984). It is common on Rimitara and there are an estimated 1,000 (minimum) and 200 on Washington and Fanning respectively (Garnett 1983, Holyoak and Thibault 1984), but all populations must remain vulnerable to the possibility of introduced predators.

Henderson Lorikeet *Vini stepheni* is restricted to and rather uncommon on Henderson Island in the **Pitcairn Islands (to U.K.)**, a small uninhabited raised-reef island in the central Pacific Ocean, whose biological fragility was exposed in 1982-1983 when a millionaire sought to make it his home (Bourne and David 1983, Fosberg *et al.* 1983, Serpell *et al.* 1983).

Blue Lorikeet *Vini peruviana* was formerly widespread in the **Cook Islands (to New Zealand)**, **Society Islands (to France)** and the northern atolls of the **Tuamotu Archipelago (to France)**, declining and disappearing with the spread through Polynesia of the Swamp Harrier *Circus approximans* and possibly of mosquito-borne avian malaria (King 1978-1979). It has been found on at least 23 islands (to some of which it was or may have been introduced), but is extinct on 15 of these, while being recently recorded from Aitutaki, Bellingshausen (possibly up to 250 pairs), Scilly (300-400 pairs), Rangiroa, Arutua and Tikehau (30 pairs), with two further localities (Apataki and Kaukura) unvisited since 1923 and several other suitable islands that remain unsurveyed for birds (Holyoak and Thibault 1984, Thibault in press).

Ultramarine Lorikeet *Vini ultramarina* occurs on Ua Pou, Nuku Hiva and Ua Huka in the **Marquesas Islands (to France)** (King 1978-1979). On Ua Pou it frequents montane forest between 700 and 1,000 m, but has been noted visiting banana plantations and flowering trees in coastal areas (Hay 1986). The population was estimated to be 250-300 pairs in 1975, but the past 15 years have seen an unexplained decline by 60 per cent in this population (Thibault in press). On Nuku Hiva an estimated 70 birds are restricted to high valleys and ridges at the north-western end of the island (Holyoak and Thibault 1984). It was introduced to Ua Huka where the population had risen to around 200-250 pairs in the early 1970s, and was still strong in 1987 (Thibault in press). However, the continued degradation of the remaining forest by introduced mammals and possibly the introduction of avian malaria have been thought seriously to threaten the species (King 1978-1979), but the causes of its decline on Ua Pou and its restricted range on Nuku Hiva are essentially unknown (Thibault in press).

Blue-fronted Lorikeet *Charmosyna toxopei* is known only from seven specimens collected on the west side of Lake Rana, on Buru, **Indonesia**, between 850 and 1,000 m (White and Bruce 1986, K. D. Bishop).

New Caledonian Lorikeet *Charmosyna diadema* is known from **New Caledonia (to France)** and is treated as extinct by King (1978-1979). It was described from two specimens, both females, collected in 1859, and a subsequent observation of the species was mentioned in 1913 (Forshaw and Cooper 1981a). Stokes (1980) was advised by islanders that the species might still exist, and cites a record of two birds seen by an experienced bushman west of Mt Panie in 1976.

Yellow-crested Cockatoo *Cacatua sulphurea* is found on Sulawesi and a number of its satellite islands, and in the Lesser Sundas from Penida and Lombok east to Timor, **Indonesia** (White and Bruce 1986). It is now scarce throughout its extensive range, and the continued trapping of birds for export and the local market could eliminate the species in some areas (P. Andrew).

Salmon-crested Cockatoo *Cacatua moluccensis* is known from Seram and its satellite islands Saparua and Haruku, **Indonesia** (White and Bruce 1986). It was once common in the lowlands in Seram (White and Bruce 1986) and was described as locally common in primary forest in the interior by Smiet (1985), but rangers at the Manusela National Park have commented on a dramatic decline in the species in recent years (G. R. Milton) and it is now scarce even within the reserve (J. Bowler, J. B. Taylor). There is no doubt that trapping is responsible for the decline: numbers legally exported from Indonesia in 1984, 1985 and 1986 were 7,398, 7,525 and 7,360 respectively (S. Manan *per* C. Schouten).

White Cockatoo *Cacatua alba* is found on Halmahera and its satellite islands Ternate, Tidore, Bacan, and Obi, **Indonesia** (White and Bruce 1986). Flocks of up to 50 birds were reported from the interior of Halmahera by Smiet (1985), but at Domatu flocks of over 30 birds seen in 1986 were not found in 1987 (F. R. Lambert, D. Yong). The species is widely shot for food but trapping for both export and the internal market is probably the greatest threat: in 1984, 1985 and 1986, 7,886, 7,164 and 7,884 were exported legally (S. Manan *per* C. Schouten).

Red-vented Cockatoo *Cacatua haematuropygia* is distributed throughout the **Philippines**, where it frequents forest, forest edge and secondary growth, and visits agricultural land to raid ripening crops (Forshaw and Cooper 1981a). Delacour and Mayr (1946) described it as common and it was probably still widespread until a decade ago, but it is now very local owing to excessive trapping: on Palawan it is still traded in the bird markets, and continued trapping will eliminate the species (T. H. Fisher, R. S. Kennedy, B. F. King, J. Scharringa).

Tanimbar Corella *Cacatua goffini* is endemic to the Tanimbar Islands, **Indonesia** (White and Bruce 1986). Large numbers were reported to occur in the forested interior of the larger islands (Smiet 1985) but the species is now widely trapped, both for trade and because it raids maize crops, a staple food in Tanimbar for part of the year (F. G. Rozendaal); in 1984, 1985 and 1986, the numbers legally exported from Indonesia were 7,828, 7,314 and 8,306 respectively (S. Manan *per* C. Schouten).

Salvadori's Fig-parrot *Psittaculirostris salvadorii* occurs in northern Irian Jaya, **Indonesia**, from the Cyclops Mountains to the eastern shore of Geelvink Bay (Beehler *et al.* 1986). It affects evergreen forest to an altitude of 400 m and is rare, at least in collections (Rand and Gilliard 1967). Diamond (1985) considers it to be locally common, but large numbers are being trapped for the cage-bird trade (K. D. Bishop).

Green-headed Racquet-tailed Parrot *Prioniturus luconensis* occurs on Luzon and Marinduque in the **Philippines** (Forshaw and Cooper 1981a). In mid-century it was common in the canopy of lowland forest in Bataan (Gilliard 1950), and remains locally common in lowland forest at Quezon (B. F. King, J. Scharringa), but it is restricted to primary forest and threatened by habitat destruction, and by trapping for bird markets (R. S. Kennedy).

Buru Racquet-tailed Parrot *Prioniturus mada* is endemic to Buru, **Indonesia**, and presumably affects forest, occasionally in the lowlands but usually above 1,000 m (White and Bruce 1986). Its status is unknown.

Alexandra's Parrot *Polytelis alexandrae* is a rare inhabitant of the spinifex and casuarina deserts of Western **Australia**, Northern Territory and north-western South Australia, where it is nomadic and formerly bred colonially: some evidence of a decline this century is provided by the low number of recent breeding records involving more than one pair (Blakers *et al.* 1984). One of its remaining strongholds is the Great Sandy Desert, Western Australia (M. Fleming *per* J. Brouwer) and the remoteness of this bird's range probably favours its survival (Joseph in press).

Golden-shouldered Parrot *Psephotus chrysopterygius* was formerly found in the Cape York region, Queensland, **Australia**, as far south as Byerstown and west along the Gulf of Carpentaria to the Norman River, but is now restricted to the eastern edge of its former range between Musgrave and Koolburra (King 1978-1979, Blakers *et al.* 1984). It nests in termite mounds in waterlogged drainage depressions and affects eucalypt and paperbark woodland with a grass understorey (Blakers *et al.* 1984). The species was heavily trapped in the 1950s and 1960s (Wheeler 1975) and although now protected, illicit trapping continues (J. Brouwer).

Hooded Parrot *Psephotus dissimilis* occurs in the semi-arid north-east of Northern Territory, **Australia**, from the western edge of Arnhem Land to the Macarthur River, but is now rare except on the Arnhem Plateau (Wheeler 1975, King 1978-1979). The nest is excavated in a termite mound, and outside the breeding season flocks of over 100 birds gather in seeding grassland and around water; the species has been heavily trapped in the past and this may account for its decline, but grazing and the timing and frequency of burning of seeding grasses may be equally important (Forshaw and Cooper 1981b).

Paradise Parrot *Psephotus pulcherrimus*, from **Australia**, was last reliably recorded in 1927 and is presumed extinct (King 1978-1978). It formerly occurred in south-eastern Queensland and north-eastern New South Wales, in savanna woodlands with a grass ground-cover, feeding on grass seed and seed heads; its extinction has been attributed to the practice of firing seeding grass to provide green pick for cattle (Blakers *et al.* 1984). If the species survives, it is probably in northern Queensland where most of the unsubstantiated reports, both historical and recent, originate (Blakers *et al.* 1984).

Antipodes Parakeet *Cyanoramphus unicolor* is endemic to the uninhabited islands of the **Antipodes (to New Zealand)**, where, in 1978, its population was estimated at 2,000-3,000 birds; the species nests in underground burrows (Taylor 1985), and is threatened by the chance of accidental introductions which once seemed unlikely because of the isolated location (Williams and Given 1981), but is now a possibility owing to increased fishing in the Southern Ocean (B. D. Bell).

Orange-bellied Parrot *Neophema chrysogaster* breeds in western Tasmania, **Australia**, and migrates to the southern coast of the Australian mainland in the winter (King 1978-1979), where in 1984 a minimum of 85 birds were recorded (Jessop and Reid 1986) although Brown *et al.* (1985) estimate the population at 100-200. In Tasmania it breeds on heath and sedgelands and is protected in the South-West National Park and Conservation Area (Burbidge and Jenkins 1984). On the mainland in Victoria and South Australia it feeds on saltmarshes and coastal dunes, and the decline in the population over the past century has been correlated with the development of large areas of this habitat for saltworks and sewage farms (Cowling and Davies 1983; see also Loyn *et al.* 1986), although there are possible contributory factors in Tasmania too, including the spread of a fungus, trampling of food plants by stock, human disturbance, mineral exploration and trapping (Joseph in press; see also Brown and Wilson 1984).

Scarlet-chested Parrot *Neophema splendida* occurs very locally in the interior of **Australia**, where it has probably always been a rare species, but as it is highly prized as a cage-bird its survival could be threatened (King 1978-1979). Under suitable conditions it apparently breeds rapidly and becomes common, only to disperse and decline until the next favourable season (Blakers *et al.* 1984).

Ground Parrot *Pezoporus wallicus* was formerly found in coastal heath and sedgelands in **Australia** from southern Queensland to south-eastern South Australia, in Tasmania, and in Western Australia from near Geraldtown to Cape Arid (King 1978-1979). It is restricted to heath that provides thick cover and a high density of food plants, factors that are affected by fire; moreover, drainage of swamps and trampling by cattle have eliminated some populations (Blakers *et al.* 1984). Its range is now fragmented: only two populations of the race *flaviventris* were found in a recent survey of Western Australia and nominate *wallicus* appears extinct in South Australia, but locally common in isolated pockets in Victoria and New South Wales (Burbidge and Jenkins 1984, Joseph in press).

Night Parrot *Geopsittacus occidentalis* has been recorded in arid central **Australia** from central Western Australia to south-west Queensland, western New South Wales and north-western Victoria; the species was presumably more abundant in the 1870s when 16 specimens were collected in the Lake Eyre region, compared to a total of six reliable records between 1935 and 1984 in the whole of Australia (Blakers *et al.* 1984). It is thought to be nomadic and may feed almost exclusively on spinifex within samphire flats and associated lake systems (King 1978-1979, Blakers *et al.* 1984) but reasons for its apparent decline are not known.

Black-cheeked Lovebird *Agapornis nigrigenis* has a total range of about 6,000 sq km in mopane woodland almost exclusively in southern **Zambia**, but extending along the Zambezi in northern Zimbabwe, and possibly occurring in northern **Botswana** and **Namibia**'s Caprivi Strip (whence there are old records) (Collar and Stuart 1985). It is now extinct in Zimbabwe (D. Rockingham-Gill).

Sangihe Hanging-parrot *Loriculus catamene* is endemic to Sangihe in the Sangihe Islands, **Indonesia**, where it was never common and is now believed to be rare (White and Bruce 1986). The original vegetation on the Sangihe Islands is almost completely replaced by coconut, nutmeg and the secondary vegetation of abandoned gardens (Whitten *et al.* 1987). However, the species has been regularly observed in coconut groves and might survive the loss of habitat (F. G. Rozendaal).

Rothschild's Parakeet *Psittacula intermedia* was long based on seven skins of uncertain provenance (Ali and Ripley 1984) but recently one or two live specimens, reputed to have come from the plains of Uttar Pradesh, have appeared each year in bird markets in **India** (Sane *et al.* 1986).

Nicobar Parakeet *Psittacula caniceps* is an endemic resident of Great Nicobar, Montschall and Kondul in the **Nicobar Islands (to India)**, where it is apparently restricted to forest (Ali and Ripley 1984). The status of the species is wholly unknown, but island development may be a threat (B. F. King) although the species's principal food, the fruit of *Pandanus*, is abundant on the unhabited islands (Forshaw and Cooper 1981a).

Mauritius Parakeet *Psittacula eques* survives in very low numbers (under 10) in the forested upland regions of south-west **Mauritius**, where it suffers almost total breeding failure (Collar and Stuart 1985; see also Jones 1987). Eight birds were seen and nine estimated to be the total population in 1986 (Cheke 1987d). One bird was trapped in 1987 to found a captive breeding attempt (D. V. Merton), but died the same year; however, one pair produced two young, now in captivity, and eight birds (minimum), five males and three females, remain in the wild (C. G. Jones).

Hyacinth Macaw *Anodorhynchus hyacinthinus*, the largest parrot in the world, affects dry forest and wet forest edge in central **Brazil** and the adjacent Pantanal regions of easternmost **Bolivia** and north-east **Paraguay**, and has greatly declined owing to trading and hunting (Ridgely 1981b, Sick 1985, A. D. Johns, P. Roth), such that now only some 2,500-5,000 birds are estimated to remain, the vast majority of them in Brazil (Munn *et al.* 1987).

Glaucous Macaw *Anodorhynchus glaucus* of south-east **Brazil**, south-east **Paraguay**, north-east **Argentina** and possibly northern **Uruguay** is almost certainly now extinct (King 1978-1979, Ridgely 1981b, Chebez 1986).

Indigo Macaw *Anodorhynchus leari* is restricted to caatinga (thorn scrub) adjacent to a set of sandstone cliffs in one small part of Bahia state, north- east **Brazil** (King 1978-1979, Sick 1979b), where the total population is not known to be more than 60 birds (Yamashita 1987).

Little Blue Macaw *Cyanopsitta spixii* stands now at the very brink of extinction in its small area of interior north-east **Brazil** (King 1978-1979, Ridgely 1981b), having declined mainly through hunting and trapping to a few individuals in the wild (P. Roth). Initiatives to provide effective protection for these last wild birds have signally failed, as have endeavours to establish a captive-breeding pro-gramme using the stock (perhaps no more than 20 in total) held in private collections around the world (Thomsen and Munn 1988).

Blue-throated Macaw *Ara glaucogularis* (formerly called Caninde or Wagler's Macaw *A. caninde*: King 1978-1979) is known with certainty only from a very restricted part of **Bolivia** in Beni and Santa Cruz, where its numbers are (or were) only between 500 and 1,000 birds (Ingels *et al.* 1981, Lanning 1982, Nores and Yzurieta 1984, Remsen *et al.* 1986) and it is still heavily exploited for the cage-bird trade (B. Woods E.).

Red-fronted Macaw *Ara rubrogenys* is restricted to a small area of east-central **Bolivia** with a total population not exceeding 5,000 birds, which is being heavily trapped for export (Ridgely 1981b, Lanning 1982, Nores and Yzurieta 1984) and even persecuted for claimed crop damage (J. V. Remsen, B. Woods E.)

Golden Conure *Guaruba guarouba* occurs in a small area of north **Brazil** from western Para to western Maranhao in terra firme (dryland forest), or adjacent varzea (seasonally flooded forest), and has declined considerably owing to habitat loss and trapping (King 1978-1979, Oren and Novaes 1986, P. Roth) mainly in the eastern part of its range, where the creation of a secure reserve is the top priority (Oren and Novaes 1986).

Socorro Conure *Aratinga brevipes*, considered distinct from Green Parakeet *A. holochlora* based on voice, morphology and plumage, is fairly common but vulnerable on Socorro, in the **Revillagigedos Islands (to Mexico)** (S. N. G. Howell).

Cuban Conure *Aratinga euops*, although not considered in a recent review of the country's threatened birds (Garrido 1985), is restricted to and steeply declining in **Cuba**, having become extinct on the Isla de la Juventud (Isle of Pines) (Garcia undated), and now possibly only fairly common in the woods of the Zapata Swamp (C. Wotzkow).

Golden-capped Conure *Aratinga auricapilla* is restricted to forested parts of south-east **Brazil** and although still common in a few places (A. Brandt, D. M. Teixeira) must be declining owing to habitat fragmentation (Ridgely 1981b, D. M. Teixeira, C. Yamashita) and trapping in numbers for the bird-trade (C. E. Carvalho). There have apparently been no recent records of the species from the southern part of its range (Ridgely 1981b; see also Willis and Oniki 1981).

Golden-plumed Conure *Leptosittaca branickii* is a very poorly known bird with disjunct populations in the temperate-zone forests of **Colombia, Ecuador** and southern **Peru**, and is nowhere common (Forshaw and Cooper 1981a, Ridgely 1981b, Arndt 1986).

Yellow-eared Conure *Ognorhynchus icterotis* is now confined to a small area of south-west **Colombia** and adjacent northern **Ecuador**, and has seriously de-clined owing to extensive forest destruction (King 1978-1979, Ridgely 1981b, Arndt 1986). A flock of 25 on the north-east slope of Cerro Munchique, July 1978, apparently constitutes the most recent (Colombian) record (Hilty and Brown 1986).

Thick-billed Parrot *Rhynchopsitta pachyrhyncha* is endemic to the Sierra Madre Occidental, **Mexico**, where it is seriously declining owing to trapping for the cagebird trade, shooting and destruction of its pine-forest habitat (King 1978- 1979, Lanning and Shiflett 1981, 1983, Arndt 1986). A recent initiative to establish a breeding population in Arizona, U.S.A., has had some success (Koschmann and Price 1987, H. Snyder, N. F. R. Snyder).

Maroon-fronted Parrot *Rhynchopsitta terrisi* is endemic to the Sierra Madre Oriental, **Mexico**, where it numbers around 2,000 birds and suffers from considerable deforestation (King 1978-1979, Lawson and Lanning 1981, Arndt 1986).

Blue-chested Parakeet *Pyrrhura cruentata* is endemic to primary lowland forest in south-east **Brazil**, where its range is now highly fragmented and numbers have massively declined (Ridgely 1981b; also King 1978-1979), but it remains common locally in several areas, including some forest reserves, although most of these are under permanent pressure and vulnerable to cutting and bird-trapping (Gonzaga *et al.* in press).

Pearly Parakeet *Pyrrhura perlata* (not including *P. perlata perlata* [= *P. rhodogaster*] as proposed by Arndt and Roth 1986) is endemic to a small part of north **Brazil** and has declined substantially owing to forest destruction (Ridgely 1981b, P. Roth).

Yellow-sided Parakeet *Pyrrhura hypoxantha* is known from three specimens in south-western Mato Grosso, **Brazil**, and is regarded as an invalid species, the birds being aberrant Green-cheeked Parakeets *P. molinae* (Forshaw and Cooper 1981, D. M. Teixeira). However, in 1987 birds closely resembling *hypoxantha* were seen at Itacarambi, Minas Gerais (the locality for Minas Gerais Tyrannulet *Phylloscartes roquettei* and Snethlage's Woodcreeper *Xiphocolaptes franciscanus* - see under Moustached Woodcreeper *X. falcirostris*) (D. C. Oren).

White-necked Parakeet *Pyrrhura albipectus* is restricted to a small region of south-east **Ecuador** in which it is uncommon and perpetually vulnerable to habitat loss (Ridgely 1981b; also Forshaw and Cooper 1981a). It probably breeds in Cordillera Cutucu (N. Krabbe).

Flame-winged Parakeet *Pyrrhura calliptera* occupies both slopes of the Eastern Andes of **Colombia** from southern Boyaca to south-western Cundinamarca, but forest destruction has been extensive within its restricted range (Ridgely 1981b) and, although still locally numerous, it is clearly now threatened (S. L. Hilty).

Rufous-fronted Parakeet *Bolborhynchus ferrugineifrons* is endemic to high-elevation shrubland in the Central Cordillera of the Andes of **Colombia** and had not certainly been reported since 1955 (Ridgely 1981b; also King 1978-1979, Arndt 1986) until recently relocated at 3,280 to 4,000 m in the vicinity of Laguna de Otun and on Nevado del Ruiz, with an estimated population of 1,000 to 2,000 (Graves and Giraldo 1987).

Grey-cheeked Parakeet *Brotogeris pyrrhopterus* occurs in deciduous forest in south-west **Ecuador** and north-west **Peru** and has declined considerably owing apparently to habitat loss and trapping (Ridgely 1981b). No fewer than 20,000 were exported from Peru in 1984 (C. Schouten).

Brown-backed Parrotlet *Touit melanonota* is endemic to south-east **Brazil** with a now fragmented range, within which it is rare though possibly much overlooked (Ridgely 1981b; also King 1978-1979); in 1987 there were records of one to seven in Rio de Janeiro state (J. F. Pacheco).

Golden-tailed Parrotlet *Touit surda* is endemic to mainly lowland forest in eastern **Brazil** and is now probably rare, owing to extensive habitat loss (Ridgely 1981b; also King 1978-1979), but it is also certainly overlooked very often, recent records being from Ceara, Alagoas, south Bahia, north Espirito Santo and Rio de Janeiro state (C. E. Carvalho, L. P. Gonzaga, R. Otoch, J. F. Pacheco, B. M. Whitney).

Spot-winged Parrotlet *Touit stictoptera* inhabits **Colombia** (known definitely from only three localities in forested mountains), eastern **Ecuador** and northern **Peru,** but is now threatened by deforestation in Colombia (Hilty and Brown 1986).

Rusty-faced Parrot *Hapalopsittaca amazonina* occurs in humid forested highlands as four races covering **Venezuela, Colombia** and **Ecuador,** but it is now rare throughout its range and two races are seriously threatened (Ridgely 1981b, Hilty and Brown 1986).

Puerto Rican Amazon *Amazona vittata* remains critically endangered in rainforest on the Luquillo Mountains of north-eastern **Puerto Rico (to U.S.A.)** (King 1978- 1979), owing to habitat restriction compounded by scarcity of nest-sites, and in particular competition for nest-sites and predation of nests by Pearly-eyed Thrashers *Margarops fuscatus*, although intensive management has wrought a slow but steady improvement in the wild population from a low of 13 in 1975 to around 30 a decade later (Wiley 1985, Snyder *et al.* 1987).

Red-spectacled Amazon *Amazona pretrei* has a small range covering south **Brazil** and north-east **Argentina,** possibly also **Uruguay** and **Paraguay,** where it is closely associated with *Araucaria*-dominated forest and is declining seriously (Ridgely 1981b; also King 1978-1979, Silva 1981, Sick 1985).

Red-crowned (Green-cheeked) Amazon *Amazona viridigenalis* is endemic to a small area of north-east **Mexico** and has seriously declined, owing to habitat destruction and trapping (Ridgely 1981b). Several thousands remain in the wild

(Clinton-Eitniear 1986), with thousands in captivity in the **U.S.A.** where some cities even have feral populations, e.g. Miami, Los Angeles, San Diego, Brownsville (J. Clinton-Eitniear); a small population has also established itself in **Puerto Rico (to U.S.A.)** (Raffaele 1983).

Red-tailed Amazon *Amazona brasiliensis* is endemic to coastal forests of south **Brazil** where it is very rare (King 1978-1979, Ridgely 1981b), a population of no more than 4,000 being now confined to an area of approximately 600,000 ha in south-eastern Sao Paulo and north-eastern Parana, which is not yet fully protected from timber exploitation and bird-trapping, although some parts of it have been given protected status (P. Sc'erer Neto).

Red-browed Amazon *Amazona rhodocorytha* is endemic to eastern **Brazil** where it has suffered a major decline as a result of forest clearance and hunting (Ridgely 1981b); recent records are from several areas in Minas Gerais (M. A. Andrade), northern Espirito Santo (Scott and Brooke 1985, Gonzaga *et al*. in press, C. E. Carvalho, B. M. Whitney) and Rio de Janeiro state (N. C. Maciel, J. F. Pacheco, L. do Rosario Bege).

Yellow-faced Amazon *Amazona xanthops* of central **Brazil** may be locally common (Sick 1985, P. Roth, J. Vielliard, E. O. Willis) or even "still very abundant in many localities" (D. M. Teixeira), but must gradually be disappearing as its cerrado (woodland savanna) habitat is cleared for agriculture (R. Cavalcanti, T. A. Parker, E. O. Willis, C. Yamashita) and birds are trapped for the pet trade (C. E. Carvalho, R. Cavalcanti). There is a 1964 record from Beni, **Bolivia** (Remsen *et al*. 1986).

Yellow-shouldered Amazon *Amazona barbadensis* has a disjunct and highly restricted distribution in northern **Venezuela** (plus Isla de Margarita and Isla la Blanquilla) and on Bonaire in the **Netherlands Antilles (to Netherlands)** and, although still locally common on the mainland in the late 1970s (Ridgely 1981b), it is now easily found at only one locality (C. Parrish, B. Swift) although still heavily traded (R. Ramirez), on Margarita it is confined to the centre of the Macanao Peninsula and probably numbers 150-200 birds (Vierheilig and Vierheilig 1988), while on Bonaire numbers appear to be under 350, with nest-predation by people, rats and Pearly-eyed Thrashers *Margarops fuscatus* (B. A. de Boer).

Vinaceous Amazon *Amazona vinacea* occurs in south-east **Brazil**, south-east **Paraguay** and north-east **Argentina** (Misiones), where it has suffered a major decline mainly through widespread forest habitat loss (Ridgely 1981b). A relict population survives in Misiones but is gravely at risk there (J. C. Chebez, M. Nores and D. Yzurieta).

St Lucia Amazon *Amazona versicolor* is restricted to the central mountain forests of **St Lucia** (King 1978-1979). Its population was estimated to be 100 in

1977 (Butler 1981) but had risen to 250 in 1986, attributed to forest protection and the abolition of hunting (P. J. Butler).

Red-necked Amazon *Amazona arausiaca* was found in lowland forest in the northern two-thirds of **Dominica** where hunting has been the major cause of its decline (King 1978-1979). Today it only occurs around Morne Diablotin and it is seriously threatened by the rapid clearance of its habitat for banana plantations; in 1987 the population was estimated at 300 birds (Evans 1988).

St Vincent Amazon *Amazona guildingii* is confined to several valleys along the mountainous backbone of **St Vincent**, where it suffers from illegal hunting and loss of habitat (King 1978-1979). In 1979 a volcanic eruption and in 1980 a hurricane caused further habitat degradation, but forest clearance for agriculture and charcoal-burning remains the greatest threat, with capture for the pet trade adding to the problems; the population was estimated to be about 420 in 1982 (Lambert 1983, 1985).

Imperial Amazon *Amazona imperialis* is a mountain rainforest species from **Dominica**, very highly prized as a cage-bird; intense hunting for food and sport resulted in a range contraction by the 1970s to two areas (King 1978-1979). Serious hurricanes in 1979 and 1980 annihilated the southern population, whilst the northern population, found on the slopes of Morne Diablotin, is threatened by habitat destruction and in 1987 was estimated to be only 60 birds (P. G. H. Evans).

Purple-bellied Parrot *Triclaria malachitacea* is endemic to south-east **Brazil** and is declining there (Sick and Teixeira 1979a), and in recent fieldwork has been found in only Rio de Janeiro, Sao Paulo and Rio Grande do Sul states (Scott and Brooke 1985, C. E. Carvalho, J. F. Pacheco, C. Yamashita).

Kakapo *Strigops habroptilus* survives in Fiordland on South Island, **New Zealand** (at least five males, B. D. Bell), and a rediscovered population (up to 40 birds, B. D. Bell) inhabits Stewart Island (King 1978-1979, Williams and Given 1981, Best and Powlesland 1985) where cat predation is a threat (Karl and Best 1982). Birds have been transferred to Little Barrier Island (*World Birdwatch* 7 [2,1985]: 1-2), where no more than 20 birds survive and there is concern that the island may not provide adequate food to stimulate breeding (B. D. Bell: also Best 1984). An understanding of factors which control lekking behaviour, particularly those triggering the erratic and unpredictable breeding cycles, may be vital if effective conservation is to be achieved (Merton *et al.* 1984).

Order CUCULIFORMES

Family Musophagidae
Turacos

Bannerman's Turaco *Tauraco bannermani*, an arboreal forest frugivore, is restricted to the Bamenda-Banso Highlands of western **Cameroon**, where it is under very serious threat from forest clearance and is only likely to survive if forest on Mount Oku is preserved (Collar and Stuart 1985, Stuart and Jensen 1986). Intensive work has been directed towards the conservation of Mount Oku, and is continuing (e.g. Macleod 1987, Wilson in press).

Prince Ruspoli's Turaco *Tauraco ruspolii*, a very secretive arboreal frugivore, has a very small range in southern **Ethiopia** where it occurs in juniper forest, mixed broadleaf woodland and acacia woodland along streams, and may be as much at risk from competition with the White-cheeked Turaco *T. leucotis* as from any loss of its habitat (Collar and Stuart 1985).

Family Cuculidae
Cuckoos, coucals

Green-cheeked Bronze-cuckoo *Chrysococcyx rufomerus* is found on the small low islands east of Timor, from Romang to Damar, **Indonesia**, where its status is unknown and complicated by the poor understanding of its taxonomic relationship to the Pied Bronze-cuckoo *C. crassirostris* (White and Bruce 1986).

Cocos Cuckoo *Coccyzus ferrugineus* from **Cocos Island (to Costa Rica)**, is much the rarest of the endemic Cocos bird species, and merits vigilance and study (Slud 1967, F. G. Stiles).

Red-faced Malkoha *Phaenicophaeus pyrrhocephalus* is rare and local in **Sri Lanka** and southern Kerala, where it is largely restricted to wet evergreen forest, in the low country and hills to about 1,700 m, and has also been seen in western Tamil Nadu, **India** (Ali and Ripley 1984). There are scattered colonies in riverine habitats of the drier zones, but it avoids cultivation and the species has declined markedly in recent years (Hoffmann 1984).

Banded Ground-cuckoo *Neomorphus radiolosus* is restricted to wet forest, mostly in foothills and on lower slopes, in north-west **Ecuador** and south-west **Colombia**, where it is rare and local (Hilty and Brown 1986); there seem to be no recent records (R. S. Ridgely).

Sunda Ground-cuckoo *Carpococcyx radiceus* is known from Borneo and **Sumatra, Indonesia**; it affects dry, level forest, at least in Sarawak, **Malaysia** (Davison 1981), although it was heard commonly in hill-forest in Brunei (Holmes and Burton 1987) and is probably widely but thinly distributed throughout the island (Smythies 1981). There are no recent records from Sumatra (see van Marle and Voous 1988).

Snail-eating Coua *Coua delalandei*, a large terrestrial cuckoo endemic to **Madagascar**, has not been recorded since 1834 and seems likely to be extinct, but conceivably survives in one poorly explored rainforest region, the hinterland of Pointe-a-Larree (Collar and Stuart 1985).

Green-billed Coucal *Centropus chlororhynchus* is endemic to **Sri Lanka** and is found only in high humid forest with a dense undergrowth (particularly of bamboo: S. Kotegama) in the western and southern foothills of the central mountain massif to 800 m: it is rare, local and severely threatened by loss of habitat (Hoffmann 1984); recent records are from Sinharaja (P. Dukes).

Short-toed Coucal *Centropus rectunguis* is an uncommon forest resident in peninsular **Malaysia**, Borneo and Sumatra, **Indonesia** (Medway and Wells 1976). It has probably been under-recorded (Smythies 1981) but is an extreme lowland specialist (Wells 1985) and the colonizing ability and widespread occurrence of its congeners leaves it susceptible to displacement in marginal habitats (see Holmes and Burton 1987).

Black-hooded Coucal *Centropus steerii* is endemic to Mindoro in the **Philippines** and confined to forest (Delacour and Mayr 1946). It was described as common by Ripley and Rabor (1958) in the lowlands and hills to 800 m but there are no recent records. A dark-winged form of the Philippine Coucal *C. viridis* occurs in grassland and scrub on the island (R. S. Kennedy) and continued deforestation could lead to its displacement of *steerii* (P. Andrew).

Javan Coucal *Centropus nigrorufus* is known from Java and by one skin of doubtful provenance from Sumatra, **Indonesia** (Kuroda 1933-1936). On Java it affects the scrub and *Nipa* palm vegetation that is found just behind mature mangrove, a habitat largely converted to fish ponds and paddy (P. Andrew). It is currently known from a single site on the south coast of Java, where it is common (P. Andrew).

Order STRIGIFORMES

Family Tytonidae
Barn owls

Madagascar Red Owl *Tyto soumagnei* is known with certainty only from rainforest in eastern-central **Madagascar**, where it has been seen only once (in 1973) since 1934 (Collar and Stuart 1985).

Taliabu Owl *Tyto nigrobrunnea* is endemic to Taliabu in the Sula Islands, **Indonesia**, and is known by a single specimen, a female, collected in 1938; it may be a representative of the Minahassa Owl *T. inexspectata* (White and Bruce 1986).

Minahassa Owl *Tyto inexspectata* is endemic to Sulawesi, **Indonesia**, where it is only known by eleven specimens, all but one collected on the northern peninsula, in hill forest between 250 and 1,500 m; a dead bird obtained by Watling (1983) in north-central Sulawesi extends the known range but it is still believed to be a rare species (White and Bruce 1986).

Lesser Masked Owl *Tyto sororcula* is found on Buru and the Tanimbar Islands, **Indonesia**, where it presumably occurs in lowland forest but is known from few specimens and has not been observed in the field (White and Bruce 1986).

Golden Owl *Tyto aurantia* occurs in forest to an altitude of 1,800 m on New Britain, **Papua New Guinea** (Schodde 1978); it is rare, recorded in 1978 and 1984 in lowland forest edge (K. D. Bishop), but there are few other field records (J. M. Diamond).

Itombwe Owl *Phodilus prigoginei* remains known only from the type-specimen, collected in a grass clearing in montane forest at Muusi, 2,430 m, in the Itombwe Mountains, **Zaire**, although a bird almost certainly this species was observed on a tea estate in **Burundi** in the 1970s (Collar and Stuart 1985).

Family Strigidae
Owls

White-fronted Scops Owl *Otus sagittatus* is resident in Tenasserim, **Burma**, peninsular **Thailand** and **Malaysia**, and possibly northern Sumatra, **Indonesia** (one record, perhaps only a vagrant); it is restricted to evergreen forest, mainly in the lowlands, but has been recorded to 600 m (Medway and Wells 1976; also van Marle and Voous 1988). The call has only recently been identified (B. F. King, D. Yong) and consequently this species's status has not yet been determined.

Sokoke Scops Owl *Otus ireneae* is endemic to the Arabuko-Sokoke Forest in coastal **Kenya**, where the population (estimated at 1,000 pairs in 1984) is ever-decreasing with the illegal but unchecked clearance of its habitat (Collar and Stuart 1985, 1988).

Sumatran Scops Owl *Otus stresemanni* is known from one specimen collected at 920 m on Gn Kerinchi, West Sumatra, **Indonesia** (Marshall 1978). There is some doubt as to taxonomic standing: Marshall (1978) treats it as probably distinct and allied to Sandy Scops Owl *O. icterorhynchus* (Africa) and Andaman Scops Owl *O. Balli* (Andamans), but van Marle and Voous (1988) note that it might only be a pale morph of Spotted Mountain Scops Owl *O. spilocophalus*.

Javan Scops Owl *Otus angelinae* is known from two locations in western Java, **Indonesia** (Kuroda 1933-1936, K. D. Bishop). It is known to frequent forest between 1,400 and 2,000 m and is probably common within its restricted range but its status is likely to remain unknown as long as the call is not documented (Andrew and Milton 1988).

Flores Scops Owl *Otus alfredi* is endemic to Flores, **Indonesia**, and known from three specimens taken late last century, in forest above 1,000 m in the mountains of Manggarai (White and Bruce 1986). Marshall (1978) searched for this species but failed to find it, as have all subsequent observers. The species is either extinct, silent or Flores was mistaken as the locality (E. Schmutz).

Mindoro Mountain Scops Owl *Otus mindorensis* is known by the type-specimen collected in 1896 on Mindoro in the **Philippines** (Marshall 1978) and by a report that it was common in l983 on Mt Halcon; Mt Halcon was then well forested above 500 m (B. F. King) but the species is known from no other locality.

Grand Comoro Scops Owl *Otus pauliani* is restricted to the highest forests on Mount Karthala on Grand Comoro, **Comoro Islands**, where its habitat remains vulnerable (Collar and Stuart 1985). In 1985 the population was estimated to comprise several tens of pairs, preferring undisturbed forest, and at considerable risk if any clearance occurs (Louette *et al.* 1986).

Seychelles Scops Owl *Otus insularis* is endemic to upland forest in Mahe in the **Seychelles**, where its total population may be only 80 pairs yet where some logging is inevitable (Collar and Stuart 1985).

Sao Tome Scops Owl *Otus hartlaubi* is fairly widespread but uncommon in upland forest on Sao Tome, **Sao Tome e Principe**, possibly also occurring on Principe (Collar and Stuart 1985). A recent survey found its habitat in good condition (Jones and Tye 1988).

Usambara Eagle Owl *Bubo vosseleri* is endemic to the Usambara Mountains in north- east **Tanzania**, where its numbers may lie between 200 and 1,000 and it may be at some risk from forest destruction (Collar and Stuart 1985). An IUCN project aimed at reconciling conservation and development in the Usambaras (Stuart 1986) is currently being implemented (N. M. Collins).

Blakiston's Fish Owl *Ketupa blakistoni* is confined to the Soviet Far East, Sakhalin and the southern Kuril Islands, **U.S.S.R.**, northern **China** and Hokkaido, **Japan** (Flint *et al.* 1984, Brazil 1985c). In the U.S.S.R. it is considered threatened, with a population estimated at 300-400 pairs (Borodin 1984). In Japan, a survey in 1984 located 49-52 birds (Brazil 1985c), whilst in China the situation is unknown.

Rufous Fishing Owl *Scotopelia ussheri*, endemic to the Upper Guinea forest block in West Africa where it inhabits mangroves and forest bordering rivers and lakes, occurs or occurred in **Ghana** (three records up to 1941), **Guinea** (one record, in 1951), **Ivory Coast** (only one certain record, undated), **Liberia** (fairly widely distributed) and **Sierra Leone** (four records up to 1969); it appears to be at risk from habitat destruction and pollution (Collar and Stuart 1985).

Albertine Owlet *Glaucidium passerinum* is known from just five specimens, all collected in forest, in the Itombwe Mountains (two) and forest west of Lake Edward (two), **Zaire**, and the Nyungwe Forest, **Rwanda** (Collar and Stuart 1985).

Forest Owlet *Athene blewitti* is endemic to **India** where it apparently ranges the length of the Satpura Range in moist tropical and subtropical woodlands, a distance of over 1,000 km, but is known from very few specimens, the last of which was collected in 1914 (King 1978-1979).

Spotted Owl *Strix occidentalis* has three subspecies, questionably distinct, dependent on large tracts of old-growth forest from south-west **Canada**, western and south-central **U.S.A.** to central **Mexico** (apparently very rare and local: Blake 1953); commercial logging is the biggest threat, not only because of reduction of habitat but indirectly because of increased competitive displacement by Barred Owls *Strix varia* and predation by Great Horned Owls *Bubo virginianus*, both species being able to tolerate secondary growth (Wilcove 1987; see also Gutierrez and Carey 1985)).

Order CAPRIMULGIFORMES

Family Podargidae
Frogmouths

Dulit Frogmouth *Batrachostomus harterti* is a submontane resident endemic of Borneo and known from only seven specimens (Smythies 1981). It has been collected from between 300 and 1,300 m, mostly in the uplands of Sarawak, **Malaysia**, but also from Mt Liang Kubung in Central Kalimantan, **Indonesia** (Smythies 1981); this would suggest that the species is fairly widespread on the central mountain spine.

Family Nyctibiidae
Potoos

Long-tailed Potoo *Nyctibius aethereus* is known by scattered records, mostly based on skins, from **Guyana, Venezuela, Colombia, Ecuador, Peru, Brazil** and **Paraguay** (Meyer de Schauensee 1982), and is a very rare bird (T. A. Parker, R. S. Ridgely, D. A. Scott). Populations in south-east Brazil and Paraguay may be a distinct species (*aethereus*, those elsewhere *longicaudatus*) (Hilty and Brown 1986).

White-winged Potoo *Nyctibius leucopterus* (separated from Andean Potoo *Nyctibius maculosus*, itself described as "very rare": Hilty and Brown 1986) is known from only two specimens in **Brazil**, one of them from Bahia (Schulenberg *et al.* 1984).

Rufous Potoo *Nyctibius bracteatus* of **Colombia, Ecuador** and **Peru** (recorded once in **Guyana** and **Brazil**) is known from only a small number of skins and records and is judged very rare (Hilty and Brown 1986, R. O. Bierregaard, R. S. Ridgely, D. A. Scott).

Family Caprimulgidae
Nightjars

Satanic Nightjar *Eurostopodus diabolicus* is endemic to Sulawesi, **Indonesia**, and known only from the type, a female collected at 250 m in forest on the northern peninsula (White and Bruce 1986). A number of unidentified calls have been attributed to the species (Holmes and Wood 1980, White and Bruce 1986).

Jamaican Pauraque *Siphonorhis americanus* has been treated as extinct on **Jamaica** (Morony *et al.* 1975, King 1978-1979), as a result of "interference by introduced mammals" (Greenway 1967), but hope has not been entirely abandoned and an unidentified nightbird has been glimpsed (Sutton 1981).

Puerto Rican Whippoorwill *Caprimulgus noctitherus* inhabits semi-deciduous forest in just three localities in the arid south-west of **Puerto Rico (to U.S.A.)**, with a total of around 500 pairs (King 1978-1979, Raffaele 1983).

White-winged Nightjar *Caprimulgus candicans* is a very little-known bird from central and south **Brazil** (Sao Paulo, Mato Grosso, and recently Goias) and eastern **Paraguay**, but is definitely a distinct species (Sick 1985, R. S. Ridgely, *contra* Short 1975). It was recently found in Emas National Park in southern Goias (Redford 1987, R. S. Ridgely).

Vaurie's Nightjar *Caprimulgus centralasicus* is known from a single female taken in west Xinjiang Uygur, **China**, and is probably a bird of the sandy foothills and plains of the Kunlun Shan and Tarim basin (Meyer de Schauensee 1984).

Salvadori's Nightjar *Caprimulgus pulchellus* is a little-known montane resident of Sumatra and Java, **Indonesia** (Kuroda 1936). The only recent records are of a bird taped at 2,000 m (Marshall 1978) and of up to five individuals regularly seen feeding about a cliff face at 1,400 m, on Gn Pangrango, West Java (Andrew 1985), and of an incubating bird in Aceh, Sumatra (van Marle and Voous 1988) but in all three cases identification is best treated as tentative (P. Andrew).

Long-trained Nightjar *Macropsalis creagra* is endemic to forest edge and second growth up to above 1,800 m in south-east **Brazil** and north-east **Argentina** where it is probably threatened (Sick 1985). Although it is rare in Rio Grande do Sul (W. Belton) and Argentina (M. Nores and D. Yzurieta), it seems locally secure in Parana (F. C. Straube) and Sao Paulo (see Willis and Oniki 1981), but the overall population is apparently small (Sick 1985).

Sickle-winged Nightjar *Eleothreptus anomalus*, of **Brazil, Uruguay, Paraguay** and **Argentina**, is possibly rare and certainly extremely little known (D. A. Scott), having been recorded from gallery forest, marshland and campo (Sick 1985, L. P. Gonzaga, A. R. de Meijer, M. Nores and D. Yzurieta). It is known from nearly eighteen skins, most of them collected in Sao Paulo, Brazil (N. J. Collar, L. P. Gonzaga).

Order APODIFORMES

Family Apodidae
Swifts

White-chested Swift *Cypseloides lemosi* is confined to the middle and upper Cauca Valley of **Colombia**, between Cali and Popayan, 1,000-1,300 m, where it is apparently very local and its needs and movements are not understood (Hilty and Brown 1986).

Waterfall Swift *Hydrochous gigas* is apparently a rare and local resident of peninsular **Malaysia**, Sumatra, Java, **Indonesia** and probably Borneo (Smythies 1981). The one well-known breeding colony is at the Cibereum waterfall on Gn Pangrango, West Java, where the birds nest and roost under and adjacent to the upper part of the waterfall (Somadikarta 1968, King 1987d).

Seychelles Swiftlet *Collocalia elaphra*, an aerial insectivorous species endemic to **Seychelles**, has a low total population (under 1,000 birds) and its few nest-caves are vulnerable to disturbance or vandalism (Collar and Stuart 1985).

Tahiti Swiftlet *Aerodramus leucophaeus* is now known to breed only on Tahiti, **Society Islands (to France)**, where it is widespread in valleys but only numbers between 200 and 500 birds; it was formerly encountered on Huahine and Bora Bora, while records from Moorea in 1973 may have referred to vagrants from Tahiti (Holyoak and Thibault 1984, Pratt *et al.* 1987, Thibault in press, M. K. Poulsen).

Atiu Swiftlet *Aerodramus sawtelli* was collected in 1973 from the Anataketake Cave on Atiu in the **Cook Islands (to New Zealand)**: the cave contained about 60 nests and the local inhabitants reported that there were a few smaller colonies elsewhere on the island (Holyoak 1974). The population is undoubtedly small but apparently stable (Pratt *et al.* 1987).

Schouteden's Swift *Schoutedenapus schoutedeni* is known from only five records at low and intermediate altitudes to the east and north-east of the Itombwe Mountains in eastern **Zaire** (Collar and Stuart 1985).

Fernando Po Swift *Apus sladeniae* is known from only ten specimens from **Bioko (Equatorial Guinea)**, **Cameroon**, **Nigeria** and **Angola**, and its true status remains a mystery (Collar and Stuart 1985).

Dark-rumped Swift *Apus acuticauda* is known to breed only in the Khasi Hills, Meghalaya, **India**, where it is restricted to the rocky cliffs and deep gorges around Cherrapunji (Ali and Ripley 1984) and Lilancote (T. P. Inskipp), although the type-specimen is from **Nepal** (Inskipp and Inskipp 1985a). Non-breeding birds appear in winter in north-west **Thailand** (B. F. King, I. S. Robertson).

Family Trochilidae
Hummingbirds

Hook-billed Hermit *Glaucis dohrnii* remains endangered in south-east **Brazil**, where a decade ago it appeared to be restricted to two patches of lowland forest in Espirito Santo and Bahia (King 1978-1979). Although its survival in these areas is in some doubt, another apparently strong population has been discovered in the CVRD Porto Seguro Reserve, which must now assume a central importance for the conservation of the species (Collar 1987, Gonzaga *et al.* in press).

White-tailed Sabrewing *Campylopterus ensipennis* is restricted to forest in north-east **Venezuela** (Meyer de Schauensee and Phelps 1978), where rainforest on the Paria Peninsula is likely to be its last refuge (B. Swift), and this has been cleared below 800 m (G. Medina Cuervo). However, fieldword in secondary forests in Monagas and Sucre, 1985-1986, showed the species to be well adapted to such habitat (R. Ramirez). The species was feared exterminated from Tobago, **Trinidad and Tobago**, by a hurricane (ffrench 1973) but it is now known to have survived (V. C. Quesnel).

Coppery Thorntail *Popelairia letitiae* is known from two males without precise locality from **Bolivia** (Meyer de Schauensee 1982), and is considered possibly a hybrid (K.-L. Schuchmann). However, a specimen in AMNH is surprisingly distinctive (R. Bleiweiss).

Sapphire-bellied Hummingbird *Lepidopyga lilliae* is rare and local in coastal mangroves in the vicinity of Cienaga Grande and at the Rancheria estuary (Guajira), **Colombia** (Hilty and Brown 1986), its habitat at one site now ruined by a pipeline (M. K. Rylander).

Honduran Emerald *Amazilia luciae* is the only bird species endemic to **Honduras**, where it is known from 11 specimens in the north-central region, and remains extremely little known (Monroe 1968).

Tachira Emerald *Amazilia distans* is known by a single specimen from Burgua, south-west Tachira, **Venezuela**, collected in rainforest at 300 m (Meyer de Schauensee and Phelps 1978), and by a possible sighting on the north slope of Tachira in 1974; it could occur in adjacent Colombia (Hilty and Brown 1986).

Mangrove Hummingbird *Amazilia boucardi* is confined to mangroves and adjacent partly open habitat on the Pacific coast of **Costa Rica** from the Gulf of Nicoya to the Golfo Dulce region (AOU 1983), where it is highly vulnerable to habitat destruction (F. G. Stiles).

Chestnut-bellied Hummingbird *Amazilia castaneiventris* remains little known with an extremely limited distribution (two definite localities only) on the west slope of the Eastern Andes in northern Boyaca and southern Bolivar, **Colombia**, (Hilty and Brown 1986).

White-tailed Hummingbird *Eupherusa poliocerca* is resident in open woodland, forest edge and clearings in semi-arid situations in Guerrero and western Oaxaca, **Mexico** (AOU 1983), where habitat destruction has rendered it highly endangered (S. N. G. Howell).

Oaxaca Hummingbird *Eupherusa cyanophrys* is restricted to open woodland, humid montane forest and forest edge in the Sierra de Miahuatlan, central Oaxaca, **Mexico** (AOU 1983), where it is still fairly common but suffering from steady removal of its limited habitat (S. N. G. Howell).

Scissor-tailed Hummingbird *Hylonympha macrocerca* is endemic to the forest at 900-1,200 m on the (narrow, 100 km long) Paria Peninsula in north-east **Venezuela** (Meyer de Schauensee and Phelps 1978), where forest clearance has reached as high as 800 m (G. Medina Cuervo).

Purple-backed Sunbeam *Aglaeactis aliciae* appears to be a very rare species known only from montane scrub in the upper Maranon valley, **Peru** (Zimmer 1951, Parker *et al.* 1982), with relatively few records since early this century (K.-L. Schuchmann, D. A. Wiedenfeld).

Black Inca *Coeligena prunellei*, although confined to the west slopes of the Eastern Andes of **Colombia** and believed greatly threatened by deforestation (King 1978-1979), has recently been found much more widely than was believed (D. W. Snow). It is present in the forest at Virolin that holds the Gorgeted Wood-quail *Odontophorus strophium* (G. Arango, M. de L. Brooke).

Juan Fernandez Firecrown *Sephanoides fernandensis* is endemic to the **Juan Fernandez Islands (to Chile)**, where in 1983 it was found extinct (race *leyboldi*) on Masafuera and of very limited range (nominate *fernandensis*) on Robinson Crusoe (W. R. P. Bourne). A survey in 1986 estimated 250 birds surviving on Masafuera and recommended urgent detailed study of the species to determine its needs and threats (Brooke 1987). A further survey in 1987 put the population at 200-500 and provided detailed guidelines for follow-up work (Stiles 1987), now being pursued (B. Araya).

Royal Sunangel *Heliangelus regalis* is known only from the vicinity of the type-locality above San Jose de Lourdes at 1,950-2,200 m on the southern extremity of the Cordillera del Condor, Cajamarca, **Peru**, where it appears to be most numerous on the brushy slopes bordering forest edge and along steep ravine banks (Fitzpatrick *et al.* 1979). This habitat requires conservation (J. P. O'Neill, T. A. Parker).

Black-breasted Puffleg *Eriocnemis nigrivestis* is known only from Volcan Pichincha and Volcan Atacazo in north-central **Ecuador**, and is threatened by habitat destruction owing to the close proximity of the capital city, Quito (Bleiweiss and Olalla 1983).

Turquoise-throated Puffleg *Eriocnemis godini*, not definitely an authentic species and extremely hard to separate from Glowing Puffleg *E. vestitus*, is known from north-west **Ecuador** at 2,100-2,300 m (no recent records) and some ancient trade-skins from **Colombia** (Hilty and Brown 1986, R. Bleiweiss).

Colourful Puffleg *Eriocnemis mirabilis* is known from wet forest and adjacent forest borders at a single locality, Charguayaco, 2,200 m, on the Pacific slope in Cauca, **Colombia** (Hilty and Brown 1986).

Black-thighed Puffleg *Eriocnemis derbyi* occupies humid forest borders and bushy pastures and ravines, usually above 2,900 m and up to 3,600 m, in central **Colombia** and northern **Ecuador**, where it is uncommon and local (Hilty and Brown 1986, R. S. Ridgely).

Hoary Puffleg *Haplophaedia lugens* occurs in humid and wet forest borders in lower highlands (1,100-1,400 m) in south-west **Colombia** and north-west **Ecuador** (Hilty and Brown 1986), where its status gives some cause for concern (S. L. Hilty). It was not rare in importations into West Germany, 1984 (K.-L. Schuchmann).

Neblina Metaltail *Metallura odomae* is confined to elfin forest on Cerro Chinguela, Piura department, **Peru** (Graves 1980), where, despite its reasonable numerical abundance (Parker *et al.* 1985), it may be vulnerable owing to its restricted distribution (J. Fjeldsa, J. P. O'Neill).

Violet-throated Metaltail *Metallura baroni* inhabits arid country in Cuenca and Loja provinces, south-west **Ecuador**, where it is uncommon to rare (Ridgely 1980, Ortiz-Crespo 1984, Barnett and Gretton 1987, J. Fjeldsa).

Grey-bellied Comet *Taphrolesbia griseiventris* is a rare species of montane scrub in central **Peru** (Parker *et al.* 1982), and its habitat is threatened (J. P. O'Neill).

Hyacinth Visorbearer *Augastes scutatus* is restricted to mountain ranges in north Minas Gerais, **Brazil** (Sick 1985), where it occurs in one national park and three other protected areas but does not seem to be common (M. A. Andrade, W. Bokermann, G. T. Mattos) in spite of hundreds of specimens having been collected in the past (Grantsau 1967, M. A. Andrade, L. P. Gonzaga).

Marvellous Spatuletail *Loddigesia mirabilis* is an uncommon bird of forest edge and montane scrub in the Chachapoyas region on the east side of the Utcubamba valley in southern Amazonas, **Peru** (Taczanowski and Stolzmann 1881, Meyer de Schauensee 1982, Parker *et al.* 1982; see also Boeke 1978), and its habitat is threatened (J. P. O'Neill).

Bee Hummingbird *Calypte helenae* is endemic to **Cuba** and, although formerly widespread and not considered in a recent review of the country's threatened birds (Garrido 1985), is now rare and restricted to isolated woodland patches (Garrido and Garcia 1975, Garcia undated).

Chilean Woodstar *Eulidia yarrellii*, regarded as endangered in northern **Chile** (King 1978-1979), is now also known from southernmost **Peru** (Parker 1982). It was observed commonly around its stronghold, Arica in Chile, in October 1986 (D. A. Scott).

Little Woodstar *Acestrura bombus* of forest and scrub in the tropical zone of east and west **Ecuador** and northern **Peru** (Meyer de Schauensee 1982) used to be common but appears to have become rare with no recent observations (R. S. Ridgely), although it has been fairly common in recent importations into West Germany (K.-L. Schuchmann).

Esmeraldas Woodstar *Acestrura berlepschi* is restricted to the tropical zone of western **Ecuador** (Meyer de Schauensee 1982) and has not been observed for many years (R. S. Ridgely).

Glow-throated Hummingbird *Selasphorus ardens* is known only from forest edge, clearings and bushy areas in the highlands of eastern Chiriqui (Cerro Flores) and century-old specimens from Veraguas, western **Panama** (Ridgely 1981a, AOU 1983).

Order TROGONIFORMES

Family Trogonidae
Trogons

Resplendent Quetzal *Pharomachrus mocinno* is an uncommon bird throughout its range in **Mexico, Guatemala, Honduras, El Salvador, Nicaragua, Costa Rica** and **Panama** (King 1978-1979). A study in Costa Rica showed it to be a specialised fruit-eater, requiring seasonal migrations to feed on an annual total of at least 41 species; although reserves have been established, these tend to be small and include limited representation of critical habitats (Wheelwright 1983).

Eared Trogon *Euptilotis neoxenus* is found in western and northern **Mexico** (AOU 1983) where it is rather rare and local (S. N. G. Howell, T. A. Parker) and it is also recorded in Arizona, **U.S.A.** (Zimmerman 1978).

Baird's Trogon *Trogon bairdii* is found in humid lowland and foothill forest on the Pacific slope of south-west **Costa Rica** and western **Panama** (AOU 1983). It is becoming rare in Panama owing to forest clearance (Ridgely 1981a).

Order CORACIIFORMES

Family Alcedinidae
Kingfishers

Blyth's Kingfisher *Alcedo hercules* is known from east **Nepal** (one record: Inskipp and Inskipp 1985), Sikkim in **Bhutan**, north-east **India**, **Bangladesh**, **Burma** except Tennasserim (King 1975), south Yunnan and Hainan, **China** (Meyer de Schauensee 1984), northern **Thailand** (one record: Boonsong and Cronin 1984), northern **Laos** and **Viet Nam** (King *et al.* 1975). It frequents streams in forest in hills to 1,200 m; much of the species's range has not been visited by ornithologists in recent years but hill forest is vulnerable and it occurs at low density (S. C. B. Harrap, N. J. Redman).

Cinnamon-banded Kingfisher *Halcyon australasia* is found on Lombok, Sumba, Timor, Wetar and the small intervening islands east to Tanimbar, **Indonesia**, where it is a woodland species occurring to at least 750 m (White and Bruce 1986); it evidently feeds exclusively in forest usually in the canopy and is not uncommon on Tanimbar (F. G. Rozendaal), but already very local on Lombok, Timor and Sumba (P. Andrew, K. D. Bishop, D. Yong).

Mangaia Kingfisher *Halcyon ruficollaris* is endemic to Mangaia, **Cook Islands (to New Zealand)**, where it was fairly common in 1973 although possibly reduced since the introduction of the Indian Myna *Acridotheres tristis* (Holyoak and Thibault 1984, Pratt *et al.* 1987).

Tuamotu Kingfisher *Halcyon gambieri* is endemic to and widespread in the gardens and coconut groves of Niau, **Tuamotu Archipelago (to France)**, where the race *gertrudae* was represented by 400-600 birds in 1974, the nominate *gambieri* having become extinct on Mangareva probably before 1922 (Holyoak and Thibault 1984, Pratt *et al.* 1987).

Marquesas Kingfisher *Halcyon godeffroyi* is endemic to two of the **Marquesas Islands (to France)**, with less than 50 pairs on Hiva Oa, where it may have suffered through the introduction of the Great Horned Owl *Bubo virginianus* and Indian Myna *Acridotheres tristis*, and 300-500 pairs on Tahuata (records from Fatu Iva, Mohotani and Ua Pou apparently being erroneous) (Holyoak and Thibault 1984, Thibault in press).

Moustached Kingfisher *Halcyon bougainvillei* is found on Bougainville, **Papua New Guinea**, and Guadalcanal, **Solomon Islands**, where it affects forest to an altitude of 1,000 m (Schodde 1978) but has not been reliably reported since 1953 (Diamond 1987).

Blue-capped Wood Kingfisher *Halcyon hombroni* is confined to Mindanao in the **Philippines**, where it inhabits forest (Delacour and Mayr 1946) and is apparently rare and certainly little known: a specimen was taken at 1,100 m on Mt Apo in 1980 (R. S. Kennedy) and one was seen along a forested stream on Mt Katanglad in 1982 (T. H. Fisher).

Biak Paradise Kingfisher *Tanysiptera riedelii* is endemic to Biak Island, Irian Jaya, **Indonesia**, where it has been recorded in forest along rocky streams (White and Bruce 1986) and in 1986 at forest edge (K. D. Bishop). It is apparently rare and restricted to forest, unlike the Numfor Paradise Kingfisher *T. carolinae* which is reported to be common and widespread on that island (Beehler *et al.* 1986, K. D. Bishop).

Family Momotidae
Motmots

Keel-billed Motmot *Electron carinatum* is found locally in humid lowland and montane forest on the Caribbean slopes in **Mexico, Belize, Guatemala, Honduras, Nicaragua, Costa Rica** (AOU 1983). It appears very rare throughout its range (D. A. Scott), its habitat in Mexico is rapidly disappearing (S. N. G. Howell), and it has not been seen in Belize for 7-8 years (D. Weyer).

Family Coraciidae
Rollers, ground-rollers

Short-legged Ground-roller *Brachypteracias leptosomus* occurs in the centre and north-east of the rainforest belt of **Madagascar**, where it is rare and threatened by forest destruction (Collar and Stuart 1985). Its presence in Zahamena Reserve has been confirmed (Thompson 1987), and it is recorded from three other protected areas (O. Langrand, M. E. Nicoll). Recent records from as far north as Vohimarina (B. Lenormand *per* O. Langrand) and as far south as Ranomafana (L. Wilme *per* O. Langrand) and Midongy (O. Langrand) represent considerable range extensions.

Scaly Ground-roller *Brachypteracias squamiger* occurs in the centre and north-east of the rainforest belt of **Madagascar**, where it is rare and threatened by forest destruction, village dogs and human exploitation for food (Collar and Stuart 1985; also Dee 1986). It is recorded from one protected area (O. Langrand, M. E. Nicoll).

Rufous-headed Ground-roller *Atelornis crossleyi* occurs in the centre (south to Vondrozo) and north-east of the rainforest belt of **Madagascar**, where it is rare and threatened by forest destruction (Collar and Stuart 1985, Dee 1986). It is recorded from three protected areas (O. Langrand, M. E. Nicoll).

Long-tailed Ground-roller *Uratelornis chimaera* is a largely terrestrial bird of subdesert scrub in south-west **Madagascar** where, like the Subdesert Mesite *Monias benschi*, it is confined to the coastal hinterland between the Mangoky and Fiherenana rivers and is subject to hunting, trapping and habitat destruction (Collar and Stuart 1985). It occurs in no protected area and tree removal for charcoal production is increasing (O. Langrand).

Family Bucerotidae
Hornbills

Rufous-necked Hornbill *Aceros nipalensis* was formerly widespread from **Nepal** through north-east **India**, **Burma**, **Thailand**, south-west Yunnan in **China**, southern **Laos**, **Kampuchea** and southern **Viet Nam** (King *et al.* 1975, Meyer de Schauensee 1984). It is probably extinct in Nepal (Inskipp and Inskipp 1985a), reportedly declining in India (Ali and Ripley 1984) and restricted to two forest reserves in south-west Thailand (Round in press). The species's range overlaps closely with that of upland shifting cultivators and its position in Burma, Laos, Kampuchea and Viet Nam is probably vulnerable (Round in press).

Wrinkled Hornbill *Aceros corrugatus* is recorded from peninsular **Thailand** (close to extinction), peninsular **Malaysia** (local), Borneo (scarce) and Sumatra, **Indonesia** (Medway and Wells 1976, Smythies 1986). In southern Sumatra it is common, even in selectively logged forest, but as a lowland specialist it is probably vulnerable to deforestation (Wells 1985).

Plain-pouched Hornbill*Aceros subruficollis* is an enigmatic species known from Tenasserim, **Burma**, south-west and peninsular **Thailand**, peninsular **Malaysia**, and Sumatra, **Indonesia**; its status remains essentially unknown, largely because field characters separating it from the widespread Wreathed Hornbill *A. undulatus* have only recently been defined (Kemp in prep.).

Narcondam Hornbill*Aceros narcondami* is an endemic resident of Narcondam in the **Andaman Islands (to India)** where in 1905 the population was estimated to be about 200 individuals (Ali and Ripley 1984) but more recently 400 (Hussain 1984). The island is 682 ha and uninhabited but coming under increasing human pressure (Hussain 1984).

Sumba Hornbill *Rhyticeros everetti* is endemic to Sumba, **Indonesia**, and is restricted to the few remaining wooded areas on the island (White and Bruce 1986). Despite being local and uncommon (UNDP/FAO 1982) and obviously vulnerable to further habitat loss, birds are often trapped at fruiting figs and nest holes and offered for sale at local hotels (B. F. King, D. Yong).

Sulu Hornbill *Anthracoceros montani* is restricted to Jolo and the Tawi Tawi Islands in the Sulu Archipelago, **Philippines**; it was observed at Balimbing on Tawi Tawi in 1987 and reportedly common in the interior (J. Hornskov, S. Jensen), but must remain vulnerable to forest destruction in its very limited range.

Helmeted Hornbill *Rhinoplax vigil* is resident in extreme southern **Burma**, peninsular **Thailand**, peninsular **Malaysia**, Borneo and Sumatra (**Indonesia**), where it is believed to be declining owing to forest clearance and hunting for its bony casque (King 1978-1979, Smythies 1986). However, it remains not uncommon in parts of Sumatra (van Marle and Voous 1988) and is probably still moderately numerous in southern Thailand (P. D. Round).

Family Galbulidae
Jacamars

Three-toed Jacamar *Jacamaralcyon tridactyla* is restricted to south-east **Brazil** where it is quite local, although apparently not rare or forest-dependent (Sick 1985, A. Brandt, G. T. Mattos, J. F. Pacheco), but there is only one recent record of it from Parana (P. Scherer Neto) and none from Sao Paulo (E. O. Willis).

Family Capitonidae
Barbets

White-mantled Barbet *Capito hypoleucus* occupies humid forest, mainly in foothills (200-1,500 m), in the lower Cauca and middle Magdalena Valleys of central **Colombia**, where it is now rare, local and in urgent need of assistance (Hilty and Brown 1986, S. L. Hilty).

Toucan Barbet *Semnornis ramphastinus* occurs in wet forest and edges in western **Colombia** and western **Ecuador**, where in some parts of its range it is threatened by trapping for the cage-bird market (King 1978-1979), although in others it remains common (Hilty and Brown 1986). Recent studies show it to be a cooperative breeder, chiefly frugivorous, occupying territories of roughly 3-6 ha, with low reproductive success (Restrepo and Mondragon 1987).

Black-banded Barbet *Megalaima javensis* is endemic to Java, **Indonesia**, where it is widespread, but not known to occur above 1,200 m and consequently rather locally distributed in the isolated pockets of forest that remain in the lowlands and hills (P. Andrew).

White-chested Tinkerbird *Pogoniulus makawai* remains known only from the type- specimen, collected in *Cryptosepalum* thicket in north-western **Zambia**, despite repeated attempts to relocate it (Collar and Stuart 1985).

Family Indicatoridae
Honeyguides

Yellow-footed Honeyguide *Melignomon eisentrauti* has been collected in forest in **Cameroon** and **Liberia**, with a sighting in **Ghana**, although it probably occurs more widely in West African forests (Collar and Stuart 1985). New information and a further review are provided in Colston and Curry-Lindahl (1986).

Family Ramphastidae
Toucans

Yellow-browed Toucanet *Aulacorhynchus huallagae* is uncommon and restricted to humid montane forest in one department of central **Peru** (Meyer de Schauensee 1982, Parker *et al.* 1982), where its habitat is threatened (J. P. O'Neill).

Family Picidae
Woodpeckers

Cuban Flicker *Colaptes fernandinae* is endemic to **Cuba**, where its rarity may be due to habitat specialization, although the populations appear stable within their limit areas of occurrence (Garrido 1985).

Red-cockaded Woodpecker *Picoides borealis* is scarce and local in mature open pine-forests in south-eastern **U.S.A.**, where it has declined with the disappearance of its habitat, once maintained by recurring natural fires, but now clearcut and replaced by faster-growing species (King 1978-1979). The population is estimated at between 3,000 and 4,400 birds (Judge 1987). Detrimental management practices continue, and remaining populations are becoming smaller and increasingly isolated; the Red-cockaded Woodpecker recovery plan (USFWS 1985) has been reviewed and further multiple approaches suggested (Ligon *et al.* 1986, Jackson 1986, Judge 1987).

Helmeted Woodpecker *Dryocopus galeatus* is highly threatened in south **Brazil**, **Paraguay** and **Argentina** (King 1978-1979), where a breeding population seems to be now restricted to Iguazu National Park in Misiones (Chebez 1986). The last records in Parana and Santa Catarina are from 1954 and 1946 respectively (Sick 1985), in Rio Grande do Sul from 1928 (Belton 1984) and in Sao Paulo from 1987 (E. O. Willis).

Ivory-billed Woodpecker *Campephilus principalis* is critically threatened in **Cuba** where the race *bairdii* survives in the eastern highlands only, and in southeastern **U.S.A.** where unconfirmed sightings and tape-recordings of nominate *principalis* sustain minimal hopes of its continued existence; shooting, collecting and loss of mature forest have contributed to the decline (King 1978- 1979, Garrido 1985). In April 1986 three birds were observed in northern Oriente Province, eastern Cuba, and management practices have been altered to preserve appropriate habitat (*World Birdwatch* 8,2 [1986]: 1-2).

Imperial Woodpecker *Campephilus imperialis* is quite possibly extinct in **Mexico**, where formerly it ranged through uncut pine forests above 2,300 m from north- west Chihuahua to Michoacan; its disappearance is attributable to habitat clearance and human exploitation for food (King 1978-1979, Short 1982).

Red-collared Woodpecker *Picus rabieri* is confined to forest, feeding mostly on the ground, in eastern **Laos** and **Viet Nam** (Short 1982) and south-east Yunnan, **China** (Meyer de Schauensee 1984). It is generally rare, and one of the least known of all woodpeckers (Short 1982).

Okinawa Woodpecker *Sapheopipo noguchii* is a rare and local resident of dense evergreen hill forest in Yamburu, the northern third of **Okinawa (to Japan)**, where substantial and continuing habitat loss renders the population, put variously at 40 to 200, in grave danger of extinction (Short 1973, 1982, King 1978-1979, Brazil 1985a, Collar 1987, M. A. Brazil).

Order PASSERIFORMES

Family Eurylaimidae
Broadbills

African Green Broadbill *Pseudocalyptomena graueri* is known from only three mountain ranges, the Itombwe Mountains and mountains west of Lake Kivu in eastern **Zaire**, and Bwindi (Impenetrable) Forest in south-west **Uganda**; while it is common in parts of the Itombwe Mountains, it is threatened by habitat destruction (Collar and Stuart 1985).

Family Dendrocolaptidae
Wood-hewers

Moustached Woodcreeper *Xiphocolaptes falcirostris* (here including the recently rediscovered Snethlage's Woodcreeper *X. franciscanus*) is known from few specimens collected over a large area in central and interior north-east **Brazil** where it seems to be rare (L. P. Gonzaga). It inhabits both semi-deciduous dry forests and humid forests isolated in caatinga (thorn scrub), which are threatened by deforestation for charcoal, timber and cultivation (Andrade *et al.* 1987, R. Cavalcanti, R. Otoch, P. Roth).

Family Furnariidae
Ovenbirds

White-bellied Cinclodes *Cinclodes palliatus* has a fairly wide range at altitudes of 4,400 to 5,000 m in the north and central parts of western **Peru** (Vaurie 1980), but it is extremely rare, apparently because it is ecologically tied to mineral-rich bogs (J. Fjeldsa; also D. Wiedenfeld).

Stout-billed Cinclodes *Cinclodes aricomae*, here treated as distinct from *C. excelsior*, is known from a few high-altitude woodland localities in **Peru** (one in **Bolivia**) and must be exceptionally rare, with possibly only 10 sq km of *Polylepis* woodland (and hence 10-20 pairs) in the whole Cordillera Vilcanota, where clearance for firewood is a serious threat (J. Fjeldsa; see Fjeldsa *et al.* 1987).

Masafuera Rayadito *Aphrastura masafuerae* was recently judged possibly extinct on Masafuera, **Juan Fernandez Islands (to Chile)** (Vaurie 1980), but subsequent fieldwork resulted in a rough estimate of around 500 birds (and probably under 1,000) distributed throughout areas of unbroken fern cover above 600 m, with probably little change this century, although the effect of goats in trampling and fragmenting fern forest requires investigation (Brooke 1987, 1988).

White-browed Tit-spinetail *Leptasthenura xenothorax*, a valid species (J. Fjeldsa, J. P. O'Neill, *contra* Morony *et al.* 1975, Vaurie 1980, Meyer de Schauensee 1982) is endemic to a few *Polylepis* woodlands in the Urubamba drainage in Cuzco department, **Peru** (Parker and O'Neill 1980). In 1987 it was found common in two woods, each 1 sq km, 10 pairs in one, 15 pairs in the other, both being cleared (Fjeldsa 1987, J. Fjeldsa); apparently only one other location is known with certainty (B. P. Walker).

Plain Spinetail *Synallaxis infuscata* is restricted to a small region near the coast in eastern Pernambuco and adjacent Alagoas, north-east **Brazil** (Vaurie 1980). It is considered very local and forest-dependent, although not rare (J. Vielliard) but also locally common (A. G. Coelho, D. M. Teixeira).

Apurimac Spinetail *Synallaxis courseni* is known only from the type-locality and one other forest patch in the mountains around Abancay, south **Peru**, with a population of 250-300 pairs at the type-locality (Vaurie 1980, Fjeldsa and Krabbe 1986, Fjeldsa 1987). Felling of humid forest in this region is drastic (B. P. Walker, J. P. O'Neill).

Chestnut-throated Spinetail *Synallaxis cherriei* occurs very locally in dense undergrowth in forest and savanna from eastern **Ecuador** south through eastern **Peru** into western **Brazil** (Vaurie 1980, Meyer de Schauensee 1982); its habitat in Peru is being destroyed (J. P. O'Neill, J. W. Terborgh).

Russet-bellied Spinetail *Synallaxis zimmeri* is a rare bird with a small range in montane scrub on the western slope of the Andes in Ancash department, **Peru** (Vaurie 1980, J. P. O'Neill, B. P. Walker). However, it may be in no immediate danger, its habitat being extensive (T. A. Parker).

White-tailed Asthenes *Asthenes usheri*, although not recognised even as a race by Vaurie (1980), is a good species and occupies only 10 sq km of open semi-arid montane forest in valley bottom at 2,200-2,770 m in Ninabamba and Mutca, Apurimac, **Peru** (Fjeldsa 1987, J. Fjeldsa, N. Krabbe).

Austral Canastero *Asthenes anthoides* requires lush grasslands and thickets in the Andean foothills of southern **Chile** and **Argentina** south to Tierra del Fuego (Araya Modinger *et al.* 1986, Narosky and Yzurieta 1987), and has become extremely rare owing to grazing and associated vegetation changes (J. Fjeldsa, R. S. Ridgely).

Line-fronted Canastero *Asthenes urubambensis* occurs probably discontinu-

ously in two subspecies, *huallagae* from the Andes of northern **Peru** and
urubambensis from the Andes of central Peru (Cuzco) and north-west and
central **Bolivia** (La Paz, Cochambamba) (Parker and O'Neill 1980, Vaurie 1980,
Remsen *et al*. 1986). It lives in treeline forest edge and small patches of humid
Polylepis woodland, and is known from very few places (Parker and O'Neill 1980,
J. Fjeldsa).

Orinoco Softtail *Thripophaga cherriei* remains known only from the type-
locality, Capuano, on the right bank of the Orinoco 35 km above the rio Vichada
confluence, in south-west **Venezuela**, where it occupies rainforest and clearings
along river banks and small canos (streams) (Meyer de Schauensee and Phelps
1978, Vaurie 1980). Extensive habitat is probably available, however, and the
species seems unlikely to be suffering (T. A. Parker, R. S. Ridgely).

Striated Softtail *Thripophaga macroura* is restricted to eastern **Brazil** in south-
eastern Bahia, Espirito Santo, eastern Minas Gerais (Pinto 1978) and northern
Rio de Janeiro (C. E. Carvalho, J. F. Pacheco), in both lowland and montane
humid forest (Sick 1985). It may be found in disturbed forest but not in second
growth, thus being threatened although locally common or fairly common (G.
T. Mattos, D. M. Teixeira).

Canebrake Groundcreeper *Clibanornis dendrocolaptoides* is a little-known bird
(Sick 1985) endemic to south **Brazil**, in Rio Grande do Sul, Parana and southern
Sao Paulo, south-eastern **Paraguay** and north-east **Argentina** in Misiones
(Vaurie 1980). There are no recent records from Argentina (J. C. Chebez, M.
Nores and D. Yzurieta, A. Tarak) and none is known either from Paraguay or
Sao Paulo (see, e.g., Willis and Oniki 1981, 1985); there is a record from Parana
in 1984 (L. dos Anjos) and in Rio Grande do Sul the species is rare, occurring
in thickets and bamboo tangles near streams (Belton 1984).

White-throated Barbtail *Margarornis tatei* has two subspecies in cloud-forest
and forest edge in north-eastern **Venezuela**, nominate *tatei* in the coastal
cordillera from Anzoategui to Sucre and Monagas at 1,200-1,700 m, and race
pariae on the Paria Penisula at 900-1,200 m (Meyer de Schauensee and Phelps
1978). Both areas are at risk from habitat destruction (G. Medina Cuervo, B.
Swift).

Alagoas Foliage-gleaner *Philydor novaesi* was described from two specimens
collected in 1979 in montane (550 m) forest undergrowth at Murici, north-east
Brazil (Teixeira and Gonzaga 1983a), and four additional specimens were
obtained in subsequent years from the type-locality (Teixeira 1987a, Teixeira *et
al*. 1987), where the species remains threatened, not being observed there in early
1987 (D. M. Teixeira).

Rufous-necked Foliage-gleaner *Automolus ruficollis* has two subspecies, race
celicae from south-western **Ecuador** and nominate *ruficollis* from north-western

Peru (Zimmer 1935; subspeciation not recognised by Vaurie 1980). Its restricted geographical and elevational ranges lie in densely settled regions, and its humid montane forest habitat is being degraded by cattle and cleared (Parker *et al.* 1982, 1985).

Henna-hooded Foliage-gleaner *Automolus erythrocephalus* is restricted to dry deciduous forest of the arid tropical zone of south-west **Ecuador** and north-west **Peru** (Vaurie 1980, Parker *et al.* 1982, Wiedenfeld *et al.* 1985), where it is seriously at risk from habitat destruction (T. A. Parker, J. P. O'Neill, R. S. Ridgely).

Great Xenops *Megaxenops parnaguae* is apparently rare and little known in the caatinga (thorn scrub) of interior north-east **Brazil** (Vaurie 1980, P. T. Z. Antas and C. Yamashita) where it has been recorded locally in recent years (Vaurie 1980, A. G. Coelho, R. Otoch, P. Roth).

Family Formicariidae
Antbirds

White-bearded Antshrike *Biatas nigropectus* is an easily overlooked, but also seemingly scarce species (T. A. Parker) restricted to south-east **Brazil** and north-east **Argentina** (Meyer de Schauensee 1982); it is considered rare both in Brazil (Sick and Teixeira 1979), where a few recent records are from Minas Gerais (G. T. Mattos) and Rio de Janeiro (J. F. Pacheco, T. A. Parker), and in Argentina (J. C. Chebez, M. Nores and D. Yzurieta), where the most recent records date from the late 1950s and 1960 (specimens in AMNH: N. J. Collar).

Cocha Antshrike *Thamnophilus praecox* is known only from an adult female collected at the mouth of the rio Lagartococha on the rio Aguarico in Napo, easternmost **Ecuador** on the Peru border (Zimmer 1937, Paynter and Traylor 1977, Meyer de Schauensee 1982), and by observations made at the type-locality (R. S. Ridgely). It is expected to occur in Peru (Zimmer 1937).

Recurve-billed Bushbird *Clytoctantes alixii* occurs from westernmost **Venezuela** (Perija Mountains in Zulia) into northern **Colombia**, where it requires dense young regrowth in humid areas, 180-1,000 m, and is possibly more numerous than records suggest (Hilty 1985, Hilty and Brown 1986).

Speckled Antshrike *Xenornis setifrons* favours heavy undergrowth in humid forest on slopes well above streams in foothills and lower mountains, eastern **Panama** and north-west **Colombia**, where it is little known, secretive, local and rare (Ridgely 1981a, Hilty and Brown 1986, T. A. Parker).

Plumbeous Antshrike *Thamnomanes plumbeus* is being taxonomically revised so that the current nominate race from south-east **Brazil** becomes a full species (R. S. Ridgely), and since it has a very restricted range there, it must be at risk (see Sick and Teixeira 1979, Scott and Brooke 1985).

Salvadori's Antwren *Myrmotherula minor* of south-east **Brazil** seems to be little known and largely restricted to lower elevation forests and old second-growth in the states of Espirito Santo, Rio de Janeiro, Sao Paulo (Willis and Oniki 1981, Scott and Brooke 1985, Sick 1985), Minas Gerais and Santa Catarina (old specimens in MNRJ: L. P. Gonzaga). It may be locally fairly common (Scott and Brooke 1985) although as a rule few individuals have been observed (C. E. Carvalho, J. F. Pacheco) or collected at any given locality (L. P. Gonzaga).

Ashy Antwren *Myrmotherula grisea*, on current evidence, occurs primarily in forest in the lower elevation foothills and valleys of the Yungas region of **Bolivia**, in La Paz, Santa Cruz and Cochabamba (Remsen *et al.* 1982). Its range is basically 900-1,500 m in the drier foothill forests, and these are the first to be cut (J. V. Remsen).

White-browed Antwren *Herpsilochmus pileatus* is (through taxonomic revision in the description of Ash-troated Antwren *H. parkeri*) now known only from two localities in caatinga (thorn scrub) in Bahia, **Brazil** (Davis and O'Neill 1986).

Pectoral Antwren *Herpsilochmus pectoralis* is a very poorly known species recorded from only a few dry-forest localities in Maranhao, Rio Grande do Norte (G. T. Mattos) and Bahia, **Brazil** (Sick 1985).

Ash-throated Antwren *Herpsilochmus parkeri* is a recently discovered species from northern **Peru**, known from one low range east of Moyobamba in San Martin and possibly restricted to it (Davis and O'Neill 1986).

Black-hooded Antwren *Formicivora erythronotos* (here transferred from the genus *Myrmotherula*: L. P. Gonzaga) is known only from Nova Friburgo in Rio de Janeiro, **Brazil**, and had been feared extinct through forest destruction there, the last reliable record being from the second half of the last century (King 1978-1979, Scott and Brooke 1985). In September 1987 it was rediscovered in a secondary swampy wood near the mangrove line at sea level on the southern coast of Rio state (J. F. Pacheco; also *World Birdwatch* 9,4 [1987]: 4).

Narrow-billed Antwren *Formicivora iheringi* is restricted to and declining in a few localities of south-central Bahia and north-east Minas Gerais, **Brazil** (King 1978-1979, Sick 1985), although it is common locally in remaining patches of dry forest rich in lianas and huge terrestrial bromeliads (Willis and Oniki 1981, Teixeira 1987) and considered not under serious threat (G. T. Mattos).

Yellow-rumped Antwren *Terenura sharpei* is known only from Puno, south-east

Peru, and Cochabamba and La Paz in northern **Bolivia**, the only observations indicating that it forages in mixed-species flocks in dense canopy foliage of humid forest at 1,350 m (Remsen *et al.* 1982). Huge areas of forest within the bird's geographical and altitudinal range have been cleared and this destruction is continuing rapidly (J. V. Remsen).

Orange-bellied Antwren *Terenura sicki* was described from a single female collected in 1979 in montane (550 m) forest at Murici, north-east **Brazil** (Teixeira and Gonzaga 1983b), and additional birds, (including males) were obtained in subsequent years from the type-locality (specimens in MNRJ: L. P. Gonzaga). Although not restricted to primary humid forest and occurring over a larger area than previously thought, this species is seriously threatened owing to heavy habitat destruction in its range (Teixeira 1987, D. M. Teixeira).

Rio De Janeiro Antbird *Cercomacra brasiliana* is known from a few localities in south-east **Brazil**, where it has been recorded from forest edge, second-growth tangles, dry woodland, caatinga (thorn scrub), and bamboo thickets up to nearly 1,000 m (Sick 1985, G. T. Mattos). This bird is currently known only from north-east Minas Gerais and southern Bahia, in a transitional area between Atlantic forest and dry woodlands which has been partially occupied by coffee plantations, but it is not considered to be under serious threat there (G. T. Mattos).

Rio Branco Antbird *Cercomacra carbonaria* is known only from specimens collected in 1831 and 1962 at rio Branco and rio Mucajai, Roraima, northern **Brazil** (Pinto 1978).

Fringe-backed Fire-eye *Pyriglena atra* is known only from the vicinity of Salvador, **Bahia**, **Brazil**, where it survived until at least 1977 (Sick and Teixeira 1979) and remains threatened despite its abundance in second-growth, since not even this has escaped the spread of Bahian agriculture (King 1978-1979, Sick and Teixeira 1979, Willis and Oniki 1981, J. Vielliard).

Slender Antbird *Rhopornis ardesiaca* is restricted to and declining in a few localities of south-central Bahia, **Brazil** (King 1978-1979), and was known until 1977 from only four specimens, although it is common locally in remaining patches of dry forest rich in lianas and huge terrestrial bromeliads (Willis and Oniki 1981, Sick 1985, Teixeira 1987b). Its plight (owing to deforestation) is regarded as serious (Teixeira 1987b) and none of its habitat is in a reserve, but the species is protected by Brazilian law.

Scalloped Antbird *Myrmeciza ruficauda* occurs in the fragmented lowland forests of eastern and south-eastern **Brazil** (Sick 1985) where it may still be locally common (A. G. Coelho, J. Vielliard) and present also in degraded areas with secondary growth (Gonzaga *et al.* in press, D. M. Teixeira). However, it is probably restricted now to a few areas in its former range (Scott and Brooke

1985, Gonzaga *et al.* in press) and its status is insufficiently known (C. E. Carvalho, T. A. Parker, D. M. Teixeira).

Grey-headed Antbird *Myrmeciza griseiceps* is restricted to forest in south-west **Ecuador** and north-west **Peru** (Meyer de Schauensee 1982, Wiedenfeld *et al.* 1985). Its restricted geographical and elevational ranges lie in densely settled regions, and its humid montane forest habitat (it is primarily a bamboo species) is being degraded by cattle and cleared (Parker *et al.* 1982, 1985).

Spot-breasted Antbird *Myrmeciza stictothorax* is known only from the type-locality on the Tapajoz river, **Brazil** (Meyer de Schauensee 1982), where, although much forest remains, it could not be found in 1985 by one field worker (T. A. Parker).

White-breasted Antbird *Rhegmatorhina hoffmannsi* is restricted to the rivers Madeira, Aripuana and Gi-parana in western **Brazil** (Pinto 1978). Heavy deforestation is occurring in its range (J. M. C. da Silva) and, while it is not in immediate danger, in 20-30 years little forest will be left (E. O. Willis).

Argus Bare-eye *Phlegopsis barringeri* remains known by the type-specimen from rio Rumiyaco, a tributary of rio San Miguel, south-east Narino, **Colombia**, on the border with Ecuador; it presumbaly inhabits humid forest undergrowth, possibly in foothills rather than lowlands, although it has been suggested the type is a hybrid (Hilty and Brown 1986).

Rufous-fronted Antthrush *Formicarius rufifrons* was known from two females from Madre de Dios, south-east **Peru**, until its rediscovery in Manu National Park, where it may prove to be restricted to river-edge forest (Parker 1983).

Giant Antpitta *Grallaria gigantea*, a floor-dweller of humid highland forest, has three subspecies (Peters 1951): *ichmanni* from one area on the east slope of the Central Andes of **Colombia** (no recent records: Hilty 1985, Hilty and Brown 1986); *hylodroma* from the west slopes of the Andes of **Ecuador**; and *gigantea* from the east slopes of the Andes of Ecuador, this last population being particularly threatened by habitat loss (J. Fjeldsa).

Moustached Antpitta *Grallaria alleni* is known only from the type-specimen from the western slope of the Central Andes, **Colombia** (King 1978-1979), and a second skin collected in Cueva de los Guacharos National Park, Huila (also Central Andes), in very humid montane forest (Hilty and Brown 1986).

Tachira Antpitta *Grallaria chthonia* is known only from the rio Chiquito, south-west Tachira, **Venezuela**, where it forages in the mossy undergrowth of high dense cloud-forest at 1,800-2,100 m (Meyer de Schauensee and Phelps 1978).

Bicoloured Antpitta *Grallaria rufocinerea* is recorded from just four widely separate localities in the Central Andes of **Colombia**, where it affects the undergrowth of humid montane forest (Hilty and Brown 1986).

Brown-banded Antpitta *Grallaria milleri* has not been seen since the type-material was collected in 1911 at Laguneta, above Salento, on the west slope of the Central Andes in Quindio, **Colombia**, an area of humid montane forest now mostly cleared (King 1978-1979, Hilty and Brown 1986).

Crescent-faced Antpitta *Grallaricula lineifrons* is known only from cold dense elfin woodland (3,000-3,200 m) in south-west **Colombia** (two records from the same region) and north-east **Ecuador** (one record) (Hilty and Brown 1986), and although its habitat may be secure the species remains too little known for confidence (J. Fjeldsa).

Hooded Antpitta *Grallaricula cucullata* is a very local inhabitant of humid forest undergrowth on the eastern slopes of the Western and Central Andes, and at the head of the Magdalena Valley, in **Colombia**, being common in Cueva de los Guacharos National Park at about 2,000 m but known from only a few other localities (Hilty and Brown 1986). A subspecies, *venezuelana*, is known only from dense cloud-forest at 1,800 m on the rio Chiquito, south-west Tachira, **Venezuela** (Meyer de Schauensee and Phelps 1978).

Family Conopophagidae
Gnateaters, antpipits

Hooded Gnateater *Conopophaga roberti* of northern **Brazil** is known from the Tocantins river eastwards to Ceara but must be losing its forest habitat and may only persist in Gorupi reserve (A. D. Johns); still in small disturbed woodlots east of Sao Luis, Maranhao, though not common (P. Roth), but very common in old but unprotected secondary growth in eastern Para (J. M. C. da Silva).

Family Rhinocryptidae
Tapaculos

Stresemann's Bristlefront *Merulaxis stresemanni* is known from two specimens from humid forest in coastal Bahia, eastern **Brazil** (King 1978-1979), where little apparently suitable habitat remains and recent brief surveys have failed to find it (L. P. Gonzaga).

Brasilia Tapaculo *Scytalopus novacapitalis* is known from around Brasilia, Distrito Federal, central **Brazil** (King 1978-1979), where it was recently rediscovered (Sick 1985), and from the same localities in Minas Gerais as the Brazilian Merganser *Mergus octosetaceus*: in the Serra da Canastra National Park (Gonzaga 1984) and in the upper rio Paranaiba (G. T. Mattos). In the Distrito Federal it is protected by the Brasilia National Park (P. T. Z. Antas) and in two other reserves (R. Cavalcanti), and is fairly common at least locally, but threatened by clearance of its gallery forest habitat (D. M. Teixeira).

Family Cotingidae
Cotingas

Shrike-like Cotinga *Laniisoma elegans* is restricted to forest in the coastal mountains of south-east **Brazil** (nominate *elegans*), and to a narrow belt along the eastern base of the Andes of **Bolivia** (race *cadwaladeri*, known from one specimen and two localities), **Peru** (rare) and **Venezuela** (south Tachira in the race *venezuelensis*), **Colombia** (one record) and **Ecuador** (race *buckleyi*) (Meyer de Schauensee and Phelps 1978, Parker *et al*. 1982, Snow 1982, Hilty and Brown 1986). It is too little known to be confident of its security (T. A. Parker).

Swallow-tailed Cotinga *Phibalura flavirostris* occupies an extensive range in open country with trees in eastern **Brazil**, breeding in mountains and then descending to the lowlands (Snow 1982, Sick 1985), but it has now become rare and appears to be found regularly only in Itatiaia National Park (L. P. Gonzaga). The population in north-east **Argentina** has become extremely difficult to locate (M. Nores) and there are three specimens from **Bolivia** (Krabbe 1984).

Grey-winged Cotinga *Tijuca condita* is a rare species, restricted to elfin cloud-forest above 1,300 m in the Serra dos Orgaos and Serra do Tingua near Rio de Janeiro, **Brazil** (Snow 1980, 1982, Scott and Brooke 1985), where the total area of suitable habitat is small but not obviously threatened (Scott and Brooke 1985).

Black-headed Berryeater *Carpornis melanocephalus* is endemic to lowland forest in south-east **Brazil** (Snow 1982), with a record now from Alagoas (Teixeira *et al*. 1986), and although present in several areas in Sao Paulo (E. O. Willis), Rio de Janeiro (C. E. Carvalho, J. F. Pacheco) and Espirito Santo (C. E. Carvalho, B. M. Whitney) and considered locally fairly common or not rare, the species is insufficiently known and apparently threatened by habitat loss (Teixeira *et al*. 1986, C. E. Carvalho, D. M. Teixeira, B. M. Whitney).

White-cheeked Cotinga *Ampelion stresemanni* is confined to *Polylepis* woodland in perhaps less than 10 localities in **Peru** (Snow 1982, Fjeldsa 1987). It is a mistletoe specialist and undertakes vertical migrations (Parker 1981), these facts plus the clearance of *Polylepis* rendering the species distinctly vulnerable (P. K. Donahue, J. Fjeldsa, J. P. O'Neill).

Buff-throated Purpletuft *Iodopleura pipra* is a very small and little-known cotinga endemic to south-east **Brazil** (Snow 1982), where it has been found, rarely, in old second-growth and forest treetops, feeding mainly on fruits of mistletoes (Camargo and de Camargo 1964), and apparently undertaking seasonal movements (Sick 1985), breeding in coastal lowland forest in winter (Willis and Oniki 1987; also 1985).

Kinglet Cotinga *Calyptura cristata* is only known from the mountains of Nova Friburgo, Rio de Janeiro state, **Brazil**, and has not been seen this century (King 1978-1979), but the recent rediscovery of the Black-hooded Antwren *Formicivora erythronotus*, also originally reported from Nova Friburgo, gives hope of the species's survival elsewhere.

Cinnamon-vented Piha *Lipaugus lanioides* is endemic to south-east **Brazil** (Snow 1982) and has been recently recorded from only one locality in Sao Paulo (E. O. Willis) and some forest reserves in Rio de Janeiro (J. F. Pacheco, T. A. Parker), Espirito Santo (Scott and Brooke 1985, C. E. Carvalho, T. A. Parker) and Minas Gerais (A. Brandt), being locally uncommon (Scott and Brooke 1985) or common (T. A. Parker, D. M. Teixeira).

Turquoise Cotinga *Cotinga ridgwayi* is confined to a very restricted area of humid forest on the Pacific side of eastern **Costa Rica** and extreme western **Panama** (Snow 1982). Its inadequately protected habitat is disappearing (T. A. Parker, F. G. Stiles).

Banded Cotinga *Cotinga maculata* remains threatened in eastern **Brazil** owing to forest destruction (King 1978-1979) and has been recently encountered only in the Sooretama Biological Reserve and CVRD's forest reserves at Linhares and Porto Seguro (Scott and Brooke 1985, Collar *et al.* 1987, Gonzaga *et al.* in press).

White-winged Cotinga *Xipholena atropurpurea* remains threatened in eastern **Brazil** owing to forest destruction (King 1978-1979) but has been found to be much less restricted than was previously believed, with recent records from remaining patches of suitable habitat up to 700 m throughout its range, including forest reserves in Bahia, Espirito Santo and Rio de Janeiro (Collar *et al.* 1987, Gonzaga *et al.* in press, C. E. Carvalho, A. G. Coelho).

Yellow-billed Cotinga *Carpodectes antoniae* is endemic to the Pacific side of **Costa Rica** and extreme western **Panama**, where it seems to be associated with coastal mangroves, possibly making vertical migrations into the hills to breed (Snow 1982). Its habitat is not adequately protected and is disappearing (T. A. Parker, R. S. Ridgely, F. G. Stiles).

Bare-necked Umbrellabird *Cephalopterus glabricollis* occurs up to 3,000 m in the mountains of **Costa Rica** and western **Panama**, apparently breeding in the humid subtropical belt, mainly on the Caribbean slopes, and moving (at least in Costa Rica) to low levels in the off-season (Snow 1982). Its habitat is not adequately protected and is disappearing (T. A. Parker, F. G. Stiles).

Long-wattled Umbrellabird *Cephalopterus penduliger* remains threatened by the combination of habitat loss and cage-bird trade pressure in humid and wet montane forest in western **Colombia** and north-west **Ecuador** (King 1978-1979, Hilty and Brown 1986). In Ecuador, an important population remains along the rio Pitsara (J. Carrion).

Family Pipridae
Manakins

Golden-crowned Manakin *Pipra vilasboasi* is known only from the headwaters of Rio Tapajoz, **Brazil** (Meyer de Schauensee 1982). The area is believed to be still largely intact, and has remained unexplored since this species was discovered, so that there are strong expectations that the bird is safe (L. P. Gonzaga)

Black-capped Manakin *Piprites pileatus* (to be reclassified as a cotinga: L. P. Gonzaga) seems exceedingly rare and local, being known from a few mountain localities in south-east **Brazil** (Pinto 1944, 1954, Sick 1985, L. dos Anjos) and only one specimen from north-east **Argentina** (J. C. Chebez, M. Nores and D. Yzurieta).

Family Tyrannidae
Tyrant-flycatchers

White-tailed Shrike-tyrant *Agriornis albicauda* (= *andicola*), of open bushy scrub in the high Andean steppes of **Ecuador, Peru, Bolivia, Argentina** and **Chile**, appears to have become very rare and local, having once been common (R. S. Ridgely, D. A. Scott). In 1987 a survey of the High Andes of Peru and Bolivia showed it to be very rare (Fjeldsa 1987).

Black-and-white Monjita *Xolmis dominicana* of southern **Brazil, Uruguay, Paraguay** and eastern **Argentina** is in steep decline everywhere and seems to be common only in one part of Rio Grande do Sul (R. S. Ridgely; also M. Nores).

Strange-tailed Tyrant *Yetapa risoria* of **Brazil, Paraguay, Uruguay** and **Argentina** is little known (Sick 1985), and has not been recorded recently in either Rio Grande do Sul (Belton 1985) or Uruguay (Cuello and Gerzenstein 1962), being apparently restricted now in Argentina to north Corrientes and south Misiones where it is probably in steep decline (M. Nores and D. Yzurieta).

Grey-breasted Flycatcher *Empidonax griseipectus* is one of the least common of birds endemic to deciduous woodland in north-west **Peru** and south-west **Ecuador**, a habitat rapidly being cleared (R. S. Ridgely, D. A. Scott).

Russet-winged Spadebill *Platyrinchus leucoryphus* of south-east **Brazil**, east **Paraguay** and north-east **Argentina** (Olrog 1979, Sick 1985) has been recorded very locally in heavily shaded forest with only moderate undergrowth (Belton 1985, L. P. Gonzaga) and is possibly threatened (Scott and Brooke 1985), being known currently from one locality in Espirito Santo (J. Vielliard, C. E. Carvalho), one in Rio de Janeiro (L. P. Gonzaga) and three in Sao Paulo (E. O. Willis).

Short-tailed Tody-flycatcher *Todirostrum viridanum* occupies a restricted range in north-west **Venezuela** in the coastal part of Falcon and Zulia, where it inhabits semi-arid country (Meyer de Schauensee and Phelps 1978). Its status is unknown.

Fork-tailed Pygmy-tyrant *Ceratotriccus furcatus* is known from a few localities on the coasts of Sao Paulo and Rio de Janeiro states, **Brazil** (Pinto 1944, 1954), and maybe in real danger (Scott and Brooke 1985), having been recorded more recently at only one locality in Sao Paulo (E. O. Willis) and one in Rio de Janeiro (C. E. Carvalho, J. F. Pacheco), but it is quite inconspicuous in bamboo thickets inside forest and might often be overlooked (C. E. Carvalho).

Kaempfer's Tody-tyrant *Idioptilon kaempferi* is known from a single specimen from near Joinvile, Santa Catarina, southern **Brazil** (Fitzpatrick and O'Neill 1979), where recent attempts to find it have failed, although some apparently suitable but unprotected habitat remains (M. A. da Re).

Sao Paulo Tyrannulet *Phylloscartes paulistus* occurs in south-east **Brazil**, eastern **Paraguay** (Sick 1985) and has only recently been recorded from north-east **Argentina** (J. C. Chebez, B. M. Whitney), inhabiting forest interior (A. M. Olalla, T. A. Parker, E. O. Willis), tall second-growth (B. M. Whitney) but also forest edge and young secondary growth (Scott and Brooke 1985). The species may be locally fairly common (Willis and Oniki 1981, L. dos Anjos, D. M. Teixeira) but is insufficiently known (T. A. Parker, D. M. Teixeira) and seems to be restricted to a few areas.

Minas Gerais Tyrannulet *Phylloscartes roquettei* is known from the type-specimen collected in 1926 in Minas Gerais, **Brazil** (Meyer de Schauensee 1982) and was present in woodlots near the type-locality in 1977 (E. O. Willis) but not found there in 1985, 1986 or 1987 (M. A. Andrade, G. T. Mattos). Its presumed habitat, semi-deciduous forest, is the most threatened of all in central Brazil owing to its valuable *aroeira* wood and fertile soils (R. Cavalcanti).

Long-tailed Tyrannulet *Phylloscartes ceciliae* seems to be confined to highland forest in Alagoas, north-east **Brazil**, where it is common in the type-locality

(Teixeira 1987c), but may be threatened by heavy habitat destruction; its range is wider than initially thought (D. M. Teixeira).

Bearded Tachuri *Polystictus pectoralis*, of **Guyana, Suriname, Venezuela, Brazil, Colombia, Paraguay, Uruguay, Bolivia** and **Argentina**, is very locally distributed throughout natural grassland and savanna habitats, which are rapidly being destroyed everywhere in South America (R. S. Ridgely; also Hilty and Brown 1986). The very restricted local race *bogotensis*, known from two localities in Colombia (King 1978-1979), was searched for without success in 1981 and may well be extinct (J. Fjeldsa).

Grey-backed Tachuri *Polystictus superciliaris* is restricted to the border of Minas Gerais and Bahia, **Brazil** (Meyer de Schauensee 1982), where it occurs in semi-open habitat in hill-tops; currently it is under little pressure (E. O. Willis), but nonetheless highly limited in range and rare (L. P.Gonzaga).

Sharp-tailed Tyrant *Culicivora caudacuta*, of **Brazil, Paraguay, Bolivia** and **Argentina**, merits careful monitoring because of the disappearance of its campos (fields) habitat (R. S. Ridgely, E. O. Willis), although it may remain secure in Bolivia (J. V. Remsen).

Ash-breasted Tit-tyrant *Anairetes alpinus* is endemic to a small number of *Polylepis* groves at high altitudes in Ancash and Cuzco, **Peru**, and apparently only one (race *boliviana*) in La Paz, northern **Bolivia** (Parker and O'Neill 1980, Fjeldsa 1987). Extensive habitat remains in Ancash (T. A. Parker), less in Cuzco and with only 1-2 pairs per wood (J. Fjeldsa). The Bolivian population may be extinct (J. V. Remsen), but birds from Cuzco appear to represent the race *boliviana* rather than nominate *alpinus* (Parker and O'Neill 1980).

Bananal Tyrannulet *Serpophaga araguayae* appears to remain known only from the type-specimen from Ilha do Bananal, Goias, **Brazil** (Traylor 1979). Up to at least 1985 it had not been found despite several searches (D. M. Teixeira).

Family Phytotomidae
Plantcutters

Peruvian Plantcutter *Phytotoma raimondii* (to be reclassified, like all plantcutters, as a cotinga: J. Fjeldsa) inhabits scrub and riparian thickets in the desert of coastal north-west **Peru** from Tumbes to northern Lima (Meyer de Schauensee 1982, Parker *et al.* 1982). It may be reliant on a small number of plant species for food, and its habitat along the densely populated coast probably faces considerable pressure (D. A. Wiedenfeld).

Family Pittidae
Pittas

Schneider's Pitta *Pitta schneideri* is endemic to the mountains of Sumatra, **Indonesia**, from Gn Sibayak south to Gn Dempu (van Marle and Voous 1988). It was described as very common on Gn Kerinci in 1914 but has not be recorded at any locality since (K. H. Voous).

Whiskered Pitta *Pitta kochi* is known from the mountains of northern Luzon in the **Philippines**, where it affects oak forest in steep terrain usually above 1,000 m, although there are records from lowland forest (Dickinson *et al*. in press). It has long been considered rare and there appear to be no recent records (R. S. Kennedy); it may still occur in the Sierra Madre.

Bar-bellied Pitta *Pitta ellioti* is a lowland forest resident of **Kampuchea, Laos** and **Viet Nam** (King *et al*. 1975), confined to forest from sea-level to 400 m, a habitat that is vulnerable throughout the region (see, e.g., Wells 1985). It is already very local (Vo Quy *per* F. G. Rozendaal) but known to occur in Gia Lai- Koutum (L. S. Stepanyan *per* F. G. Rozendaal).

Gurney's Pitta *Pitta gurneyi* is a lowland rainforest resident in southern Tenasserim, **Burma** (last recorded 1914), and peninsular **Thailand**, from which it has almost totally disappeared owing to habitat destruction (King 1978-1979, Collar *et al*. 1986). At least 16 pairs survive in two tiny pockets of forest but they are critically endangered by further deforestation and trapping (Round and Treesucon 1986, Gretton 1987, C. R. Robson, J. Parr). Ongoing studies by ICBP will seek to provide complete distributional data for both the species and its habitat and lead to the development and implementation of a recovery programme to ensure its survival (M. R. W. Rands).

Fairy Pitta *Pitta nympha* breeds in southern **Japan** (Sonobe 1982), islands off **South Korea** (Gore and Won 1971), and Anhui, Henan, Guangdong and east Guangxi in eastern **China** (Meyer de Schauensee 1984), and **Taiwan** (Mees 1977). The northern population is migratory and has been recorded in east China and Taiwan, south- east China and northern **Viet Nam** but winters mainly in Borneo (**Indonesia** and **Malaysia**); the population in south-east China is resident (Meyer de Schauensee 1984). It is uncommon, except, at least formerly, as a migrant in Taiwan (Severinghaus and Blackshaw 1976); it is known by nine specimens from Borneo but is described as locally common (Smythies 1981); it inhabits hill forest and woodland and the populations in China are believed threatened by habitat destruction (P. R. Kennerley).

Superb Pitta *Pitta superba* is known from Manus in the Admiralty Islands, **Papua New Guinea** (Traylor 1979). A number of observers have failed to locate the species (J. M. Diamond), although it is reportedly moderately common in forest near Lorengau (K. D. Bishop).

Steere's Pitta *Pitta steerii* occurs on Mindanao, Bohol, Leyte and Samar in the **Philippines** (duPont 1971). It is partial to montane forests on broken ground with a dense undergrowth (Delacour and Mayr 1946), but the only recent record indicates it favours limestone country and may be locally common even in degraded forest: it was found common at Bilar on Bohol in 1987 (J. Hornskov, S. Jensen), and thus although long considered rare (R. S. Kennedy) it may prove common in suitable habitat on other islands that are rarely visited by ornithologists.

Solomons Pitta *Pitta anerythra* is known from Bougainville, **Papua New Guinea**, and Santa Isabel, **Solomon Islands**, and was formerly described as common, with 18 being collected in the first decade of this century, but it has not been recorded since 1936 (Diamond 1987) despite prolonged searches (K. D. Bishop, E. Harding).

Family Acanthisittidae
New Zealand Wrens

Bush Wren *Xenicus longipes* is endemic to **New Zealand** and thought to be extinct (Williams and Given 1981, B. D. Bell). It declined rapidly following the introduction of predatory mammals, the North Island race *stokcsi* last being recorded in 1949, the Stewart Island race *variabilis* in 1965, and the South Island race *longipes* in 1972 (King 1987-1979, Williams and Given 1981).

Family Philepittidae
Asitys

Yellow-bellied Sunbird-asity *Neodrepanis hypoxantha*, endemic to the central part of the rainforest belt of **Madagascar** but difficult to distinguish from its only congener, is known from 13 specimens collected before 1933 and the observation of a nesting pair above Perinet in 1976 (Collar and Stuart 1985; also Longmore 1985, Dee 1986). In the past few years the species has been found breeding in the Andringitra Mountains (south-east of Fianarantsoa) at 2,000 m (O. Langrand, M. E. Nicoll).

Family Atrichornithidae
Scrub-birds

Rufous Scrub-bird *Atrichornis rufescens* occurs in isolated populations in the highlands of the Great Dividing Range in New South Wales, **Australia**, where it affects dense undergrowth in rainforest and eucalyptus forest, and was formerly locally common in natural clearings within this habitat; a census of known populations in 1980 located 172 breeding pairs, the decline attributed to the removal of lowland rainforest, but selective logging that increases forest ground-cover might actually benefit the species (King 1978-1979, Blakers *et al.* 1984).

Noisy Scrub-bird *Atrichornis clamosus* was formerly distributed through the high rainfall areas of south-west Western **Australia**, from near Perth to Albany, but was not reported between 1889 and 1961, when a population was located in gullies in eucalyptus forest on Mt Gardener (King 1978-1979), recently estimated at 74 pairs (Blakers *et al.* 1984). A population has been established at Lake Gardener, a kilometer to the north-west, and translocations have apparently been successful to at least one other site though breeding remains to be proved (A. Burbidge; also Burbidge and Jenkins 1984).

Family Alaudidae
Larks

Ash's Lark *Mirafra ashi* is known only from arid coastal grassy plains just north of Uarsciek in southern **Somalia** (Collar and Stuart 1985).

Degodi Lark *Mirafra degodiensis* is known from only two specimens collected together in light bush (low acacias on bare soil) near Bogol Manya in the Degodi region of southern **Ethiopia** (Collar and Stuart 1985).

Somali Long-clawed Lark *Heteromirafra archeri* is a secretive grassland species known only from an exceptionally restricted area west of Hargeisa and Buramo in north-west **Somalia** along the Ethiopian frontier, and has been seen only once, in 1955, since 1922; its habitat may have been seriously disrupted by cultivation and settlement (Collar and Stuart 1985).

South African Long-clawed Lark *Heteromirafra ruddi* inhabits high-altitude grasslands in **South Africa, Lesotho** and perhaps Swaziland, and appears to have deserted much of the southern part of its range in response to habitat degradation (Collar and Stuart 1985; also Brooke 1984).

Sidamo Long-clawed Lark *Heteromirafra sidamoensis* is known only from two specimens, collected in open grassland savanna near Neghelli in Sidamo province, southern **Ethiopia**, in May 1968 and April 1974 (Collar and Stuart 1985; also Ash and Olson 1985).

Botha's Lark *Spizocorys fringillaris* is confined to high-altitude grasslands in northern Orange Free State and south-eastern Transvaal, **South Africa**, where it is rare and seldom reported (Collar and Stuart 1985; also Brooke 1984).

Raso Lark *Alauda razae* is only found on part of the very small, arid island of Raso in the **Cape Verde Islands**, where its population fluctuates with climate, reaching a low of only around 20 pairs in the early 1980s (Collar and Stuart 1985). In early 1985, however, a survey showed at least 150 birds to be present (M. A. S. Beaman; see *World Birdwatch* 7,2 [1985]: 4).

Family Hirundinidae
Swallows, martins

White-eyed River-martin *Pseudochelidon sirintarae* is known only as a winter visitor to Lake Boraphet, central **Thailand** (King 1978-1979). It has not been reliably reported since 1980 (Sophasan and Dobias 1984), although one was reputedly trapped by a local in 1986 (Ogle 1986), and the concentrations of roosting Barn Swallows *Hirundo rustica* with which it formerly associated have been reduced as a result of the harvesting of reeds *Phragmites* and disturbance caused by illegal bird trapping (Round in press). Evidence to support speculation that the species breeds in China (Dickinson 1986) has been found wanting (Parkes 1987).

Bahama Swallow *Tachycineta cyaneoviridis* is an uncommon aerial feeder confined as a breeding bird to pine woodlands (with one instance of nesting on a building) in the northern **Bahama Islands** of Grand Bahama, Great Abaco, Andros and New Providence, wintering sparingly throughout the Bahamas and eastern **Cuba** over marshes and old fields, and irregular on passage in Florida, U.S.A. (Brudenell-Bruce 1975, Emlen 1977, AOU 1983, Buden 1987). Its modern status is uncertain.

White-tailed Swallow *Hirundo megaensis* occupies an area of roughly 10,000 sq km in open country around Mega and Yavello in southern **Ethiopia**, where it remains putatively at risk from any development of its habitat (Collar and Stuart 1985).

Red Sea Cliff Swallow *Hirundo perdita* is known from the type-specimen found dead in May 1984 at Sanganeb Lighthouse, north-east of Port Sudan, **Sudan**; the species is judged most likely to be found in the Red Sea hills of Sudan or **Ethiopia** (Fry and Smith 1985)

Family Motacillidae
Wagtails, pipits

Sokoke Pipit *Anthus sokokensis* occurs in three coastal forest sites, the Arabuko-Sokoke Forest in **Kenya**, which is suffering illegal but unchecked clearance, the Pugu Hills, where the area of forest is small and the species very rare, and a site near Moa, probably now cleared, both in **Tanzania** (Collar and Stuart 1985).

Yellow-breasted Pipit *Anthus chloris*, mistakenly omitted from Collar and Stuart (1985), occupies open dense grasslands usually at high altitudes in eastern **South Africa** and **Lesotho**, where burning and grazing diminish its habitat (Brooke 1984).

Chaco Pipit *Anthus chacoensis* is a grassland species known only from wintering birds in Chaco and Formosa, **Argentina**, and eastern **Paraguay**, and breeding birds (January) collected near Leones, Cordoba, Argentina (Short 1975, 1976). It appears genuinely rare with few if any recent records (J. C. Chebez, M. Nores and D. Yzurieta), but part of the problem may be identification (P. Canevari).

Ochre-breasted Pipit *Anthus nattereri* of south-east **Brazil**, **Paraguay** and **Argentina** is little known (Sick 1985), rare and local (Belton 1985, M. Nores and D. Yzurieta, J. F. Pacheco) and probably threatened by overgrazing (J. C. Chebez) and habitat loss through massive agricultural development with eucalyptus, pines, sugarcane and soybeans (E. O. Willis).

Family Campephagidae
Cuckoo-shrikes

Slaty Cuckoo-shrike *Coracina schistacea* is known from the Banggai and Sula Islands, **Indonesia** (White and Bruce 1986). The status of the species and its habitat are unknown.

Mauritius Cuckoo-shrike *Coracina typica* is an insectivorous, forest-dwelling species, endemic to **Mauritius**, that continues to suffer from habitat loss and heavy predation of its nests by introduced animals (Collar and Stuart 1985; see also Cheke 1987a). The species is now known to be more widely distributed than previously described, with a total number possibly in excess of 200 pairs (C. G. Jones).

Reunion Cuckoo-shrike *Coracina newtoni* is an insectivorous, forest-dwelling species, endemic to **Reunion (to France)** and restricted to one very small and inadequately protected area in the north-west where it is at some risk from poachers and its habitat is being degraded by introduced deer (Collar and Stuart 1985; see also Cheke 1987b).

Black Cuckoo-shrike *Coracina coerulescens* is known from Luzon and formerly Cebu (now extinct) in the **Philippines**, where it affects the canopy of lowland forest (Delacour and Mayr 1946, duPont 1971); Gilliard (1950) described it as abundant on the Bataan Peninsula and it is still locally common in undisturbed lowland forest at Quezon (J. Scharringa), but must remain vulnerable to further destruction of habitat.

Sula Cuckoo-shrike *Coracina sula* is known from the Sula Islands, **Indonesia** (White and Bruce 1986). The status of the species and its habitat are unknown.

White-winged Cuckoo-shrike *Coracina ostenta* occurs on the middle islands of the **Philippines**, Panay, Guimaras and Negros, where it is apparently restricted to forest and is known to be declining as habitat is removed (R. S. Kennedy). It survives around Mt Canlaon on northern Negros, but recent surveys of southern Negros (Erickson and Heideman 1983) and of Panay have failed to locate the species (R. Sison *per* R. S. Kennedy), and it may no longer survive on Guimaras as the island is nearly devoid of indigenous vegetation (R. S. Kennedy).

Western Wattled Cuckoo-shrike *Campephaga lobata* is confined to and rare in the Upper Guinea forest block of West Africa where it is known from **Ghana** (one record this century), **Ivory Coast** (Tai Forest), **Liberia** (Mount Nimba and Grand Gedeh County) and **Sierra Leone** (Gola Forest) (Collar and Stuart 1985; see also Colston and Curry-Lindahl 1986).

Family Pycnonotidae
Bulbuls

Wattled Bulbul *Pycnonotus nieuwenhuisii*, from **Indonesia**, is known from two specimens, one (nominate *nieuwenhuisii*) collected at 600 m in north-east Kalimantan in 1900 and one (race *inexspectatus*) collected at 700 m in northern Sumatra in 1937 (Chasen and Hoogerwerf 1941, van Marle and Voous 1988).

Prigogine's Greenbul *Chlorocichla prigoginei* occurs in patches of forest at intermediate elevations to the north-west of Lake Edward and on the Lendu

Plateau in eastern **Zaire**, and is under serious threat from forest destruction (Collar and Stuart 1985).

Spot-winged Greenbul *Phyllastrephus leucolepis* is a new and obviously very rare species known only from Upper Guinea rainforest north-west of Zwedru, Grand Gedeh County, south-east **Liberia** (Gatter 1985).

Appert's Greenbul *Phyllastrephus apperti* is a ground-haunting, dry-forest bulbul known with certainty from only two remote unprotected localities in south-west **Madagascar**, where it is exceptionally rare and faces the danger of habitat destruction by fire (Collar and Stuart 1985). It is recorded from no protected area and forest clearance for charcoal production is increasing in its range (O. Langrand).

Dusky Greenbul *Phyllastrephus tenebrosus* is a mysterious bulbul of rainforest undergrowth, known from eight skins and two adjacent localities in eastern-central **Madagascar** (Collar and Stuart 1985), with a third locality, Maroantsetra, recently determined further to the North (O. Langrand; see Dee 1986). It is recorded from one protected area (O. Langrand, M. E. Nicoll).

Grey-crowned Greenbul *Phyllastrephus cinereiceps* appears to be confined to the eastern rainforest belt of **Madagascar**, but had been encountered only twice since the early 1930s (Collar and Stuart 1985) until it was found breeding and not uncommon at Ranomafana (O. Langrand; see Dee 1986, Collar and Stuart 1988). It is recorded from two protected areas (O. Langrand, M. E. Nicoll).

Yellow-throated Olive Greenbul *Criniger olivaceus* is confined to and rare in the Upper Guinea forest block of West Africa where it is known from **Ghana** (1870s), **Guinea** (one record, 1930), **Ivory Coast** (two records), **Liberia** (at least four localities in recent decades), **Senegal** (one nineteenth-century record) and **Sierra Leone** (two localities) (Collar and Stuart 1985; see also Colston and Curry-Lindahl 1986). Of the two records from Ivory Coast, one is from Tai, the other a recent observation (January 1988) of several at Yapo, 40 km north of Abidjan (C. Balchin, S. Cook, B. Reed).

Mottle-breasted Bulbul *Hypsipetes siquijorensis* is a rare and little-known species of Cebu, Siquijor, Romblon and Tablas in the **Philippines** (Delacour and Mayr 1946). It is extinct on Cebu and probably in trouble on Siquijor where only a fragment of the original forest remains (P. Magsalay *per* R. S. Kennedy). Its status on Romblon and Tablas is unknown.

Mauritius Black Bulbul *Hypsipetes olivaceus*, a primarily frugivorous forest-dwelling species endemic to **Mauritius**, was reduced to some 200 pairs in the mid- 1970s and has probably declined further since, with nest predation and competition from introduced birds the major threats (Collar and Stuart 1985; see also Cheke 1987a).

Family Laniidae
Shrikes

Gabela Helmet-shrike *Prionops gabela* remains known only from a small area of forest and thicket near Gabela on the scarp of **Angola** (Collar and Stuart 1985).

Mount Kupe Bush-shrike *Malaconotus kupeensis* has remained undetected since its discovery in 1949 and relocation in 1951 in primary forest on Mount Kupe, western **Cameroon**, where the area of habitat covers a mere 21 sq km (Collar and Stuart 1985).

Green-breasted Bush-shrike *Malaconotus gladiator*, a rare inhabitant of montane forest canopy, occurs at a few localities, some of them under severe threat of clearance, in western **Cameroon** and eastern **Nigeria** (Collar and Stuart 1985). The species is rare on Mount Oku, Cameroon (Stuart and Jensen 1986), such that it could not be found in four weeks of fieldwork in 1985 (Wilson in press).

Monteiro's Bush-shrike *Malaconotus monteiri* is known only from a few forested sites on the scarp of **Angola** (no record since 1954) and a nineteenth-century specimen from Mount Cameroon, **Cameroon** (Collar and Stuart 1985).

Uluguru Bush-shrike *Malaconotus alius* is an elusive, low-density inhabitant of the forest canopy in the Uluguru Mountains, **Tanzania**, where a dense human population is steadily clearing the lower slopes (Collar and Stuart 1985).

Sao Tome Fiscal Shrike *Lanius newtoni* was last seen in 1928 and all records are from the southern, wet part of Sao Tome, **Sao Tome e Principe**, where the reasons for its rarity are obscure (Collar and Stuart 1985).

Family Vangidae
Vangas

Van Dam's Vanga *Xenopirostris damii*, an insectivorous bird of deciduous forest, is known this century from a single site (Ankarafantsika) in north-west **Madagascar** which is, however, a protected area (Collar and Stuart 1985).

Pollen's Vanga *Xenopirostris polleni* occurs throughout the eastern rainforest belt of **Madagascar**, but is everywhere very rare (Collar and Stuart 1985; see Dee 1986). It is recorded from two protected areas (O. Langrand, M. E. Nicoll).

Family Cinclidae
Dippers

Rufous-throated Dipper *Cinclus schulzii* was believed to be very sparsely distributed in north-west **Argentina** (Jujuy, Salta, Tucuman, Catamarca) (King 1978-1979), but has now been recorded in adjacent Tarija, **Bolivia** (Remsen and Traylor 1983). Moreover, recent fieldwork in Argentina has shown the bird to be fairly common if local, being found along fast-flowing permanent streams within alder-dominated woodland between 1,400 and 2,700 m, the total population perhaps being in the low thousands (Salvador *et al.* 1986, Nores *et al.* 1987). Clearance, cattle encroachment and water utilization may be local threats (R. Vides Almonacid; also Beltran 1987).

Family Troglodytidae
Wrens

Slender-billed Wren *Hylorchilus sumichrasti* occupies dense humid lowland forest, generally in areas with rocky outcrops, in west-central Veracruz, extreme north- western Oaxaca and western Chiapas, **Mexico** (AOU 1983). Within the limestone outcrop areas it is locally still quite common, and it appears to survive in shaded coffee plantations, but habitat destruction is now extending even into the steep outcrops (at least in Veracruz), and the species's requirements remain essentially unknown (S. N. G. Howell).

Apolinar's Wren *Cistothorus apolinari* occurs very locally in tall cattails and bullrushes bordering montane lakes and lagoons (2,500-4,000 m, though as low as 2,000 m at one new locality: Fjeldsa and Krabbe 1986) at a scatter of localities in the Eastern Andes of **Colombia** (King 1978-1979, Hilty and Brown 1986), and has suffered much habitat destruction (J. Fjeldsa).

Zapata Wren *Ferminia cerverai* is restricted to the Zapata Swamp, **Cuba**, where it declined to near-extinction in the 1960s and 1970s owing possibly to burning of habitat by local people (King 1978-1979), but some records in the 1980s offer hope that it may be recovering (Garrido 1985).

Niceforo's Wren *Thryothorus nicefori* is known only from the type-locality, a region of light woodland and coffee plantations by the rio Fonce (1,100 m) on the west slope of the Eastern Andes in Santander province, **Colombia** (Hilty and Brown 1986).

Socorro Wren *Thryomanes sissonii* (probably a *Trodlodytes*: Jehl and Parkes 1982, S. N. G. Howell) is endemic to Socorro in the **Revillagigedos Islands (to Mexico)**, where it is common (Jehl and Parkes 1982) but now vulnerable to introduced mammalian predators (S. N. G. Howell).

Clarion Wren *Troglodytes tanneri* is confined to Clarion Island in the **Revillagigedos Islands (to Mexico)** (AOU 1983), where in January 1986 up to 20 birds were noted and numbers were considered substantially lower than previously reported (Everett 1988). It was considered common but vulnerable in February 1988 (S. N. G. Howell).

Family Mimidae
Thrashers, mockingbirds

Socorro Mockingbird *Mimodes graysoni* is endemic to Socorro Island in the **Revillagigedos Islands (to Mexico)** where, despite being judged at no risk (King 1978-1979), it was in serious danger of extinction by 1981, probably owing to the introduction of feral cats with the establishment of a military garrison in 1958 (Jehl and Parkes 1982, 1983, Jehl 1983, 1984). Only a single bird could be found during a partial survey in 1984 (K. C. Parkes), but several birds and, at one locality, three pairs were located in February 1988 (S. N. G. Howell, S. Webb).

White-breasted Thrasher *Ramphocinclus brachyurus* was judged as at great risk on both **Martinique (to France)** (nominate *brachyurus*, restricted to the Caravelle Peninsula on the east coast), with no records since 1966, and **St Lucia** (race *sanctaeluciae*, restricted to valleys on the north-east coast), where last surveyed in 1971 (King 1978-1979). A pair of nominate *brachyurus* was found on the Caravelle Peninsula in 1983 (D. A. Scott) and three were found there (outside the nature reserve) in July 1986 (Wood 1987), but the species evidently remains extremely rare. On St Lucia in 1987, race *santaeluciae* was recorded in valleys from Petite Anse south to the second valley south of Louvet, with an estimated total population of 60 pairs, much riverine forest habitat destruction being in evidence (P. Wood).

Family Muscicapidae

Subfamily Turdinae
Thrushes, robins, chats

Rusty-bellied Shortwing *Brachypteryx hyperythra* is a rare and little-known species of dense undergrowth and thickets, recorded from Sikkim, Arunachal Pradesh and Nagaland, **India** (Ali and Ripley 1984), and extreme north-west Yunnan, **China** (Meyer de Schauensee 1984).

Swynnerton's Forest Robin *Swynnertonia swynnertoni* is a ground-haunting bird of middle-altitude and montane forests, restricted to Chirinda and a few other tiny forest patches in eastern **Zimbabwe** (nominate *swynnertoni*), Mount Gorongosa in **Mozambique** (race *umbratica*) and the Uzungwa escarpment in **Tanzania** (race *rodgersi*) (Collar and Stuart 1985).

Gabela Akalat *Sheppardia gabela* is known only from the understorey of forest patches near Gabela on the scarp of **Angola**, where there is good evidence that its habitat has been largely removed (Collar and Stuart 1985).

East Coast Akalat *Sheppardia gunningi* is a ground-haunting bird of small, mostly coastal lowland forests in eastern Africa, with populations around Beira in **Mozambique** (nominate *gunningi*), in the lower Tana River forests, the Arabuko-Sokoke forest, the Shimba Hills and a few other patches in **Kenya** and the Pugu Hills in **Tanzania** (race *sokokensis*), and a number of mountains in **Malawi** (race *bensoni*) (Collar and Stuart 1985).

Rufous-headed Robin *Erithacus ruficeps* is known from three specimens from the Qinling Shan in south Shaanxi, **China** (Meyer de Schauensee 1984). A migrant was netted and released at 2,000 m in peninsular **Malaysia** (Medway and Wells 1976), and three were found at Jiuzhaigou, Sichuan, in 1985 (M. A. S. Beaman) and others seen in subsequent years, e.g. six singing males in 1987 (F. G. Rozendaal). The species is also known from Baihe, Sichuan (B. F. King).

Black-throated Robin *Erithacus obscurus* is known in **China** from south-east Gansu, from the Qinling Shan in south Shaanxi, and as a rare migrant from Yunnan, and also **Thailand** (Meyer de Schauensee 1984). It was located at Jiuzhaigou, Sichuan, in 1985 (M. A. S. Beaman) but not seen there subsequently: one male was at Baihe, Sichuan in 1985 (B. F. King). The species is presumably very local, as there are no other records.

White-headed Robin-chat *Cossypha heinrichi* haunts the undergrowth of one area in northern **Angola** and a few forest patches 500 km to the north in western **Zaire**, but remains very poorly known (Collar and Stuart 1985).

Dappled Mountain Robin *Modulatrix orostruthus*, so elusive that it has barely ever been observed in the field, occurs at very low densities at intermediate elevations in montane forest on Mount Namuli in **Mozambique** (nominate *orostruthus*), in the East Usambaras (race *amani*) and in the Uzungwa escarpment (race *sanjei*), both in **Tanzania** (Collar and Stuart 1985). An IUCN project aimed at reconciling land-use pressures in the Usambaras (Stuart 1986) is currently being implemented (N. M. Collins). The rarity of the species, for which the new genus *Arcanator* is proposed, may be due to ecological specialization unrelated to competitive factors (Irwin and Clancey 1986).

Usambara Ground Robin *Dryocichloides montanus*, although numerically strong (the total population is conservatively estimated to be 28,000), only occurs in the West Usambaras in **Tanzania** where natural forest is being converted to softwood plantations (Collar and Stuart 1985).

Iringa Ground Robin *Dryocichloides lowei* is known from only six areas of mainly dry montane forest in southern **Tanzania** and requires improved habitat protection to be secure (Collar and Stuart 1985).

Thyolo Alethe *Alethe choloensis* is a ground-haunting bird known from 15 small patches of submontane evergreen forest, 13 of them in southern **Malawi** and two in adjacent **Mozambique**, with the bulk of the estimated 1,500 pairs being on Malawi's Mount Mulanje (1,000 pairs) and Mount Thyolo (200 pairs) where, as at most other sites, habitat clearance is occurring (Collar and Stuart 1985).

Seychelles Magpie-robin *Copsychus sechellarum* survives only on Fregate (around 20 birds) and Aride (one bird) in the **Seychelles**, where its populations have been exterminated by feral cats; however, although cats were entirely eradicated from Fregate in 1981, the island's declining Magpie-robin population merely levelled out rather than increased (Collar and Stuart 1985). In early 1985 25 birds were counted on Fregate (M. C. Garnett, A. Seddon); in early 1987 20 birds were found there (M. R. W. Rands, G. F. Rands) and later that year 23 birds, including six immatures, were recorded (I. Bullock, J. Komdeur, V. Laboudallon). A major review of the species is in Watson *et al.* (in press).

Black Shama *Copsychus cebuensis* is endemic to Cebu in the **Philippines**, where no original forest remains (Rabor 1962), but though it has been listed as extinct (King 1978-1979), it still survives, primarily in bamboo thickets (P. Magsalay *per* R. S. Kennedy).

Luzon Water-redstart *Rhyacornis bicolor* is restricted to clear mountain streams and rivers on Luzon in the **Philippines**, where it feeds largely on insects taken from boulders amongst the torrents (Delacour and Mayr 1946); it is still locally common but intolerant of disturbance to its habitat (R. S. Kennedy) and shot by local sportsmen (J. Hornskov, S. Jensen).

Sumatran Cochoa *Cochoa beccarii* (a good species: Collar and Andrew 1987) is endemic to the mountains of Sumatra, **Indonesia**, where it is known from four specimens, all males and collected between 1,200 and 1,600 m in West Sumatra (Robinson and Kloss 1918). There are two recent sight records, one of a presumed immature from North Sumatra (van Marle and Voous 1988).

Javan Cochoa *Cochoa azurea* is a rare endemic of the mountains of West and Central Java, **Indonesia**, where it affects forest between 900 and 3,000 m (Kuroda 1933), and is currently known from only three locations in West Java (P. Andrew; see Collar and Andrew 1987).

Kamao *Myadestes myadestinus* is endemic to Kauai in the **Hawaiian Islands (to U.S.A.)** where it occurs in dense montane forest; it has declined drastically in recent years (Pratt *et al*. 1987).

Olomao *Myadestes lanaiensis*, a shy and retiring bird of the forest canopy, is known from Lanai (last seen 1933), Maui (extirpated by historic times) and Molokai (only a few scattered individiuals remaining) in the **Hawaiian Islands (to U.S.A.)** (Pratt *et al*. 1987).

Puaiohi *Myadestes palmeri* is confined to a small portion of the Alakai swamp on Kauai in the **Hawaiian Islands (to U.S.A.)**; it is an extremely secretive species, keeping to undergrowth in dense forest, and has apparently always been rare with only a few dozen (or fewer) living individuals (King 1978-1979, Pratt *et al*. 1987).

Stoliczka's Bushchat *Saxicola macrorhyncha* is a rare and local resident of the semi-deserts of **Pakistan** and north-west **India**, mainly from the Indus through Haryana, western Uttar Pradesh and Rajasthan, and Gujarat, although known by two records from **Afghanistan** (Ali and Ripley 1984). It is one of the most threatened of the Indus basin endemics (Gaston 1984), possibly dependent on grassland which has been mostly eliminated by heavy overgrazing (B. F. King).

Hodgson's Bushchat *Saxicola insignis* breeds very locally in the mountains of Kazakhstan in **Mongolia** and Inner Mongolia, **China**, and winters in the grasslands of the Gangetic plain of northern **India**, **Nepal**, the Sikkim foothills in north- east India and **Bhutan** (Ali and Ripley 1984, T. P. Inskipp).

Fuerteventura Stonechat *Saxicola dacotiae*, an insectivorous, scrub-haunting bird endemic to Fuerteventura in the **Canary Islands (to Spain)**, was believed to be widely but very locally distributed with a low total population (Collar and Stuart 1985). However, a survey in February and March 1985 yielded an estimated 650-850 pairs (Bibby and Hill 1987).

Timor Bushchat *Saxicola gutturalis* is found on Timor and its satellite islands of Roti and Semau, **Indonesia**, in scrubby savanna on Roti and in the lowlands and up to 1,200 m on Timor (White and Bruce 1986). In West Timor it is common in the few remnant pockets of woodland but is largely excluded from savanna and open scrub by the Pied Bushchat *S. caprata* (P. Andrew).

Benson's Rockthrush *Monticola bensoni* is only known from arid rocky country between the Mangoky and Onilahy rivers in south-west **Madagascar**, chiefly in and around the Isalo Massif, and although no threats are apparent (the region is protected by a national park) total numbers of the species may prove small (Collar and Stuart 1985, Collar and Tattersall 1987).

Sri Lanka Whistling Thrush *Myiophoneus blighi* is a shy, rare bird of streams in dense mountain forest between 1,000 and 2,000 m in **Sri Lanka** (Ali and Ripley

1984), where it is declining, probably as a result of the loss of natural forest, monoculture plantations being largely devoid of undergrowth and hence unsuitable habitat (Hoffmann 1984).

Slaty-backed Thrush *Zoothera schistacea* is found in the Tanimbar Islands, **Indonesia** (White and Bruce 1986). It is common in lowland forest, even regularly found in secondary forest, and is presumably secure as long as the islands remain forested; but all forest is lowland and consequently commercially valuable (F. G. Rozendaal).

Orange-banded Thrush *Zoothera peronii* occurs in lowland woodland on Timor, Wetar and the small islands of Romang, Damar and Babar, **Indonesia**, although it has been recorded to 1,200 m (White and Bruce 1986). On Timor it is locally common in the few remnants of deciduous forest below 600 m, all recent records being from Baun, Bipolo, Camplong and Kapan in four patches of forest that are tiny, and vulnerable and comprise the entire remaining lowland forest of West Timor (P. Andrew).

Everett's Thrush *Zoothera everetti* is a rare endemic of the mountains of Borneo, known only from the spinal range between Mt Dulit and Kinabalu, **Malaysia**, and found usually between 1,300 and 2,300 m (Smythies 1981).

Amami Thrush *Zoothera amami*, treated in King (1978-1979) as a race of White's Thrush *Z. dauma* but here separated (see Ishihara 1986), is endemic to Amami-oshima, **Japan**, where it occurs at very low densities and only in primary forest, and is at some risk from habitat destruction (M. A. Brazil).

Fawn-breasted Thrush *Zoothera machiki* was long known from just three specimens collected on Lara in the Tanimbar Islands, **Indonesia** (White and Bruce 1986), but has recently been found locally common in primary forest and occasionally secondary scrub on Vamdena (F. G. Rozendaal). All forest in the Tanimbars is lowland and hence commercially valuable (F. G. Rozendaal).

Forest Ground-thrush *Turdus oberlaenderi* has only been recorded in the Ituri Forest, Itombwe Mountains and Semliki valley in **Zaire** and in the Semliki (Bwamba) Forest in **Uganda**; forest destruction, which was thought likely to have eliminated the species from Bwamba (Collar and Stuart 1985), has not been as serious there as previously reported, but still remains the main threat (Collar and Stuart 1988).

Kibale Ground-thrush *Turdus kibalensis* is known simply from two specimens netted together in 1966 amid thick secondary growth in Kibale Forest, **Uganda**, where steady encroachment continues to pose a threat (Collar and Stuart 1985, 1988).

Spotted Ground-thrush *Turdus fischeri*, a remarkably elusive thrush of the forest floor, requiring deep shade and deep leaf-litter, has an extraordinary distribution: there are two migratory coastal subspecies (nominate *fischeri* wintering in **Kenya** and **Tanzania** and probably breeding in Mozambique; *natalicus* mostly breeding south-west of Durban and wintering north-east of Durban, **South Africa**), one resident race (*belcheri*, restricted to four small mountains in **Malawi** and numbering 30-40 pairs in all), and two races known from single specimens, *maxis* from the Imatong Mountains in **Sudan** and *lippensi* from the Upemba National Park, **Zaire** (Collar and Stuart 1985; also Prigogine and Louette 1984, Bennun 1987).

Taita Thrush *Turdus helleri* is apparently confined to the forest on the Taita Hills and Mount Kasigau in south-east **Kenya**, available habitat in the former covering less than 3 sq km and being under serious threat (Collar and Stuart 1985). In Ngaongao Forest (one of the two relatively intact patches remaining), a total of 90-190 was estimated in 1985 (McGuigan 1987).

Yemen Thrush *Turdus menachensis* is restricted to **North Yemen** and south-west **Saudi Arabia** (Bowden 1987). The species is strictly montane, confined to areas of remnant, dense, "natural" vegetation above 1,200 m., and believed to occur at low densities in suitable habitat which is threatened by the collection of firewood (Bowden 1987).

Grey-sided Thrush *Turdus feae* has a restricted breeding range in Hebei, in north-east **China**, and winters south to north-east **India**, **Burma** and northern **Thailand** (Meyer de Schauensee 1984). It inhabits forest but its distribution is poorly known; it was noted in May 1985 at Pangquanguo in the Luliang Shan, west central Shanxi, and may breed there (King 1987).

Subfamily Orthonychinae
Logrunners

Western Whipbird *Psophodes nigrogularis*, considered out of danger in King (1978- 1979), occurs in five isolated populations in south and south-west **Australia**; it is locally common on the Yorke and Eyre peninsulas of South Australia but rare and declining near Albany, Western Australia, in north-west Victoria and south- east South Australia (Blakers *et al.* 1984). The western race, *leucogaster*, is seriously threatened and if the clearing of heath and mallee continues the species will decline further (J. Brouwer; see also McNee 1985).

Subfamily Timaliinae
Babblers

Marsh Babbler *Pellorneum palustre* is confined to the tracts of reeds and wet grasslands in the lowlands and foothills to 800 m of Arunachal Pradesh and

Assam in north-east **India**, and in **Bangladesh**, where it is locally not uncommon (Ali and Ripley 1984), but several grassland species in the region appear vulnerable.

Black-browed Babbler *Trichastoma perspicillatum* is known from the type-specimen collected in Kalimantan, **Indonesia**, in the middle of the last century, unless regarded as conspecific with Vanderbilt's Babbler *T. vanderbilti* (Smythies 1981) or Horsfield's Babbler *T. sepiarium* (Hoogerwerf 1966).

Vanderbilt's Babbler *Trichastoma vanderbilti* is known from the type-specimen collected at 900 m on a steep slope in primary forest, northern Sumatra, **Indonesia**, unless regarded as conspecific with the Black-browed Babbler *T. perspicillatum* (Smythies 1981) or Horsfield's Babbler *T. sepiarium* (Hoogewerf 1966; also, tentatively, van Marle and Voous 1988).

Bagobo Babbler *Leonardina woodi* represents an endemic genus and was described in 1905 from a specimen taken at 1,200 m on Mt Apo on Mindanao in the **Philippines** (Delacour and Mayr 1946). It was subsequently recorded from several localities on Mindanao but records this decade are solely from 1,000 m on Mt Apo (J. Scharringa, A. Wassink).

Short-tailed Scimitar-babbler *Jabouilleia danjoui* is a rare endemic resident of the mountains of central and south Annam, **Viet Nam** (King *et al.* 1975). The status of the species and its habitat are unknown.

Luzon Wren-babbler *Napothera rabori* is endemic to Luzon in the northern **Philippines**, being first described in 1960 and known only from the type-localities of the three recognized subspecies. It has apparently not been observed in the field as all specimens have been taken in nets or rat-traps (R. S. Kennedy); it may be secure in the Sierra Madre.

Rufous-throated Wren-babbler *Spelaeornis caudatus* is a scarce resident of the upper Mai Valley, **Nepal**, Sikkim, **India**, **Bhutan** and Arunachal Pradesh (Ripley 1982, Ali and Ripley 1984, Inskipp and Inskipp 1986).

Rusty-throated Wren-babbler *Spelaeornis badeigularis* is known only from the type-specimen, taken at 1,600 m in the Mishmi Hills, eastern Arunachal Pradesh, north-east **India** (Ripley 1982).

Tawny-breasted Wren-babbler *Spelaeornis longicaudatus* is a scarce endemic resident of oak and rhododendron forests between 1,000 and 2,000 m in Meghalaya, the Cachar Hills of Assam and Manipur, in north-east **India** (Ali and Ripley 1984).

Wedge-billed Wren-babbler *Sphenocichla humei* has been collected in Sikkim (not recorded since 1875), the Aka (a winter record at 1,200 m) and Mishmi Hills (not recorded since 1879), Arunachal Pradesh and Nagaland, Manipur, Meghalaya and Cachar hills in Assam in north-east **India**, and north-east **Burma** (Ali and Ripley 1984), with few recent records (Ripley 1982) although one was observed near Darjeeling in 1973 (B. F. King).

Deignan's Babbler *Stachyris rodolphei* is an endemic resident of bamboo forest between 1,000 and 2,000 m on Doi Chiang Dao in north-west **Thailand** (King *et al.* 1975).

Flame-templed Babbler *Stachyris speciosa* is found on Negros and has recently been discovered on Panay, **Philippines** (R. Sison *per* R. S. Kennedy). It is still moderately common in remnant lowland and hill forest on Negros but deforestation there is proceeding rapidly (R. S. Kennedy). Its status on Panay is unknown.

Negros Babbler *Stachyris nigrorum* is known from the type-locality in the mountains of southern Negros (duPont 1971) and from Panay in the **Philippines** (R. Sison *per* R. S. Kennedy). It is locally common in southern Negros (J. Hornskov, S. Jensen) but restricted to islands suffering severe deforestation (see Cox 1988).

White-breasted Babbler *Stachyris grammiceps* is endemic to west and central Java, **Indonesia** (Kuroda 1933-1936. It is locally common in patches of forest on the southern volcanic slopes of West Java, up to at least 800 m, but this habitat is now so fragmented that it remains one of the most threatened endemic species on the island (P. Andrew, K. D. Bishop).

Sooty Babbler *Stachyris herberti* is an endemic resident at low elevations in central **Laos** (King *et al.* 1975). The status of the species and its habitat are unknown.

Snowy-throated Babbler *Stachyris oglei* is a rare endemic resident of the Patkai and Mishmi hills in eastern Arunachal Pradesh, north-east **India** (Ali and Ripley 1984).

Jerdon's Babbler *Moupinia altirostris* is found in three disjunct populations: in **Pakistan** on the plains of the Indus, in north-east **India** in the Ganges basin, and on the Irrawaddy plains of south-central **Burma**, though the last population might be extinct (Ali and Ripley 1984). It affects expanses of elephant-grass, reeds and marshland, it is uncommon and local and the western race *scindicum* appears especially vulnerable (Gaston 1984).

Hinde's Pied Babbler *Turdoides hindei* occurs in a small area of **Kenya** south and east of Mount Kenya, where it is a bird of secondary vegetation and open woodland on steep-sided valleys and along gullies; there is evidence of a considerable contraction of range this century (Collar and Stuart 1985).

Ashy-headed Laughingthrush *Garrulax cinereifrons* is endemic to **Sri Lanka** and confined to undisturbed evergreen forest of the foothills and mountains to 1,600 m (Ali and Ripley 1984); the species has declined markedly in recent years and is apparently intolerant of forest degradation, particularly that caused by firewood collectors (Hoffmann 1984).

Black-hooded Laughingthrush *Garrulax milleti* is an endemic forest resident of the hills of central and southern Annam, **Viet Nam** (King *et al.* 1975). Its status is unknown.

Sukatschev's Laughingthrush *Garrulax sukatschewi* is endemic to south-west Gansu in central **China** (Meyer de Schauensee 1984) and northern Sichuan at Jiuzhaigou and Wanglang (B. F. King). Subsequent records suggest it is locally common in the bamboo undergrowth of mixed forest.

Biet's Laughingthrush *Garrulax bieti* is resident in Yunnan, from east of the Mekong Jiang to south-west Sichuan, **China** (Meyer de Schauensee 1984) and Jiuzhaigou, north Sichuan (P. R. Kennerley). Its status is unknown.

Collared Laughingthrush *Garrulax yersini* is known only from the Langbian plateau in southern Annam, **Viet Nam** (King *et al.* 1975). The status of the species and its habitat are unknown.

Emei Shan Liocichla *Liocichla omeiensis* is known from Emei Shan in central Sichuan, **China** (Meyer de Schauensee 1984). It is fairly common but unobtrusive in dense secondary growth and bamboo (C. R. Robson, P. Alstrom) and was recently found at other localities south of Emei Shan in Sichuan (B. F. King), but its range remains extremely restricted.

Gold-fronted Fulvetta *Alcippe variegaticeps* is resident in the broadleaf forests of southern Sichuan (including Emei Shan) and the Yao Shan in Guangxi, **China** (Meyer de Schauensee 1984, King and Li Guiyan in press). It affects forest undergrowth, usually between 1,000 and 2,000 m, but the only recent records are from southern Sichuan where the patches of remnant forest are likely to disappear within a decade; it was recorded in May 1986 in Dafengding Panda Reserve in south-central Sichuan (King and Li Guiyan in press).

White-throated Mountain Babbler *Lioptilus gilberti* appears to be dependent on primary montane forest and is restricted to a few localities in western **Cameroon** and eastern **Nigeria** (Collar and Stuart 1985, Stuart and Jensen 1986).

Grey-crowned Crocias *Crocias langbianis* is a rare endemic of the Langbian Plateau in southern Annam, **Viet Nam**, so little known that even the condition of its habitat is uncertain (King *et al.* 1975).

Madagascar Yellowbrow *Crossleyia xanthophrys*, a distinctive babbler in its own genus, is known from rainforest in central-eastern **Madagascar**, with one record from the north; it had been seen only twice since 1930 (Collar and Stuart 1985), until observed in small flocks with breeding proved at Ranomafana (O. Langrand; see Dee 1986, Collar and Stuart 1988). It is recorded from two protected areas (O. Langrand, M. E. Nicoll).

Subfamily Panurinae
Parrotbills

Black-breasted Parrotbill *Paradoxornis flavirostris* occurs in **Nepal**, east through **Bhutan** and Arunachal Pradesh, north-east **India** and **Bangladesh** to west **Burma** (Ripley 1982), and west Yunnan, **China** (C. R. Robson) but there are no records this century from Nepal (Inskipp and Inskipp 1984) and its status in the entire remainder of its range is unknown. It affects reeds and wet grassland from the plains to 1,900 m (Ali and Ripley 1984).

Crested Parrotbill *Paradoxornis zappeyi* is known from Emei Shan and Wa Shan in Sichuan (Meyer de Schauensee 1984) and western Guizhou (Cheng 1987), **China**. It is not uncommon near the summit of Emei Shan, in dwarf bamboo and scrub (P. Alstrom, C. R. Robson, M. D. Williams), even on the outskirts of villages (F. G. Rozendaal), but all recent records are from the one mountain.

Przevalski's Parrotbill *Paradoxornis przewalskii* is resident in south-east Gansu, south-east Qinghai and adjacent Sichuan, in **China**, where it affects bamboo undergrowth in fir and spruce forest, between 2,500 and 3,000 m (Meyer de Schauensee 1984); it is scarce at Jiuzhaigou (M. A. S. Beaman, B. F. King, C. R. Robson).

Short-tailed Parrotbill *Paradoxornis davidianus* is known from east **Burma** (one record: Smythies 1986), north-west **Thailand**, southern Yunnan, Zhejiang and Fujian in **China** (Meyer de Schauensee 1984), northern **Laos** and northern Tonkin, **Viet Nam** (King *et al.* 1975). It frequents bamboo in lowlands to 1,800 m (Meyer de Schauensee 1984); despite so wide a range, it is apparently very rare throughout (C. R. Robson).

Greater Rufous-headed Parrotbill *Paradoxornis ruficeps* occurs in the eastern Himalayas from Sikkim, **India**, through **Bhutan**, Arunachal Pradesh and the hills south of the Brahmaputra to **Burma**, south-east Xizang Zizhiqu, **China**, north-west Yunnan, and northern **Laos** and **Viet Nam** (Ripley 1982). It is found in reeds, bamboo and dense grassland in the foothills up to 1,400 m (Meyer de Schauensee 1984), and within its extensive range it is very local and there appear to be no recent records (C. R. Robson).

Subfamily Picathartinae
Picathartes

White-necked Picathartes *Picathartes gymnocephalus* breeds colonially in caves and on rock-faces in the Upper Guinea forest block from **Ghana, Ivory Coast, Liberia** and **Guinea** into **Sierra Leone,** and is threatened by forest clearance, hunting and zoo-collecting (Collar and Stuart 1985; see also Colston and Curry-Lindahl 1986). Records from Togo are in error, although suitable habitat exists (Cheke 1986).

Grey-necked Picathartes *Picathartes oreas* breeds colonially in caves and on rock faces in southern **Cameroon,** north-eastern **Gabon** and possibly continental Equatorial Guinea, with new records from **Bioko (Equatorial Guinea)** (T. M. Butynski) and south-east **Nigeria,** where no fewer than 91 breeding sites were located in September and October 1987 (Ash 1987b), but it remains threatened by forest clearance and hunting (Collar and Stuart 1985). New breeding data for Gabon are in Brosset and Erard (1986).

Subfamily Polioptilinae
Gnatcatchers

Cuban Gnatcatcher *Polioptila lembeyei,* although not considered in a recent review of the country's threatened birds (Garrido 1985), has a restricted range on the north and south coasts of **Cuba,** and is rare everywhere except in one small locality around Baitiquiri (Garrido and Garcia 1975, Garcia undated).

Subfamily Sylviinae
Old World warblers

Grauer's Swamp Warbler *Bradypterus graueri* is known from a few highland swamps in eastern **Zaire,** south-western **Uganda, Rwanda** and northern **Burundi,** and although common it is in severe danger from swamp drainage (Collar and Stuart 1985).

Dja River Warbler *Bradypterus grandis* is an apparently rare bird of dense undergrowth, known only from a few localities in southern **Cameroon** and **Gabon** (Collar and Stuart 1985).

Large-billed Bush-warbler *Bradypterus major* is an extremely local bird in the Himalayas of **Pakistan, India** and **China,** and, in the race *innae,* in the **U.S.S.R.** and China (Mayr and Cottrell 1986). Its range is contracting in Kashmir, possibly due to change in agricultural practice (R. F. Grimmett, B. F. King, C. R. Robson).

Aquatic Warbler *Acrocephalus paludicola* breeds possibly only in **Austria, East Germany, Hungary, Poland** and the **U.S.S.R.** (Flint *et al.* 1984, Jacob *et al.* 1985, Grimmett and Jones in prep.). In Europe it is known to breed at a limited number of localities (Grimmett and Jones in prep.), with 1,300-1,500 pairs in Poland (mainly Biebrze Marshes) (T. Wesolowski) and 30-40 pairs in East Germany (Dornbusch 1985), whilst in the U.S.S.R. it is described as rare (Flint *et al.* 1984). The species winters in Africa but its distribution is very poorly known; two of the few records are from Mali (Curry and Sayer 1979).

Speckled Reed Warbler *Acrocephalus sorghophilus* may breed in Liaoning and north-east Hebei, China (Meyer de Schauensee 1984) but this range is in doubt (P. Alstrom). It has been recorded on passage in east **China** at Beijing (P. R. Kennerley). Small numbers are recorded in the **Philippines**, which may prove to be the main wintering grounds; it is fairly common in the marshes of Luzon (B. F. King).

Nauru Reed Warbler *Acrocephalus rehsei* is endemic to **Nauru**, where in 1983 island residents reported that it was still present in the remaining bushy areas (Pratt *et al.* 1987).

Nihoa Reed Warbler (Millerbird) *Acrocephalus familiaris* is known in two races (sometimes regarded as separate species) from the north-western **Hawaiian Islands (to U.S.A.)** of Laysan and Nihoa; the nominate form was extirpated from Laysan between 1912 and 1923 following the destruction of the indigenous vegetation by introduced rabbits, whilst the population of the race *kingi* on Nihoa (0.64 sq km) fluctuates between 200 and 600 individuals (King 1978-1979, Pratt *et al.* 1987).

Rodrigues Warbler *Acrocephalus rodericanus* retains a population of only some 20-25 birds on Rodrigues, **Mauritius**, following the clearance and disturbance of its dense thicket habitat coupled with the impact of cyclones in the past two decades; habitat creation and conservation are urgently needed and the Black Rat *Rattus rattus* is feared to have colonised the island recently (Collar and Stuart 1985; see also Cheke 1987c).

Seychelles Warbler *Acrocephalus sechellensis* is confined to the tiny (27 ha) island of Cousin, **Seychelles**, where, following ICBP management as a nature reserve and the associated recovery of the *Pisonia* woodland, it is now relatively common, with some 250-300 birds present in 1981 (Collar and Stuart 1985).

Aldabra Warbler *Nesillas aldabranus*, if it is not by now extinct, must be the rarest, most restricted and highly threatened species of bird in the world, being found only in a 10 ha strip of coastal vegetation on Aldabra, **Seychelles**, where no more than five birds were ever seen and, since 1977, only two, both males; rat predation on nests is perhaps the main cause of the species's plight (Collar and

Stuart 1985; see also Hambler *et al.* 1985). Searches from July to November 1986 produced no records and the species is feared extinct (Roberts 1987).

Papyrus Yellow Warbler *Chloropeta gracilirostris* occurs mainly in papyrus swamps, but occasionally other marshy habitats, in areas of high rainfall in **Burundi, Kenya, Rwanda, Uganda, Zaire** and **Zambia,** and is threatened by attempts to drain and exploit papyrus swamps (Collar and Stuart 1985).

Kolombangara Warbler *Phylloscopus amoenus* is endemic to Kolombangara, **Solomon Islands,** where it is found in forest in the mountainous interior, a single bird being observed in 1974 (J. M. Diamond). A report that Kolombangara is now entirely deforested appears to be exaggerated, but almost all forest below 400 m has been cleared (G. Baines).

Socotra Cisticola *Cisticola haesitata* is confined to **Socotra (South Yemen),** where it is unaccountably rare (Collar and Stuart 1985: 717). Its modern status is unknown.

Tana River Cisticola *Cisticola restricta* is known from a small number of specimens, all collected in the lower Tana River basin in eastern **Kenya,** though it may also be found in **Somalia;** recent attempts to locate the species in the field have been unsuccessful (Collar and Stuart 1985).

River Prinia *Prinia "fluviatilis",* for which a full description is awaited, has been found in only a few localities in **Niger, Chad** and northern **Cameroon,** but nothing is known of its status (Collar and Stuart 1985).

Long-tailed Prinia *Prinia burnesii* is resident in two disjunct populations, in the plains of the Indus in **Pakistan** and in the Brahmaputra in north-east **India** (Ali and Ripley 1984). Its distribution parallels that of Jerdon's Babbler *Moupinia altirostris;* it remains locally common in the wet grasslands of north- east India but the nominate race in Pakistan is vulnerable (Gaston 1984).

White-winged Apalis *Apalis chariessa* is known only from the lower Tana River in coastal **Kenya** (nominate *chariessa*), now possibly extinct, the Uluguru and Uzungwa Mountains in **Tanzania,** Mount Chiperone in **Mozambique** and eleven small forests in southern **Malawi** (where the national total is about 100 pairs and under severe threat), all the race *macphersoni* (Collar and Stuart 1985: 717-718).

Karamoja Apalis *Apalis karamojae* is a very poorly known warbler largely associated with riverine acacia in north-east **Uganda** (nominate *karamojae*) and northern **Tanzania** (race *stronachi*) (Collar and Stuart 1985, Stuart and Collar 1986).

Kungwe Apalis *Apalis argentea* appears to be in danger from forest clearance throughout its fragmented range, nominate *argentea* being confined to Mount Mahale (or Kungwe) and environs in western **Tanzania** and the race *eidos* occurring on Idjwi Island in Lake Kivu, eastern **Zaire**, Nyungwe Forest, **Rwanda** and the tiny Bururi Forest in **Burundi** (Collar and Stuart 1985).

Kabobo Apalis *Apalis kaboboensis* is known only from montane forest on Mount Kabobo, west of Lake Tanganyika, in eastern **Zaire**, with no recent (post-1957) information on its status (Collar and Stuart 1985).

Long-billed Apalis *Apalis moreaui* is a low-density species known from two widely separated montane forests, the East Usambaras in **Tanzania** (nominate *moreaui*) and the Njesi Plateau in northern **Mozambique** (race *sousae*), a site not visited since 1945; although chiefly a bird of forest clearings and edges, it remains vulnerable to forest destruction (Collar and Stuart 1985). However, an IUCN project aimed at reconciling land-use pressures in the Usambaras (Stuart 1986) is currently being implemented (N. M. Collins).

Mrs Moreau's Warbler *Bathmocercus winifredae* occurs in three montane forests in eastern **Tanzania**, the Ulugurus, Ukagurus and Uzungwas, the first and last of which require major conservation attention (Collar and Stuart 1985).

Turner's Eremomela *Eremomela turneri* has a patchy distribution and is very poorly known in western **Kenya** (nominate *turneri* in Kakamega Forest and environs) and eastern **Zaire** in the south-eastern corner of the equatorial forest belt, with one record from south-westernmost **Uganda** (race *kalindei*) (Collar and Stuart 1985).

Pulitzer's Longbill *Macrosphenus pulitzeri* is known only from two general forest areas on the scarp of **Angola**, with no recent information on its status (Collar and Stuart 1985).

Sao Tome Short-tail *Amaurocichla bocagii* is a remarkable little forest bird of puzzling affinities and apparently both tree-creeping and ground-haunting habits, confined to southern Sao Tome, **Sao Tome e Principe**, where it has been collected once this century, in 1928 (Collar and Stuart 1985). In April 1987 in the south-east of the island, a bird that could only have been this species was seen at dusk chasing a kingfisher by a river before disappearing into the crown of a palm (S. D. Eccles; see also Jones and Tye 1988).

Bristled Grass-warbler *Chaetornis striatus* ranges from **Pakistan** east to Assam and **Bangladesh** and south to Tamil Nadu, **India** (Ali and Ripley 1984) and has recently been found nesting in **Nepal** (P. Heath, D. Thorns); it is a rare and local inhabitant of grassland although the species is hard to locate and may be commoner than it seems (Gaston 1984).

Japanese Marsh Warbler *Megalurus pryeri* breeds in east Liaoning and north-east Hebei, in north-east **China**, and on Honshu, **Japan** (King 1978-1979, Meyer de Schauensee 1984). In Japan it breeds in only three areas (Sonobe 1982), its population maybe in the low hundreds, its wintering areas are poorly known, and it is dependent on reedbeds which are liable to drainage (M. A. Brazil). In China it is known to breed at Zhalong, west Heilongjiang (A. Goodwin, V. Olsson, P. Alstrom) and to winter at Lake Poyang (Kennerley 1987).

Fly River Grassbird *Megalurus albolimbatus* is known from two localities in extreme south-western **Papua New Guinea**, from Lake Daviumbu on the middle Fly River and from the Bensbach River (Beehler *et al.* 1986). It affects inundated reeds and sedges along rivers and lakes and although locally common it apparently has a very restricted distribution (Rand and Gilliard 1967); grazing by feral deer is degrading the grassland (K. D. Bishop).

Long-legged Warbler *Trichocichla rufa* is endemic to **Fiji**, where it is known from Viti Levu by four specimens collected between 1890 and 1894, and from Vanua Levu by a specimen taken in 1974 (King 1978-1979).

Subfamily Malurinae
Australian warblers

Purple-crowned Fairy-wren *Malurus coronatus* from **Australia** occurs in two subspecies, *coronatus* in the Kimberleys, Western Australia, to the lower Victoria River area of Northern Territory, and *macgillivrayi* in eastern Northern Territory and north-west Queensland (Pizzey 1980). It inhabits canegrass and thickets in the vicinity of water, and occasionally mangroves (Burbidge and Jenkins 1984). The decline in range and numbers of *coronatus* has been linked to pastoral development, and could be critical if cattle densities increase (I. Rowley *per* J. Brouwer); though no corresponding contraction in range has been noted for *macgillivrayi*, its relict populations do not appear to recolonise areas, even when the vegetation has regenerated (Blakers *et al.* 1984).

Thick-billed Grass-wren *Amytornis textilis* inhabits areas of thick shrub, most notably saltbush and bluebush, in **Australia** and has declined where grazing has prevented young plants from maturing into suitably thick old bushes (Blakers *et al.* 1984). In Western Australia nominate *textilis* once ranged across much of the southern interior but relict populations are now known only from Shark Bay and the Nullarbor Plain (Burbidge and Jenkins 1984). In South Australia a similar decline has occurred in *modestus*, which is now largely confined to the Lake Eyre, Lake Torrens and Lake Frome basins (Parker and Reid 1979). The population *myall* is probably still well distributed in parts of southern South Australia but there are few recent records (Blakers *et al.* 1984).

Eyrean Grass-wren *Amytornis goyderi* was collected in 1874 and rediscovered in

1961 on the Macumba River on the north side of Lake Eyre, South **Australia** (King 1978-1979). In 1976 it was found commonly in the southern Simpson Desert and regarded as no longer threatened with extinction (Parker and Reid 1979). Although local abundance appears to vary greatly with season, it is now thought to be widespread in the northern Lake Eyre region in dense tussocks of canegrass (Blakers *et al.* 1984).

Grey Grass-wren *Amytornis barbatus* was first recorded in 1921 but not described until 1967, being known from a small number of locations in north-west New South Wales, south-west Queensland and north-east South **Australia** (Blakers *et al.* 1984) and may prove to be more widespread than first supposed (Parker and Reid 1979). It inhabits dense stands of lignum, usually interspersed with canegrass or sedge, and is locally nomadic in periods of drought (Blakers *et al.* 1984).

Carpentarian Grass-wren *Amytornis dorotheae* is thinly distributed in a long but very narrow belt of outcropping sandstone in the McArthur river region of Northern Territory, **Australia**; it is known from six localities but a recent study by the Northern Territory Conservation Commission confirmed that the species requires old hummock spinifex as its preferred habitat and that this is threatened by current fire regimes (Blakers *et al.* 1984, J. Brouwer).

Gouldian Finch *Stipiturus mallee* occurs in northern **Australia**, from Derby, Western Australia, east through Northern Territory to the Atherton Tablelands of Queensland (Blakers *et al.* 1984). The decline in this species has been alarming; the main problem, exacerbated by trapping, appears to be an introduced lung-mite infection that threatens the population, particularly in the Northern Territory (S. Tidemann).

Eastern Bristlebird *Dasyornis brachypterus* occurs in isolated and scattered populations in the adjacent coastal regions of eastern Victoria, New South Wales and southern Queensland, **Australia**, where it lives in rank vegetation bordering on heath and in the northern part of its range is found up to 600 m (Blakers *et al.* 1984). The frequent burning and grazing of the heath vegetation within this limited range has led to a decline, although infrequent burning might be advantageous as thick low vegetation is a successional stage reached within a few years of a fire (Blakers *et al.* 1984).

Western Bristlebird *Dasyornis longirostris* was formerly found in coastal southwest Western **Australia**, from Perth to Esperance, but is now restricted to the southern coastal areas around Albany (King 1978-1979, Burbidge and Jenkins 1984). It inhabits dense coastal heath, reedbeds and grassland scrub, and its decline is attributed to the indiscriminate burning of these habitats, although it will survive even in small pockets of unburnt country (Blakers *et al.* 1984; see also McNee 1986).

Biak Gerygone *Gerygone hypoxantha* is endemic to Biak Island, Irian Jaya,

Indonesia, and although it is now judged a race of Large-billed Gerygone *G. magnirostris* (Beehler *et al.* 1986), it has not been recorded in three visits to Biak in the 1980s (K. D. Bishop).

Chestnut-breasted Whiteface *Aphelocephala pectoralis* is found in South Australia, Australia, but is still little known, and its nest and eggs were not described until 1968; it feeds on the ground among shrubs on stony rises or gibber plains but is nomadic and recorded very rarely and incidentally (Blakers *et al.* 1984), though its status and habitat have probably changed little since settlement (J. Brouwer).

Subfamily Muscicapinae
Old World flycatchers

Nimba Flycatcher *Melaenornis annamarulae* is known only from lowland rainforest at the foot of Mount Nimba in **Liberia** and from a skin collected in Tai Forest in **Ivory Coast**; it must be very rare, and greatly threatened by habitat destruction throughout the Upper Guinea forest block (Collar and Stuart 1985; see also Colston and Curry-Lindahl 1986).

Brown-chested Flycatcher *Rhinomyias brunneata* is a woodland bird from greatly deforested south-east **China**, from Henan and Jiangsu south to Guangxi and Guangdong (Meyer de Schauensee 1984); it is common at Bu Buo Shan, Guangdong (P. R. Kennerley). The species is known to winter in peninsular **Malaysia**, but may reach Sumatra, Indonesia (Medway and Wells 1976). The population in the **Andaman Islands (to India)** may be resident and represent another species (B. F. King).

Henna-tailed Jungle-flycatcher *Rhinomyias colonus* is known from Mangole and Sanana in the Sula Islands and Peleng and doubtfully eastern Sulawesi, **Indonesia**, this last locality being based on a single specimen lost in 1945 (White and Bruce 1986). Its status is unknown.

White-throated Jungle-flycatcher *Rhinomyias albigularis* is confined to lowland and hill forest on Guimaras and Negros in the **Philippines**, where it was described as rare by Delacour and Mayr (1946). The fragments of standing forest on the islands are being cleared and where the species survives its population must be very small (R. S. Kennedy); there are recent records from Negros in 1987 (J. Hornskov, S. Jensen).

Damar Blue Flycatcher *Ficedula henrici* is endemic to Damar, **Indonesia**, and known from nine specimens collected in 1899 (White and Bruce 1986). The status of the species and its habitat are unknown.

Lompobattang Flycatcher *Ficedula bonthaina* is endemic to Sulawesi, **Indone-**

sia, and known only from Gn Lompobattang at the tip of the south-west peninsula (White and Bruce 1986). It was evidently common in dense forest undergrowth at about 1,100 m, as a long series was obtained in 1931 (White and Bruce 1986), but its current status is unknown; the surrounding lowlands have been cleared to 1,000 m and represent one of the more densely populated areas of Sulawesi (Whitten *et al.* 1987).

Sumba Flycatcher *Ficedula harterti* is endemic to Sumba, **Indonesia**, where it has been collected at approximately 500 m (White and Bruce 1986), with a recent record of a single bird in remnant evergreen forest at 600 m (B. F. King); its habitat requirements are otherwise unknown but it is presumably threatened by forest destruction.

Black-banded Flycatcher *Ficedula timorensis* is endemic to Timor, **Indonesia**, where it frequents forest undergrowth and is locally common but restricted to remnant patches (Baun, Bipolo, Camplong, Kapan and Besi Pae) of deciduous forest up to 1,200 m; the ground vegetation in all these patches of forest is grazed by cattle (P. Andrew, J. McKean, D. Yong).

Matinan Flycatcher *Cyornis sandfordi* is endemic to Sulawesi, **Indonesia**, and long known only from the Matinan mountains on the northern peninsula (White and Bruce 1986). Its presence was confirmed in 1985 and it presumably occurs throughout the northern peninsula in montane forest (F. G. Rozendaal).

Rueck's Blue Flycatcher *Cyornis ruecki* is known from Sumatra, **Indonesia**, by two specimens collected in 1917 and doubtfully from peninsular Malaysia by two trade skins (Medway and Wells 1976); it is probably from lowland or coastal forest or mangrove, but its status, habitat and range remain essentially unknown and its taxonomic status is questioned (van Marle and Voous 1988).

Blue-breasted Flycatcher *Cyornis herioti* is endemic to Luzon in the **Philippines**, where it is a rare species of hill forest (R. S. Kennedy); there is one recent record from the Sierra Madre (J. Hornskov, S. Jensen).

Chapin's Flycatcher *Muscicapa lendu* is known with certainty from the Lendu Plateau (now largely deforested) and Itombwe Mountains in eastern **Zaire**, the Bwindi (Impenetrable) Forest in **Uganda** and Kakamega Forest in **Kenya**, and is rare throughout this fragmented range (Collar and Stuart 1985).

Grand Comoro Flycatcher *Humblotia flavirostris*, a distinctive flycatcher in its own genus, occurs only in forest and heath on Mount Karthala, Grand Comoro **Comoro Islands**, where its habitat is somewhat vulnerable and insufficiently protected (Collar and Stuart 1985). However, study in 1985 indicated several thousand pairs to be present over a fairly large area of the mountain (Louette *et al.* 1986).

Red-tailed Newtonia *Newtonia fanovanae* is known from the type-specimen only, collected in December 1931 in Fanovana Forest (now cleared), eastern-central **Madagascar**; it is either greatly overlooked, genuinely rare, or extinct (Collar and Stuart 1985).

Chatham Island Black Robin *Petroica traversi* was restricted to Little Mangere in the **Chatham Islands (to New Zealand)** but, following deterioration of its scrub- forest habitat, the entire remnant population of seven birds was transferred to Mangere (King 1978-1979, Williams and Given 1981). An egg-manipulating, cross- fostering programme had resulted in 38 birds by 1987/1988, now distributed between Mangere and Rangatira (Diamond 1984, D. V. Merton).

Subfamily Platysteirinae
Puffback-flycatchers, wattle-eyes

Gabon Batis *Batis minima* is endemic to **Gabon** where it was recently reported to be common and tolerant of forest disturbance (Collar and Stuart 1985: 719), but more recently still the same informants have described it as rare, localised and known only from the Makokou region (Brosset and Erard 1986).

Banded Wattle-eye *Platysteira laticincta* is restricted to the Bamenda-Banso Highlands of western **Cameroon**, where it is under very serious threat from forest clearance and is only likely to survive if forest on Mount Oku is preserved (Collar and Stuart 1985, Stuart and Jensen 1986). Intensive work has been directed towards the conservation of Mount Oku, and is continuing (e.g. Macleod 1987, Wilson in press).

Subfamily Monarchinae
Monarchs, paradise-flycatchers

Seychelles Paradise-flycatcher *Terpsiphone corvina* inhabits mature stands of indigenous *Calophyllum* and *Terminalia* on La Digue, **Seychelles**, where its population numbers about 60; very small, probably unviable populations occur on Praslin and possibly Felicite (Collar and Stuart 1985). A population census in February 1988 found between 72 and 75 individuals (I. Bullock, J. Komdeur, M. Komdeur, V. Laboudallon, G. Lewis).

Caerulean Paradise-flycatcher *Eutrichomyias rowleyi* is endemic to Sangihe in the Sangihe Islands, **Indonesia**, and known only by the type, probably a female, and one record of a single bird sighted in 1978 on the forested slopes of Gn Awu at the northern end of the island (White and Bruce 1986). If it survives it is presumably restricted to the few remaining patches of forest on Sangihe although all apparently suitable habitat has been searched in recent years without success (Whitten *et al.* 1987, F. G. Rozendaal).

Short-crested Monarch *Hypothymis helenae* is known from North Camiguin, Luzon, the Polillo Islands, Samar, Dinagat and north-eastern Mindanao in the **Philippines**, where it affects lowland forest (Delacour and Mayr 1946), and though rare on the larger islands it is still locally common on the tiny islands of Dinagat and North Camiguin (R. S. Kennedy); it may prove common on Samar where Cox (1988) confirms large tracts of lowland forest remain.

Celestial Monarch *Hypothymis coelestis* is known from Basilan, Mindanao, Dinagat, Negros, Samar, Sibuyan and Luzon in the **Philippines**, but is a rare bird of the forest canopy (Delacour and Mayr 1946) and has been observed by few ornithologists in the past decade (R. S. Kennedy).

Rarotonga Monarch *Pomarea dimidiata* is restricted to the forested interior of Rarotonga, **Cook Islands (to New Zealand)** (King 1978-1979). It has probably been rare for most of this century and a survey in 1983 located only 21 birds and two nests, the first ever recorded; the bulk of the population occurs in the Totokoitu and Taipara Valleys and preservation of these areas is essential to the species's survival (Hay 1986). In 1987 researchers from Cambridge, U.K., and New Zealand found 34 birds in the 1.25 sq km of available habitat (M. Bryan, S. Mitchell).

Tahiti Monarch *Pomarea nigra* is endemic to but close to extinction on Tahiti, **Society Islands (to France)**, the single specimen collected in 1823 on Maupiti in the same group now being recognised as a full (extinct) species (Holyoak and Thibault 1984; also King 1978-1979). The recent view that 100-500 birds probably survive (Holyoak and Thibault 1984, Hay 1986) has sadly received no support from recent investigations, with four to six birds on Mt Marau and a pair in Papehue Valley, 1984 (M. K. Poulsen), and but a single pair seen in 1985 and none found in 1986 and 1987 (Thibault in press). The species never occurred on Tonga (Todd 1984).

Marquesas Monarch *Pomarea mendozae* was formerly widespread in the central **Marquesas Islands (to France)**, occurring in four subspecies, all but one (*motanensis*) considered threatened by the late 1970s (King 1978-1979). It is still fairly common (*motanensis*) on Mohotani where the population is estimated at between 250 and 350 pairs, and on Ua Pou (*mira*) with a population of between 150 and 200 pairs, but endangered (nominate *mendozae*) on Hiva Oa (one seen 1975, but population on Tahuata extinct) and feared extinct (*nukuhivae*), though reported by locals in 1987, on Nuku Hiva (Holyoak and Thibault 1984, Thibault in press). The species was common in the 1920s and its decline is probably linked to the deforestation and overgrazing of the wooded valleys it favours (Hay 1986).

Iphis Monarch *Pomarea iphis* is endemic to Ua Huka, **Marquesas Islands (to France)**, where several hundred pairs were present in 1975 (Holyoak and Thibault 1984). The race *fluxa*, reported as probably surviving (King 1978-1979) and "much reduced but still present on Eiao" (Pratt *et al.* 1987), was found to be extinct in July 1987 (Thibault in press).

Fatu Iva Monarch *Pomarea whitneyi* is endemic to Fatu Iva, **Marquesas Islands (to France)**, where several hundred pairs were present in 1975 (Holyoak and Thibault 1984). There have been no reports since then, and given the island's small size (only 100 sq km) and the genus's history of decline and extinction, the species is viewed with some concern (J.-C. Thibault).

Rennell Shrikebill *Clytorhynchus hamlini* is known from Rennell, **Solomon Islands**, where it affects lowland forest and occasionally secondary vegetation, and is vulnerable to forest fragmentation (Diamond 1984). The island is well forested but a bauxite mining scheme, currently shelved, and a proposed forestry scheme could adversely affect the species (J. M. Diamond).

Truk Monarch *Metabolus rugensis* is confined to the high islands and a few low islets within the lagoon of Truk, **Federated States of Micronesia (to U.S.A.)**, where it affects upland forest and mangroves and only occasionally the agricultural vegetation that predominates on the islands (Pratt *et al.* 1987). It appears that the species has recovered since 1945 but is still threatened by deforestation (King 1978-1979, Engbring and Pratt 1985).

Black-chinned Monarch *Monarcha boanensis* is known only from the holotype collected on Boano, a small island at the western end of Seram, **Indonesia** (White and Bruce 1986). Its status is unknown but some forest remains in the centre of the island (D. A. Holmes *per* K. D. Bishop).

White-tipped Monarch *Monarcha everetti* is known only from Tanahjampea, **Indonesia**, in the Flores Sea (White and Bruce 1986). Its status is unknown: there is thought to be no forest left on the island (K. D. Bishop).

Biak Monarch *Monarcha brehmii* is confined to Biak Island, Irian Jaya, **Indonesia**, where it affects lowland and hill forest to an altitude of 600 m (Schodde 1978). It is probably rare as it is poorly represented in collections (Rand and Gilliard 1967); the undescribed female was recorded in disturbed lowland forest on Supiori in 1984 (K. D. Bishop).

Guam Flycatcher *Myiagra freycineti* is endemic to **Guam (to U.S.A.)**, where it was once widespread in wooded areas, but the population has crashed over the last decade and it is now either restricted to the mature forest around limestone cliffs on the northern end of the island or extinct (Jenkins 1983, Engbring and Pratt 1985). The decline of almost all the forest birds on Guam has been dramatic and is as yet unexplained (Pratt *et al.* 1987), but is most likely due to depredation by the introduced Brown Tree Snake *Boiga irregularis* (W. C. Gagne).

Biak Black Flycatcher *Myiagra atra* is known from Biak and Numfor Islands,

Irian Jaya, **Indonesia**, and by one specimen from neighbouring Rani Island, being largely confined to the interior hills where it feeds in the canopy of forest, but is occasionally recorded in mangrove (Beehler *et al*. 1986). In a survey of Biak in 1982 it was found only in forest on adjacent Supiori and considered unlikely to survive in secondary vegetation on Biak (K. D. Bishop).

Subfamily Rhipidurinae
Fantails

Malaita Fantail *Rhipidura malaitae* has not been recorded since its discovery in 1930, in mountain forest on Malaita, **Solomon Islands** (Diamond 1987). The mountains of Malaita have not been visited by ornithologists since 1930, but the forest habitat is reported to be undisturbed and the species may therefore be at no risk (J. M. Diamond).

Subfamily Pachycephalinae
Whistlers

Red-lored Whistler *Pachycephala rufogularis* is restricted to a relatively small area of eastern South Australia and adjacent north-western Victoria, **Australia**, where it feeds largely on terrestrial insects and is found only in mallee with low ground-cover, particularly of the creeper *Cassytha*, consequently being sensitive to the clearing and burning of the ground vegetation; the species is declining and several populations that survived into the 1970s are thought to have disappeared in the past decade (Blakers *et al*. 1984).

Vogelkop Whistler *Pachycephala meyeri* is found in the mountains of Vogelkop, Irian Jaya, **Indonesia**, where it occurs in lower mountain forest and thickets, between 970 and 1,450 m (Beehler *et al*. 1986). There is some overlap at its upper limit with the high-mountain Regent Whistler *P. schlegelii*; it is known from few specimens and presumably occurs at very low density, but it may occur in the Foya Mountains (Diamond 1985).

Family Paridae
Titmice, chickadees

White-winged Tit *Parus nuchalis* is found in thick scrub and deciduous woodland in the semi-deserts of Kutch and parts of Gujarat and Rajasthan in north-west **India**, and in the Eastern Ghats in peninsular India (Ali and Ripley 1984). It is already extremely rare in southern India (Ali and Ripley 1984) and in the north-west it is patchily distributed and susceptible to habitat degradation (Gaston 1984).

Yellow Tit *Parus holsti* occurs chiefly in primary broadleaf forest between 1,000 and 2,300 m on **Taiwan**, where it is rare (Severinghaus and Blackshaw 1976) and considered at risk from forest destruction and other human activities (L. L. Severinghaus).

Family Sittidae
Nuthatches

White-browed Nuthatch *Sitta victoriae* is known only from Mt Victoria in the Chin Hills, **Burma**, where its current status is unknown (Paynter 1967, Smythies 1986), although the Himalayan Nuthatch *S. himalayensis*, then treated as conspecific, was once described as common in the Chin Hills (Smythies 1953).

Algerian Nuthatch *Sitta ledanti* maintains a population of around 80 pairs in summit forest on Mont Babor, **Algeria**, where it is threatened by loss of habitat although the site has national park status (Collar and Stuart 1985).

Yunnan Nuthatch *Sitta yunnanensis* is a resident of mountain pine forests in southern Sichuan and northern Yunnan, **China** (Meyer de Schauensee 1984). It is locally common in relict pine forest at Lijiang, north-west Yunnan, but may be dependent on mature pines which are disappearing (C. R. Robson, D. S. Farrow, F. G. Rozendaal).

Yellow-billed Nuthatch *Sitta solangiae* is known from the Fansipan mountains in north-eastern Tonkin (nominate *solangiae*) and from the Langbian plateau in south-central Annam (race *fortior*), in **Viet Nam** (Paynter 1967).

Giant Nuthatch *Sitta magna* is resident in east **Burma**, north-west **Thailand** and south-west **China** north to the Xue Shan ("Likiang mountains") in north-west Yunnan, where it affects forest above 1,300 m (King *et al*. 1975, Meyer de Schauensee 1984). Its status in Burma is not known but it is rare and local in Thailand (P. D. Round) and in China the only recent record is from relict pine forest at Lijiang (i.e. near Xue Shan), Yunnan (A. Goodwin).

Beautiful Nuthatch *Sitta formosa* is found in the eastern Himalayas, from Sikkim and **Bhutan**, through north-east **India**, **Burma** to west and south Yunnan in south-west **China**, northern **Laos** and northern **Viet Nam** (King *et al*. 1975, Ali and Ripley 1984). It affects forest between 1,300 and 2,000 m, and sometimes descends to the lowlands in the winter (Meyer de Schauensee 1984). It is rare throughout its extensive range (many observers); the first record for **Thailand** was in the north-west in January 1986 (*Oriental Bird Club Bull*. 3 [1986]: 35).

Family Rhabdornithidae
Philippine creepers

Long-billed Creeper *Rhabdornis grandis* is found in northern Luzon in the **Philippines** (Dickinson *et al.* 1988). It is known only from two specimens but may prove to be widespread in the remnant mountain forests of north-eastern Luzon (R. S. Kennedy); it was recorded from Mt Polis in 1986 (B. F. King) though not located there in 1985 (J. Scharringa); it is presumably very local.

Family Dicaeidae
Flowerpeckers

Brown-backed Flowerpecker *Dicaeum everetti* is found in peninsular **Malaysia**, the Natuna Islands, **Indonesia**, and Borneo, a lowland forest resident that is either rare or overlooked, being known only from Selangor in peninsular Malaysia (Medway and Wells 1976) and Kuching in Sarawak (Smythies 1981).

Forty-spotted Pardalote *Pardalotus quadragintus* is endemic to Tasmania, **Australia**; it was formerly widespread and locally common from sea level up to 1,000 m in the eastern half of the island, but is now restricted to the coastal south-east where eight populations survive on islands and coastal peninsulas in the vicinity of Hobart (Blakers *et al.* 1984). It affects open forest, particularly that dominated by *Eucalyptus viminalis*, and its decline has been linked to habitat destruction, unsuitable fire regimes and competition from the Striated Pardalote *P. striatus* with which it is sympatric (Burbidge and Jenkins 1984).

Family Nectariniidae
Sunbirds

Amani Sunbird *Anthreptes pallidigaster* occurs up to 900 m in the East Usambara Mountains in **Tanzania**, where suitable habitat covers only 130 sq km, and in 67 sq km of the Arabuko-Sokoke Forest in **Kenya**; forest clearance is its principal threat (Collar and Stuart 1985). An IUCN project aimed at reconciling land-use pressures in the Usambaras (Stuart 1986) is currently being implemented (N. M. Collins)

Banded Green Sunbird *Anthreptes rubritorques* is a middle-altitude species of four forest areas - the Usambara, Nguru, Uluguru and Uzungwa mountains - in eastern **Tanzania**, but is only common in the first of these where, however, it is most at risk from forest destruction (Collar and Stuart 1985), although an IUCN project aimed at reconciling land-use pressures (Stuart 1986) is currently underway (N. M. Collins).

Giant Sunbird *Dreptes thomensis*, the largest representative of its family outside the Oriental genus *Arachnothera*, is restricted to forest in the centre and west of Sao Tome, Sao Tome e Principe, where it has been reported reasonably common (Collar and Stuart 1985: 720). It was not encountered, however, in a recent survey (Jones and Tye 1988).

Apricot-breasted Sunbird *Nectarinia buettikoferi* is endemic to Sumba, **Indonesia** (White and Bruce 1986). It is locally common but apparently restricted to patches of monsoon forest, the further loss of which could seriously threaten the species (B. F. King, D. Yong).

Marungu Sunbird *Nectarinia prigoginei* occurs only in riparian forest patches in the Marungu Highlands of south-eastern **Zaire**, where habitat clearance is proceeding apace (Collar and Stuart 1985).

Rockefeller's Sunbird *Nectarinia rockefelleri* occupies high montane forest and afroalpine moorland on the Itombwe Mountains, mountains west of Lake Kivu, and Mount Karisimbi (north of Lake Kivu), eastern **Zaire**, with no recent information on the conservation status of these areas (Collar and Stuart 1985).

Rufous-winged Sunbird *Nectarinia rufipennis* is known only from the Mwanihana Forest on the eastern scarp of the Uzungwa Mountains in eastern **Tanzania**, for which national park status has been proposed (Collar and Stuart 1985).

Elegant Sunbird *Aethopyga duyvenbodei* is endemic to the Sangihe Islands and known from Sangihe and Siau, **Indonesia** (White and Bruce 1986). It is apparently restricted to the remnant patches of forest on Sangihe, common at the forest edge on Gn Sahendaruman (F. G. Rozendaal) but already rare in remnant forest on Gn Awu (K. D. Bishop): most members of the genus cope well in secondary habitats, but this species appears to be an exception (Whitten *et al.* 1987).

Family Zosteropidae
White-eyes

Javan White-eye *Zosterops flavus* was formerly known from the north-western coast of Java, **Indonesia**, and in Borneo by four specimens from the coast of southern Kalimantan and one specimen from Kuching (Sarawak), **Malaysia** (Mees 1969). The population on Java is apparently small (Allport and Milton

1988) but recent records from Kalimantan suggest the species might be locally common in mangrove on the south coast (Holmes and Burton 1987).

Golden-bellied White-eye *Zosterops uropygialis* is endemic to Kai Kecil and Tual in the Kai Islands, **Indonesia** (White and Bruce 1986). Its status is unknown, but the larger island, Kai Kecil, is well-populated and habitat destruction is considerable (K. D. Bishop).

Lemon-throated White-eye *Zosterops anomalus* is endemic to Sulawesi, **Indonesia**, but known only from the south-west peninsula, from the lowlands to 1,350 m (White and Bruce 1986); recent records are from dry scrub forest near Ujungpandang (B. F. King, D. Yong) where it is unobtrusive but not uncommon (see Whitten *et al.* 1987).

Sudest White-eye *Zosterops meeki* is confined to Sudest (Tagula) Island in the Louisiade Archipelago, **Papua New Guinea**, where it affects lowland forest and forest edge to an altitude of 300 m according to Schodde (1978). The status of the species and its habitat are unknown (J. M. Diamond).

Ambon Yellow White-eye *Zosterops kuehni* occurs on Ambon and, doubtfully, Seram, **Indonesia** (White and Bruce 1986). On Ambon it is locally common but restricted to hill forest and threatened by habitat destruction on this densely populated island (J. Bowler, J McKean, J. B. Taylor).

Gizo White-eye *Zosterops luteirostris* is confined to Gizo and Ranongga in the **Solomon Islands** (Paynter 1967). It is known to survive on Gizo but is uncommon since most of the island has been logged; further removal of forest could seriously endanger the species (J. M. Diamond).

Nendo White-eye *Zosterops sanctaecrucis* is endemic to Nendo in the Santa Cruz Islands, **Solomon Islands** (Mees 1961). Its status and that of its habitat are unknown (J. M. Diamond).

White-breasted White-eye *Zosterops albogularis* is endemic to **Norfolk Island (to Australia)**, and, though common until the end of the 1880s, is now confined to the remoter forests of the Mt Pitt Reserve (King 1978-1979). The population was estimated at 50 in 1962 but a survey conducted in 1985 failed to locate the species (Johnson 1987; see also Rooke 1986). Its decline coincided with the arrival of the Silvereye *Z. lateralis*, which is now abundant on the island, and was probably hastened by the clearing of the natural vegetation (Schodde *et al.* 1983).

Sao Tome White-eye *Zosterops ficedulinus* is confined to forest on Sao Tome and Principe, **Sao Tome e Principe**, and was reported to have declined seriously on the latter, worryingly on the former (Collar and Stuart 1985). However, a recent survey found that, while the species is indeed rare on Principe, it is abundant in parts of Sao Tome (Jones and Tye 1988).

Seychelles White-eye *Zosterops modestus* occurs in three tiny areas of mixed secondary forest in central Mahe, **Seychelles**, where since the mid-1970s, when a population of around 100 was guessed, it appears to have been declining inexorably towards extinction (Collar and Stuart 1985).

Mount Karthala White-eye *Zosterops mouroniensis* is restricted to the single small area of *Philippia* heath at the top of Mount Karthala, Grand Comoro, **Comoro Islands**, where it is permanently vulnerable (Collar and Stuart 1985, Louette *et al*. 1986).

Mauritius Olive White-eye *Zosterops chloronothus* has suffered until very recently from habitat clearance on its native **Mauritius**, and there are now probably only some 275 pairs remaining (Collar and Stuart 1985; see also Cheke 1987a). However, this figure is regarded as too optimistic (C. G. Jones).

Fernando Po Speirops *Speirops brunneus* is known only from the higher slopes of Pico de Santa Isabel, above 1,900 m, on **Bioko (Equatorial Guinea)**, where it inhabits lichen forest and montane heathland and is permanently vulnerable (Collar and Stuart 1985). However, recent fieldwork has confirmed that the species is common and suggested that its habitat is at little potential risk (T. M. Butynski).

Principe Speirops *Speirops leucophaeus* is endemic to Principe, **Sao Tome e Principe**, in the Gulf of Guinea, where a recent survey found evidence of local persecution and of a possible decline since the early 1970s (Jones and Tye 1988).

Sanford's White-eye *Woodfordia lacertosa* is endemic to Nendo in the Santa Cruz Islands, **Solomon Islands** (Mees 1969). Its status is unknown.

Great Truk White-eye *Rukia ruki* is confined to the islands of Tol, Polle, Onei and Pata in the lagoon of Truk, **Federated States of Micronesia (to U.S.A.)**, and is rare on all the islands except Tol (thought to be the only locality: King 1978-1979), where it is locally common in a tiny patch of forest near the island's summit (Engbring and Pratt 1985). The cause of the species scarcity is unknown although disturbance to the indigenous forest is undoubtedly important (Hay 1986).

Great Pohnpei White-eye *Rukia longirostra* is endemic to the island of Pohnpei, **Federated States of Micronesia (to U.S.A.)**, where it was long thought to be rare and restricted to forest above 500 m (King 1978-1979). A survey in 1983 found it common at higher elevations but also present in the lowlands, and its reported scarcity probably resulted from its inconspicuous nature (Engbring and Pratt 1985).

Rufous-throated White-eye *Madanga ruficollis* is known by four specimens taken at 840 and 1,550 m in the mountains of north-west Buru, **Indonesia**, and has not been recorded since its description in 1923 (White and Bruce 1986).

Spot-breasted White-eye *Heleia muelleri* is endemic to Timor, **Indonesia** (White and Bruce 1986), and is scarce in remnant pockets of deciduous woodland in the lowlands (P. Andrew) but has been recorded to 850 m (Mayr 1944).

Family Meliphagidae
Honeyeaters

Black-chested Honeyeater *Lichmera notabilis* is endemic to Wetar, **Indonesia**, where the status of the species and its habitat are unknown (White and Bruce 1986).

Crimson-hooded Honeyeater *Myzomela kuehni* is endemic to Wetar, **Indonesia**, and has not been recorded for over fifty years (White and Bruce 1986).

Sudest Meliphaga *Meliphaga vicina* is endemic to Sudest (Tagula) in the East Papuan Islands, **Papua New Guinea**, where it affects lowland forest and forest edge in the lowlands to 800 m (Schodde 1978). The status of the species and its habitat are unknown (J. M. Diamond).

Bonin Islands Honeyeater *Apalopteron familiare* is extinct (nominate *familiare*) on Chichijima and apparently also Muko-jima, surviving only on Haha-jima (race *hahasima*) and possibly its offshore islands in Ogasawara-shoto, i.e. **Bonin Islands (to Japan)** (Greenway 1967, King 1978-1979, Sonobe 1982, M. A. Brazil). Although it is apparently common and widespread in almost all habitats on Haha- jima, an elderly local has described it as far less common than in his childhood, presumably owing to the total loss of primary forest; this and the extinction of the nominate race are grounds for concern (M. A. Brazil).

Stitchbird *Notiomystis cincta* is a forest-dwelling species from **New Zealand** surviving only on Little Barrier Island; it is thought to have been exterminated from North Island as a result of predation, disease and collecting (King 1978-1979, Williams and Given 1981). The population is estimated at 4,000-5,000 birds; attempts have been made to establish the species on other smaller islands, but these populations may not persist because of the large variety of food sources required (Angehr 1985).

Brass's Friarbird *Philemon brassi* is only known from a small area of flooded canegrass and dense secondary forest around a lagoon on the Idenburg River, a tributary of the Mamberamo River in north-east Irian Jaya, **Indonesia** (Beehler 1985). The species has not been recorded since its discovery but ornithologists have not revisited the type-locality (J. M. Diamond).

Dusky Friarbird *Philemon fuscicapillus* is found on Halmahera and its satellite islands of Bacan and Morotai, **Indonesia** (White and Bruce 1986); it is an enigmatic species, reasonably well represented in museum collections and yet now rarely reported by field ornithologists (F. G. Rozendaal, D. Yong).

Long-bearded Melidectes *Melidectes princeps* has a restricted distribution in the highlands of **Papua New Guinea**, being recorded from mossy woodlands near the treeline between 3,500 and 4,200 m in the Kratke, Kubor, Hagen and Bismarck ranges (Beehler *et al*. 1986). It is thinly distributed and suffers disturbance to its limited habitat (J. M. Diamond).

Kauai Oo *Moho braccatus* is endemic to Kauai in the **Hawaiian Islands (to U.S.A.)** and now confined to the Alakai Swamp (King 1978-1979). It was not uncommon early this century but in the last decade has succumbed, probably to avian malaria, and now numbers a few individuals (Pratt *et al*. 1987).

Bishop's Oo *Moho bishopi*, from the **Hawaiian Islands (to U.S.A.)**, is known from Molokai, where it was last recorded in 1904 (treated as extinct by King 1978-1979), and Maui, where it was rediscovered in 1981; it survives as a rare inhabitant of the forest on the north-eastern slope of Haleakala (Pratt *et al*. 1987).

Regent Honeyeater *Xanthomyza phrygia* occurs in south-east **Australia**, mostly in coastal regions, from south-east Queensland more or less continuously through New South Wales, and Victoria to South Australia (Blakers *et al*. 1984). It is believed extinct in South Australia and to have declined seriously over the past decade in much of its range; insufficient flowering in one or two breeding seasons could reduce the species to critical levels (J. Brouwer).

Black-eared Miner *Manorina melanotis* occurs in small and very local colonies in a contiguous area of south-west New South Wales, north-west Victoria and eastern South Australia, **Australia** (Blakers *et al*. 1984). It is only known from three colonies, the largest of which contains nine birds, in Victoria, and is possibly extinct in South Australia; it favours mallee and is being displaced or genetically swamped by the Yellow-throated Miner *M. flavigula* as its habitat is cleared (J. Brouwer).

Family Emberizidae

Subfamily Emberizinae
Buntings

Japanese Yellow Bunting *Emberiza sulphurata* is an uncommon and very local summer visitor to a few prefectures in central Honshu, **Japan**, where it occupies deciduous and mixed deciduous-coniferous forests in low mountains (Sonobe 1982, M. A. Brazil). It winters in eastern **China**, but no details are known (Meyer de Schauensee 1984).

Guadalupe Junco *Junco insularis*, regarded as distinct from Dark-eyed Junco *J. hyemalis* on the basis of voice, morphology and plumage (S. N. G. Howell), is uncommon to fairly common on **Guadalupe Island, (Mexico)**, where once it was abundant (Jehl and Everett 1985), but its habitat is now severely threatened (S. N. G. Howell).

Sierra Madre Sparrow *Xenospiza baileyi* occupies bunch-grass areas, generally in regions of highland pine, in Durango, Jalisco, Morelos and the Distrito Federal, **Mexico** (AOU 1983). It is locally fairly common, but skulking and hard to see; nevertheless its habitat is being cleared and burnt for agriculture (S. N. G. Howell).

Zapata Sparrow *Torreornis inexpectata* occurs in three races in three widely scattered but very restricted localities on **Cuba**, nominate *inexpectata* in the Zapata Swamp, *sigmani* along the arid south-easternmost coast (where it is greatly at risk from fire) and *varonai* on Cayo Coco off the central-north coast (King 1978-1979, Garrido 1985).

Gough Bunting *Rowettia goughensis* is endemic to Gough Island in the **Tristan da Cunha group (to U.K.)**, South Atlantic Ocean, where its 200 pairs are permanently at risk from the introduction of mammalian predators (Collar and Stuart 1985).

Tristan Bunting *Nesospiza acunhae* occurs widely on Inaccessible and Nightingale (also Middle and Stoltenhoff) Islands in the **Tristan da Cunha group (to U.K.)**, South Atlantic Ocean, where its populations (although totalling several thousands) remain at risk from the introduction of mammalian predators (Collar and Stuart 1985).

Grosbeak Bunting *Nesospiza wilkinsi* is restricted to woodland on Inaccessible and Nightingale Islands in the **Tristan da Cunha group (to U.K.)**, South Atlantic Ocean, with a total population in the low hundreds permanently at risk from the introduction of mammalian predators and the loss of its habitat (Collar and Stuart 1985).

Slender-billed Finch *Xenospingus concolor* occurs on the coast and west slope of the Andes of **Peru**, from Lima south to the Tarapaca-Antofagasta border in **Chile** (Meyer de Schauensee 1982). There are still places where it is fairly common (R. A. Hughes) but its riparian habitat is rapidly disappearing (T. A. Parker).

Grey-winged Inca-finch *Incaspiza ortizi* is restricted to montane scrub in the adjacent departments of Piura and Cajamarca, northern **Peru**, where it is uncommon (Parker *et al*. 1982, 1985).

Plain-tailed Warbling-finch *Poospiza alticola* is restricted to montane scrub and *Polylepis* woodland in the adjacent departments of La Libertad and Ancash, western **Peru**, where it is local and uncommon (Meyer de Schauensee 1982, Parker *et al*. 1982). In 1987 a survey of *Polylepis* woodlands in Peru yielded records from only a single site (Fjeldsa 1987).

Rufous-breasted Warbling-finch *Poospiza rubecula* is restricted to montane scrub on both sides of the western cordillera from La Libertad south to Lima, **Peru**, but it is local and rare (Meyer de Schauensee 1982, Parker *et al*. 1982). It remains little known, and its habitat is disappearing (J. Fjeldsa, J. P. O'Neill, R. S. Ridgely).

Cochabamba Mountain-finch *Poospiza garleppi* is restricted to *Polylepis* woodland and adjacent cultivations in Cochabamba, **Bolivia** (Meyer de Schauensee 1982), where it is known from only six localities (J. V. Remsen; also Fjeldsa 1987).

Tucuman Mountain-finch *Poospiza baeri* occupies an extremely small range in bushy valleys at 2,000-3,000 m on the east slope of the Nevada de Aconquija in Tucuman, north-west **Argentina**, although within its habitat it is relatively common and the habitat itself appears as secure as it is impenetrable (Narosky and Yzurieta 1987, M. Nores).

Entre Rios Seedeater *Sporophila zelichi* is restricted to the east-central part of Entre Rios, **Argentina**, where it prefers marshes around crystalline springs, but was never common (Narosky 1977); it may now be very seriously threatened by trappers (T. Narosky, S. Salvador). Its taxonomic status requires evaluation (M. Nores).

Buffy-throated Seedeater *Sporophila frontalis* is (or was) known to occur in large numbers locally in rice-fields and bamboo-flowerings in south-east **Brazil** (Sick 1985), and has been recorded also in eastern **Paraguay** and north-east **Argentina** (Meyer de Schauensee 1966) and, although it has been considered still locally very common (T. A. Parker, D. M. Teixeira, J. Vielliard) it must be in trouble even with moderate deforestation (E. O. Willis) and with heavy trapping (C. E. Carvalho). The species has not been seen at all in Sao Paulo by one long-term field worker (E. O. Willis), but small numbers have recently been recorded from the wild in Rio de Janeiro (C. E. Carvalho, J. F. Pacheco) and Minas Gerais (M. A. Andrade, A. Brandt).

Temminck's Seedeater *Sporophila falcirostris* is a bamboo-flower follower endemic to eastern **Brazil** that must be in trouble even with moderate deforestation (E. O. Willis) and has already been on lists of threatened birds (Greenway 1958, Sick 1969), although it has subsequently been considered common locally

(T. A. Parker, D. M. Teixeira, J. Vielliard). The species has disappeared from certain localities in Sao Paulo (Sick 1985) and has not been seen at all in this state by one long-term field worker (E. O. Willis) but a few individuals have been occasionally encountered in Rio de Janeiro and Bahia (J. F. Pacheco, L. P. Gonzaga).

Tumaco Seedeater *Sporophila insulata* is only known from the type-series collected in 1912 on the then undeveloped shrubby island of Tumaco off the coast of Narino, **Colombia**, where now a large city stands (King 1978-1979, Hilty and Brown 1986).

Rufous-rumped Seedeater *Sporophila hypochroma* occupies extensive grasslands in Santa Cruz and southern Beni, **Bolivia** (Meyer de Schauensee 1982, J. V. Remsen) and is otherwise known from two captive specimens in Corrientes, **Argentina** (M. Nores) and recently from Emas National Park, Southern Goias, **Brazil** (Redford 1987). The species appears to tolerate some grazing (J. V. Remsen), but the pressure on grasslands throughout South America is a source of concern for all species dependent on them (R. S. Ridgely).

Marsh Seedeater *Sporophila palustris*, of grasslands and marshes in **Brazil**, **Paraguay**, **Uruguay** and **Argentina**, is rare (Belton 1985, Sick 1985) and threatened mainly by trapping in Argentina (J. C. Chebez, A. R. M. Gepp, M. Nores and D. Yzurieta). Individuals recorded in central Brazil may be migrants (Sick 1985). There are recent records from Uruguay (R. Vaz-Ferreira).

Chestnut Seedeater *Sporophila cinnamomea* is a rare species, known from Rio Grande do Sul, Mato Grosso, Goias and Minas Gerais, **Brazil** (Sick 1985), east of Villarica, eastern **Paraguay**, and Entre Rios, and Corrientes, **Argentina** (Meyer de Schauensee 1982, M. Nores and D. Yzurieta).

Blackish-blue Seedeater *Amaurospiza moesta* is a local forest species endemic to **Brazil**, east **Paraguay** and north-east **Argentina** (Sick 1985), which has been rarely recorded from Brazil in recent years (Belton 1985, L. dos Anjos, C. E. Carvalho, J. F. Pacheco, P. Scherer Neto, B. M. Whitney, E. O. Willis) but is not yet rare in its limited range in Argentina (J. C, Chebez, M. Nores and D Yzurieta).

St Lucia Black Finch *Melanospiza richardsoni* is endemic to **St Lucia** in the Lesser Antilles, where a recent study found it widespread in all habitats yet, possibly as a result of mongoose *Herpestes auropunctatus* predation on nestlings, everywhere uncommon, with only one concentration of birds (at La Sorciere Forest Reserve) (Trail and Baptista in press, P. W. Trail).

Floreana Tree-finch *Camarhynchus pauper* is endemic to Floreana in the **Galapagos Islands (to Ecuador)**, where it is (or was) common in the highlands and uncommon or rare on the coast (Harris 1982). However, although recently it was asserted that none of the Galapagos finches is known to have become extinct (Grant 1986), one report refers to this species as extinct (D. C. Duffy), another as at best indeterminate, with no recent information (M. H. Wilson).

Mangrove Finch *Camarhynchus heliobates* is restricted to mangrove on two islands, Fernandina and Isabela, in the **Galapagos Islands (to Ecuador)**, where its total population in 1974 was an estimated 100-200 birds (King 1978-1979). There has been no new survey of the species (D. C. Duffy, M. H. Wilson).

Olive-headed Brush-finch *Atlapetes flaviceps*, though reported as not seen since first collected in Tolima, **Colombia**, in 1911 (King 1978-1979), was in fact netted and photographed in northern Huila in December 1967, but this remains the only recent record and the species is apparently very rare (Hilty and Brown 1986).

Pale-headed Brush-finch *Atlapetes pallidiceps* is restricted to scrub in the arid tropical and subtropical zones of Azuay, south-west **Ecuador** (Meyer de Schauensee 1982), where it is at considerable risk from habitat loss (T. A. Parker, R. S. Ridgely).

Tanager-finch *Oreothraupis arremonops* occupies undergrowth in wet mossy forest (cloud-forest) in the Andes of north-west **Ecuador** and two areas of **Colombia**, 1,700-2,500 m (Hilty and Brown 1986), but appears to be very rare (D. A. Scott) with no recent records from Ecuador (R. S. Ridgely) and only one regular site, the western slopes of Cerro Munchique (Hilty and Brown 1986).

Black-masked Finch *Coryphaspiza melanotis* of **Brazil, Bolivia, Paraguay** and **Argentina** is a local, terrestrial bird, apparently restricted to near-virgin grassland, a threatened ecosystem (Sick 1985, T. A. Parker, E. O. Willis).

Yellow Cardinal *Gubernatrix cristata* of **Argentina, Uruguay** and southern **Brazil** has disappeared from or become rare in almost every part of its former range owing to intensive trapping for the pet-trade (F. Achaval, W. Belton, J. C. Chebez, A. R. M. Gepp, M. Nores and D. Yzurieta, T. A. Parker), so that the species was included in Appendix II of Cites in 1987 (*Traffic Bull.* 8,4 [1987]: 4).

Subfamily Thraupinae
Tanagers

Cone-billed Tanager *Conothraupis mesoleuca* seems still to be known only from the type-specimen taken amidst bushy vegetation in dry forest near Cuyaba, Mato Grosso, **Brazil** (Meyer de Schanensee 1982, Isler and Isler 1987).

Yellow-green Bush-tanager *Chlorospingus flavovirens* is an extremely local bird recorded from north-west **Ecuador** in Pichincha province (two specimens) and in Valle, **Colombia**, where it inhabits mossy forest and forest edge at 950-1,050 m (Isler and Isler 1987).

Cherry-throated Tanager *Nemosia rourei* is known only from the type-specimen from **Brazil**, collected in 1870 from the Muriae river region on the north bank of the rio Paraiba do Sul, Rio de Janeiro state, and a flock of eight seen in forest canopy in Jatiboca, Espirito Santo, around 1940 (King 1978-1979, Sick 1979a, Isler and Isler 1987); examination of the type by H. Sick is 1976 indicated that the "Muriae" in question is not, as has been assumed, in Minas Gerais (L. P. Gonzaga).

Black-cheeked Ant-tanager *Habia atrimaxillaris* is known only from the lowlands of south-west **Costa Rica** around the Golfo Dulce region in southern Puntarenas, where it inhabits undergrowth of tall secondary forest and streamside woodlands (Isler and Isler 1987). It is rare, decreasing and not adequately protected (F. G. Stiles).

Sooty Ant-tanager *Habia gutturalis* occupies (often streamside) undergrowth in tall secondary forest and patchy woodland within a restricted range in north-west **Colombia** (Isler and Isler 1987), where it is now judged rare and threatened (S. L. Hilty) despite a report that it might have benefited from forest destruction (Willis 1972).

Black-and-gold Tanager *Buthraupis melanochlamys* occurs at 1,300-2,450 m in humid forest with heavy undergrowth in two small areas of west-central **Colombia** where it is threatened by deforestation (Hilty 1985, Isler and Isler 1987).

Gold-ringed Tanager *Buthraupis aureocincta* is known only from wet mossy forest in the Cerro Tatama and north Valle, **Colombia**, where it is threatened by deforestation (Hilty 1985, Isler and Isler 1987).

Golden-backed Mountain-tanager *Buthraupis aureodorsalis* inhabits patches and islands of elfin forest at 3,150-3,500 m on the east Andean slope from La Libertad to Huanuco, **Peru** (Isler and Isler 1987), and while its habitat is relatively secure its restriction to only a few localities and general low numbers are a source of concern (J. Fjeldsa, J. P. O'Neill).

Green-throated Euphonia *Euphonia chalybea* is endemic to lowland forest, forest edge and old plantations in south-east **Brazil**, eastern **Paraguay** and north-east **Argentina** (Isler and Isler 1987), but appears very little known, being uncommon in Rio Grande do Sul (Belton 1985, R. S. Ridgely) and not encountered at all by one field worker in Sao Paulo state (E. O. Willis). However, small numbers are still to be found in Iguazu National Park in western Parana and north-east Argentina (J. C. Chebez, R. S. Ridgely) and there are recent records also from Itatiaia National Park (J. F. Pacheco) and Serra dos Orgaos National Park in Rio de Janeiro (L. P. Gonzaga).

Multicoloured Tanager *Chlorochrysa nitidissima* is endemic to humid and wet montane forest on both slopes of the Western Andes of **Colombia**, but now has a highly fragmented range owing to extensive habitat clearance (Hilty 1985, Isler and Isler 1987).

Azure-rumped Tanager *Tangara cabanisi* occupies a restricted range in southern **Mexico** and adjacent western **Guatemala**, where it inhabits the canopy of tall humid forest, mostly above 1,200 m (Isler and Isler 1987). A dearth of records before the 1970s led to the species being considered threatened (King 1978- 1979).

Seven-coloured Tanager *Tangara fastuosa* is declining owing to habitat destruction and the cagebird trade in its limited range in north-east **Brazil** (King 1978- 1979), where it inhabits forest and bushy second-growth up to at least 850 m (Isler and Isler 1987).

Green-capped Tanager *Tangara meyerdeschauenseei* is a recently discovered species of semi-arid montane scrub restricted to a single valley in south **Peru** (Schulenberg and Binford 1985).

Black-backed Tanager *Tangara peruviana* is endemic to coastal lowlands (to 600 m) in south-east **Brazil**, where it affects semi-open areas including hedgerows, streamside vegetation, woodland edge and restinga (littoral scrub) (Isler and Isler 1987), yet remains little known and "may be in real danger" (Scott and Brooke 1985).

Sira Tanager *Tangara phillipsi* is a new species known only from the slopes of the Cerros de Sira, Huanuco, **Peru**, at 1,300-1,570 m, where it is a fairly common member of mixed-species flocks in cloud-forest canopy (Graves and Weske 1987).

White-bellied Dacnis *Dacnis albiventris* of the Amazonian lowlands (to 400 m) in south-east **Colombia**, southernmost **Venezuela**, western **Brazil**, eastern **Ecuador** and north-east **Peru** is a rare and local bird within its large range (Isler and Isler 1987, R. S. Ridgely).

Turquoise Dacnis *Dacnis hartlaubi* is rare and local with a very fragmented range on the west slopes of the West, Central and East Andes in **Colombia**, where it inhabits humid forest edge and nearby isolated trees (Isler and Isler 1987, S. L. Hilty).

Black-legged Dacnis *Dacnis nigripes* is endemic to the coastal belt (to 1,000 m) of south-east **Brazil**, where it is scarce and local (apparently with seasonal movements to the lowlands) and found in clearings and old second-growth edge (Gonzaga 1983, Willis and Oniki 1985, Isler and Isler 1987, E. O. Willis).

Scarlet-breasted Dacnis *Dacnis berlepschi* is a rare and local bird of restricted distribution in south-west **Colombia** and north-west **Ecuador**, where it has been encountered at wet forest edge and in tall second-growth (Isler and Isler 1987).

Venezuelan Flowerpiercer *Diglossa venezuelensis* is restricted to cloud-forest, forest edge and shrubbery at 1,600-2,500 m in the coastal cordillera of north- east **Venezuela**, on Cerro Turumiquire in Sucre and at Caripe and on Cerro el Negro in Monagas (Meyer de Schauensee and Phelps 1978), though with a recent (1985) record from Cerro Humo on the Paria Peninsula (M. L. Goodwin *per* B. Swift). All these localities are under severe pressure from cattle-farming and related deforestation (G. Medina Cuervo), and the Cerro el Negro population, despite being within the El Guacharo National Park, is highly threatened (R. Ramirez).

Family Parulidae
New World warblers

Bachman's Warbler *Vermivora bachmanii* is possibly extinct, having bred in south- eastern **U.S.A.** and wintered on **Cuba** and the Isla de Juventud (Isle of Pines) (AOU 1983). Habitat destruction in its restricted breeding and wintering areas is thought to have been responsible for its decline (King 1978-1979), and this is reinforced by speculation that the species was a bamboo-thicket specialist for, although swampy forest is still present, canebrakes of sufficient territorial size have virtually disappeared (Remsen 1986). Climatic factors may also have been significant, particularly those resulting in post-glacial rises in sea levels; the reduced Caribbean winter range may have increased the amplitude of population fluctuations resulting from winter mortality owing to hurricanes (Hamel 1986). In the past decade Bachman's Warbler has been reported from five localities, the most recently confirmed in Florida in 1977 (Barber 1985).

Golden-cheeked Warbler *Dendroica chrysoparia* occupies a very restricted breeding range in central Texas, **U.S.A.**, where it inhabits oak-cedar woodland, and winters in montane pine-oak woodland in **Guatemala**, **Honduras** and **Nicaragua** (AOU 1983) and southern **Mexico** (Braun *et al.* 1986).

Vitelline Warbler *Dendroica vitellina* occurs in three subspecies, nominate *vitellina* on Grand Cayman and race *crawfordi* on Cayman Brac and Little Cayman, **Cayman Islands (to U.K.)**, both of which are locally common (Bradley 1985), and race *nelsoni* on Big Swan and Little **Swan Islands (Honduras)**, which is or was common on both (Monroe 1968). However, the species is threatened throughout the Caymans by proposed habitat conversion (P. Bradley) and in 1987 the Swan Islands were being utilized for the training of Nicaraguan counter-revolutionaries (S. Thorn).

Kirtland's Warbler *Dendroica kirtlandii* has a severely restricted breeding distribution in jack-pine woods in Michigan, **U.S.A.**, and has also been recorded in **Canada**, wintering in the **Bahama Islands** and the **Turks and Caicos Islands (to U.K.)**; breeding success has been reduced because of brood-parasitism by the Brown-headed Cowbird *Molothrus ater* (King 1978-1979). Cowbird control has not resulted in a significant increase in the warbler population, which had remained at an average of 207 singing males for 10 years (Kelly and DeCapita 1982), and in 1987 only 167 singing males were located (Weinrich 1987). Other factors which have contributed to the species's decline include habitat matura-tion and fragmentation, pairing success, fledging mortality and breeding disper-sal (Probst 1986). Pairing success may be particularly important in revising past productivity estimates: many males in marginal habitat do not pair successfully, thus possibly retarding the recovery of the population, and improving the quality of the habitat may therefore be a crucial factor in the management of the species (Probst and Hayes 1987).

Whistling Warbler *Catharopeza bishopi* is restricted to **St Vincent**, where it is sparse and localized in forest areas at higher levels (M. G. Kelsey).

Altamira Yellowthroat *Geothlypis flavovelata* is resident in marshes in southern Tamaulipas, extreme eastern San Luis Potosi and northern Veracruz, **Mexico**, (AOU 1983). However, its populations are all too small to be considered viable, except that in Laguna Champayan, Altamira (Tamaulipas), where the species is reasonably abundant; but industrial development is seriously affecting the Altamira region, with much drainage in the past 20 years, and the future of Laguna Champayan is uncertain (P. Escalante).

Black-polled Yellowthroat *Geothlypis speciosa* is resident in the highland marshes and wetlands of eastern Michoacan (Lago Patzcuaro, Lago Cuitzeo), southern Guanajuato (Lago Yuriria, Presa Solis), Mexico state (upper rio Lerma, Lago Zumpango) and Distrito Federal (Lago Texcoco), **Mexico** (AOU 1983). Only Lagos Patzcuaro, Cuitzeo and Yuriria are known to continue to hold the species, but are very shallow lakes that undergo drastic changes in water level; there is government interest in the conservation of Lago Cuitzeo, but no action has yet been taken (P. Escalante).

Semper's Warbler *Leucopeza semperi* remains endangered on **St Lucia**, where as a forest understorey bird it is suspected of having fallen victim to the introduced mongoose *Herpestes auropunctatus*, with a last sighting in 1972 (King 1978-1979). A concerted 10-day search with mist-nets in the forests around Piton Flore in 1987 produced no evidence of its survival (P. Wood).

Yellow-faced Redstart *Myioborus pariae* is endemic to the Paria Peninsula, north- west **Venezuela**, where it inhabits humid cloud-forest at 800-1,200 m on Cerro Humo and Cerro Azul (Meyer de Schauensee and Phelps 1978). It is common within this habitat, but human pressure in the region is intense and the species is greatly at risk (G. Medina Cuervo).

Grey-headed Warbler *Basileuterus griseiceps* occupies a narrow altidudinal band (1,200-1,600 m) in cloud-forest and second-growth on the coastal cordillera in three states of northern **Venezuela** (Meyer de Schauensee and Phelps 1978), where it is threatened by habitat destruction (G. Medina Cuervo).

Grey-throated Warbler *Basileuterus cinereicollis* has two subspecies: *pallidus* from the subtropical zone of extreme western **Venezuela** and north-east **Colombia**, *cinereicollis* from the subtropical zone of the eastern Andes of Colombia from Santander del Norte south to Meta (Peters 1968). There is practically no recent information on this bird, which may now be rare in much of its range owing to habitat loss (Hilty and Brown 1986, S. L. Hilty).

White-winged Ground-warbler *Xenoligea montana* is restricted to woods and thickets in the mountains of **Haiti** and **Dominican Republic** (Bond 1979), but is now greatly at risk from habitat loss in Haiti (Woods and Ottenwalder undated) and is vulnerable though more widespread in the Dominican Republic, being dependent on certain species of tree (A. Stockton de Dod).

Pearly-breasted Conebill *Conirostrum margaritae* of north-east **Peru** (Loreto) and western Amazonian **Brazil** is threatened by the destruction of its varzea (seasonably flooded forest) habitat through developing pulpwood industries (A. D. Johns, T. A. Parker; see Remsen and Parker 1983).

Tamarugo Conebill *Conirostrum tamarugense* is found in the high shrub zone of southern **Peru** and northern **Chile** (see Mayr and Vuilleumier 1983), where locally common (D. A. Scott) although possibly linked ecologically to *Prosopis* trees, much exploited for firewood in mines (J. C. Torres-Mura); moreover, the species may only breed in a few patches of *Polylepis/Gynoxis* scrub, the only such patch known for it being about 5 ha (J. Fjeldsa).

Family Drepanididae
Hawaiian honeycreepers

Akepa *Loxops coccineus* is known from Oahu (considered extinct by King 1978-1979), Maui (rare and patchily distributed above 1,100 m on Haleakala) and Hawaii (locally common) in the **Hawaiian Islands (to U.S.A.)** (Pratt *et al.* 1987).

Akikiki *Oreomystis bairdi* is restricted to the high-elevation rainforest of the Alakai swamp area on Kauai, **Hawaiian Islands (to U.S.A.)** (King 1978-1979), where it is uncommon (Pratt *et al.* 1987).

Kakawahie *Paroreomyza flammea* is endemic to Molokai in the **Hawaiian Islands (to U.S.A.)**, where it was once common and widespread, but has suffered a catastrophic drop in numbers this century and was last seen in 1963, so is probably extinct (King 1978-1979, Pratt *et al.* 1987).

Oahu Creeper *Paroreomyza maculata* is endemic to Oahu in the **Hawaiian Islands (to U.S.A.)** and is now extremely rare, last reported in the Koolau Mountains (King 1978-1979, Pratt *et al.* 1987).

Akialoa *Hemignathus obscurus* was known from all of the larger **Hawaiian Islands (to U.S.A.)** except Maui; it had been extirpated on most islands early this century, the Kauai form surviving into the 1960s in the Alakai Swamp, but is now possibly extinct (King 1978-1979, Pratt *et al.* 1987).

Nukupuu *Hemignathus lucidus* is endemic to the **Hawaiian Islands (to U.S.A.)** where it is extinct on Oahu and has probably already disappeared from the Alakai Swamp on Kauai, but a small population was discovered in 1967 on the northeast slope of Haleakala on Maui (King 1978-1979). It was also reported recently from Kohala on Hawaii (Pratt *et al.* 1987).

Akiapolaau *Hemignathus munroi* is endemic to Hawaii in the **Hawaiian Islands (to U.S.A.)** where it was formerly widespread on the island but is now restricted to fragments of forest; an estimated 1,500 individuals survive, mostly in the Kau Forest Reserve and the upper Hamakua area (King 1978-1979, Pratt *et al.* 1987).

Maui Parrotbill *Pseudonestor xanthophrys* is endemic to Maui in the **Hawaiian Islands (to U.S.A.)** where it is found on the eastern slopes of Haleakala between 1,200 and 2,150 m; a recent survey estimated the population to be about 500 individuals (King 1978-1979, Pratt *et al.* 1987).

Ou *Psittirostra psittacea* was known from Kauai, Oahu, Molokai, Lanai, Maui and Hawaii in the **Hawaiian Islands (to U.S.A.)**; it now occurs locally in the Alakai Swamp at about 1,200 m on Kauai (King 1978-1979), and between 1,300 and 1,500 m in the Hamakua on Hawaii; the population on Hawaii is estimated at 400 but is noticeably declining (Pratt *et al.* 1987).

Nihoa Finch *Telespyza ultima* is endemic to Nihoa in the **Hawaiian Islands (to U.S.A.)**; it is common but the island has an area of 0.64 sq km (King 1978-1979) and an attempted introduction to French Frigate Shoals failed (Pratt *et al.* 1987).

Laysan Finch *Telespyza cantans* is confined to Laysan in the **Hawaiian Islands**

(to U.S.A.) with small numbers persisting on Hermes and Pearl Atoll from an introduction in 1967; it is said to have survived the defoliation of Laysan caused by rabbits (and resulting in the elimination of the Millerbird *Acrocephalus familiaris*) by feeding on seabird eggs; it has also been introduced to Midway Island but the population succumbed to rats (Pratt *et al.* 1987).

Palila *Loxioides bailleui* is restricted to Hawaii in the **Hawaiian Islands (to U.S.A.)**; it was abundant though locally distributed until the turn of the century (King 1978-1979), but is now confined to the upper slopes, between 2,000 and 3,000 m, on Mauna Kea; the population apparently fluctuates between 2,000 and 6,000 individuals (Pratt *et al.* 1987). Breeding data are in van Riper (1980), population and habitat data in Scott *et al.* (1984).

Poo Uli *Melamprosops phaeosoma* was discovered in 1973 in the Koolau Forest Reserve on the north-eastern flanks of Haleakala on Maui in the **Hawaiian Islands (to U.S.A.)**; it is rare in the remote forest of the type-locality between 1,500 and 2,000 m (King 1978-1979, Pratt *et al.* 1987).

Crested Honeycreeper *Palmeria dolei* is known from Maui and Molokai in the **Hawaiian Islands (to U.S.A.)**; it is probably extinct on Molokai where it was last observed in 1907, but is still locally common between 1,800 and 2,150 m on the eastern slopes of Haleakala on Maui (King 1978-1979, Pratt *et al.* 1987).

Family Vireonidae
Vireos

Black-capped Vireo *Vireo atricapillus* breeds in Oklahoma and Texas, U.S.A., and northern **Mexico**, and winters in western Mexico (AOU 1983). A key element in the decline of the species (fewer than 30 pairs in Oklahoma) appears to be brood- parasitism by the Brown-headed Cowbird *Molothrus ater*, as well as difficulty in obtaining mates and the need for stimulation from conspecific birds nearby to continue nesting throughout the season (Grzybowski *et al.* 1986). The last stronghold for the species may be the Edward's Plateau, Texas, where continuous brushland is less suitable feeding habitat for Brown-headed Cowbirds and parasitism is less severe (Collar 1986b).

Family Icteridae
New World blackbirds and orioles, cowbirds

Chestnut-mantled Oropendola *Psarocolius cassini* remains known from only three specimens in the humid lowlands of northern Choco, north-west **Colom-**

bia, where (if it is a good species) it is evidently rare and local (Hilty and Brown 1986, S. L. Hilty).

Para Oropendola *Psarocolius bifasciatus* appears to be restricted to a relatively small area (Rio Tocantins to east of Sao Luis, Maranhao) in northern **Brazil**, where it is uncommon or fairly common even in disturbed habitats (A. D. Johns, P. Roth) but vulnerable to agricultural clearance (A. D. Johns, J. M. C. da Silva).

Selva Cacique *Cacicus koepckeae* appears to remain known only from humid low- lying forest at the type-locality at Balta, rio Curanja, in Loreto, eastern **Peru** (Meyer de Schauensee 1982, Parker *et al.* 1982).

Martinique Oriole *Icterus bonana* is endemic to **Martinique (to France)**, where it is most numerous in the semi-arid hills of the southern half of the island (Bond 1979). In 1986 a survey of the species indicated that it occurs in four forest types on the island (mangrove, dry, moist and rain-, but not cloud-forest) but that it has declined, not owing to habitat loss or hunting, but to extensive brood-parasitism by the recently established Shiny Cowbird *Molothrus bonariensis*, a species that requires urgent control (Wood 1987).

Montserrat Oriole *Icterus oberi* is endemic to **Montserrat (to U.K.)**, where it inhabits forested mountain slopes down to 800 m (Bond 1979). In 1984 it was found to be commonest in wet forests but present over a wide altitudinal and ecological range; nevertheless, it is threatened by unchecked habitat destruction (Faaborg and Arendt 1985).

Saffron-cowled Blackbird *Xanthopsar flavus* of bushy marshes amongst grass-lands in southern **Brazil, Uruguay, Paraguay, Bolivia** and **Argentina** is vulnerable to habitat transformation for grazing and agriculture and has suffered a major decline, being restricted now to only a few localities (F. Achaval, J. C. Chebez, M. Nores and D. Yzurieta, T. A. Parker, M. Rumboll). In 1987, however, it was fairly abundant in part of Uruguay (R. Vaz-Ferreira).

Yellow-shouldered Blackbird *Agelaius xanthomus*, from **Puerto Rico (to U.S.A.)**, has two subspecies, both gravely threatened: nominate *xanthomus* from the main islands of Puerto Rico has declined because of wetland drainage, predation by rats, nest competition from Pearly-eyed Thrashers *Margarops fuscatus*, and brood- parasitism by Shiny Cowbirds *Molothrus bonariensis*; the race *monensis* from adjacent Mona Island is threatened by development plans and potential brood- parasitism (King 1978-1979). The total population in 1982 on Puerto Rico was estimated to be about 720 birds with recruitment below that needed for population maintenance, and on Mona Island between 220-500 birds (U.S. Fish and Wildlife Service 1983).

Pampas Meadowlark *Sturnella defilippi* of south **Brazil, Uruguay** and **Argentina**

occurs sporadically in Parana (Sick 1985) and is extremely rare in Rio Grande do Sul (Belton 1985) and Argentina (J. C. Chebez, M. Nores and D. Yzurieta), where the causes of its apparent decline are not known (J. C. Chebez). Its habitat includes native open grassland with thickets and cultivated fields, within which its distribution is clumped (Gochfeld 1978, Sick 1985).

Red-bellied Grackle *Hypopyrrhus pyrohypogaster* is a rare and local bird of humid forest canopy in the foothills and mountains of central and south-east **Colombia**, where it has suffered seriously from deforestation (Hilty 1985, Hilty and Brown 1986).

Forbes's Blackbird *Curaeus forbesi* is restricted to marshes along forest edge at three localities in eastern **Brazil** (J. Vielliard; also L. P. Gonzaga) and, although one of these is Rio Doce State Park (M. A. Andrade), the species remains vulnerable to habitat destruction and cowbird parasitism (J. Vielliard).

Bronze-brown Cowbird *Molothrus armenti* is restricted to a very small area of the north coast of **Colombia**, with the majority of its population in the Isla de Salamanca National Park (Hilty and Brown 1986). This park is now being destroyed by a road and by mangrove die-off owing to a mismanaged water regime in the Cienaga Grande (J. Botero).

Family Fringillidae
Grosbeaks, finches

Blue Chaffinch *Fringilla teydea*, from the **Canary Islands (to Spain)**, occupies the pine forest regions of Tenerife (nominate *teydea*) and Gran Canaria (race *polatzeki*) and is in decline on the latter (Collar and Stuart 1985; see also Martin 1987). Anomalous nesting in laurel forest on the Anaga Peninsula has been claimed (de Naurois 1986). The piping of water from forested slopes, which in the early 1960s was judged to be reducing the number of the species's drinking places in high summer (see Collar and Stuart 1985), has now resulted in all streams running dry on Gran Canaria with the consequent extinction of an endemic blackfly (*Oryx* 21 [1987]: 205); the consequence for *polatzeki* may ultimately be the same, although there are still several viable drinking places that it uses (A. Martin).

Ankober Serin *Serinus ankoberensis* is a small, cliff-frequenting, montane finch, as yet known only from a single small area around Ankober, Shoa province, eastern **Ethiopia** (Collar and Stuart 1985).

Yellow-throated Serin *Serinus flavigula* remains known from three century-old specimens taken in one small area of Shoa province, eastern **Ethiopia** and requires new searches to confirm its survival (Collar and Stuart 1985).

Sao Tome Grosbeak *Neospiza concolor*, a remarkable bird of uncertain affinities, is known only from three nineteenth-century specimens from forest in southern Sao Tome, **Sao Tome e Principe** (Collar and Stuart 1985). It was not encountered in a recent survey of the island (Jones and Tye 1988).

Yellow-faced Siskin *Carduelis yarrellii* of northern **Venezuela** and north-eastern **Brazil** is scarce in the former (M. L. Goodwin) and very restricted in the latter (Sick 1985) where it is common locally but greatly trapped (A. G. Coelho, C. E. Carvalho, R. Otoch).

Red Siskin *Carduelis cucullata*, a semi-nomadic finch which formerly occupied a continuous range across northern Venezuela into north-eastern Colombia, with isolated populations on the islands of Gasparee, Monos and Trinidad, has a much reduced distribution in the northern cordilleras of **Venezuela**, with an estimated total population of 600-800 birds in 1981 (Coats and Phelps 1985). The species has suffered from long-term exploitation because of the popularity of the male as a cage-bird, and the ease of hybridization with the domestic canary to introduce genes for red plumage (King 1978-1979). Populations on several Caribbean islands, probably descendants of captive birds, have been systematically poached (Amos 1985/1986) although the escaped population on **Puerto Rico (to U.S.A.)** may once have outnumbered the indigenous population (Raffaele 1983); the status of the species on **Cuba** is unknown (Garrido and Garcia 1975). The species is legally protected, but trapping continues and is even more deleterious as aviculturists are now breeding Red Siskin in their own right and both males and females are sought (Frey 1985).

Saffron Siskin *Carduelis siemiradzkii* has a very small range in arid scrub in Guayaquil and on Puna Island, south-west **Ecuador** (Meyer de Schauensee 1982). It also occurs in deciduous forest in the region and is definitely at risk there (R. S. Ridgely), but may also occur in north-east Peru (Wiedenfeld *et al.* 1985).

Warsangli Linnet *Acanthis johannis*, recorded from five sites (numerous only in one: Daloh Forest Reserve, Erigavo) in two small areas of the northern **Somalia** highlands, occurs in both open country and juniper forest, but its long-term security depends on fuller knowledge of its needs (Collar and Stuart 1985).

Family Estrildidae
Waxbills

Anambra Waxbill *Estrilda poliopareia* occurs in long grass and herbage along rivers and on lagoon sandbanks in southern **Nigeria**, where it remains known from only a few localities (Collar and Stuart 1985).

Black-lored Waxbill *Estrilda nigriloris* is restricted to level grassy plains around the Lualaba River and Lake Upemba in southern **Zaire**, where its status requires elucidation (Collar and Stuart 1985).

Green Munia *Estrilda formosa* is a very local and unevenly distributed resident of central **India** (Ali and Ripley 1984). There are isolated records from Lahore, **Pakistan**, and Delhi and Lucknow, and it is possible that a scattered population exists north of the Vindhyas (Gaston and Macrell 1980). It affects grassland, cane and scrub jungle (Ali and Ripley 1984), but no reason for the species's scarcity has been suggested (Gaston 1984).

Green-faced Parrotfinch *Erythrura viridifacies* is known to occur in the vicinity of Manila on Luzon in the **Philippines**, congregating where grasses or bamboos are seeding and has been observed in savanna, at the forest edge and in bamboo (Goodwin 1982). The nest has not been described and its status is unknown (R. S. Kennedy).

Mindanao Parrotfinch *Erythrura coloria* is known from Mt Katanglad and Mt Apo, on Mindanao, in the **Philippines** (Goodwin 1982, Dickinson *et al.* in press). It affects forest, the few recent records being from above 1,000 m (R. S. Kennedy); the status of the species is unknown but damage to the forest on Mt Apo has been extensive and is continuing (Cox 1988).

Pink-billed Parrotfinch *Erythrura kleinschmidti* is endemic to Viti Levu, **Fiji**, where it is largely confined to the Nadrau Plateau; it has always been considered rare (King 1978-1979) but it is probably more widespread than previously thought and there are records from secondary scrub (Watling 1982) and plantations (Hay 1986).

Family Ploceidae

Subfamily Ploceinae
Weavers

Bannerman's Weaver *Ploceus bannermani* occupies forest-edge habitat in a few montane areas of western **Cameroon**, chiefly in the Bamenda Highlands and notably at Mount Oku, and of eastern **Nigeria**, notably on the Obudu Plateau; while relatively common, its habitat is steadily disappearing (Collar and Stuart 1985; also Stuart and Jensen 1986, Wilson in press).

Bates's Weaver *Ploceus batesi* is a rarely recorded species from lowland rainforest in southern **Cameroon**, where it remains known from only a few localities (Collar and Stuart 1985).

Black-chinned Weaver *Ploceus nigrimentum* occurs very sparsely above 1,500 m in the Bailundu Highlands of western **Angola** (one post-1927 observation or set of observations) and on the Baleke Plateau (750 m) in **Congo** (one record in November 1951) (Collar and Stuart 1985).

Loango Slender-billed Weaver *Ploceus subpersonatus* is known only from the coastal strip from **Gabon** and **Zaire** (no records yet from Congo) into Cabinda (**Angola**) and remains little known (Collar and Stuart 1985). It has recently been studied in Gabon, where it appears to be thinly spread in suitable habitat (swamp-forest, savanna) along the coast, without any obvious threats (P. D. Alexander-Marrack).

Lake Lufira Weaver *Ploceus ruweti* is restricted to the swamps bordering Lake Lufira in southern **Zaire**, with no recent information on its status (Collar and Stuart 1985).

Clarke's Weaver *Ploceus golandi* is known only from the Arabuko-Sokoke Forest in south-east **Kenya**, where illegal but persistent logging is taking place (Collar and Stuart 1985, 1988).

Golden-naped Weaver *Ploceus aureonucha* has been found only in a small part of the Ituri Forest, north of Beni in eastern **Zaire**, where up to the mid-1980s it had not been seen since 1926 (Collar and Stuart 1985), until encountered several times during 1986, once in a flock of up to 60 birds, in forest edge in the Beni region (*World Birdwatch* 8,3 [1986]: 5; 9,1 [1987]: 5).

Finn's Baya Weaver *Ploceus megarhynchus* is a very local resident of Uttar Pradesh in northern **India**, and West Bengal and Assam in north-eastern India; it affects seasonally inundated grassland and marshes, particularly tree-dotted expanses of *Imperata arundinacea* and *Saccharum spontaneum* grasslands and marshes (Ali and Ripley 1984).

Yellow-legged Weaver *Ploceus flavipes* is known only from the Ituri Forest in eastern **Zaire** where it appears to be rare and up to the mid-1980s had not been seen since 1953 (Collar and Stuart 1985), but it has recently been recorded regularly (J. Hart, T. Hart). A specimen from Lima, taken in 1959, has recently come to light and represents a new locality for the species in Ituri (Louette 1988).

Tanzanian Mountain Weaver *Ploceus nicolli*, a low-density forest species, inhabits the East and West Usambara Mountains (nominate *nicolli*) and the Uluguru and Uzungwa Mountains (race *anderseni*), **Tanzania**, and is under some threat from forest destruction (Collar and Stuart 1985). An IUCN project aimed at reconciling land-use pressures in the Usambaras (Stuart 1986) is currently underway (N. M. Collins).

Entebbe Weaver *Ploceus victoriae* is a new species known only from Entebbe, **Uganda**, where it is "undoubtedly rare" and encountered on only a few occasions, February 1983 - January 1984) (Ash 1986; also Ash 1987a, Louette 1987).

Ibadan Malimbe *Malimbus ibadanensis* seems likely to be seriously threatened by the massive habitat destruction that has occurred within its small range in south-western **Nigeria**, where the most recent records are from forest patches around Ibadan (Collar and Stuart 1985). In November 1987 four birds, including a male feeding a juvenile, were observed in secondary woodland in Ibadan, but this was the only record in ten days intensive searching, suggesting that the species has indeed become very rare (Ash 1987b).

Gola Malimbe *Malimbus ballmanni* is confined to the Upper Guinea forest block in **Ivory Coast** (one record north-west of Tai), eastern **Liberia** (Grand Gedeh County) and **Sierra Leone** (Gola Forest), and is at great risk from the massive forest clearance within its range (Collar and Stuart 1985).

Mauritius Fody *Foudia rubra* suffered catastrophically from the clearance of its upland forest habitat in south-west **Mauritius** in the 1970s, and continues to sustain heavy nest losses to introduced predators (Collar and Stuart 1985; see also Cheke 1987a).

Seychelles Fody *Foudia sechellarum* survives on three rat-free islands, Cousin, Cousine and Fregate, in the **Seychelles**, but may still face competition and predation from introduced birds (Collar and Stuart 1985). The population on Cousin was around 1,300 birds in the late 1970s (Brooke 1985).

Rodrigues Fody *Foudia flavicans* survives in a small area on the northern slopes of Rodrigues, **Mauritius**; in 1983 approximately 100 birds survived in patches of mixed evergreen forest, facing possible annihilation by a cyclone and several new threats from introduced predators and competitors (Collar and Stuart 1985; see also Cheke 1987c).

Family Sturnidae
Starlings

Santo Mountain Starling *Aplonis santovestris* is endemic to Espiritu Santo, **Vanuatu**, and restricted to forest above 1,000 m in the interior of the island (King 1978-1979). The type and a second specimen were collected at 1,300 m on

Vutimele in 1934 and a third specimen was taken a year earlier on Tabwemasana (Pickering 1985). The only subsequent observations of the species, by H. L. Bregulla, were in the mid-1970s in cloud-forest undergrowth above the abandoned village of Nokovula on Tabwemasana, and several other searches, including one in 1985, have failed to find it, although habitat remains intact (Pickering 1985).

Pohnpei Mountain Starling *Aplonis pelzelni* is restricted to the montane forest of Pohnpei, **Federated States of Micronesia (to U.S.A.)** and has declined drastically since 1932, when 59 specimens were collected (King 1978-1979). It was apparently once widespread on the island but the last specimen was taken in 1956 and it was not located in a survey conducted in 1983; the interior of the island is still forested and no convincing reason can be found for the species's disappearance (Engbring and Pratt 1983).

Rarotonga Starling *Aplonis cinerascens* is restricted to the forested interior of Rarotonga in the **Cook Islands (to New Zealand)**; it was regarded as abundant early this century and still not uncommon in 1973, but conservative estimates made in 1984 put the population at 100 (Hay 1986).

Abbott's Starling *Cinnyricinclus femoralis* is known from a few mountain forests in **Kenya**, including Mount Kenya National Park, and **Tanzania**, including Arusha National Park and Mount Kilimanjaro National Park, but the Arusha population may be only seasonal in occurrence and those in the other two may be subject to decline from habitat destruction (Collar and Stuart 1985). However, the species is now also known from and common (flocks of up to 40) in Kikuyu Escarpment Forest (southern Aberdares), Kenya, being present throughout the year (Taylor and Taylor in press).

Bali Starling *Leucopsar rothschildi* is endemic to Bali, **Indonesia**, and confined to a small area of deciduous forest and acacia savanna on the island's extreme north-western tip (King 1978-1979). The area is now a national park but trapping for the cage-bird trade, the chief threat to the species, was prevalent in 1982 (Ash 1984). In 1984 the wild population was estimated to be between 125 and 180 individuals (van Helvoort 1987) and by 1988 it had further declined to less than 100 birds, possibly as few as 55 (B. van Helvoort). However, there is a considerable captive population in the world's zoos, and ICBP, in collaboration with the Indonesian government and American and English zoos, launched a three-year programme in 1987 to enhance the wild population on Bali and establish a captive-breeding programme in Indonesia with a view to reintroduction (M. R. W. Rands).

Helmeted Myna *Basilornis galeatus* is known from the Banggai and Sula Islands, **Indonesia** (White and Bruce 1986). It was located in heavily disturbed forest on Banggai in the 1980s (K. D. Bishop), but its status on the other islands is unknown.

Bare-eyed Myna *Streptocitta albertinae* is found on the Sula Islands, **Indonesia** (White and Bruce 1986). The status of the species and its habitat are unknown.

Family Oriolidae
Orioles

Isabella Oriole *Oriolus isabellae* has been collected in the mountains of northern Luzon in the **Philippines**, where it is threatened by destruction of its forest habitat (R. S. Kennedy, T. H. Fisher).

Silver Oriole *Oriolus mellianus* breeds in **China**, in northern Guangdong, in Guangxi in the Yao Shan, and in Sichuan, and winters south, but rarely, to southeast **Thailand** and **Kampuchea** (Meyer de Schauensee 1984); in 1987 it was recorded from Ba Boa Shan, Guangdong, in forest that is scheduled for logging within three years, but in no other reserve in the province (P. R. Kennerley); it occurs in remnant broadleaf forest in south Sichuan but is threatened by deforestation (King and Li Guiyian in press), and on Emei Shan (B. F. King).

Family Dicruridae
Drongos

Grand Comoro Drongo *Dicrurus fuscipennis* has a highly localised distribution within the 500-900 m altitudinal zone around Mount Karthala, Grand Comoro, **Comoro Islands**, and is everywhere rare (Collar and Stuart 1985). In 1985 it was concluded that little more than 100 birds exist, but because they appear to prefer forest edge they are probably at no great risk (Louette *et al.* 1986).

Mayotte Drongo *Dicrurus waldeni* is sparsely and locally distributed in forest on **Mayotte (to France)** in the Comoros (Collar and Stuart 1985). It is now restricted to areas with large trees and descends nowhere below 200 m (Louette *et al.* 1986).

Family Callaeidae
New Zealand wattlebirds

Kokako *Callaeas cinerea* from **New Zealand** has suffered from predation by introduced mammals, competition for food from exotic herbivores and destruction of forest (King 1978-1979, Williams and Given 1981, Hay *et al.* 1985). The

South Island race *cinerea* has recently been rediscovered on Stewart Island but numbers are not known (B. D. Bell). The North Island race *wilsoni* has a fragmented and declining range, and is vulnerable to habitat destruction and deterioration (O'Donnell 1984). Several pairs have been transferred to Little Barrier Island where they are known to have bred (B. D. Bell).

Saddleback *Creadion carunculatus* inhabits coastal scrub forest and understorey vegetation in **New Zealand**; after the introduction of predators, the range of the North Island race *rufusater* contracted to Hen Island, and that of the South Island race *carunculatus* to three islets off Stewart Island; reintroductions to other islands have proved successful (King 1978-1979) and resulted in an increase in population to about 2,000 *rufusater* and 300 *carunculatus* (Williams and Given 1981).

Family Ptilonorhynchidae
Bowerbirds

Golden-fronted Bowerbird *Amblyornis flavifrons* was until recently known only from the three or four specimens of unknown provenance, acquired from a plume dealer in 1895 (Schodde 1978). It is now known to occur in the Foya Mountains in north Irian Jaya, **Indonesia**, in forest between 1,000 and 2,000 m (Diamond 1982, Beehler *et al.* 1986); it occurs at reasonable density in a restricted but inaccessible area and is not immediately threatened (J. M. Diamond).

Adelbert Bowerbird *Sericulus bakeri* inhabits montane forest in the Adelbert Mountains in north-west **Papua New Guinea**, where it is fairly common within its very restricted range (only 1,200 sq km: R. D. Mackay) (Rand and Gilliard 1967), but occupies a narrow altitudinal band of between 900 and 1,400 m and is replaced at higher altitudes by the widespread Macgregor's Bowerbird *Amblyornis macgregoriae* (Beehler *et al.* 1986). Although the range is not heavily populated, local villagers rely on hunting (R. D. Mackay).

Family Paradisaeidae
Birds of paradise

Long-tailed Paradigalla *Paradigalla carunculata* occurs in the Arfak Mountains, in the Vogelkop, and in the western Snow Mountains, Irian Jaya, **Indonesia** (Beehler *et al.* 1986). It is poorly known (Rand and Gilliard 1967) and apparently rare, though no reason for its scarcity is known. Beehler (1985) suggests that it might be an unsuccessful member of a species pair, for the very similar Short-tailed Paradigalla *P. brevicauda* is widely distributed in western and central New Guinea.

Black Sicklebill *Epimachus fastuosus* is patchily distributed in the mountains of western and central New Guinea, from the Tamrau and Arfak Mountains in Vogelkop, Irian Jaya, **Indonesia**, to the Kubor and Kratke ranges and a few localities in the Torricelli and Bewani mountains in **Papua New Guinea** (Rand and Gilliard 1967, B. M. Beehler). It is the largest plumed member of its family and is much hunted both for its tail feathers and for food (Beehler 1985).

Ribbon-tailed Astrapia *Astrapia mayeri* is known from montane forest between 2,400 and 3,400 m in the central mountains of **Papua New Guinea**, from Mt Hagen and Mt Giluwe and approximately 130 km further west, although the western limits of its range are unclear (Beehler *et al.* 1986). Beehler (1985) considers hybridization with, and competition from Stephanie's Astrapia *A. stephaniae* as threatening *mayeri* at the eastern end of its range although Schodde (1978) had argued against this view; but in any case the species is threatened by habitat destruction and hunting (J. M. Diamond).

Wahnes's Parotia *Parotia wahnesi* is known from the mountains of the Huon Peninsula and the Adelbert Mountains, **Papua New Guinea** (Beehler *et al.* 1986). It is rarely hunted but apparently requires primary forest on valley floors at 1,200 to 1,800 m which are the optimum altitudes for indigenous agriculture and settlement (Schodde 1978).

Goldie's Bird Of Paradise *Paradisaea decora* is restricted to Fergusson and Normanby in the East Papuan Islands, **Papua New Guinea**, where it is found in forest and at forest edge on ridges and is apparently limited to an altitudinal range of between 300 and at least 700 m (Beehler *et al.* 1986; G. R. Kula). It is not known to visit native gardens, even those abandoned and overgrown, and the preservation of undisturbed forest is essential to the species (LeCroy *et al.* 1984).

Family Corvidae
Crows

Beautiful Jay *Cyanolyca pulchra* is rare and local in wet mossy forest, forest edge and taller second-growth, 900-2,300 m, on the Pacific slope of western **Colombia** and north-east **Ecuador** (Hilty and Brown 1986, R. S. Ridgely).

Dwarf Jay *Cyanolyca nana* is resident in humid montane pine-oak and fir forest in the mountains of Veracruz, Puebla and Oaxaca, southern **Mexico**, although it may now be restricted to Oaxaca (AOU 1983). The habitat with this restricted range is being logged out (S. N. G. Howell, T. A. Parker).

White-throated Jay *Cyanolyca mirabilis* is resident in humid pine-oak and probably montane forest in the mountains of Guerrero (Sierra Madre del Sur) and Oaxaca (Sierra de Miahuatlan and Sierra de Yucuyacua), **Mexico** (AOU 1983). The habitat within this restricted range is being cleared and grazed out rapidly (S. N. G. Howell).

Azure Jay *Cyanocorax caeruleus* of south-east **Brazil** and northern **Argentina** is in steep decline, extremely rare in Argentina (M. Nores) and now apparently in satisfactory numbers only in Rio Grande do Sul and Parana (R. S. Ridgely, P. Scherer Neto).

Sichuan Grey Jay *Perisoreus internigrans* is endemic to the spruce and pine forests of the mountains of central **China** (Meyer de Schauensee 1984). It is found in north-west Sichuan and east Qinghai (Goodwin 1976), usually above 3,000 m, and is now thought to be rare (C. R. Robson); there is one recent record from Jiuzhaigou, Sichuan (B. F. King).

Sri Lanka Magpie *Urocissa ornata* is endemic to **Sri Lanka**, in wet forest, from the foothills to over 2,000 m (Ali and Ripley 1984) and is disappearing from areas in which it was formerly found, probably owing to the degradation of native forest by wood collectors and villagers; timber monocultures do not appear to support the species (Hoffmann 1984, S. Kotagama).

Hooded Treepie *Crypsirina cucullata* was a common bird of the dry zone of central **Burma** (Smythies 1986), but its woodland habitat has been disappearing and the species is no longer to be found near Mandalay (B. F. King).

Ethiopian Bush-crow *Zavattariornis stresemanni*, remarkable both for its habits (possibly a cooperative breeder) and for its uncertain affinities (probably a crow, possibly a starling), is confined to around 6,000 sq km of park-like thorn-bush and short-grass savanna around Yavello and Mega, southern **Ethiopia**, and could easily suffer from habitat alteration (Collar and Stuart 1985).

Banggai Crow *Corvus unicolor* is endemic to Banggai in the Banggai Islands, **Indonesia**, and known from two specimens; its status is unknown but the widespread and common Slender-billed Crow *C. enca* might have replaced *unicolor* in the more disturbed lowland areas (White and Bruce 1986).

Flores Crow *Corvus florensis* is endemic to Flores, **Indonesia**, and known from few specimens (White and Bruce 1986). It is found in forest to at least 700 m (Schmutz 1977) but is local; recent observations are from coastal forest at Nanga Rawa and lowland forest at Kisol, and further loss of lowland forest will threaten the species as it has not adapted to agricultural land (K. D. Bishop, B. F. King, D. Yong).

Marianas Crow *Corvus kubaryi* affects woodland on the islands of **Guam (to**

U.S.A.) and Rota in the **Northern Marianas Islands (to U.S.A.)**; there were an estimated 350 birds on Guam in 1981 but numbers are known to have declined since then and the population is in danger of extinction; the Rota population is thought to have remained stable since 1945 and was estimated at 1,300 in 1982 (Engring and Pratt 1985), although Jenkins (1983) suggests it may be declining there too. Ecological studies are by Tomback (1986) and Michael (1987).

Hawaiian Crow *Corvus hawaiiensis* is endemic to the island of Hawaii in the **Hawaiian Islands (to U.S.A.)**, where in the mid-1970s possibly 70 birds survived (King 1978-1979). The situation continued to deteriorate despite studies and attempts at captive-breeding (see, e.g., Buhl 1983, Sakai *et al.* 1986), and by 1987 the species was virtually extinct in the wild, with the four pairs in captivity failing to breed (Pratt 1987). The wild population is currently estimated at less than 10 birds (W. C. Gagne).

REFERENCE LIST

REFERENCE LIST

Ahmad, A. (in prep.) Occurrence and problems of migratory White-headed Duck *Oxyura leucocephala* in Pakistan.

Akcakaya, H. R. and Akcakaya, R. (1986) Concern for Turkey's last Bald Ibises. *WWF Monthly Reports* September: 243-245.

Albuquerque, J. L. B. (1986) Conservation and status of raptors in southern Brazil. *Birds of Prey Bull.* 3: 88-94.

Alexander, C. (1985) The St.Helena Wirebird, its status and distribution. Unpublished.

Ali, S., Daniel, J. C. and Rahmani, A. R. (1986) *Study of ecology of certain endangered species of wildlife and their habitats. The Floricans.* Annual Report 1. Bombay: Bombay Natural History Society.

Ali, S. and Ripley, S. D. (1984) *Handbook of the birds of India and Pakistan.* Compact edition. Bombay: Oxford University Press.

Allport, G. and Milton, G.R. (1988) A note on the recent sighting of *Zosterops flava* Javan White-eye. *Kukila* 3: 142-149.

Amos, S. H. (1985/86) Efforts to aid the endangered Black-hooded Red Siskin. *AFA Watchbird* 12(6): 19.

Andrade, M. A., Freitas, M. V. and Mattos, G. T. (1987) Dados preliminares sobre a distribuicao e conservacao de *Xiphocolaptes franciscanus* Snethlage: Dendrocolaptidae endemico do Brasil. *III Congreso de Ornitologia Neotropical: Resumenes.* Unpublished.

Andrew, P. (1985) An annotated checklist of the birds of Cibodas-Gunung Gede Nature Reserve. *Kukila* 2: 10-28.

Andrew, P. and Milton, G. R. (1988) A note on the Javan Scops-owl *Otus angelinae* Finsch. *Kukila* 3: 79.

Andrusaitis, G. ed. (1985) *Red data book of the Latvian SSR: rare and endangered species of animals and plants.* (In Latvian and Russian.) Riga: Zinatne.

Angehr, G. R. (1985) *Stitchbird.* Dunedin, New Zealand: John McIndoe and New Zealand Wildlife Service.

AOU (1983) *Check-list of North American birds.* Sixth edition. American Ornithologists' Union.

Appert, O. (1985) Zur Biologie der Mesitornithiformes (Nakas oder "Stelzenrallen") Madagaskars und erste fotografische Dokumente von Vertretern der Ordnung. *Orn. Beob.* 82: 31-54.

Araya Modinger, B. (1983) A preliminary report on the status and distribution of the Humboldt Penguin in Chile. Pp. 125-140 in *Proceedings [of the] Jean Delacour/IFCB Symposium on breeding birds in captivity.* North Hollywood, California: International Foundation for the Conservation of Birds.

Araya Modinger, B., Millie Holman, G. and Bernal Morales, M. (1986) *Guia de campo de las aves de Chile.* Santiago: Editorial Universitaria.

Archibald, G. (1988) Whooping Crane update. *ICF Bugle* 14(1): 4-6.

Archibald, G. W. and Pasquier, R. F. (1987) *Proceedings of the 1983 International Crane Workshop.* Baraboo, Wisconsin: International Crane Foundation.

Arndt, T. (1986) *Sudamerikanische Sittiche,* 5. Bomlitz, West Germany: Horst Muller-Verlag.

Arndt, T. and Roth, P. (1986) Der Rotbauchsittich *Pyrrhura rhodogaster* im Vergleich mit den verschiedenen Unterarten des Blausteisssittichs *Pyrrhura perlata*: Vorschlag fur nomenklatorische und systematische Anderungen. *Ver. Orn. Ges. Bayern* 24: 313-317.

Ash, J. S. (1984) Bird observations on Bali. *Bull. Brit. Orn. Club* 104: 24-35.

Ash, J. S. (1986) A *Ploceus* sp. nov. from Uganda. *Ibis* 128: 330-336.

Ash, J. S. (1987a) *Ploceus victoriae. Ibis* 129: 406-407.

Ash, J. S. (1987b) Surveys of *Picathartes oreas, Malimbus ibadanensis* and other species in Nigeria. International Council for Bird Preservation and Nigerian Conservation Foundation, unpublished report.

Ash, J. S. and Olson, S. L. (1985) A second specimen of *Mirafra (Heteromirafra) sidamoensis* Erard. *Bull. Brit. Orn. Club* 105: 141-143.

Bannikov, A. S. ed. (1978) *Red data book of USSR: rare and endangered species of animals and plants.* (In Russian.) Moscow: Promyshlennost.

Barber, R. D. (1985) A recent record of the Bachman's Warbler in Florida. *Florida Field Nat.* 13: 64-66.

Barnett, A. and Gretton, A. (1987) Rio Mazan - a people's forest. *World Birdwatch* 9(1): 3-4.

Beaman, M. ed. (1975) *Turkey Bird Report 1970-1973*. Sandy: Ornithological Society of Turkey.

Beaman, M. and Porter, R. F. (1985) Status of birds of prey in Turkey. *Bull. World Working Group on Birds of Prey* 2: 52-56.

Becking, J. H. (1976) Feeding range of Abbott's Booby *Sula abbotti* at the coast of Java. *Ibis* 118: 589-590.

Beehler, B. M. (1978) Notes on the mountain birds of New Ireland. *Emu* 78: 65-70.

Beehler, B. M. (1985) Conservation of New Guinea rainforest birds. Pp. 233-247 in A. W. Diamond and T. E. Lovejoy, eds. *Conservation of tropical forest birds*. Cambridge, U.K.: International Council for Bird Preservation (Techn. Publ. 4).

Beehler, B. M., Pratt, T. K. and Zimmerman, D. A. (1986) *Birds of New Guinea*. Princeton: Princeton University Press.

Beichle, U. (1982) Untersuchungen zur Biologie und Systematik der Zahntaube *Didunculus strigirostris* (Jardine 1845). Kiel: Christian-Albrechts Universitat doctoral dissertation.

Beichle, U. (1987) Lebensraum, Bestand und Nahrungsaufnahme der Zahntaube, *Didunculus strigirostris*. *J. Orn.* 128: 75-89.

Bell, B. D. (1986) *The conservation status of New Zealand wildlife*. Wellington: New Zealand Wildlife Service Occ. Publ. no. 12.

Belton, W. (1984) Birds of Rio Grande do Sul, Brazil, part 1: Rheidae through Furnariidae. *Bull. Amer. Mus. Nat. Hist.* 178(4).

Belton, W. (1985) Birds of Rio Grande do Sul, Brazil, part 2: Formicariidae through Corvidae. *Bull. Amer. Mus. Nat. Hist.* 180(1).

Beltran, J. (1987) El Mirlo de Agua (*Cinclus schulzi*). *Nuestras Aves* 5(13): 23-25.

Bennun, L. A. (1987) Ringing and recapture of Spotted Ground Thrushes *Turdus fischeri fischeri* at Gede, Kenya Coast: indications of site fidelity and population size stability. *Scopus* 11: 1-5.

van den Berg, A. B. and Bosman, C. A. W. (1986) Supplementary notes on some birds of Lore Lindu Reserve, central Sulawesi. *Forktail* 1: 7-13.

Best, H. A. (1984) The foods of Kakapo on Stewart Island as determined from their feeding sign. *New Zealand J. Ecol.* 7: 71-83.

Best, H. and Powlesland, R. (1985) *Kakapo*. Dunedin, New Zealand: John McIndoe and New Zealand Wildlife Service.

Bhushan, B. (1986a) Rediscovery of the Jerdon's or Double-banded Courser *Cursorius bitorquatus* (Blyth). *J. Bombay Nat. Hist. Soc.* 83: 1-14.

Bhushan, B. (1986b) Photographic record of the Jerdon's or Double-banded Courser *Cursorius bitorquatus*. *J. Bombay Nat. Hist. Soc.* 83 (Suppl.): 159-162.

Bibby, C. J. and Hill, D. A. (1987) Status of the Fuerteventura Stonechat *Saxicola dacotiae*. *Ibis* 129: 491-498.

Bierregaard, R. O. (1984) Observations of the nesting biology of the Guiana Crested Eagle (*Morphnus guianensis*). *Wilson Bull.* 96: 1-5.

Bishop, K. D. (1983) Some notes on non-passerine birds of West New Britain. *Emu* 83: 235-241.

Blake, E. R. (1953) *Birds of Mexico*. Chicago: University of Chicago Press.

Blake, E. R. (1977) *Manual of Neotropical birds*. Chicago: University of Chicago Press.

Blakers, M., Davies, S. J. J. F. and Reilly, P. N. (1984) *The atlas of Australian birds*. Victoria: Royal Australian Ornithologists' Union.

Bleiweiss, R. and Olalia P., M. (1983) Notes on the ecology of the Black-breasted Puffleg on Volcan Pichincha, Ecuador. *Wilson Bull.* 94: 656-661.

Blockstein, D. E. (1987) *Endangered birds of Grenada, West Indies*. Progress report.

Blot, J. (1985) Contribution a la connaissance de la biologie et de l'ecologie de *Francolinus ochropectus* Dorst et Jouanin. *Alauda* 53: 244-256.

Boeke, J. D. (1978) A food source of the Marvellous Spatuletail *Loddigesia mirabilis*. *Ibis* 120: 551.

Bond, J. (1979) *Birds of the West Indies*. Fourth edition. London: Collins.

Booth, D. T. (1987) Home range and hatching success of Malleefowl,, *Leipoa ocellata* Gould (Megapodiidae), in Murray Mallee near Renmark, S.A. *Aust. Wildl. Res.* 14: 95-104.

Borello, W. (1985) The distribution and status of Cape Vulture colonies in Botswana in 1984. *Vulture News* 14: 19-22.

Borello, W. (1986) First protected Cape Vulture breeding site in Botswana. *Vulture News* 15: 19-20.

Borello, W. and Borello, R. (1987) The Cape Vulture colonies in Botswana in 1985 and 1986. *Vulture News* 17: 37-42.

Borodin, A. M. ed. (1984) *Red data book of the USSR: rare and endangered species of animals and plants. Vol. 1: animals.* (In Russian.) 2nd edition. Moscow: Promyshlennost.

Boshoff, A. F. and Robertson, A. S. (1985) A conservation plan for the Cape vulture colony at Potberg, de Hoop Nature Reserve, southwestern Cape Province. *Bontebok* 4: 25-31.

Boshoff, A. F. and Vernon, C. J. (1987) The Cape Vulture colonies at Karnmelkspruit (1984-1986) and Balloch (1978-1986), north-eastern Cape Province. *Vulture News* 17: 31-36.

Boswell, J. (1986) *Bird conservation in the People's Republic of China.* Part 2.

Bourne, W. R. P. (1976) on subfossil bones of Abbott's Booby *Sula abbotti* from the Mascarene Islands, with a note on the proportions and distribution of the Sulidae. *Ibis* 118: 119-123.

Bourne, W. R. P. and David, A. C. F. (1983) Henderson Island, central South Pacific, and its birds. *Notornis* 30: 233-243.

Bowden, C. G. R. (1987) The Yemen Thrush in North Yemen. *Sandgrouse* 9: 87-89.

Bradley, P. (1985) *Birds of the Cayman Islands.* George Town, Grand Cayman: P. E. Bradley.

Braun, M. J., Braun, D. D. and Terrill, S. B. (1986) Winter records of the Golden-cheeked Warbler (*Dendroica chrysoparia*) from Mexico. *Amer. Birds* 40(3): 564-566.

Brazil, M. (1984a) Observations on the behaviour and vocalizations of the Okinawa Rail *Rallus okinawae. J. College of Dairying* (Ebetsu, Hokkaido) 10: 437-499.

Brazil, M. (1984b) One on tape is worth three in the bush. *BBC Wildlife* 2: 574-575.

Brazil, M. (1985a) The endemic birds of the Nansei Shoto. Pp. 11-35 in *Conservation of the Nansei shoto,* 2. Tokyo: World Wildlife Fund Japan.

Brazil, M. (1985b) Notes on the Okinawa Rail *Rallus okinawae*: observations at night and at dawn. *Tori* 33: 125-126.

Brazil, M. (1985c) Owl of the setting sun. *BBC Wildlife* 3: 110-115.

Brazil, M. (1986) Sea Eagle sunrise. *BBC Wildlife* 4(12): 588-592.

Brazil, M. (1987) Where have all the Baikal Teals gone? *Oriental Bird Club Bull.* 5: 29.

Bregulla, H. L. (1987) Zur Biologie des Kagu, *Rhinochetus jubatus. Zool. Garten* N.F. 57: 349-365.

Bregulla, H. L. (in press) Birds of Vanuatu.

Broni, S. C. (1985) Social and spatial foraging patterns of the jackass penguin *Spheniscus demersus. S. Afr. J. Zool.* 20: 241-245.

Brooke, M. de L. (1985) The annual cycle of the Toc-toc *Foudia sechellarum* on Cousin Island, Seychelles. *Ibis* 127: 7-15.

Brooke, M. de L. (1987) *The birds of the Juan Fernandez Islands, Chile.* Cambridge, U.K.: International Council for Bird Preservation (Study Report 16).

Brooke, M. de L. (1988) Distribution and numbers of the Masafuera Rayadito *Aphrastura masafuerae* on Isla Alejandro Selkirk, Juan Fernandez archipelago, Chile. *Bull. Brit. Orn. Club* 108: 4-9

Brooke, R. K. (1984) *South African Red Data Book - birds.* Pretoria: South African National Scientific Programmes Report no. 97.

Brooks, D. J., Evans, M. I., Martins, R. P. and Porter, R. F. (1987) The status of birds in North Yemen and the records of OSME Expedition in 1985. *Sandgrouse* 9: 4-66.

Brosset, A. and Erard, C. (1986) *Les oiseaux des regions forestieres du nord-est du Gabon,* 1. Paris: Societe Nationale de Protection de la Nature.

Brown, C. J. (1985) The status and conservation of the Cape Vulture in SWA/Namibia. *Vulture News* 14: 4-15.

Brown, L. H. and Amadon, D. (1968) *Hawks, eagles and falcons of the world.* London, New York: Hamlyn, McGraw-Hill.

Brown, P. B. and Wilson, R. I. (1984) *Orange-bellied Parrot recovery plan.* Tasmania: National Parks and Wildlife Service.

Brown, P., Wilson, R., Loyn, R., Murray, N. and Lane, B. (1985) *The Orange-bellied Parrot - an RAOU conservation statement.* Melbourne: Royal Australasian Ornithologists' Union.

Brudenell-Bruce, P. G. C. (1975) *The birds of New Providence and the Bahama Islands.* London: Collins.

Bruning, D. (1983) Breeding condors in captivity for release into the wild. *Zoo Biology* 2: 245-252.

Buden, D. W. (1987) *The birds of the southern Bahamas.* London: British Ornithologists' Union (Check-list 8).

Buhl, K. (1983) Trouble in paradise ... the Hawaiian Crow. *AFA Watchbird* 10(3): 26-30.

Burbidge, A. A. and Jenkins, R. W. G. eds (1984) *Endangered vertebrates of Australia and its island territories*. Canberra: Australian National Parks and Wildlife Service.

Butler, P. J. (1981) The St. Lucia Amazon (*Amazona versicolor*): its changing status and conservation. Pp. 171-180 in R. F. Pasquier, ed. *Conservation of New World parrots*. Washington D. C.: Smithsonian Institution Press for the International Council for Bird Preservation (Techn. Publ. 1).

Cade, T. J. (1982) *The falcons of the world*. London: Collins.

Caleda, M., Lanante, R. and Viloria, E. (1986) Preliminary studies of the Palawan Peacock Pheasant *Polyplectron emphanum*. In M. Ridley, ed. *Pheasants in Asia 1986*. Basildon, U.K.: World Pheasant Association.

Camargo, H. F. de A. and de Carmargo, E. A. (1964) Occorencia de *Iodopleura p. pipra* no Estado de Sao Paulo, Brasil, e algumas notas sobre *Iodopleura isabellae*. *Pap. Dep. Zool. Sao Paulo* 16: 45-55.

Carp, E. (1980) *Directory of wetlands of international importance in the western Palearctic*. Gland: IUCN and UNEP.

Chasen, F.N. (1935) A handlist of Malaysian birds. *Bull. Raffles Mus.* 11: 1-389.

Chasen, F. N. and Hoogerwerf, A. (1941) Birds of the Netherlands Indian Mt. Leuser expedition 1937 to North Sumatra. *Treubia* 18: (Supplement).

Chebez, J. C. (1986) Nuestras aves amenazadas. 13. Carpintero cara canela (*Dryocopus galeatus*). *Nuestras Aves* 4(10): 16-8.

Cheke, A. S. (1987a) The ecology of the smaller land-birds of Mauritius. Pp. 151-207 in A. W. Diamond, ed. *Studies of Mascarene Island birds*. Cambridge, U.K.: Cambridge University Press.

Cheke, A. S. (1987b) The ecology of the surviving native land-birds of Reunion. Pp. 301-358 in A. W. Diamond, ed. *Studies of Mascarene Island birds*. Cambridge, U.K.: Cambridge University Press.

Cheke, A. S. (1987c) Observations on the surviving endemic birds of Rodrigues. Pp. 364-402 in A. W. Diamond, ed. *Studies of Mascarene Island birds*. Cambridge, U.K.: Cambridge University Press.

Cheke, A. S. (1987d) The legacy of the Dodo - conservation in Mauritius. *Oryx* 21: 29-36.

Cheke, R. A. (1986) The supposed occurrence of the White-necked Picathartes *Picathartes gymnocephalus* in Togo. *Bull. Brit. Orn. Club* 106: 152.

Chebez, J. C. (1986) El Guacamayo Violaceo (*Anodorhynchus glaucus*). *Nuestras Aves* 4(9): 17-20.

Child, P. (1986) Black-fronted Tern breeding at high altitude. *Notornis* 33(3): 193-194.

Clark, W. S. (1986) What is *Buteo ventralis*? *Birds of Prey Bull.* 3: 115-118.

Clements, F. A. and Bradbear, N. J. (1986) Status of wintering Black-necked Cranes *Grus nigricollis* in Bhutan. *Forktail* 2: 103-107.

Clinton-Eitniear, J. (1986) Status of the Green-cheeked Amazon in north-eastern Mexico. *AFA Watchbird* 12(6): 22-24.

Coats, S. and Phelps, W. H. (1985) The Venezuelan Red Siskin: case history of an endangered species. Pp. 977-985 in P. A. Buckley, M. S. Foster, E. S. Morton, R. S. Ridgely and F. G. Buckley, eds. *Neotropical ornithology*. Washington, D. C.: American Ornithologists' Union.

Collar, N. J. (1979) The world status of the Houbara: a preliminary review. 12pp (unpaginated) in C. L. Coles and N. J. Collar, eds. *Symposium papers: the Great Bustard (Otis tarda), Sofia, Bulgaria, May 26th, 1978 [and] the Houbara Bustard (Chlamydotis undulata), Athens, Greece, May 24th 1979.* [Fordingbrige, U.K.: The Game Conservancy.]

Collar, N. J. (1985) The world status of the Great Bustard. *Bustard studies* 2: 1-20.

Collar, N. J. (1986a) Threatened raptors of the Americas: work in progress from the ICBP/IUCN Red Data Book. *Birds of Prey Bull.* 3: 13-20.

Collar, N. J. (1986b) Red Data Bird: Black-capped Vireo. *World Birdwatch* 8(2): 5.

Collar, N. J. (1987) Rising sun, falling trees. *World Birdwatch* 9(1): 6-7.

Collar, N. J. and Andrew, P. (1987) Red data birds: the cochoas. *World Birdwatch* 9(4): 5.

Collar, N. J. and Gonzaga, L. P. (in press) Cracids at risk: the global perspective. In S. D. Strahl, ed. [Proceedings of the Second International Cracid Symposium, Caracas, Venezuela, 1988].

Collar, N. J., Gonzaga, L. A. P., Jones, P. J. and Scott, D. A. (1987) Avifauna da Mata Atlantica. Pp. 73-84 in *Seminario sobre desenvolvimento economico e impacto ambiental em areas do tropico umido brasileiro, 1. Belem, 1986.* Rio de Janerio: Companhia Vale do Rio Doce.

Collar, N. J. and Goriup, P. D., eds. (1983) Report of the ICBP Fuerteventura Houbara Expedition, 1979. *Bustard Studies* 1.

Collar, N. J., Round, P. D. and Wells, D. R. (1986) The past and future of Gurney's Pitta *Pitta gurneyi*. *Forktail* 1: 29-51.

Collar, N. J. and Stuart, S. N. (1985) *Threatened birds of Africa and related islands. The ICBP/IUCN Red Data Book*. Cambridge, U.K.: International Council for Bird Preservation and International Union for the Conservation of Nature.

Collar, N. J. and Stuart, S. N. (1988) *Threatened birds and biodiversity: seventy-five forests important for bird species at risk in the Afrotropical and Malagasy realm*. Cambridge, U.K.: International Council for Bird Preservation.

Collar, N. J. and Tattersall, I. (1987) J. T. Last and the type-locality of Benson's Rockthrush *Monticola bensoni*. *Bull. Brit. Orn. Club* 107: 55-59.

Colston, P. R. and Curry-Lindahl, K. (1986) *The birds of Mount Nimba, Liberia*. London: British Museum (Natural History).

Cooper, J. (1985) New breeding locality data for southern African seabirds: Jackass Penguin *Spheniscus demersus*. *Cormorant* 13: 81.

Cowling, S. J. and Davies, S. J. J. F. (1983) *Status of Australian birds with special reference to captive breeding*. Melbourne: Department of Conservation.

Coulter, M. C. (1984) Seabird conservation in the Galapagos Islands, Ecuador. Pp. 237-244 in J. P. Croxall, P. G. H. Evans and R. W. Schreiber, eds. *Status and conservation of the world's seabirds*. Cambridge, U.K.: International Council for Bird Preservation (Techn. Publ. 2).

Coulter, M. C., Cruz, F. and Cruz, J. (1985) A programme to save the Dark-rumped Petrel, *Pterodroma phaeopygia*, on Floreana Island, Galapagos, Ecuador. Pp 177-180 in P. J. Moors, ed. *Conservation of island birds*. Cambridge, U.K.: International Council for Bird Preservation (Techn. Publ. 3).

Cox, R. (1988) The conservation status of biological resources in the Philippines: a report by the IUCN Conservation Monitoring Centre (for the International Institute for Environment and Development). Unpublished.

Cramp, S. and Simmons, K. E. L. (1977-1983) *Handbook of the birds of Europe, the Middle East and North Africa*. Vols. 1-3. Oxford: Oxford University Press.

Cramp, S. (1985) *Handbook of the birds of Europe, the Middle East and North Africa*. Vol. 4. Oxford: Oxford University Press.

Cramp, S. ed. (1985) *The birds of the western Palearctic*, 4. Oxford: Oxford University Press.

Crivelli, A. J. (1987) The ecology and behaviour of the Dalmatian Pelican, *Pelecanus crispus* Bruch. A world-endangered species. Commission of the European Communities and Station Biologique de la Tour de Valat, unpublished report.

Crivelli, A. J. and Schreiber, R. W. (1984) Status of the Pelecanidae. *Biol. Conserv*. 30: 147-156.

Crivelli, A. J. and Vizi, O. (1981) The Dalmatian Pelican *Pelecanus crispus* Bruch 1832, a recently world endangered bird species. *Biol. Cons*. 20: 297-310.

Crockett, D. E. (1979) Rediscovery of the Chatham Island taiko solved century-old mystery. *Forest and Bird* 13(4): 8-13.

Crockett, D. E. (1986) *Taiko research project*. 1985-1986 expedition report. Unpublished.

Cruz, J. B. and Cruz, F. (1987) Conservation of the Dark-rumped Petrel *Pterodroma phaeopygia* in the Galapagos Islands, Ecuador. *Biol. Conserv*. 42: 303-311.

Curry, P. J. and Sayer, J. A. (1979) The inundation zone of the Niger as an environment for Palearctic migrants. *Ibis* 121: 20-40.

Darby, J. (1985) The great Yellow-eyed Penguin count. *Forest & Bird* 16(2): 16-18.

Davies, A. G. (1987) *The Gola Forest Reserves, Sierra Leone: wildlife conservation and forest management*. Gland, Switzerland, and Cambridge, U.K.: International Union for Conservation of Nature and Natural Resources.

Davis, F. W., Hilgartner, W. B. and Steadman, D. W. (1985) Notes on the diets of *Geotrygon montana* and *Columba caribaea* in Jamaica. *Bull. Brit. Orn. Club* 105: 130-133.

Davis, T. J. and O'Neill, J. P. (1986) A new species of antwren (Formicariidae: *Herpsilochmus*) from Peru, with comments on the systematics of other members of the genus. *Wilson Bull*. 98: 337-352.

Davison, G. W. H. (1981) A survey of terrestrial birds in the Gunung Mulu National Park, Sarawak. *Sarawak Mus. Journal* 27: 283-293.

Davison, G. W. H. (1982) Systematics within the genus *Arborophila* Hodgson. *Federation Mus. Journal* 27: 125-134.

Dee, T. J. (1986) *The endemic birds of Madagascar*. Cambridge, U.K.: International Council for Bird Preservation.

Dekker, R. W. R. J. and Wattel, J. (1987) Egg and image: new and traditional uses for the Maleo (*Macrocephalon maleo*). Pp. 83-87 in A. W. Diamond and F. L. Finion, eds. *The value of birds*. Cambridge, U.K.: International Council for Bird Preservation.

Delacour, (1927) *Arborophila davidi* sp. n. *Bull. Brit. Orn. Club* 47: 169.

Delacour, J. (1951) *The pheasants of the world*. London: Country Life Limited.

Delacour, J. and Mayr, E. (1946) *Birds of the Philippines*. New York: Macmillan.

Delibes, M. (1978) Ecologia alimenticia del aguila imperial iberica (*Aquila adalberti*) en el Coto Donana durante la crianza de los pollos. *Donana, Acta Vertebrata* 5: 35-60.

Desfayes, M. (1987) Evidence for the ancient presence of the Bald Ibis *Geronticus eremita* in Greece. *Bull. Brit. Orn. Club* 107: 93-94.

Devillers, P. (1977) Observations at a breeding colony of *Larus (belcheri) atlanticus*. *Gerfaut* 67: 22-43.

Diamond, J. M. (1976) *Recommendations for minimising enviromental costs of mining on Rennell*. Report to the Central Planning Office, Goverment of the Solomon Islands.

Diamond, J. M. (1982) Rediscovery of the Yellow-fronted Gardener Bowerbird. *Science* 216 (4544): 431-434.

Diamond, J. M. (1984) Back from the brink of extinction. *Nature* 309: 308.

Diamond, J. M. (1985) New ditributional records and taxa from the outlying mountain ranges of New Guinea. *Emu* 85: 65-91.

Diamond, J. M. (1987) Extant unless proven extinct? Or, extinct unless proven extant? *Conserv. Biol.* 1: 77-79.

Dickinson, E. C. (1986) Does the White-eyed River-martin *Pseudochelidon sirintarae* breed in China? *Forktail* 2: 95-96.

Dickinson, E. C. and Eck, S. (1984) Notes on Philippine birds, 2. A second Philippine record of *Sterna bernsteini*. *Bull. Brit. Orn. Club* 104: 72.

Dickinson, E. C., Kennedy, R. S. and Parkes, K. C. (in press) *Check-list of the birds of the Philippines*. London: British Ornithologists' Union.

Dornbusch, M. (1985) Die gegenwartige Situation vom Aussterben bedrohter Tierarten in der DDR. *Hercynia* (N.F.) 22: 221-227.

Draulans, D. (1986) On the distribution and foraging behaviour of the Malagasy Heron *Ardea humbloti*. *Ostrich* 57: 249-251.

Duffy, D. C., Hays, C. and Plenge, M. A. (1984) The conservation status of Peruvian seabirds. Pp. 245-259 in J. P. Croxall, P. G. H. Evans and R. W. Schreiber, eds. *Status and conservation of the world's seabirds*. Cambridge, U.K.: International Council for Bird Preservation (Techn. Publ. 2).

Duffy, D. C., Wilson, R. P., Ricklefs, R. E., Broni, S. C., and Veldhuis, H. (1987) Penguins and purse-seiners: competition or co-existence? *Natn. Geogr. Res.* 3: 480-488.

duPont, J. E. (1971) *Philippine birds*. Greenville, Delaware: Delaware Museum of Natural History.

Eck, S. (1986) *Eutriorchis astur* im Dresdner Tierkunde-Museum. *J. Orn.* 127: 93-94.

Eley, J. W. (1982) Systematic relationships and zoogeography of the White-winged Guan (*Penelope albipennis*) and related forms. *Wilson Bull.* 94: 241-259.

Emlen, J. T. (1977) *Land bird communities of Grand Bahama Island: the structure and dynamics of an avifauna*. American Ornithologists' Union (Orn. Monogr. 24).

Emmerson, K. W., Martin, A., Delgado, G., and Quilis, V. (1986) Distribution and some aspects of the breeding biology of Bolle's Pigeon (*Columba bollii*) on Tenerife. *Vogelwelt* 107: 52-65.

Engbring, J. and Pratt, H. D. (1985) Endangered birds in Micronesia: their history, status and future prospects. *Bird Conserv.* 2: 71-105.

Erickson, K. R. and Heideman, P. D. (1983) Notes on the avifauna of the Balinsasayao rainforest region, Negros Oriental, Philippines. *Silliman J.* 30: 63-72.

Escalante, R. (1980) Notas sobre algunas aves de la vertiente atlantica de Sud America (Rallidae, Laridae). *Resumenes, 1 Jornadas de Ciencias Naturales, Montevideo*: 33-34.

Escott, C. J. and Holmes, D. A. (1980) The avifauna of Sulawesi, Indonesia: faunistic notes and additions. *Bull. Brit. Orn. Club* 100: 189-194.

Estudillo Lopez, J. (1983) Considerations in regard to rare and endangered species of cracids both in nature and captivity. Pp. 45-61 in *Proceedings [of the] Jean Delacour/IFCB Symposium on breeding birds in captivity*. North Hollywood, California: International Foundation for the Conservation of Birds.

Evans, P. G. H. (1986) Monitoring seabirds in the north Atlantic. Pp. 179-206 in Medmaravis and Monbailliu, X. eds. *Mediterranean Marine avifauana*. Medmaravis, Berlin: Springer-verlag.

Everett, W. T. (1988) Notes from Clarion Island. *Condor* 90: 512-513.

Faaborg, J. (1983) Why share a mate? *Living Bird Quarterly* 2(2): 14-17.

Faaborg, J. (1984) Potential for restocking Galapagos Hawks on islands where they have been extirpated. *Noticias de Galapagos* 39: 28-30.

Faaborg, J. (1985) Reproductive success and survivorship of the Galapagos Hawk *Buteo galapagoensis*: potential costs and benefits of cooperative polyandry. *Ibis* 128: 337-347.

Faaborg, J. R. and Arendt, W. J. (1985) *Wildlife assessments in the Caribbean*. San Juan, Puerto Rico: Institute of Tropical Forestry.

Fernandez-Cruz, M. and Arauio, J. eds. (1985) *Situacion de la avifauna de la Peninsula Iberica, Baleares y Macaronesia*. Madrid: Sociedad Espanola de Ornitologia.

ffrench, R. (1973) *A guide to the birds of Trinidad and Tobago*. Wynnewood, Penn: Livingston Publishing Company.

Fiebig, J. and Jander, G. (1985) Der Steppenschlammlaufer, *Limnodromus semipalmatus*, als mongolischer Brutvogel. *Ann. Orn.* 9: 107-111.

Fisher, D. J. (1985) Observations on Relict Gull in Mongolia. *Dutch Birding* 7: 117-120.

Fitzpatrick, J. W. and O'Neill, J. P. (1979) A new tody-tyrant from northern Peru. *Auk* 96: 443-447.

Fitzpatrick, J. W., Willard, D. E. and Terborgh, J. W. (1979) A new species of hummingbird from Peru. *Wilson Bull.* 91: 177-186.

Fjeldsa, J. (1981) *Podiceps taczanowskii* (Aves, Podicipedidae), the endemic grebe of Lake Junin, Peru. A review. *Steenstrupia* 7(11): 237-259.

Fjeldsa, J. (1983) A Black Rail from Junin, central Peru: *Laterallus jamaicensis tuerosi* ssp. n. (Aves, Rallidae). *Steenstrupia* 8(13): 277-282.

Fjeldsa, J. (1984) Three endangered South American grebes (Podiceps): case histories and the ethics of saving species by human intervention. *Ann. Zool. Fennici* 21: 411-416.

Fjeldsa, J. (1986) Feeding ecology and possible life history tactics of the Hooded Grebe *Podiceps gallardoi*. *Ardea* 74: 40-58.

Fjeldsa, J. (1987) Relict forests in the High Andes of Peru and Bolivia. Technical report from the *Polylepis* forest expedition of the Zoological Museum [University of Copenhagen] 1987, with some preliminary suggestions for habitat conservation. Unpublished.

Fjeldsa, J. and Krabbe, N. (1986) Some range extensions and other unusual records of Andean birds. *Bull. Brit. Orn. Club* 106: 115-124.

Fjeldsa, J., Krabbe, N. and Parker, T. A. [not W.] (1987) Rediscovery of *Cinclodes excelsior aricomae* and notes on the nominate race. *Bull. Brit. Orn. Club* 107: 112-114.

Flint, V. E., Boehme, R. L., Kostin, Y. V., and Kuznetzov, A. A. (1984) *A field guide to birds of the USSR*. Princeton: Princeton University Press.

Folkestad, A. O. (1984) Situasjonen for havorna *Haliaeetus albicilla* i Norge. *Var Fuglefauna* 7: 209-216.

Forshaw, J. M. and Cooper, W. T. (1981a) *Parrots of the world*. Second edition. Melbourne: Lansdowne Press.

Forshaw, J. M. and Cooper, W. T. (1981b) *Australian parrots*. Melbourne: Lansdowne.

Fosberg, F. R., Sachet, M.-H. and Stoddart, D. R. (1983) Henderson Island (southeastern Polynesia): summary of current knowledge. *Atoll Res. Bull.* 272.

Frey, H. (1985) The Black-hooded Red Siskin, an endangered species, an interview with Pat Dempko. *AFA Watchbird* 12(4): 40-42.

Friedman, H. (1950) The birds of North and Middle America, 11. *U.S. Natn. Mus. Bull.* 50.

Fry, C. H., Hosken, J. H. and Skinner, D. (1986) Further observations on the breeding of Slaty Egrets *Egretta vinaceigula* and Rufousbellied Herons *Ardeola rufiventris*. *Ostrich* 57: 61-64.

Fry, C. H. and Smith, D. A. (1985) A new swallow from the Red Sea. *Ibis* 127: 1-6.

Fujimaki, Y. (1987) Joint survey report of Japan and USSR on Steller's Sea-Eagle. Summary, p. 49 in *The Third Japan-USSR Bird Protection Symposium, 21 November 1986*. [Tokyo:] Wild Bird Society of Japan.

Fullager, P. J. and Disney, H. J. de S. (1975) The birds of Lord Howe Islands: a report on the rare and endangered species. *Bull. ICBP 12*: 187-202.

Gallagher, M. D., Scott, D. A., Ormond, R. F. G., Connor, R. J. and Jennings, M. C. (1984). The distribution and conservation of seabirds breeding on the coasts and islands of Iran and Arabia. Pp. 421-456 in J. P. Croxall, P. G. H. Evans and R. W. Schreiber, eds. *Status and conservation of the world's seabirds*. Cambridge, U.K.: International Council for Bird Preservation (Techn. Publ. 2).

Garcia, F. (undated) *Las aves de Cuba, 1: especies endemicas*. La Habana: Gente Nueva.

Garnett, M. C. (1983) A management plan for nature conservation in the Line and Phoenix Islands, Part 1: description. Unpublished.

Garrido, O. H. (1985) Cuban endangered birds. Pp. 992-999 in P. A. Buckley, M. S. Foster, E. S. Morton, R. S. Ridgely and F. G. Buckley, eds. *Neotropical ornithology*. Washington, D. C.: American Ornithologists' Union (Orn. Monogr. 36).

Garrido, O. H. (1986) *Las Palomas*. La Habana: Editorial Cientifico-Tecnica.

Garrido, O. H. and Garcia, F. (1975) Catalogo de las aves de Cuba. La Habana: Academia de Ciencias de Cuba.

Garson, P. J. (1983) The Cheer Pheasant *Catreus wallichii* in Himachal Pradesh, Western Himalayas: an update. *World Pheasant Assoc. J.* 8: 29-39.

Gast, S. E. and King, B. (1985) Notes on Philippine birds, 7. Recent records of the Chinese Egret *Egretta eulophotes* from Luzon, Mindoro and Palawan, Philippines. *Bull. Brit. Orn. Club* 105: 139-141.

Gaston, A. J. (1984) Is habitat destruction in India and Pakistan beginning to affect the status of endemic passerine birds? *J. Bombay Nat. Hist. Soc.* 81(3): 636-641.

Gaston, A. J. and Singh, J. (1980) The status of the Cheer Pheasant *Catreus wallichii* in the Chail Wildlife Santuary, Himachal Pradesh. *World Pheasant Assoc. J.* 5: 68-73.

Gaston, A. J. and Macrell, J. (1980) Green Munia (*Estrilda formosa*) at Delhi, and other interesting records for 1978. *J. Bombay Nat. Hist. Soc.* 77: 144-145.

Gaston, A. J., Garson, P. J. and Hunter, M. L. (1981) Present distribution and status of pheasants in Himachal Pradesh, western Himalayas. *World Pheasant Assoc. J.* 6: 10-30.

Gaston, A. J., Islam, K. and Crawford, J. A. (1983) The current status of the Western Tragopan *Tragopan melanocephalus*. *World Pheasant Assoc. J.* 8: 40-49.

Gatter, W. (1985) Ein neuer Bulbul aus Westafrika (Aves, Pycnonotidae). *J. Orn.* 126: 155-161.

Gensbol, B. (1986) *Collins Guide to the birds of prey of Britain and Europe, North Africa and the Middle East*. London: Collins.

Gilliard, E. T. (1950) Notes on a collection of birds from Bataan, Luzon, Philippine Islands. *Bull. Amer. Mus. Nat. Hist.* 94: 457-504.

Gilliard, E. T. and LeCroy, M. (1967) Results of the 1958-1959 Gilliard New Britain Expedition, 4: annotated list of birds of the Whiteman Mountains, New Britain. *Bull. Amer. Mus. Nat. Hist.* 135: 173-216.

Gochfeld, M. (1978) Social facilitation of singing: group size and flight song rates in the Pampas Meadowlark *Sturnella defilippii*. *Ibis* 120: 338-339.

Gollop, J. B., Barry, T. W. and Iversen, E. H. (1986) *Eskimo Curlew. A vanishing species?* Regina, Saskatchewan: Saskatchewan Natural History Society (Spec. Publ. 17).

Gonzaga, L. P. (1983) Notas sobre *Dacnis nigripes* Pelzeln, 1856 (Aves, Coerebidae). *Iheringia* Ser. Zool. 63: 45-58.

Gonzaga, L. P. (1984) Voa araponga, voa macuco, que o homem vem ai... *Ciencia Hoje* 2(11): 18-24.

Gonzaga, L. P., Scott, D. A. and Collar, N. J. (in press) The status and birds of some forest fragments in eastern Brazil.

Gonzalez, L. M., Gonzalez, J. L., Garzon, J. and Heredia, B. (1987) Censo y distribucion del Aguila Imperial Iberica, *Aquila (heliaca) adalberti* Brehm, 1861, en Espana durante el periodo 1981-1986. *Bol. Est. Cent. Ecol.* 16(31): 99-109.

Gonzalez Garcia, F. (1984) Aspectos biologicos del Pavon *Oreophasis derbianus* G. R. Gray (Aves: Cracidae) en la Reserva Natural "El Triunfo", Municipio del Angel Albion Corzo, Chiapas, Mexico. Tesis profesional, Facultad de Ciencias Biologicas, Universidad Veracruzana, Xalapa, Veracruz, Mexico.

Goodwin, D. (1976) *Crows of the world*. London: British Museum (Natural History).

Goodwin, D. (1982) *Estrildid finches of the world*. London: British Museum (Natural History) and Oxford University Press.

Goodwin, D. (1983) *Pigeons and doves of the world*. Third edition. London: British Museum (Natural History).

Gore, M. E. J. and Won, Pyong-Oh. (1971) *The birds of Korea*. Seoul: Royal Asiatic Society.

Goriup, P. D., ed. (1983) *The Houbara Bustard in Morocco: report of the Al-Areen/ICBP March 1982 preliminary survey*. [Cambridge, U.K.: International Council for Bird Preservation, on behalf of Al-Areen Wildlife Park, Bahrain.]

Goriup, P. D. and Karpowicz, Z. J. (1985) A review of the past and recent status of the Lesser Florican. *Bustard Studies* 3: 163-182.

Goriup, P. D. and Vardhan, H., eds. (1983) *Bustards in decline*. Jaipur: Tourism and Wildife Society of India.

Grant, P. R. (1986) *Ecology and evolution of Darwin's finches*. Princeton: Princeton University Press.

Grantsau, R. (1967) Sobre o genero *Augastes*, com a descricao de uma subespecie nova (Aves, Trochilidae). *Pap. Avuls. Zool.* 21: 21-31.

Graves, G. R. (1980) A new species of metaltail hummingbird from northern Peru. *Wilson Bull.* 92: 1-7.

Graves, G. R. and Giraldo O., J. A. (1987) Population status of the Rufous-fronted Parakeet (*Bolborhynchus ferrugineifrons*), a Colombian endemic. *Gerfaut* 77: 89-92.

Graves, G. R. and Weske, J. S. (1987) *Tangara phillipsi*, a new species from the Cerros del Sira, eastern Peru. *Wilson Bull.* 99: 1-6.

Greenway, J. C. (1958) *Extinct and vanishing birds of the world*. New York: American Committee for International Wildlife Protection (Ser. Publ. 13).

Greenway, J. C. (1967) *Extinct and vanishing birds of the world*. Second edition. New York: Dover Publications.

Gretton, A. (1987) Gurney's Pitta: the struggle to survive. *World Birdwatch* 9(4): 6-7.

Grimmett, R. (1986) News and views: White-winged Ducks in Thailand. *Bull. Oriental Bird Club* 3: 7.

Grimmett, R. and Jones, T. (in prep.) Important bird areas of Europe.

Grzybowski, J. A., Clapp, R. S. and Marshall, J. T. (1986) History and current population status of the Black-capped Vireo in Oklahoma. *Amer. Birds* 40(5): 1151-1161.

Gutierrez, R. J. and Carey, A. B., eds. (1985) *Ecology and management of the Spotted Owl in the Pacific northwest*. Oregon: United States Department of Agriculture (General Technical Report PNW-185).

Hadden, D. (1981) *Birds of the north Solomons*. Papua New Guinea: Wau Ecology Institute (Handbook no. 8).

Haig, S. M. and Oring, L. W. (1985) Distribution and status of the Piping Plover throughout the annual cycle. *J. Field Orn.* 56(4): 334-345.

Hambler, C., Hambler, K. and Newing, J. M. (1985) Some observations on Nesillas aldabranus, the endangered brush warbler of Aldabra Atoll, with hypotheses on its distribution. *Atoll Res. Bull.* 290.

Hamel, P. B. (1986) *Bachman's Warbler. A species in peril*. Washington, D. C.: Smithsonian Institution Press.

Hamsch, S. (1987) Zur Biologie der Mesitornithiformes Madagaskars. *Falke* 160-162.

Hancock, J. and Kushlan, J. (1984) *The herons handbook*. London: Croom Helm.

Haney, J. C. (1987) Aspects of the pelagic ecology and behaviour of the Black-capped Petrel (*Pterodroma hasitata*). *Wilson Bull.* 99: 153-168.

Hannecart, F. (in press) Les oiseaux menaces de la Nouvelle-Caledonie et des iles proches. In *Livre rouge des oiseaux menaces des regions francaises outre-mer*. Conseil International pour la Protection des Oiseaux.

Harris, M. P. (1979) Population dynamics of the Flightless Cormorant *Nannopterum harrisi*. *Ibis* 122: 135-146.

Harris, M. (1982) *A field guide to the birds of Galapagos*. Revised edition. London: Collins.

Harrison, C. S., Naughton, M. B. and Fefer, S. I. (1984) The status and conservation of seabirds in the Hawaiian archipelago and Johnston atoll. Pp. 513-562 in J. P. Croxall, P. G. H. Evans and R. W. Schreiber, eds. *Status and conservation of the world's seabirds*. Cambridge, U.K.: International Council for Bird Preservation (Techn. Publ. 2).

Harrison, P. (1983) *Seabirds*. Beckenham: Croom Helm Ltd.

Harvey, W.G. (1986) A taste of Karamay. *Oriental Bird Club Bull.* 4: 8-10.

Hasegawa, H. (1982) The breeding status of the Short-tailed Albatross *Diomedea albatrus*, on Torishima, 1979/80-1980/81. *J. Yamashina Inst. Ornith.* 14: 16-24.

Hasegawa, H. (1984) Status and conservation of seabirds in Japan, with special attention to the Short-tailed Albatross. Pp. 487-500 in J. P. Croxall, P. G. H. Evans and R. W. Schreiber, eds. *Status and conservation of the world's seabirds*. Cambridge, U.K.: International Council for Bird Preservation (Techn. Publ. 2).

Haverschmidt, F. (1968) *Birds of Surinam*. Edinburgh and London: Oliver and Boyd.

Haverschmidt, F. (1972) *Accipiter poliogaster* in Surinam. *J. Orn.* 113: 338-339.

Hay, R. (1984) The Tuamotu Sandpiper: little known, little cared for. *Forest and Bird* 15(4): 17.

Hay, R. (1986) *Bird conservation in the Pacific Islands*. Cambridge, U.K.: International Council for Bird Preservation (Study Report 7).

Hay, J. R., Best, H. A. and Powlesland, R. G. (1985) *Kokako*. Dunedin, New Zealand: John McIndoe and New Zealand Wildlife Service.

Hayman, P., Marchant, J. and Prater, T. (1986) *Shorebirds*. London: Croom Helm.

Hays, C. (1984) The Humboldt penguin in Peru. *Oryx* 18: 92-95.

Hays, C. (1986) Effects of the 1982-83 El Nino on Humboldt Penguin colonies in Peru. *Biol. Conserv.* 36: 169-180.

Helander, B. (1980) Fargringmarkning av havsorn - en lagesrapport. *Fauna och Flora* 4: 183-187.

Helander, B. (1983) *Reproduction of the White-tailed Sea Eagle Haliaeetus albicilla (L.) in Sweden, in relation to food and residue levels of organochlorine and mercury compounds in the eggs*. Stockholm: University of Stockholm and Swedish Society for the Conservation of Nature.

Helander, B., Olsson, M. and Reutergardh, L. (1982) Residue levels of organochlorine and mercury compounds in unhatched eggs and the relationships to breeding success in White-tailed Sea Eagles *Haliaeetus albicilla* in Sweden. *Holarctic Ecology* 5(4): 349-366.

Helvoort, B. van (1987) Status and conservation needs of the Bali Starling. *Bull. Oriental Bird Club* 5: 9-12.

Henry, G. M. (1955) *A field guide to the birds of Ceylon*. Oxford: Oxford University Press.

Heredia, B., Gonzalez, L. M., Gonzalez, J. L. and Alonso, J. C. (1985) La emancipacion y dispersion de los jovenes de Aguila Imperial en el Parque Nacional de Donana. *Vida Silvestre* 53: 37-43.

Hermes, N. (1980) Endangered species. In Haigh, C. ed. *Endangered animals of New South Wales*. Sydney: National Parks and Wildlife Service.

Hernandez-Camacho, J. I. and Rodriguez-Mahecha J. V. (1986) Satus geografico y taxonomico de *Molothrus armenti* Cabanis 1851 (Aves: Icteridae). *Caldasia* 15: 655-664.

Hicks, J. and Yorkston, H. (1982) Notes on the breeding of the Christmas Island Imperial Pigeon *Ducula whartoni*. *Australian Bird Watcher* 9(8): 247-251.

Hillgarth, N., Stewart-Cox. B. and Thouless, C. (1986) The decline of the Green Peafowl *Pavo muticus*. In M. Ridley, ed. *Pheasants in Asia 1986*. Basildon, U.K.: World Pheasant Association.

Hilty, S. L. (1985) Distributional changes in the Colombian avifauna: a preliminary blue list. Pp. 1000-1012 in P. A. Buckley, M. S. Foster, E. S. Morton, R. S. Ridgely and F. G. Buckley, eds. *Neotropical ornithology*. Washington, D. C.: American Ornithologists' Union (Orn. Monogr. 36).

Hilty, S. L. and Brown, W. L. (1986) *A guide to the birds of Colombia*. Princeton: Princeton University Press.

Hockey, P. A. R. (1986) The Canary Islands Expedition. *Quagga* 16: 22-23.

Hockey, P. A. R. (1987) The influence of coastal utilisation by man on the presumed extinction of the Canarian Black Oystercatcher *Haematopus meadewaldoi* Bannerman. *Biol. Conserv.* 39: 49-62.

Hoffmann, T. W. (1984) *National red data list of endangered and rare birds of Sri Lanka*. Colombo: Ceylon Bird Club.

Hollom, P. A. D., Porter, R. F., Christensen, S. and Willis, I. (1988) *Birds of the Middle East and North Africa*. Calton: T. and A. D. Poyser.

Holmes, D. A. (1977) Faunistic notes and further additions to the Sumatran avifauna. *Bull. Brit. Orn. Club* 97: 68-71.

Holmes, D. A. and Burton, K. (1987) Recent notes on the avifauna of Kalimantan. *Kukila* 3: 2-32.

Holmes, P. and Wood, H. (1980) *The report of the ornithological expedition to Sulawesi*. Middlesex.

Holyoak, D. T. (1974) Undescribed land birds from the Cook Islands, Pacific Ocean. *Bull. Brit. Orn. Club* 94: 145-150.

Holyoak, D. T. and Thibault, J.-C. (1984) Contribution a l'etude des oiseaux de Polynesie orientale. *Mem. Mus. Natn. Hist. Nat.* Ser. A., Zool. 127: 1-209.

Hoogendoorm, W. and Mackrill, E. J. (1987) Audouin's Gull in southwestern Palearctic. *Dutch Birding* 9: 99-107.

Hoogerwerf, A. (1966) Some notes on the genus *Trichostoma* especially on the validity of *T. sepiarium minus* from east Java and about the status of *T. vanderbilti* and *T. liberale* from northern Sumatra. *Yamashina's Institute for Ornithology and Zoology* 4: 294-300.

Hopkinson, G. and Masterson, A. (1984) The occurrence and ecological preferences of certain Rallidae near Salisbury, Zimbabwe. Pp. 425-440 in J. Ledger, ed. *Proc. Fifth Pan Afr. Orn. Congr.* Johannesburg: Southern African Ornithological Society.

HOS (Hellenic Ornithological Society) (1987) Decrease in the population of the Lesser Kestrel (*Falco naumanni*). *Nature* 37: 35.

Howes, J. (1986) Identification of Cox's Sandpiper *Calidris paramelanotos*. *Interwader Newsletter* 7: 13.

Howes, J. (1988) Nordmann's Greenshank *Tringa guttifer*: status and threats. *Asian Wetland News* 1: 12.

Howes, J. and Lambert, F. (1987) Some notes on the status, field identification and foraging characteristics of Nordmann's Greenshank. *Wader Study Group Bull.* 49: 14-17.

Huizinga, M. (1984) Bolle's Laurel Pigeon and Laurel Pigeon on La Palma. *Dutch Birding* 6: 134-135.

Hunter, L. A. (in press) Status of the endemic Atitlan Grebe of Guatemala: is it extinct? [*Auk.*]

Hussain, S. A. (1984) Some aspects of the biology and ecolgy of Narcondan Hornbill (*Rhyteceros nardonami*). *J. of Bombay Nat. Hist. Soc.* 81: 1-18.

Imber, M. J. (1987) Breeding ecology and conservation of the Black Petrel (*Procellaria parkinsoni*). *Notornis* 34(1): 19-39.

Ingels, J., Parkes, K. C. and Farrand, J. (1981) The status of the macaw generally but incorrectly called *Ara caninde* (Wagler). *Gerfaut* 71: 283-294.

Inskipp, C. and Collar, N. J. (1984) The Bengal Florican: its conservation in Nepal. *Oryx* 18: 30-35.

Inskipp, C. and Inskipp, T. (1983) *Results of a preliminary survey of Bengal Floricans Houbaropsis bengalensis in Nepal and India, 1982.* Cambridge, U.K.: International Council for Bird Preservation (Study Report 2).

Inskipp, C. and Inskipp, T. (1985a) *A guide to the birds of Nepal.* London: Croom and Helm.

Inskipp C, and Inskipp, T. (1985b) A survey of Bengal Floricans in Nepal and India, 1982. *Bustard Studies* 3: 141-160.

Inskipp, C. and Inskipp, T. P. (1986) Birds and forests in Nepal. *Forktail* 1: 53-64.

Irwin, M. P. S. and Clancey, P. A. (1986) A new generic status for the Dappled Mountain Robin. *Bull. Brit. Orn. Club* 106: 111-115.

Ishihara, T. (1986) The Amami Ground Thrush distinct from the White's Ground Thrush. *Strix* 5: 60-61.

Islam, K. and Crawford, J. A. (1985) Brood habitat and roost sites of Western Tragopans in northeastern Pakistan. *World Pheasant Assoc. J.* 10: 7-14.

Islam, K. and Crawford, J. A. (1986) Summary of Western Tragopan Project in Pakistan with recommendation for conservation of the species. In M.Ridley, ed. *Pheasants in Asia 1986.* Basildon, U.K.: World Pheasant Association.

Isler, M. L. and Isler, P. R. (1987) *The tanagers: natural history, distribution and identification.* Washington, D. C.: Smithsonian Institution Press.

Jackson, J. A. (1986) Biopolitics, management of federal lands, and the conservation of the Red-cockaded Woodpecker. *Amer. Birds* 40(5): 1162-1168.

Jacob, J.-P., Lafontaine, R. -M., Chiwy, B., Divillers, P, de Visscher, N. -M. and Ledant, J.-P. (1985) Fiches d'information sur les especes enumerees dans l'annexe 1 de la directive 79/409/CEE. Unpublished report to EEC.

James, P. C. (1984) The status and conservation of seabirds in the Mediterranean Sea. Pp. 371-375 in: Croxall, J. P., Evans, P. G. H., and Schreiber, R. W. eds. *Status and conservation of the world's seabirds.* Cambridge, U.K.: International Council for Bird Preservation (Techn. Publ.

2).

Jehl, J. R. (1972) On the cold trail of an extinct petrel. *Pacific Discovery* 25(6): 24-29.

Jehl, J. R. (1982) The biology and taxonomy of Townsend's Shearwater. *Gerfaut* 72: 121-135.

Jehl, J. R. (1983) Can the Socorro Dove and Socorro Mockingbird be saved? Pp. 5-9 in *Proceedings [of the] Jean Delacour/IFCB Symposium on breeding birds in captivity.* North Hollywood, California: International Foundation for the Conservation of Birds.

Jehl, J. R. (1984) Comings and goings on a desert isle. *Natural History* 93(2): 6-12.

Jehl, J. R. and Everett, W. T. (1985) History and status of the avifauna of Isla Guadalupe, Mexico. *Trans. San Diego Soc. Nat. Hist.* 20(17): 313-336.

Jehl, J. R. and Parkes, K. C. (1982) The status of the avifauna of the Revillagigedo Islands, Mexico. *Wilson Bull.* 94: 1-19.

Jehl, J. R. and Parkes, K. C. (1983) "Replacements" of landbird species on Socorro Island, Mexico. *Auk* 100: 551-559.

Jenkins, J. M. (1983) *The native forest birds of Guam.* Washington, D.C.: American Ornithologists' Union (Orn. Monogr. 31).

Jennings, M. C., Heathcote, P. C., Parr, D. and Baha el Din, S. M. (1985) *Ornithological survey of the Ras Dib area and the islands at the mouth of the Gulf of Suez, Egypt.* Report prepared for B.P. Petroleum Development Co. (Egypt) Ltd.

Jenny, J. P. and Cade, T. J. (1986) Observations on the biology of the Orange-breasted Falcon *Falco deiroleucus. Birds of Prey Bull.* 3: 119-124.

Jenny, J. P. and Burnham, W. A. (1987) Preliminary observations on the biology of the Orange-breasted Falcon (*Falco deiroleucus*). III Congress de Ornitologia Neotropical: Resumenes. Unpublished.

Jessop, A. E. and Reid, T. (1986) *Winter surveys of the Orange-bellied Parrot Neophema chrysogaster in Victoria, 1984 and 1985.* Victoria, Australia: Royal Australasian Ornithologists' Union.

Johnsgard, P. A. (1986) *The pheasants of the world.* Oxford: Oxford University Press.

Johnson, A. and Chebez J. C. (1985) Sobre la situacion de *Mergus octosetaceus* Vieillot (Anseriformes: Anatidae) en la Argentina. *Historia Natural* Supl. no. 1: 1-16.

Johnson, T. (1987) Red Data Bird: White-breasted White-eye. *World Birdwatch* 9(3): 5.

Jones, C. G. (1987) The larger land-birds of Mauritius. Pp.208-300 in A. W. Diamond, ed. *Studies of Mascarene Island birds.* Cambridge, U.K.: Cambridge University Press.

Jones, P. J. and Tye, A. (1988) *A survey of the avifauna of Sao Tome and Principe.* Cambridge, U.K.: International Council for Bird Preservation (Study Report 24).

Jouanin, C. and Mougin, J. -L. (1979) Order Procellariiformes. Pp. 48-118 in E. Mayr and G. W. Cottrell, eds. *Checklist of birds of the world.* Vol. 1. 2nd Edition. Cambridge, Massachusetts: Museum of Comparative Zoology.

Joseph, L. (in press) A review of the conservation status of Australian Parrots in 1987. [*Biol. Cons.*].

Jouventin, P., Stahl, J. C., Weimerskirch, H. and Mougin, J. L. (1984) The seabirds of the French subantarctic islands and Adelie land, their status and conservation. Pp. 609-625 in J. P. Croxall, P. G. H. Evans and R. W. Schreiber, eds. *Status and conservation of the world's seabirds.* Cambridge, U.K.: International Council for Bird Preservation (Techn. Publ. 2).

de Juana, E., Varela, J. and Witt, H. -H. (1984) The conservation of seabirds at the Chafarinas islands. Pp. 363-370 in Croxall, J. P., Evans, P. G. H. and Schreiber, R. W., eds. *Status and conservation of the world's seabirds.* Cambridge, U.K.: International Council for Bird Preservation (Techn. Publ. 2).

de Juana, E. and Varela, J. M. (1987) Audouin's Gull, Chafarinas, 1987. *Seabird Group Newsletter* 50: 16.

Judge, R. P. (1987) Topics in endangered species management and policy. Phd dissertation, Dept. of Economics, Duke University.

Karl, B. J. and Best, H. A. (1982) Feral cats on Stewart Island; their foods, and their effects on Kakapo. *New Zealand J. of Zoology* 9: 287-294.

Kasparek, M. and van der Ven, J. (1983) *Birds of Turkey. 1: Ercek Golu.* Published by the authors, Heidelburg.

Kelly, S. T. and DeCapita, M. E. (1982) Cowbird control and its effect on Kirtland's Warbler reproductive success. *Wilson Bull.* 94(3): 363-365.

Kemp, A. C. (in prep.) The systematics and zoogeography of Oriental and Australasian hornbills (Aves: Bucerotidae).

Kemp, A. C. anc Crowe, T. M. (1985) The systematics and zoogeography of Afrotropical hornbills (Aves: Bucerotidae). Pp 279-324 in K.-L. Schuchmann, ed. *Proceedings of the International Symposium on African Vertebrates*. Bonn: Zoologisches Forschungsinstitut und Museum Alexander Koenig.

Kennerley, P. R. (1987) A survey of the birds of the Poyang Lake Nature Reserve, Jiangxi Province, China, 29 December 1985 - 4 January 1986. *Hong Kong Bird Report* 1984/1985: 97-111.

Kennerley, P. R. and Bakewell, D. N. (1987) Nordmann's Greenshank in Hong Kong: a review of the identification and status. *Hong Kong Bird Report* 1986: 83-100.

Khan, M. A. R. (1986) The threatened White-winged Wood Duck *Cairina scutulata* in Bangladesh. *Forktail* 2: 97-101.

King, B. (1985) Wild sighting of Hume's Pheasant in Burma. *WPA News* 8: 21.

King, B. F. (1986) Report on pheasants at Jiuzhaigou and Baihe Panda Reserves in north-west Sichuan, southern China. *WPA News* 11: 20-22.

King, B. (1987a) Some bird observations at Pangquanguo Reserve in west central Shanxi Province in NE China. *Hong Kong Bird Report* 1984-1985: 112-114.

King, B. (1987b) Some notes on the birds of the Yi Shan area of NW Jiangxi Province, China. *Hong Kong Bird Report* 1984-1985: 115-119.

King, B. (1987c) Wild sighting of Cabot's Tragopan. *WPA News* 18: 21-23.

King, B. (1987d) The Waterfall Swift *Hydrochous gigas*. *Bull. Brit. Orn. Club* 107: 36-37.

King, B. F., Dickinson, E. C. and Woodcock, M. W. (1975) *A field guide to the birds of South-East Asia*. London: Collins.

King, W. B. (1978-1979) *Red data book, 2. Aves*. Morges, Switzerland: International Union for Conservation of Nature and Natural Resources.

Kitson, A. R. (1980) *Larus relictus* - a review. *Bull. Brit. Orn. Club* 100(3): 178-185.

Knoder, C. E. (1983) Elliot's Pheasant conservation. *World Pheasant Assoc. J.* 8: 11-28

Kolosov, A. M. ed. (1983) *Red data book of the RSFSR: animals*. (In Russian). Moscow: Rossel 'khozizdat.

Kooiman J. G. (1940) Mededeelingen over het voorkomen in Oostjava vor dit gewest nog niet in de literatuur genoemde vogels. *Ardea* 29: 98-108.

Koschmann, J. R. and Price, P. L. (1987) The Thick-billed Parrot. *AFA Watchbird* 14(1): 48-53.

Krabbe, N. (1984) An additional specimen of the Swallow-tailed Cotinga *Phibalura flavirostris boliviana*. *Bull. Brit. Orn. Club* 104: 68-69.

Kumerloeve, H. (1984) The Waldrapp, *Geronticus eremita* (Linnaeus, 1758): historical review, taxonomic history, and present status. *Biol. Conserv.* 30: 363-373.

Kuroda, N. (1933-1936) *Birds of the island of Java*. Tokyo.

Kyllingstad, H. C. (1986) A record of Bald Ibis from the Sinai Mountains. *O.S.M.E. Bull.* 17: 1-2.

La Cock, G. D. (1986) The Southern Oscillation, environmental anomalies, and mortality of two southern African seabirds. *Climatic Change* 8: 173-184.

La Cock, G. D., Duffy, D. C. and Cooper, J. (1987) Population dynamics of the African Penguin *Spheniscus demersus* at Marcus Island in the Benguela Upwelling ecosystem: 1979-85. *Biol. Conserv.* 40: 117-126.

Lambert, F. (1983) *Report of an expedition to survey the status of the St Vincent Parrot Amazona guildingii*. Cambridge, U.K.: International Council for Bird Preservation (Study Report 3).

Lambert, F. (1985) The St Vincent parrot, an endangered Caribbean bird. *Oryx* 19: 34-37.

Lane, B. (1987) *Shorebirds in Australia*. Melbourne: Nelson Publishers.

Langrand, O. (1987) Distribution, status and conservation of the Madagascar Fish-eagle *Haliaeetus vociferoides* Desmurs, 1845. *Biol. Conserv.* 42: 73-77.

Lanning, D. V. (1982) Survey of the Red-fronted Macaw (*Ara rubrogenys*) and Caninde Macaw (*Ara caninde*) in Bolivia, December 1981 - March 1982. Unpublished.

Lanning, D. V. and Shiflett, J. T. (1981) Status and nesting ecology of the Thick-billed Parrot (*Rhynchopsitta pachyrhyncha*). Pp. 393-401 in R. F. Pasquier, ed. *Conservation of New World parrots*. Washington, D. C.: Smithsonian Institution Press for the International Council of Bird Preservation (Techn. Publ. 1).

Lanning D. V. and Shiflett, J. T. (1983) Nesting ecology of Thick-billed Parrots. *Condor* 85: 66-73.

La Touche, J. D. D. (1925-34) *A handbook of the birds of eastern China*. London: Taylor and Francis.

Lavers, R. and Mills, J. (1984) *Takahe*. Dunedin, New Zealand: John McIndoe and New Zealand Wildlife Service.

Lawson, P. W. and Lanning, D. V. (1981) Nesting and status of the Maroon-fronted Parrot (*Rhynchopsitta terrisi*). Pp. 385-392 in R. F. Pasquier, ed. *Conservation of New World parrots.* Washington, D. C.: Smithsonian Institution Press for the International Council for Bird Preservation (Techn. Publ. 1).

LeCroy, M., Peckover, W. S., Kulupi, A. and Manseima, J. (1984) Bird observations on Normanby and Fergusson, D'Entrecasteaux Islands, Papua New Guinea. Baroko, PNG: Division of Wildlife (Wildlife in Papua New Guinea 83/1).

Liedel, K. (1982) Verbreitung und Oekologie des Step Penschlammlaufers, *Limnodromus semipalmatus* (Blyth). *Ann. Orn.* 6: 147-162.

Lelliott, A. D. (1981) Cheer Pheasants in west-central Nepal. *World Pheasant Assoc. J.* 6: 89-95.

Lever, C. (1987) *Naturalized birds of the world.* Harlow, U.K.: Longman Scientific and Technical.

Lewis, R. E. (1986) A rain-forest raptor in danger. *Oryx* 20: 170-175.

Ligon, J. D., Stacey, P. B., Connor, R. N., Bock, C. E. and Adkisson, C. S. (1986) Report of the American Ornithologists' Union Committee for the conservation of the Red-cockaded Woodpecker. *Auk* 103(4): 848-855.

Lobkov, E. G. and Neufeldt, I. A. (1986) Distribution and biology of the Steller's Sea Eagle - *Haliaeetus pelagicus pelagicus* (Pallas). *Proc. Zool. Inst. Acad. Sci. USSR.* 150: 107-146.

Longmore, N. W. (1985) A Sydney specimen of *Neodrepanis hypoxantha* (Philepittidae). *Bull. Brit. Orn. Club* 105: 85-86.

Louette, M. (1987) A new weaver from Uganda? *Ibis* 129: 405-406.

Louette, M. (1988) Additions and corrections to the avifauna of Zaire (2). *Bull. Brit. Orn. Club* 108: 43-50.

Louette, M., Stevens, J., Bijnens, L. and Janssens, L. (1986) *Comoro Islands endemic bird survey.* International Council for Bird Preservation final report (30 April 1986).

Love, J. A. (1983) *The return of the Sea Eagle.* Cambridge, U.K.: Cambridge University Press.

Loyn, R. H., Lane, B. A., Chandler, C. and Carr, G. W. (1986) Ecology of Orange-bellied Parrots *Neophema chrysogaster* at their main remnant wintering site. *Emu* 86: 195-206.

Lu Tai-chun, He Fen-qi and Lui Ru-sun (1986) The Chines Monal *Lophophorus lhuysii*: studies of its ecology and biology. In M. Ridley, ed. *Pheasants in Asia 1986.* Basildon, U.K.: World Pheasant Association.

Luthin, C. (1987) Rare visit to Oriental Crested Ibis. *Flying Free* 5(2): 4-5.

Luthin, C. S. (1987) Status and conservation priorities for the world's stork species. *Colonial Waterbirds* 10: 181-202.

Mackinnon, J. (1983) Methods for the conservation of Maleo birds, *Macrocephalon maleo* on the island of Sulawesi, Indonesia. *Biol. Conserv.* 20: 183-193.

Macleod, H. L. (1987) *The conservation of Oku Mountain Forest, Cameroon.* Cambridge, U.K.: International Council for Bird Preservation (Study Report 15).

Madge, S. and Birn, H. (1988) *Wildfowl.* London: Christopher Helm.

de Magalhaes, J. C. R. (1978) Especies cinegeticas e protecao a fauna na regiao sudeste, com especial referencia ao estade de Sao Paulo. Pp. 62-67 in *Seminario sobre caca amadorista.* Rio de Janeiro: Fundacao Brasileira para a Conservacao da Natureza.

Magrath, R. D., Ridley, M. W. and Woinarski, J. Z. (1985) Status and habitat requirements of Lesser Floricans in Kathiawar, western India. *Bustard Studies* 3: 185-193.

Malingreau, J.-P. and Tucker, C. J. (1988) Large-scale deforestation in the southeastern Amazon basin of Brazil. *Ambio* 17: 49-55.

Mann, C. F. (1986) Christmas Island Frigatebirds *Fregata andrewsi* on the Kenya coast. *Bull. Brit. Orn. Club* 106: 89-90.

Manry, D. E. (1985a) Reproductive performance of the Bald Ibis *Geronticus calvus* in relation to rainfall and grass-burning. *Ibis* 127: 159-173.

Manry, D. E. (1985b) Distribution, abundance and conservation of the Bald Ibis *Geronticus calvus* in southern Africa. *Biol. Conserv.* 33: 351-362.

Marchant, J., Prater, T. and Hayman, P. (1986) *Shorebirds.* London and Sydney: Croom Helm.

van Marle, J. G. and Voous, K. H. (1988) *The birds of Sumatra.* London: British Ornithologists' Union (Check-list 10).

Marshall, J. T. (1978) *Systematics of smaller Asian night birds based on voice.* Kansas: American Ornithologists' Union (Orn. Monogr. 25).

Martin, A. (1985) Premiere onservation du Pigeon Trocaz (*Columba trocaz bollii*) a l'ile de Hierro

(Iles Canaries). *Alauda* 53: 137-140.

Martin, A. (1987) *Atlas de las aves nidificantes en la isla de Tenerife*. La Laguna: Instituo de Estudios Canarios.

Martindale, J. (1986) *The Freckled Duck - an RAOU conservation statement*. Melbourne: Royal Australasian Ornithologists' Union (Report 22).

Massey Stewart, J. (1987) The 'lily of birds': the success story of the Siberian white crane. *Oryx* 21: 6-10.

Masterson, A. (1986) Wattled Cranes - hot seating? *Honeyguide* 32: 154-155.

Matthews, G. V. T. and Evans, M. E. (1974) On the behaviour of the White-headed Duck with especial reference to breeding. *Wildfowl* 25: 56-66.

Mauersberger, G., Wagner, S., Wallschlager, D. and Warthold, R. (1982) Neue Daten zur Avifauna mongolica. *Mitt. Zool. Mus. Berlin* 58: 11-74.

Mayr, E. (1944) The birds of Timor and Sumba. *Bull. Amer. Mus. Nat. Hist.* 83: 123-194.

Mayr, E. (1945) *Birds of the southwest Pacific*. New York: Macmillan.

Mayr, E. and Cottrell, G. W. (1986) *Check-list of birds of the world*, 11. Cambridge, Mass.: Museum of Comparative Zoology.

Mayr, E. and Vuilleumier, F. (1983) New species of birds described from 1966 to 1975. *J. Orn.* 124: 217-232.

McGuigan, C. (1987) Ornithology report. Pp.10-27 in S. L. Tetlow, ed. *Cambridge Conservation Study 1985: Taita Hills, Kenya*. Cambridge, U.K.: International Council for Bird Preservation, Study Report no.19.

McKean, J. L. (1987) A first record of Christmas Island Frigatebird *Fregata andrewsi*. *Kukila* 3(1-2): 47.

McNee, S. (1986) *Surveys of the Western Whipbird and Western Bristlebird in western Australia, 1985*. Victoria, Australia: Royal Australasian Ornithologists' Union (Report 18).

McNicholl, M. K. (1985) Profiles on risk status of Canadian birds: 2. Piping Plover. *Alberta Naturalist* 15(4): 135-138.

Medway, Lord and Wells, D. R. (1976) *The birds of the Malay Peninsular*, 5. London and Kuala Lumpur: H. F. and G. Witherby in association with Penerbit Universiti Malaysia.

Mees, G. F. (1961) A systematic review of the Indo-Australian Zosteropidae (Part I). *Zool. Verh.* 50: 1-168.

Mees, G. F. (1969) A systematic review of the Indo-Australian Zosteropidae (Part III). *Zool. Verh.* 102: 1-390.

Mees, G. F. (1973) Description of a new member of the *Monarcha trivigata* group from Flores, Lesser Sunda Islands (Aves, Monarchinae). *Zool. Meded.* 46: 179-181.

Melville, D. S. (1984) Seabirds of China and the surrounding seas. Pp. 501-511 in J. P. Croxall, P. G. H. Evans and R. W. Schreiber, eds. *Status and conservation of the world's seabirds*. Cambridge, U.K.: International Council for Bird Preservation (Techn. Publ. 2).

Melville, D. S. and Round, P. D. (1982) Further records of the Asian Dowitcher *Limnodromus semipalmatus* from Thailand, with notes on its distribution and identification. *Nat. Hist. Bull. Siam. Soc.* 30(2): 119-204.

Merton, D. V., Morris, R. B. and Atkinson, I. A. E. (1984) Lek behaviour in a parrot: the Kakapo *Strigops labroptilus* of New Zealand. *Ibis* 126: 277-283.

Meyburg, B.-U. (1982) Seltene und vom Aussterben bedrohte Greifvogel (III): der Spanische Kaiseradler *Aquila (heliaca) adalberti*. Der Falkner 31/32: 21-30.

Meyburg, B.-U. (1986) Threatened and near-threatened diurnal birds of prey of the world. *Birds of Prey Bull.* 3: 1-12.

Meyburg, B.-U. (1987) Clutch size, nestling aggression and breeding success of the Spanish Imperial Eagle. *Brit. Birds* 80: 308-320.

Meyburg, B.-U. and Meyburg, C. (1983) Distribution and present status of the Black Vulture *Aegypicus monachus*. *Bull. World Working Group on Birds of Prey* 1: 172.

Meyer de Schauensee, R. (1966) *The species of birds of South America and their distribution*. Narberth, Penn.: Livingston Publishing Company for the Academy of Natural Sciences of Philadelphia.

Meyer de Schauensee, R. (1982) *A guide to the birds of South America*. Philadelphia: Academy of Natural Sciences (reprinted by Pan American Section, International Council for Bird Preservation).

Meyer de Schauensee, R. (1984) *The birds of China*. Oxford: Oxford University Press.

Meyer de Schauensee, R. and Phelps, W. H. (1978) *A guide to the birds of Venezuela*. Princeton: Princeton University Press.

Mian, A. (1986) Ecological impact of Arab falconry on Houbara Bustard in Baluchistan. *Environ. Conserv.* 13: 41-46.

Michael, G. A. (1987) Notes on the breeding biology and ecology of the Mariana or Guam Crow. *Avicult. Mag.* 93(2): 73-82.

Mills, J. A., Lavers, R. B. and Lee, W. G. (1984) The Takahe - a relict of the Pleistocene grassland avifauna of New Zealand. *New Zealand J. of Ecology* 7: 57-70.

Milton, G. R. (1985) Notes on the distribution of the Masked Finfoot *Heliopias personata* in Indonesia. *Kukila* 2: 41-43.

Monroe, B. L. (1968) *A distributional survey of the birds of Honduras*. American Ornithologists' Union (Orn. Monogr. 7).

Morony, J. J., Bock, W.J. and Farrand, J. (1975) *Reference list of the birds of the world*. New York: American Museum of Natural History (Department of Ornithology).

Morris, G. E. (1987) News of Nam Cat Tien. *Garrulax* 2: 3-5.

Muller, H. H. (1988) Erster Brutnachweis des vom Aussterben bedrohten Taiko-Sturmvogels (Pterodroma magentae) auf den Chatham Islands (Neuseeland). *Seevogel* 9(1): 9-11.

Munn, C. A., Thomsen, J. B. and Yamashita, C. (1987) Survey and status of the Hyacinth Macaw (*Anodorhynchus hyacinthinus*) in Brazil, Bolivia, and Paraguay. Unpublished.

Myers, P. and Hansen, R. L. (1980) Rediscovery of the Rufous-faced Crake (*Laterallus xenopterus*). *Auk* 97: 901-902.

Nagy, K. A., Siegfried, W. R. and Wilson, R. P. (1984) Energy utilization by free-ranging Jackass Penguins, *Spheniscus demersus*. *Ecology* 65: 1648-1655.

Nakhasathien, S. (1987) The discovery of Storm's Stork *Ciconia stormi* in Thailand. *Forktail* 3: 43-49.

Narosky, S. (1977) Una nueva especie del genera *Sporophila* (Emberizidae). *Hornero* 11: 345-348.

Narosky, T. and Yzurieta, D. (1987) *Guia para la identificacion de las aves de Argentina y Uruguay*. Buenos Aires: Vazquez Mazzini Editores.

Nash, A. D. and Nash, S. V. (1985) Large Frogmouth *Batrachostomus auritus* mobbed by a Greater Rachet-tailed Drongo *Dicrurus paradiseus*. *Kukila* 2: 67.

Nash, S. V. and Nash, A. D. (1986) Records of the White-winged Duck *Cairina scutulata* in Sumatran peatswamp forest. *Oriental Bird Club Bull.* 3: 17.

de Naurois, R. (1986) Une reproduction de *Fringilla t. teydea* (Webb, Berthelot et Moquin-Tandon) dans un biotope inattendu. *Cyanopica* 3: 533-538.

Nelson, J. B. (1974) The distribution of Abbott's Booby *Sula abbotti*. *Ibis* 116: 368-369.

Nelson, J. B. and Powell, D. (1986) The breeding ecology of Abbott's Booby *Sula abbotti*. *Emu* 86(1): 33-46.

Nikolaus, G. (1987) *Distribution atlas of Sudan's birds with notes on habitat and status*. Bonn: Zoologisches Forschungsinstitut und Museum Alexander Koenig (Bonner zoologische Monographien, no. 25).

Norderhaug, A. and Norderhaug, M. (1984) Status of the Lesser White-fronted Goose *Anser erythropus*, in Fennoscandia. *Swedish Wildlife Research* 13(1): 171-185.

Nores, M. and Yzurieta, D. (1984) Distribucion y situacion actual de las parabas y parabachis en Bolivia (Aves Psittacidae). Consejo Internacional para la Preservacion de las Aves. Unpublished.

Nores, M., Yzurieta, D. and Salvador, S. A. (1987) Distribucion y situacion actual del Mirlo de Agua Pecho Rojo (*Cinclus schulzi*). III Congreso de Ornitologia Neotropical: Resumenes. Unpublished.

Nowak, E. (1983) Die Schopfkasarka, *Tadorna cristata* (Kuroda, 1917) - eine vom Aussterben bedrohte Tierart (Wissensstand und Vorschlage zum Schutz). *Bonn. zool. Beitr.* 34: 235-271.

Nowak, E. (1984a) Ueber das vermutliche Brut- und Ueberwinterungsgebiet der Schopfkasarka, *Tadorna cristata*. *J. Orn.* 125: 103-105.

Nowak, E. (1984b) Ueber einige Farbungs- und Verhaltensmerkmale der Schopfkasarka. *Falke* 31: 150-155.

O'Donnell, C. F. J. (1984) The North Island Kokako (*Callaeas cinerea wilsoni*) in the Western King Country and Taranaki. *Notornis* 31(2): 131-144.

Ogle, D. (1986) The status and seasonality of birds in Nakhon Sawan Province, Thailand. *Nat. Hist. Bull. Siam Soc.* 34(2): 115-143.

O Myong Sok (1984) Wiederentdeckung der Schopfkasarka, *Tadorna cristata*, in der Koreanischen Demokratischen Volksrepublik. *J. Orn.* 125: 102-103.

Olrog, C. C. (1985) Status of wet forest raptors in northern Argentina. Pp. 191-197 in I. Newton and R. D. Chancellor, eds. *Conservation studies on raptors.* Cambridge, U. K.: International Council for Bird Preservation (Techn. Publ. 5)

Olsen, P. D. and Olsen, J. (1986) Distribution, status, movements and breeding of the Grey Falcon *Falco hypoleucos. Emu* 86: 47-51.

Olsen, S. L. and Warheit, K. I. (1988) A new genus for *Sula abbotti. Bull. Brit. Orn. Club* 108: 9-12.

O'Neill, J. P., del Solar R., G., Ortiz T., E., Eley, J. W. and Williams, M. D. (1981) The White-winged Guan, *Penelope albipennis*, its rediscovery, status, nesting, systematics, and recommendations for its continued survival. Pp. 203-215 in *Primer Simposio Internacional de la Familia Cracidae: Memorias.* [Mexico City:] Universidad Nacional Autonoma de Mexico.

Oren, D. C. and Novaes, F. C. (1986) Observations on the Golden Parakeet *Aratinga guarouba* in northern Brazil. *Biol. Conserv.* 36: 329-337.

Ortiz-Crespo, F. I. (1984) First twentieth-century specimen of the Violet-throated Metaltail *Metallura baroni. Bull. Brit. Orn. Club* 104: 95-97.

Ortiz Tejada, E. and Purisaca Puicon, J. (1981) Estudio preliminar sobre la Pava aliblanca (*Penelope albipennis*) Taczanowski 1877. Pp. 192-202 in *Primer Simposio Internacional de la Familia Cradidae: Memorias.* [Mexico City:] Universidad Nacional Autonoma de Mexico.

Osborne, P. E. (1986) *Survey of the birds of Fuerteventura, Canary Islands, with special reference to the status of the Canarian Houbara Bustard Chlamydotis undulata.* Cambridge, U.K.: International Council for Bird Preservation (Study Report 10).

Ostapenko, W. A. and Zewenmjadag, N. (1983) Uber Verbreitung, Anzahl und Biologie der Kraniche im Ostteil der Mongolischen Volksrepublik. *Beitr. Vogelkd.* 29: 274-278.

Palma, L. (1985) The present situation of birds of prey in Portugal. Pp. 3-14 in I. Newton, and R. D. Chancellor, eds. *Conservation studies on raptors.* Cambridge, U.K.: International Council for Bird Preservation (Techn. Publ. 5).

Parker, S. A. and Reid, N. (1979) Remarks on the status of some Australian passerines. In M. J. Tyler, ed. *The status of endangered Australasian wildlife.* Adelaide: Royal Zoological Society of South Australia.

Parker, T. A. (1981) Distribution and biology of the White-cheeked Cotinga *Zaratornis stresemanni*, a high Andean frugivore. *Bull. Brit. Orn. Club* 101: 256-265.

Parker, T. A. (1982) First record of the Chilean Woodstar *Eulidia yarrellii* in Peru. *Bull. Brit. Orn. Club* 102: 86.

Parker, T. A. (1983) Rediscovery of the Rufous-fronted Antthrush (*Formicarius rufifrons*) in southeastern Paru. *Gerfaut* 73: 287-289.

Parker, T. A. and O'Neill, J. P. (1980) Notes on little known birds of the upper Urubamba Valley, southern Peru. *Auk* 97: 167-176.

Parker, T. A., Allen Parker, S. and Plenge, M. A. (1982) *An annotated checklist of Peruvian birds.* Vermillion, South Dakota: Buteo Books.

Parker, T. A., Schulenberg, T. S., Graves, G. R. and Braun, M. J. (1985) The avifauna of the Huancabamba region, northern Peru. Pp. 169-197 in P. A. Buckley, M. S. Foster, E. S. Morton, R. S. Ridgely and F. G. Buckley, eds. *Neotropical ornithology.* Washington, D. C.: American Ornithologists' Union (Orn. Monogr. 36).

Parkes, K. C. (1987) Letter: was the "Chinese" White-eyed River-Martin an Oriental Pratincole? *Forktail* 3: 68-69.

Parrot-Holden, J. (1987) The Socorro Dove - its destiny. *AFA Watchbird* 14(5): 48-49.

Pattee, O. H. (1987) The role of lead in Condor mortality. *Endangered Species Techn. Bull.* XII(9): 6-7.

Paynter, R. A., ed. (1967) *Check-list of birds of the world*, 12. Cambridge, Mass.: Museum of Comparative Zoology.

Paynter, R. A. and Traylor, M. A. (1977) *Ornithological gazetteer of Ecuador.* Cambridge, Mass.: Museum of Comparative Zoology.

Peters, J. L. (1934-1987) *Checklist of the birds of the world.* Cambridge, Mass.: Harvard University Press.

Phelps, W. H. and Phelps, W. H. (1958) Lista de las aves de Venezuela con su distribucion, 2. Parte 1. No passeriformes. *Biol. Soc. Venezolana Cienc. Nat.* 19(90).

Pickering, R. H., ed. (1985) Santo Mountains Expedition 1985, preliminary report. Port Vila: Vanuatu Natural Science Society, unpublished.

Piechocki, R., Stubbe, M., Uhlenhaut, K. and Sumjaa, D. (1981) Beitrage zur Avifauna der Mongolei. *Mitt. Zool. Mus. Berlin* 57 (suppl.: Ann. Orn. 5): 71-128.

Pierce, R. J. (1986) Differences in susceptibility to predation during nesting between Pied and Black Stilts (*Himantopus* spp.) *Auk* 103: 273-280.

Piersma, T. (1986) Coastal waders on three Canary Islands in March-April 1986. *Wader Study Group Bull.* 48: 19-20.

Pinto, O. (1937) A rolinha *Oxypelia cyanopis* Pelzeln, so conhecida do Brasil, e uma das aves mais raras que existem. *Bol. Biologico* (N. S.) 3(5): 17-18.

Pinto, O. (1944) *Catalogo das aves do Brasil. Segunda Parte.* Sao Paulo: Departamento de Zoologia.

Pinto, O. (1945) Cinquenta anos de investigacao ornitologica. *Arc. Zool. Est. Sao Paulo* 4: 261-340.

Pinto, O. (1954) Aves do Itatiaia. *Bol. Parq. Nac. Itatiaia* no. 3.

Pinto, O. (1978) *Novo catalogo das aves do Brasil.* Sao Paulo: Departmento de Zoologia.

Piper, S. E. and Ruddle, P. (1986) An initial evaluation of the Cape Vulture colonies at Mkambati, Transkei. *Vulture News* 15: 7-12.

Pizzey, G. (1980) *A field guide to the birds of Australia.* Sydney: Collins.

Pokorny, F. and Pikula, J. (1987) Artificial breeding, rearing and release of Reeves Pheasant (*Syrmaticus reevesi*) (Gray 1929) in Czechoslovakia. *World Pheasant Assoc. J.* 12: 75-80.

Potapov, R. L. and Flint, V. E. eds. (1987). *The birds of the USSR: Galliformes, Gruiformes.* (In Russian.) Leningrad: 'Nauka'.

Prater, A. J. and Scott, D. A. (In prep.) The Slender-billed Curlew *Numenius tenuirostris*: a vanishing species.

Pratt, J. D., Bruner, P. L. and Berrett, D. G. (1987) *A field guide to the birds of Hawaii and the tropical Pacific.* Princeton: Princeton University Press.

Pratt, T. K. (1987) Recent observations March through May 1987. '*Elepaio* 47: 93-95.

Prigogine, A. and Louette, M. (1984) A new race of the Spotted Ground-thrush, *Zoothera guttata*, from Upemba, Zaire. *Gerfaut* 74: 185-186.

Probst, J. R. (1986) A review of factors limiting the Kirtland's Warbler on its breeding grounds. *Amer. Midland Nat.* 116(1): 87-100.

Probst, J. R. and Hayes, J. P. (1987) Pairing success of Kirtland's Warblers in marginal vs. suitable habitat. *Auk* 104: 234-241.

Rabor, D. S. (1962) The impact of deforestation on birds of Cebu, Philippines, with new records for that island. *VIII Bull. I.C.B.P.*: 79-85.

Raffaele, H. A. (1983a) *A guide to the birds of Puerto Rico and the Virgin Islands.* San Juan: Fondo Educativo Interamericano.

Raffaele, H. A. (1983b) The raising of a ghost - *Spinus cucullatus* in Puerto Rico. *Auk* 100(3): 737-739.

Rahmani, A. (1987) Protection for the Great Indian Bustard. *Oryx* 21: 174-179.

Rand, A. L. and Gilliard, E. T. (1967) *Handbook of New Guinea birds.* London: Weidenfield and Nicolson.

Randall, R. M. and Randall, B. M. (1986) The diet of Jackass Penguins *Spheniscus demersus* in Algoa Bay, South Africa, and its bearing on population declines elsewhere. *Biol. Conserv.* 37: 119-134.

Rauzon, M. J., Harrison, C. S. and Conant, S. (1985) The status of the Sooty storm-petrel in Hawaii. *Wilson Bull* 97(3): 390-392.

Redford, K. H. (1987) Parque das Emas. *Ciencia Hoje* 7(38): 42-48.

Remsen, J. V. (1986) Was Bachman's Warbler a bamboo specialist? *Auk* 103: 216-219.

Remsen, J. V. and Parker, T. A. (1983) The contribution of river-created habitats to bird species richness in Amazonia. *Biotropica* 15(3): 223-231.

Remsen, J. V. and Traylor, M. A. (1983) Additions to the avifauna of Bolivia, part 2. *Condor* 85: 95-98.

Remsen, J. V., Parker, T. A. and Ridgely, R. S. (1982) Natural history notes on some poorly known Bolivian birds. *Gerfaut* 72: 77-87.

Remsen, J. V., Traylor, M. A. and Parks, K. C. (1986) Range extensions of some Bolivian birds, 2

(Columbidae to Rhinocryptidae). *Bull. Brit. Orn. Club* 106: 22-32.

Restrepo, C. and Mondragon, M. L. (1987) Sobre la biologia de *Semmornis ramphastinus*: resultados preliminares. *III Congreso de Ornitologia Neotropical: Resumenes*. Unpublished.

Reville, R., Tranter, J. and Yorkston, H. (1987) *Monitoring the endangered Abbott's Booby on Christmas Island 1983-1986*. Canberra: Australian National Parks and Wildlife Service (Occasional Paper No. 11).

Ridgely, R. S. (1980) Notes on some rare or previously unrecorded birds in Ecuador. *Amer. birds* 34: 242-248.

Ridgely, R. S. (1981a) *A guide to the birds of Panama*. Third printing, with corrections and additions. Princeton: Princeton University Press.

Ridgely, R. S. (1981b) The current distribution and status of mainland Neotropical parrots. Pp. 233-384 in R. F. Pasquier, ed. *Conservation of New World parrots*. Washington, D. C.: Smithsonian Institution Press for the International Council for Bird Preservation (Techn. Publ. 1).

Rinke, D. (1986) The status of wildlife in Tonga. *Oryx* 20(3): 146-151.

van Riper, C. (1980) Observations on the breeding of the Palila *Psittirostra bailleui* of Hawaii. *Ibis* 122: 462-475.

Ripley, S. D. (1977) *Rails of the world*. Toronto: M. F. Feheley.

Ripley, S. D. (1982) *A synopsis of the birds of India and Pakistan*. Second edition. Bombay: Bombay Natural History Society.

Ripley, S. D. and Rabor, D. S. (1958) Notes on a collection of birds from Mindoro Island, Philippines. *Bull. Peabody Mus. Nat. Hist.* 13: 1-83.

Roberts, P. (1987) Is the Aldabra brush warbler extinct? *Oryx* 21: 209-210.

Roberts, T. J. (1985) Zangi Nawar - portrait of a unique lake in the desert. *J. Bombay. Nat. Hist. Soc.* 82(3): 540-547.

Robertson, A. S. (1986) Notes on the breeding cycle of Cape Vultures (*Gyps coprotheres*). *Raptor Research* 20: 51-60.

Robertson, A. S. and Boshoff, A. S. (1986) The feeding ecology of Cape Vultures *Gyps coprotheres* in a stock-farming area. *Biol. Conserv.* 35: 63-86.

Robertson, A. and February, E. (1986) Towards an historical perspective of Cape Vultures and domestic stock: a view from the southwestern Cape. *Vulture News* 15: 4-6.

Robertson, C. J. R. ed. (1985) *Complete book of New Zealand birds*. Sydney: Reader's Digest.

Robertson, C. J. R. and Bell, B. D. (1984) Seabird status and conservation in the New Zealand region. Pp. 573-586 in J. P. Croxall, P. G. H. Evans and R. W. Schreiber, eds. *Status and conservation of the world's seabirds*. Cambridge, U.K.: International Council for Bird Preservation (Techn. Publ. 2).

Robinson, H. C. and Boden Kloss, C. (1918) Results of an expedition to Korinchi Peak, Sumatra. Part 2: Birds. *J. Fed. Malay States Mus.* 8: 81-284.

Robson, C. R. (1986) Recent observations of birds in Xizang and Qinghai provinces, China. *Forktail* 2: 67-82.

Robson, C. (1987) Pheasants in Vietnam. *Garrulax* 3: 2-3.

Romero-Zambrano, H. (1983) Revision del status zoogeografico y redescripcion de *Odontophorus strophium* (Gould) (Aves: Phasianidae). *Caldasia* 13(65): 777-786.

Rooke, I. (1986) *Survey of the White-breasted White-eye and the Norfolk Island Boobook Owl on Norfolk Island, October - November 1985*. Victoria, Australia: Royal Australasian Ornithologists' Union (Report 20).

Rosenberg, D. K. and Harcourt, S. A. (1987) Population sizes and potential conservation problems of the endemic Galapagos Penguin and Flightless Cormorant. *Noticias de Galapagos* 45: 24-25.

Round, P. D. (1985) Records of the Asian Dowitcher *Limnodromus semipalmatus* in Thailand. *Oriental Bird Club Bull.* 1: 5-7.

Round, P. D. (in press) *The status and conservation of forest birds in Thailand*. Cambridge: International Council for Bird Preservation.

Round, P. D. and Treesucon, U. (1986) The rediscovery of Gurney's Pitta *Pitta gurneyi*. *Forktail* 2: 53-66.

Sakai, H. F., Ralph, C. J. and Jenkins, C. D. (1986) Foraging ecology of the Hawaiian Crow, an endangered generalist. *Condor* 88: 211-219.

Salvador, S., Narosky, S. and Fraga, R. (1986) First description of the nest and eggs of the Rufous-throated Dipper (*Cinclus schulzi*) in northwestern Argentina. *Gerfaut* 76: 63-66.

Salter, R. E. (1983) Summary of currently available information on internationally threatened wildlife species in Burma. Rangoon: Food and Agricultural Organisation of the United Nations (Working People's Settlement Board: Nature Conservation and National Parks Project, Burma, FO: Buar/80/006 Field Document 7/83).

Sane, S. R., Kannan, P., Rajendran, C. G., Ingle, S. T. and Bhagwat, A. M. (1986) On the taxonomic status of *Psittacula intermedia* (Rothschild). *J. Bombay Nat. Hist. Soc.* 83: (Supplement).

Sankaran, R. (1987) The Lesser Florican. *Sanctuary* 7: 26-37.

Sankaran, R. and Rahmani, A. R. (1986) *Study of ecology of certain endangered species of wildlife and their habitats: the Lesser Florican, annual report 2 1985-86.* [Bombay:] Bombay Natural History Society.

Sarker, S. U. and Iqbal, M. (1985) Observations on Pallas's Fish Eagle *Haliaeetus leucoryphus* in Bangladesh. *Bull. World Working Group on Birds of Prey* 2: 100-102.

Saxena, V. S. and Meena, B. L. (1985) Occurence of Lesser Floricans in forest plantations in Rajasthan, India. *Bustard Studies* 3: 183-184.

Schlatter, R. P. (1984) The status and conservation of seabirds in Chile. Pp. 261-269 in J. P. Croxall, P. G. H. Evans and R. W. Schreiber, eds. *Status and conservation of the world's seabirds.* Cambridge, U. K.: International Council for Bird Preservation (Techn. Publ. 2).

Schodde, R. (1978) The status of endangered Papuasian birds, and Appendix. Pp. 133-145 and 185-206 respectively in M. J. Tyler, ed. *The status of endangered Australasian wildlife.* Adelaide: Royal Zoological Society of South Australia.

Schodde, R., Fullagar, P. and Hermes, N. (1983) *A review of Norfolk Island birds: past and present.* Special publication no. 8. Canberra: Australian National Parks and Wildlife Service.

Schodde, R. and Mathews, S. J. (1977) *Contributions to Papuasian ornithology 5: Survey of the birds of Taam Island, Kai Group.* Division of Wildlife Research Technical Paper No. 33. Australia: CSIRO.

Schmutz, E. (1977) *Die vogel der Manggarai (Flores).* Ruteng, Flores.

Schulenberg, T. S., Allen, S. E., Stotz, D. F. and Wiedenfeld, D. A. (1984) Distributional records from the Cordillera Yanachaga, central Peru. *Gerfaut* 74: 57-70.

Schulenberg, T. S. and Binford, L. C. (1985) A new species of tanager (Emberizidae, Thraupinae, *Tangara*) from southern Peru. *Wilson Bull.* 97: 413-420.

Schulz, H. (1985) A review of the world status and breeding distribution of the Little Bustard. *Bustard Studies* 2: 131-151.

Scott, D. A. and Brooke, M. de L. (1985) The endangered avifauna of southeastern Brazil: a report on the BOU/WWF expedition of 1980/81 and 1981/82. Pp. 115-139 in A. W. Diamond and T. E. Lovejoy, eds. *Conservation of tropical forest birds.* Cambridge, U.K.: International Council for Bird Preservation (Techn. Publ. 4).

Scott, D. A. and Carbonell, M. (1986) *A directory for Neotropical wetlands.* Cambridge and Slimbridge, U.K.: International Union for Conservation of Nature and Natural Resources, and International Waterfowl Research Bureau.

Scott, D. A. and Carp, E. (1982) A midwinter survey of wetlands in Mesopotamia. Iraq: 1979. *Sandgrouse* 4: 60-76.

Scott, J. M., Mountainspring, S., van Riper, C., Kepler, C. B., Jacobi, J. D., Burr, T. A. and Giffin, J. G. (1984) Annual variation in the distribution, abundance, and habitat response of the Palila (*Loxioides bailleui*). *Auk* 101: 647-664.

Serpell, J., Collar, N., Davis, S. and Wells, S. (1983) Submission to the Foreign and Commonwealth Office on the future conservation of Henderson Island in the Pitcairn Group. Unpublished.

Severinghaus, S. R. (1978) Recommendations for the conservation of the Swinhoe's and Midako Pheasants in Taiwan. *World Pheasant Assoc. J.* 3: 79-89.

Severinghaus, S. (1986) The adaptability of Mikado and Swinhoe's Pheasants to disturbed habitats in Taiwan. Unpaginated abstract in M. Ridley, ed. *Pheasants in Asia 1986.* Basildon, U.K.: World Pheasant Association.

Severinghaus, S. R. and Blackshaw, K. T. (1976) *A new guide to the birds of Taiwan.* Taipei: Me Ya Publications.

Shi, Z. R., Thouless, C. R. and Melville, D. S. (in press) Discovery of the breeding grounds of Saunder's Gull *Larus saundersi*. *Ibis.*

Shibaev, Yu. A. (1987a) Distributional survey of Japanese Crested Ibis by questionnaire using colour postcards in Fare East USSR. Summary, p. 48 in *The Third Japan-USSR Bird Protection Symposium, 21 November 1986*. [Tokyo]: Wild Bird Society of Japan.

Shibaev, Yu. A. (1987b) Interim report on population survey of Steller's Sea-Eagle in winter in USSR. Summary, p. 48 in *The Third Japan-USSR Bird Protection Symposium, 21 November 1986*. [Tokyo]: Wild Bird Society of Japan.

Short, L. L. (1973) Habits, relationshiops and conservation of the Ocinawa Woodpecker. *Wilson Bull.* 85: 5-20.

Short, L. L. (1975) A zoogeographic analysis of the South American chaco avifauna. *Bull. Amer. Mus. Nat. Hist.* 154(3).

Short, L. L. (1976) Notes on a collection of birds from the Paraguayan chaco. *Amer. Mus. Novit.* 2597.

Short, L. L. (1982) *Woodpeckers of the world*. Greenville, Delaware: Delaware Museum of Natural History (Monog. Ser. no. 4).

Sick, H. (1969) Aves brasileiras ameacadas de extincao e nocoes gerais de conservacao de aves do Brasil. *An. Acad. Bras. Cienc.* 41 (supl.): 205-229.

Sick, H. (1979a) Notes on some Brazilian birds. *Bull. Brit. Orn. Club* 99: 115-120.

Sick, H. (1979b) Decouverte de la patrie de l'Ara de Lear *Anodorhynchus leari*. *Alauda* 47: 59-60.

Sick, H. (1985) *Ornitologia brasileira, uma introducao*. Brasilia: Editora Universidade de Brasilia.

Sick, H. and Teixeira, D. M. (1979) Notas sobre aves brasileiras raras ou ameacadas de extincao. *Publ. avuls. Mus. Nac.* 62.

Silva, F. (1981) Contribuicao ao conhecimento da biologia do papagaio charao, *Amazona pretrei* (Temminck, 1830) (Psittacidae, Aves). *Iheringia*, Ser. Zool. 58. 79-85.

Silvius, M. J. (1988) On the importance of Sumatra's east coast for waterbirds, with notes on the Asian Dowitcher *Limnodromus semipalmatus*. *Kukila* 3: 117-137.

Silvius, M. J., Verheugt, W. J. M. and Iskandar, J. (1986) *Coastal wetlands inventory of southeast Sumatra*. Study Report no. 9. Cambridge, U.K.: International Council for Bird Preservation.

Simons, T. R. (1985) Biology and behaviour of the endangered Hawain Dark-rumped Petrel *Condor* 87: 229-245.

Skokova, N. N. and Vinogradov, V. G. (1986) *Waterfowl habitat conservation*. (In Russian). Moscow: Agropromizdat.

Slud, P. (1967) The birds of Cocos Island [Costa Rica]. *Bull. Amer. Mus. Nat. Hist.* 134(4).

Smiet, A. C. (1985) Notes on the field status and trade in Moluccan parrots. *Biol. Conserv.* 34: 181-194.

Smythies, B. E. (1953) *The birds of Burma*. Edinburgh: Oliver and Boyd.

Smythies, B. E. (1981) *The birds of Borneo*. 3rd edition. Malaysia: The Sabah Society and The Malayan Nature Society.

Smythies, B. E. (1986) *The birds of Burma*. Third edition. Liss, Hampshire, U.K.: Nimrod Press; and Pickering, Ontario: Silvio Mattacchione and Co.

Snow, D. W. (1980) A new species of cotinga from southeastern Brazil. *Bull. Brit. Orn. Club* 100: 213-215.

Snow, D. (1982) *The cotingas*. London: British Museum (Natural History), and Oxford: Oxford University Press.

Snyder, N. F. R., Ramey, R. R. and Sibley, F. C. (1986) Nest-site biology of the California Condor. *Condor*. 988: 228-241.

Snyder, N. F. R., Wiley, J. W. and Kepler, C. B. (1987) *The parrots of Luquillo: natural history and conservation of the Puerto Rican Parrot*. Los Angeles: Western Foundation of Vertebrate Zoology.

Somadikarta, S. (1968) The Giant Swiftlet Collocalia gigas Hartert and Butler. *Auk* 85: 549-559.

Sonobe, K. (1982) *A field guide to the birds of Japan*. Tokyo: Wild Bird Society of Japan.

Sonobe, K. and Izawa, N. (1987) *Endangered bird species in the Korean Peninsula*. Tokyo: Museum of Korean Nature (Korea University in Tokyo), and Wild Bird Society of Japan.

Sophasan, S. and Dobias, R. (1984) The fate of the "princess bird", or White-eyed River Martin (*Pseudochelidon sirintarae*). *Nat. Hist. Bull. Siam Soc.* 32(1): 1-10.

Steadman, D. W. and Olson, S. L. (1985) Bird remains from an archaeological site on Henderson Island, South Pacific: man-caused extinctions on an "uninhabited" island. *Proc. Natn. Acad. Sci. USA* 82: 6191-6195.

Steadman, D. W., Stull, J. and Eaton, S. W. (1979) Natural history of the Ocellated Turkey. *World Pheasant Assoc. J.* 4: 15-37.

Sterbetz, I. (1982) Migration of *Anser erythropus* and *Branta ruficollis* in Hungary 1971-1980. *Aquila* 89: 107-114.

Stiles, F. G. (1987) *Observaciones sobre la situacion actual del Picaflor Rojo de Juan Fernandez (Sephanoides fernandensis), con recomendaciones para un estudio integral de su ecologia y biologia poblacional.* Santiago: Oficina Regional de la FAO para America Latina y el Caribe.

Stockton de Dod, A. (1987) *Aves de la Republica Dominicana.* Second edition. Santo Domingo: Museo Nacional de Historia Natural.

Stoddart, D. R. (1981) Abbott's Booby on Assumption. *Atoll Res. Bull.* 255: 27-32.

Stokes, T. (1979) On the possible existence of the New Caledonian Wood Rail *Tricholimnas lafresnayanus. Bull. Brit. Orn. Club* 99: 47-54.

Stokes, T. (1980) Notes on the landbirds of New Caledonia. *Emu* 80: 81-86.

Stokes, T. (1988) *A review of the birds of Christmas Island, Indian Ocean.* Canberra: Australian National Parks and Wildlife Service.

Stone, C. P., Loope, L. L. and Smith, C. W. (1988) Conservation biology in the Galapagos Archipelago: perspectives from Hawaii. *'Elepaio* 48: 1-8.

Storer, R. W. (1981) The Rufous-faced Crake (*Laterallus xenopterus*) and its Paraguayan congeners. *Wilson Bull.* 93: 137-144.

Stuart, S. N. (1986) Usambara Mountains. *World Birdwatch* 8(3): 8-9.

Stuart, S. N. and Collar, N. J. (1985) Subspeciation in the Karamoja Apalis *Apalis karamojae. Bull. Brit. Orn. Club* 105: 86-89.

Stuart, S. N. and Jensen, F. P. (1986) The status and ecology of montane forest bird species in western Cameroon. Pp. 38-105 in S. N. Stuart, ed. *Conservation of Cameroon montane forests.* Cambridge, U.K.: International Council for Bird Preservation.

Summers, R. W. (1985) Demographic variations in the movements of Upland Geese *Chloephaga picta* and Ruddy-headed Geese *Chloephaga rubidiceps* in the Falkland Islands. *J. Zool, Lond.* (A) 206: 1-15

Summers, R. W., Underhill, L. G., Middleton, D. and Buckland, S. T. (1985) Turnover in the population of Ruddy-headed Geese (*Chloephaga rubidiceps*) at Goose Green, Falkland Islands. *J. Appl. Ecol.* 22: 635-643.

Sutton, R. (1981) Hunting the Jamaican Pauraque. *Gosse Bird Club Broadsheet* 37: 4-5.

Taczanowski, L. and Stolzmann, J. (1881) Notice sur la *Loddigesia mirabilis* Bourc. *Proc. Zool. Soc. London*: 827-834.

Taylor, R. H. (1985) Status, habits and conservation of Cynoramphus parakeets in the New Zealand region. Pp 195-211 in P. J. Moors, ed. *Consercatin of island birds.* Cambridge, U.K.: Internatinal Council for Bird Preservation (Techn. Publ. 3).

Taylor, P. B. and Taylor, C. A. (in press) The status, movements and breeding of some birds in the Kikuyu Escarpment Forest, central Kenya highlands. *Tauraco* 1.

Teixeira, D. M. (1987a) Notas sobre *Terenura sicki* Teixeira & Gonzaga, 1983 (Aves, Formicariidae). *Bol. Mus. Paraense Emilio Goeldi*, Ser. Zool. 3(2): 241-251.

Teixeira, D. M. (1987b) Notas sobre o "gravatazeiro", *Rhopornis ardesiaca* (Wied, 1831) (Aves, Formicariidae). *Rev. Brasil. Biol.* 47: 409-414.

Teixeira, D. M. (1987c) A new tyrannulet (Phylloscartes) from northeastern Brazil. *Bull. Brit. Orn. Club* 107(1): 37-41.

Teixeira, D. M. and Gonzaga, L. P. (1983a) Um novo Furnariidae do nordeste do Brasil: *Philydor novaesi* sp. nov. (Aves, Passeriformes). *Bol. Mus. Paraense Emilio Goeldi* NS Zool. no.124: 1-22.

Teixeira, D. M. and Gonzaga, L. P. (1983b) A new antwren from northeastern Brazil. *Bull. Brit. Orn. Club* 103: 133-135.

Teixeira, D. M. and Negret, A. (1984) The Dwarf Tinamou (*Taoniscus nanus*) of central Brazil. *Auk* 101: 188-189.

Teixeira, D. M., Nacinovic, J. B. and Tavares, M. S. (1986) Notes on some birds of northeastern Brazil. *Bull. Brit. Orn. Club* 106: 70-74.

Teixeira, D. M., Nacinovic, J. B. and Pontual, F. B. (1987) Notes on some birds of northeastern Brazil. *Bull. Brit. Orn. Club* 107: 151-157.

van Tets, G. F. and Fullager, P. J. (1984) Status of seabirds breeding in Australia. Pp. 559-571 in

J. P. Croxall, P. G. H. Evans and R. W. Schreiber, eds. *Status and conservation of the world's seabirds*. Cambridge, U.K.: International Council for Bird Preservation (Techn. Publ. 2)

Thibault, J.-C. (in press) Menaces et conservation des oiseaux de Polynesie francaise. In *Livre rouge des oiseaux menaces des regions francaises outre mer*. Conseil Internatinal pour la Protection des Oiseaux.

Thibault, J.-C. and Guyot, I. (in press) Recent changes in the avifauna of Makatea (Tuamotu, South Pacific). *Atol Res. Bull.*

Thiede, U. (1982) "Yambaru Kuina" (*Rallus okinawae*), eine neu entdeckte Rallenart in Japan. *Vogelwelt* 103: 143-150.

Thiollay, J.-M. (1984) Raptor community structure of a primary rain forest in French Guiana and effect of human hunting pressure. *Raptor Research* 18: 117-122.

Thiollay, J.-M. (1985) Birds of prey in French Guiana - a preliminary survey. *Bull. World Working Group on Birds of Prey* 2: 11-15.

Thomsen, J. B. and Munn, C. A. (1988) *Cyanopsitta spixii*: a non-recovery report. *Parrotletter* 1(1): 6-7.

Thompson, P. M. (1987) *Zahamena Forest (Madagascar) Expedition 1985*. Cambridge, U. K.: International Council for Bird Preservation, Study Report no.20.

Todd, D. (1984) The Tahiti Flycatcher *Pomarea nigra tabuensis* in Tonga; rejection of an "extinct" subspecies. *Bull. Brit. Orn. Club* 104: 72.

Todd, D. (1983) Pritchard's Megapode on Niuafo'ou Island, Kingdom of Tonga. *World Pheasant Assoc. J.* 8: 69-68.

Tomback, D. F. (1986) Observations on the behaviour and ecology of the Mariana Crow. *Condor* 88: 398-401.

Trail, P. W. and Baptista, L. F. (in press) The behaviour, status and relationships of the endemic St Lucia Black Finch. *Natn. Georg. Res.*

Traylor, M. A. (1952) Notes on birds from the Marcapata Valley, Cuzco, Peru. *Fieldiana Zool.* 34(3): 17-23.

Traylor, M. A., ed. (1979) *Check-list of birds of the world*, 8. Cambridge, Mass.: Museum of Comparative Zoology.

UNDP/FAO (1982) National conservation plan for Indonesia, 4: Nusa Tenggara. Field report of UNDP/FAO National Parks Development Project INS/78/061. Bogor: Food and Agriculture Organization of the United Nations (Field Report 44).

U. S. Fish and Wildlife Service (1983) *Yellow-shouldered Blackbird recovery plan*. Atlanta, Georgia: U.S. Fish and Wildlife Service.

U.S. Fish and Wildlife Service (1985) *Red-cockaded Woodpecker recovery plan*. Atlanta, Georgia: U.S. Fish Wildl. Serv.

Urban, E. K., Fry, C. H. and Keith, S. (1986) *The birds of Africa*, 2. London: Academic Press.

Varty, N., Adams, J., Espin, P. and Hambler, C., eds. (1986) *An ornithological survey of Lake Tota, Colombia, 1982*. Cambridge, U.K.: International Council for Bird Preservation (Study Report 12).

Vaurie, C. (1980) Taxonomy and geographical distribution of the Furnariidae (Aves, Passeriformes). *Bull. Amer. Mus. Nat. Hist.* 166(1).

Veitch, C. R. (1985) Methods of eradicating feral cats from offshore islands in New Zealand. Pp. 125-141 in P. J. Moors, ed. *Conservation of island birds*. Cambridge, U.K.: International Council for Bird Preservation (Techn. Publ. 3).

van der Ven, J. (1984) 81 species in need of special protection in Council of Europe countries. Unpublished report to Council of Europe.

Verheugt, W. J. M. (1987) Conservation status and action program for the Milky Stork *Mycteria cinerea*. *Colonial Waterbirds* 10(2): 211-220.

Verheugt, W. (1988) Red Data Bird: Asian Dowitcher. *World Birdwatch* 10(1): 5.

Vernon, C. J. and Piper, S. E. (1986) The Cape Vulture colony at Colleywobbles, Transkei, in 1984 and 1985. *Vulture News* 15: 27-28.

Vierheilig, M. B. and Vierheilig, H. (1988) Beitrage zu Status und Biologie von Papageien der Insel Margarita, Venezuela. *Gefied. Welt* 112: 50-52, 91.

Voous, K.H. (1948) Notes on a collection of Javanese birds. *Limosa* 21: 85-100.

de Vries, T. (1984) Problems of reintroducing native animals on islands where they have been exterminated. *Noticias de Galapagos* 40: 12.

Watkins, B. P. and Furness, R. W. (1986) Population status, breeding and conservation of the Gough Moorhen. *Ostrich* 57: 32-36.

Watling, D. (1982) *Birds of Fiji, Tonga and Samoa*. Wellington, New Zealand: Millwood Press.

Watling, D. (1983a) Ornithological notes from Sulawesi. *Emu* 83: 247-261.

Watling, D. (1983b) Sandbox incubator. *Animal Kingdom* 86(3): 30-35.

Watling, D. (1986) Rediscovery of a petrel and new faunal records on Gau Island. *Oryx* 20 (1): 31-34.

Watling, D and Lewanavanua, R. F. (1985) A note to record the continuing survival of the Fiji (MacGillivray's) Petrel *Pseudobulweria macgillivrayi*. *Ibis* 127: 230-233.

Watson, J., Warman, C., Todd, D. and Laboudallon, V. (in press) The Seychelles Magpie Robin *Copsychus sechellarum*: ecology and conservation of an endangered species. [*Biol. Conserv.*]

Weinrich, J. (1987) The Kirtland's Warbler in 1987. Michigan Department of Natural Resources (Wildlife Division Report No. 3074).

Welch, G. and Welch, H. (1986) Djibouti II autumn '85. Unpublished.

Welch, G., Welch, H., Denton, M. and Coghlan [misspelt Cogilan], S. (1986) Djibouti II preliminary report. *WPA News* 12: 24-27.

Wells, D. R. (1985) The forest avifauna of western Malesia and its conservation. Pp. 213-232 in A.W. Diamond and T.E. Lovejoy, eds. *Conservation of tropical forest birds*. Cambridge, U.K.: International Council for Bird Preservation (Techn. Publ. 4).

Wheeler, W. R. (1975) Report on rare and endangered species of birds from the Australian mainland. *Bull. ICBP 12*: 159-264.

Wheelwright, N. T. (1983) Fruits and the ecology of Resplendent Quetzals. *Auk* 100: 286-301.

White, C. M. N. and Bruce, M. D. (1986) *The birds of Wallacea (Sulawesi, the Moluccas and Lesser Sunda Islands, Indonesia): an annotated checklist*. London: British Ornithologists' Union. (Checklist no. 7).

Whitten, A. J., Bishop, K. D., Nash, S. V. and Clayton, L. (1987) One or more extinctions from Sulawesi, Indonesia? *Conserv. Biol.* 1: 42-48.

Wiedenfeld, D. A., Schulenberg, T. S. and Robbins, M. B. (1985) Birds of a tropical deciduous forest in extreme northwestern Peru. Pp. 305-315 in P. A. Buckley, M. S. Foster, E. S. Morton, R. S. Ridgely and F. G. Buckley, eds. *Neotropical ornithology*. Washington, D.C.: American Ornithologists' Union (Orn. Monogr. 36).

Wilcove, D. S. (1987) Public lands management and the fate of the Spotted Owl. *Amer. Birds* 41(3): 361-367.

Wingate, D. B. (1985) The restoration of Nonsuch Island as a living museum of Bermuda's pre-colonial terrestrial biome. Pp. 225-238 in P. J. Moors, ed. *Conservation of island birds*. Cambridge, U.K.: International Council for Bird Preservation (Techn. Publ. 3).

Wiley, J. W. (1985) The Puerto Rican Parrot and competition for its nest sites. Pp. 213-223 in P. J. Moors, ed. *Conservation of island birds*. Cambridge, U.K.: International Council for Bird Preservation (Techn. Publ. 3).

Wiley, J. W. (1986) Status and conservation of raptors in the West Indies. *Birds of Prey Bull.* 3: 57-70.

Wiley, J. W. and Wiley, B. N. (1981) Breeding season ecology and behaviour of Ridgway's Hawk *Buteo ridgwayi*. *Condor* 83: 132-151.

Willgohs, J. F. (1984) *Havorn i Norge*. Trondheim: Direktoratet for Vilt og Ferskvannsfisk.

Williams, A. J. (1984) The status and conservation of seabirds on some islands in the African sector of the Southern Ocean. Pp. 627-635 in J. P. Croxall, P. G. H. Evans and R. W. Schreiber, eds. *Status and conservation of the world's seabirds*. Cambridge, U.K.: International Council for Bird Preservation (Techn. Publ. 2).

Williams, G. R. and Given, D. R. (1981) *The red data book of New Zealand*. Wellington: Nature Conservation Council.

Williams, J. (1987) Wattled Crane survey in Caprivi. *Quagga* 18: 22-23.

Williams, M. D. (1986) Preliminary report on the China Cranewatch 1986. Unpublished.

Williams, M. D., Bakewell, D. N., Carey, G. J. and Holloway, S. J. (1986) On the bird migration at Beidaihe, Hebei province, China, during spring 1985. *Forktail* 2: 3-20.

Williams, M. J. (1986) The number of Auckland Island Teal. *Wildfowl* 37: 63-70.

Willis, E. O. (1972) Taxonomy, ecology and behaviour of the Sooty Ant-tanager (*Habia gutturalis*) and other ant-tanagers (Aves). *Amer. Mus. Novit.* 2480.

Willis, E. O. and Oniki, Y. (1981) Levantamento preliminar de aves em treze areas do Estado de Sao Paulo. *Rev. Brasil. Biol.* 41: 121-135.

Willis, E. O. and Oniki, Y. (1985) Bird specimens new for the state of Sao Paulo, Brazil. *Rev. Brasil. Biol.* 45: 105-108.

Willis, E. O. and Oniki, Y. (1987) Winter nesting of *Iodopleura pipra* (Cotingidae) in southeastern Brazil. *III Congreso de Ornitologia Neotropical: Resumenes.* Unpublished.

Wilson, J. D. (in press) *The status and conservation of the montane forest avifauna of Mount Oku, Cameroon.* Cambridge, U.K.: International Council for Bird Preservation Study Report.

Wilson, R. P. (1985a) Seasonality in diet and breeding success of the Jackass Penguin *Spheniscus demersus. J. Orn.* 126: 53-62.

Wilson, R. P. (1985b) The Jackass Penguin (*Spheniscus demersus*) as a pelagic predator. *Mar. Ecol. Prog. Ser.* 25: 219-227.

Wood, P. (1987) *Report of the 1986 University of East Anglia Martinique Oriole Expedition.* Cambridge, U.K.: International Council for Bird Preservation (Study Report 23).

Woods, C. A. and Ottenwalder, J. A. (undated) *Birds of the national parks of Haiti.* Gainsville: University of Florida.

Wotzkow, C. (1985) Status and distribution of Falconiformes in Cuba. *Bull. World Working Group on Birds of Prey* 2: 1-10.

Wotzkow, C. (1986) Ecological observations of Gundlach's Hawk *Accipiter gundlachii* in Cuba. *Birds of Prey Bull.* 3: 111-114.

Wu Zhi-kang and Hsu Wei-shu (1986) The distribution and abundance of White-crowned Long-tailed Pheasants *Syrmaticus reevesi* in Guizhou province, China. In M. Ridley, ed. *Pheasants in Asia 1986.* Basildon, U.K: World Pheasant Association.

Yamashina, Y. and Mano, T. (1981) A new species of rail from Okinawa Island. *J. Yamashina Inst. Orn.* 13(3): 1-6.

Yamashita, C. (1987) Field observations and comments on the Indigo Macaw (*Anodorhynchus leari*), a highly endangered species from north-eastern Brazil. *Wilson Bull.* 99: 280-282.

Yurlov, A. K. (1981) [Asiatic Dowitcher *Limnodromus semipalmatus* in the Lake Chany region (Western Siberia).] Pp. 102-109 in Yurlov, K. T., ed. *Ekologiya i biotsenoticheskie svyazi pereletnykh ptits zapadnoi sibiri.* Novosibirsk.

Young, L., Garson, P. J. and Kaul, R. (1987) Calling behaviour and social organization in the Cheer Pheasant: implications for survey technique. *World Pheasant Assoc. J.* 12: 30-43.

Young, L., Hussain, M. and Asker, G. (1986) Margalla Hills Cheer Pheasant reintroduction project progress report - 1985. In M. Ridley, ed. *Pheasants in Asia 1986.* Basildon, U.K.: World Pheasant Association.

Zheng Guangmei, Zhao Xinru, Song Jie, Liu Zongxing and Zhou Hongqing (1985) ["On the breeding ecology of *Tragopoan caboti.*"] *Acta Ecol. Sin.* 5(4): 379-385.

Zheng Guangmei, Zhao Xinru, and Song Jie (1986) On the breeding ecology of the Cabot's Tragopan *Tragopan caboti.* In M. Ridely, ed. *Pheasants in Asia 1986.* Basildon, U.K.: World Pheasant Association.

Zheng Guangmei, Zhao Xinru, Song Jie, Liu Zongxing and Zhou Hongqing (1986) ["Feeding ecology of the Cabot's Tragopan (*Tragopan caboti*). *Acta Ecol. Sin.* 6(3): 283-288.

Zimmer, J. T. (1935) Studies of Peruvian birds. XVII. *Amer. Mus. Novit.* 785.

Zimmer, J. T. (1937) Studies of Peruvian birds. No. XXV. *Amer. Mus. Novit.* 917.

Zimmer, J. T. (1951) Studies of Peruvian birds. No. 61. *Amer. Mus. Novit.* 1540.

Zimmerman, D. A. (1978) Eared Trogon - immigrant or visitor? *American Birds* 32: 135-139.

Zino, F. and Zino, P. A. (1986) An account of the habitat, feeding habitats, density, breeding and need of protection of the Long-toed Wood Pigeon, *Columba trocaz. Bocagiana* no.97.

Zubakin, W. A. and Flint, W. E. (1980) Oekologia und Verhalten der Reliktmowe (*Larus relictus* Lonnb.). *Beitr. Vogelkd.* 26: 253-275.

APPENDICES

Appendix 1
Threatened birds by geopolitical unit

Numbers in brackets indicate the number of geopolitical units in which the species occurs: species with no number occur solely in the geopolitical unit under which they are listed. The passage and wintering ranges of Palearctic species have not been covered comprehensively.

Afghanistan
Black Vulture *Aegypius monachus* (10)
Siberian Crane *Grus leucogeranus* (5)
Houbara Bustard *Chlamydotis undulata* (23)
Stoliczka's Bushchat *Saxicola macrorhyncha* (3)

Alaska (U.S.A.)
Eskimo Curlew *Numenius borealis* (10)
Bristle-thighed Curlew *Numenius tahitiensis* (9)

Albania
Dalmatian Pelican *Pelecanus crispus* (13)
Pygmy Cormorant *Halietor pygmeus* (9)
Lesser Kestrel *Falco naumanni* (27)
Corncrake *Crex crex* (33)

Algeria
Northern Bald Ibis *Geronticus eremita* (7)
Marbled Teal *Marmaronetta angustirostris* (15)
White-headed Duck *Oxyura leucocephala* (9)
Lesser Kestrel *Falco naumanni* (27)
Houbara Bustard *Chlamydotis undulata* (23)
Audouin's Gull *Larus audouinii* (10)
Algerian Nuthatch *Sitta ledanti*

Amsterdam Island (to France)
Amsterdam Albatross *Diomedea amsterdamensis*

Andaman Islands (to India)
Dark Serpent-eagle *Spilornis elgini*
Nicobar Pigeon *Caloenas nicobarica* (7)
Narcondam Hornbill *Aceros narcondami*
Brown-chested Flycatcher *Rhinomyias brunneata* (3)

Angola
Swierstra's Francolin *Francolinus swierstrai*
Wattled Crane *Bugeranus carunculatus* (11)

Fernando Po Swift *Apus sladeniae* (4)
Gabela Helmet-shrike *Prionops gabela*
Monteiro's Bush-shrike *Malaconotus monteiri* (2)
Gabela Akalat *Sheppardia gabela*
White-headed Robin-chat *Cossypha heinrichi* (2)
Pulitzer's Longbill *Macrosphenus pulitzeri*
Black-chinned Weaver *Ploceus nigrimentum* (2)
Loango Slender-billed Weaver *Ploceus subpersonatus* (3)

Antipodes Islands (to New Zealand)
New Zealand Snipe *Coenocorypha aucklandica* (4)
Antipodes Parakeet *Cyanoramphus unicolor*

Argentina
Solitary Tinamou *Tinamus solitarius* (3)
Dwarf Tinamou *Taoniscus nanus* (2)
Hooded Grebe *Podiceps gallardoi*
Andean Flamingo *Phoenicoparrus andinus* (4)
Puna Flamingo *Phoenicoparrus jamesi* (4)
Ruddy-headed Goose *Chloephaga rubidiceps* (3)
Brazilian Merganser *Mergus octosetaceus* (3)
Grey-bellied Hawk *Accipiter poliogaster* (10)
Mantled Hawk *Leucopternis polionota* (3)
Crowned Eagle *Harpyhaliaetus coronatus* (4)
Rufous-tailed Hawk *Buteo ventralis* (2)
Crested Eagle *Morphnus guianensis* (15)
Harpy Eagle *Harpia harpyja* (18)
Orange-breasted Falcon *Falco deiroleucus* (17)
Red-faced Guan *Penelope dabbenei* (2)
Black-fronted Piping Guan *Pipile jacutinga* (3)
Austral Rail *Rallus antarcticus* (2)
Dot-winged Crake *Porzana spiloptera* (2)
Horned Coot *Fulica cornuta* (3)
Eskimo Curlew *Numenius borealis* (10)
Olrog's Gull *Larus atlanticus*
Purple-winged Ground-dove *Claravis godefrida* (3)
Glaucous Macaw *Anodorhynchus glaucus* (4)
Red-spectacled Amazon *Amazona pretrei* (4)
Vinaceous Amazon *Amazona vinacea* (3)
Long-trained Nightjar *Macropsalis creagra* (2)
Sickle-winged Nightjar *Eleothreptus anomalus* (4)
Helmeted Woodpecker *Dryocopus galeatus* (3)
Austral Canastero *Asthenes anthoides* (2)
Canebrake Groundcreeper *Clibanornis dendrocolaptoides* (3)
White-bearded Antshrike *Biatas nigropectus* (2)
Swallow-tailed Cotinga *Phibalura flavirostris* (3)

Black-capped Manakin *Piprites pileatus* (2)
White-tailed Shrike-tyrant *Agriornis albicauda* (5)
Black-and-white Monjita *Xolmis dominicana* (4)
Strange-tailed Tyrant *Yetapa risoria* (4)
Russet-winged Spadebill *Platyrinchus leucoryphus* (3)
Sao Paulo Tyrannulet *Phylloscartes paulistus* (3)
Bearded Tachuri *Polystictus pectoralis* (9)
Sharp-tailed Tyrant *Culicivora caudacuta* (4)
Chaco Pipit *Anthus chacoensis* (2)
Ochre-breasted Pipit *Anthus nattereri* (3)
Rufous-throated Dipper *Cinclus schulzii* (2)
Tucuman Mountain-finch *Poospiza baeri*
Entre Rios Seedeater *Sporophila zelichi*
Buffy-throated Seedeater *Sporophila frontalis* (3)
Rufous-rumped Seedeater *Sporophila hypochroma* (3)
Marsh Seedeater *Sporophila palustris* (4)
Chestnut Seedeater *Sporophila cinnamomea* (3)
Blackish-blue Seedeater *Amaurospiza moesta* (3)
Black-masked Finch *Coryphaspiza melanotis* (4)
Yellow Cardinal *Gubernatrix cristata* (3)
Green-throated Euphonia *Euphonia chalybea* (3)
Saffron-cowled Blackbird *Xanthopsar flavus* (5)
Pampas Meadowlark *Sturnella defilippi* (3)
Azure Jay *Cyanocorax caeruleus* (2)

Ascension Island (to U.K.)
Ascension Frigatebird *Fregata aquila*

Auckland Islands (to New Zealand)
Yellow-eyed Penguin *Megadyptes antipodes* (3)
New Zealand Brown Teal *Anas aucklandica* (3)
New Zealand Snipe *Coenocorypha aucklandica* (4)

Australia (see also Christmas Island, Lord Howe Island, Norfolk Island)
Freckled Duck *Stictonetta naevosa*
Red Goshawk *Accipiter radiatus*
Grey Falcon *Falco hypoleucos*
Malleefowl *Leipoa ocellata*
Black-breasted Button-quail *Turnix melanogaster*
Buff-breasted Button-quail *Turnix olivei*
Plains-wanderer *Pedionomus torquatus*
Hooded Plover *Charadrius rubricollis*
Asian Dowitcher *Limnodromus semipalmatus* (13)
Cox's Sandpiper *Calidris paramelanotos*
Alexandra's Parrot *Polytelis alexandrae*
Golden-shouldered Parrot *Psephotus chrysopterygius*

Hooded Parrot *Psephotus dissimilis*
Paradise Parrot *Psephotus pulcherrimus*
Orange-bellied Parrot *Neophema chrysogaster*
Scarlet-chested Parrot *Neophema splendida*
Ground Parrot *Pezoporus wallicus*
Night Parrot *Geopsittacus occidentalis*
Rufous Scrub-bird *Atrichornis rufescens*
Noisy Scrub-bird *Atrichornis clamosus*
Western Whipbird *Psophodes nigrogularis*
Purple-crowned Fairy-wren *Malurus coronatus*
Thick-billed Grass-wren *Amytornis textilis*
Eyrean Grass-wren *Amytornis goyderi*
Grey Grass-wren *Amytornis barbatus*
Carpentarian Grass-wren *Amytornis dorotheae*
Gouldian Finch *Stipiturus mallee*
Eastern Bristlebird *Dasyornis brachypterus*
Western Bristlebird *Dasyornis longirostris*
Chestnut-breasted Whiteface *Aphelocephala pectoralis*
Red-lored Whistler *Pachycephala rufogularis*
Forty-spotted Pardalote *Pardalotus quadragintus*
Regent Honeyeater *Xanthomyza phrygia*
Black-eared Miner *Manorina melanotis*

Austria

White-tailed Eagle *Haliaeetus albicilla* (22)
Lesser Kestrel *Falco naumanni* (27)
Corncrake *Crex crex* (33)
Great Bustard *Otis tarda* (18)
Aquatic Warbler *Acrocephalus paludicola* (5)

Bahama Islands

West Indian Whistling Duck *Dendrocygna arborea* (9)
Piping Plover *Charadrius melodus* (12)
Bahama Swallow *Tachycineta cyaneoviridis* (2)
Kirtland's Warbler *Dendroica kirtlandii* (4)

Bahrain

Houbara Bustard *Chlamydotis undulata* (23)

Bangladesh

White-bellied Heron *Ardea imperialis* (5)
Lesser Adjutant *Leptoptilos javanicus* (11)
Greater Adjutant *Leptoptilos dubius* (7)
White-winged Duck *Cairina scutulata* (7)
Baer's Pochard *Aythya baeri* (11)
Swamp Partridge *Francolinus gularis* (3)

Manipur Bush Quail *Perdicula manipurensis* (2)
Masked Finfoot *Heliopais personata* (6)
Spotted Greenshank *Tringa guttifer* (11)
Blyth's Kingfisher *Alcedo hercules* (9)
Marsh Babbler *Pellorneum palustre* (2)
Black-breasted Parrotbill *Paradoxornis flavirostris* (6)
Bristled Grass-warbler *Chaetornis striatus* (4)

Barbados
Piping Plover *Charadrius melodus* (12)

Belgium
Red Kite *Milvus milvus* (19)
Corncrake *Crex crex* (33)

Belize
Harpy Eagle *Harpia harpyja* (18)
Ocellated Turkey *Agriocharis ocellata* (3)
Keel-billed Motmot *Electron carinatum* (6)

Bermuda (to U.K.)
Cahow *Pterodroma cahow*
Piping Plover *Charadrius melodus* (12)

Bhutan
White-bellied Heron *Ardea imperialis* (5)
Blyth's Tragopan *Tragopan blythii* (4)
Black-necked Crane *Grus nigricollis* (5)
Wood Snipe *Gallinago nemoricola* (5)
Pale-capped Pigeon *Columba punicea* (7)
Blyth's Kingfisher *Alcedo hercules* (9)
Hodgson's Bushchat *Saxicola insignis* (5)
Rufous-throated Wren-babbler *Spelaeornis caudatus* (3)
Black-breasted Parrotbill *Paradoxornis flavirostris* (6)
Greater Rufous-headed Parrotbill *Paradoxornis ruficeps* (6)
Beautiful Nuthatch *Sitta formosa* (7)

Bioko (Equatorial Guinea)
Fernando Po Swift *Apus sladeniae* (4)
Grey-necked Picathartes *Picathartes oreas* (4)
Fernando Po Speirops *Speirops brunneus*

Bolivia
Zigzag Heron *Zebrilus undulatus* (9)
Andean Flamingo *Phoenicoparrus andinus* (4)
Puna Flamingo *Phoenicoparrus jamesi* (4)

Grey-bellied Hawk *Accipiter poliogaster* (10)
Crowned Eagle *Harpyhaliaetus coronatus* (4)
Crested Eagle *Morphnus guianensis* (15)
Harpy Eagle *Harpia harpyja* (18)
Orange-breasted Falcon *Falco deiroleucus* (17)
Red-faced Guan *Penelope dabbenei* (2)
Southern Helmeted Curassow *Pauxi unicornis* (2)
Wattled Curassow *Crax globulosa* (5)
Horned Coot *Fulica cornuta* (3)
Hyacinth Macaw *Anodorhynchus hyacinthinus* (3)
Blue-throated Macaw *Ara glaucogularis*
Red-fronted Macaw *Ara rubrogenys*
Yellow-faced Amazon *Amazona xanthops* (2)
Coppery Thorntail *Popelairia letitiae*
Stout-billed Cinclodes *Cinclodes aricomae* (2)
Line-fronted Canastero *Asthenes urubambensis* (2)
Ashy Antwren *Myrmotherula grisea*
Yellow-rumped Antwren *Terenura sharpei* (2)
Shrike-like Cotinga *Laniisoma elegans* (6)
Swallow-tailed Cotinga *Phibalura flavirostris* (3)
White-tailed Shrike-tyrant *Agriornis albicauda* (5)
Bearded Tachuri *Polystictus pectoralis* (9)
Sharp-tailed Tyrant *Culicivora caudacuta* (4)
Ash-breasted Tit-tyrant *Anairetes alpinus* (2)
Rufous-throated Dipper *Cinclus schulzii* (2)
Cochabamba Mountain-finch *Poospiza garleppi*
Rufous-rumped Seedeater *Sporophila hypochroma* (3)
Black-masked Finch *Coryphaspiza melanotis* (4)
Saffron-cowled Blackbird *Xanthopsar flavus* (5)

Bonin Islands (to Japan)
Bonin Islands Honeyeater *Apalopteron familiare*

Botswana
Slaty Egret *Egretta vinaceigula* (3)
Cape Vulture *Gyps coprotheres* (7)
Lesser Kestrel *Falco naumanni* (27)
Wattled Crane *Bugeranus carunculatus* (11)
Black-cheeked Lovebird *Agapornis nigrigenis* (3)

Brazil
Solitary Tinamou *Tinamus solitarius* (3)
Yellow-legged Tinamou *Crypturellus noctivagus*
Lesser Nothura *Nothura minor*
Dwarf Tinamou *Taoniscus nanus* (2)
Zigzag Heron *Zebrilus undulatus* (9)

Brazilian Merganser *Mergus octosetaceus* (3)
Grey-bellied Hawk *Accipiter poliogaster* (10)
White-necked Hawk *Leucopternis lacernulata*
Mantled Hawk *Leucopternis polionota* (3)
Crowned Eagle *Harpyhaliaetus coronatus* (4)
Crested Eagle *Morphnus guianensis* (15)
Harpy Eagle *Harpia harpyja* (18)
Orange-breasted Falcon *Falco deiroleucus* (17)
White-browed Guan *Penelope jacucaca*
Chestnut-bellied Guan *Penelope ochrogaster*
Black-fronted Piping Guan *Pipile jacutinga* (3)
Alagoas Curassow *Mitu mitu*
Wattled Curassow *Crax globulosa* (5)
Red-billed Curassow *Crax blumenbachii*
Rufous-faced Crake *Laterallus xenopterus* (2)
Eskimo Curlew *Numenius borealis* (10)
Blue-eyed Ground-dove *Columbina cyanopis*
Purple-winged Ground-dove *Claravis godefrida* (3)
Hyacinth Macaw *Anodorhynchus hyacinthinus* (3)
Glaucous Macaw *Anodorhynchus glaucus* (4)
Indigo Macaw *Anodorhynchus leari*
Little Blue Macaw *Cyanopsitta spixii*
Golden Conure *Guaruba guarouba*
Golden-capped Conure *Aratinga auricapilla*
Blue-chested Parakeet *Pyrrhura cruentata*
Pearly Parakeet *Pyrrhura perlata*
Yellow-sided Parakeet *Pyrrhura hypoxantha*
Brown-backed Parrotlet *Touit melanonota*
Golden-tailed Parrotlet *Touit surda*
Red-spectacled Amazon *Amazona pretrei* (4)
Red-tailed Amazon *Amazona brasiliensis*
Red-browed Amazon *Amazona rhodocorytha*
Yellow-faced Amazon *Amazona xanthops* (2)
Vinaceous Amazon *Amazona vinacea* (3)
Purple-bellied Parrot *Triclaria malachitacea*
Long-tailed Potoo *Nyctibius aethereus* (7)
White-winged Potoo *Nyctibius leucopterus*
Rufous Potoo *Nyctibius bracteatus* (5)
White-winged Nightjar *Caprimulgus candicans* (2)
Long-trained Nightjar *Macropsalis creagra* (2)
Sickle-winged Nightjar *Eleothreptus anomalus* (4)
Hook-billed Hermit *Glaucis dohrnii*
Hyacinth Visorbearer *Augastes scutatus*
Three-toed Jacamar *Jacamaralcyon tridactyla*
Helmeted Woodpecker *Dryocopus galeatus* (3)
Moustached Woodcreeper *Xiphocolaptes falcirostris*

Plain Spinetail *Synallaxis infuscata*
Chestnut-throated Spinetail *Synallaxis cherriei* (3)
Striated Softtail *Thripophaga macroura*
Canebrake Groundcreeper *Clibanornis dendrocolaptoides* (3)
Alagoas Foliage-gleaner *Philydor novaesi*
Great Xenops *Megaxenops parnaguae*
White-bearded Antshrike *Biatas nigropectus* (2)
Plumbeous Antshrike *Thamnomanes plumbeus*
Salvadori's Antwren *Myrmotherula minor*
White-browed Antwren *Herpsilochmus pileatus*
Pectoral Antwren *Herpsilochmus pectoralis*
Black-hooded Antwren *Formicivora erythronotos*
Narrow-billed Antwren *Formicivora iheringi*
Orange-bellied Antwren *Terenura sicki*
Rio De Janeiro Antbird *Cercomacra brasiliana*
Rio Branco Antbird *Cercomacra carbonaria*
Fringe-backed Fire-eye *Pyriglena atra*
Slender Antbird *Rhopornis ardesiaca*
Scalloped Antbird *Myrmeciza ruficauda*
Spot-breasted Antbird *Myrmeciza stictothorax*
White-breasted Antbird *Rhegmatorhina hoffmannsi*
Hooded Gnateater *Conopophaga roberti*
Stresemann's Bristlefront *Merulaxis stresemanni*
Brasilia Tapaculo *Scytalopus novacapitalis*
Shrike-like Cotinga *Laniisoma elegans* (6)
Swallow-tailed Cotinga *Phibalura flavirostris* (3)
Grey-winged Cotinga *Tijuca condita*
Black-headed Berryeater *Carpornis melanocephalus*
Buff-throated Purpletuft *Iodopleura pipra*
Kinglet Cotinga *Calyptura cristata*
Cinnamon-vented Piha *Lipaugus lanioides*
Banded Cotinga *Cotinga maculata*
White-winged Cotinga *Xipholena atropurpurea*
Golden-crowned Manakin *Pipra vilasboasi*
Black-capped Manakin *Piprites pileatus* (2)
Black-and-white Monjita *Xolmis dominicana* (4)
Strange-tailed Tyrant *Yetapa risoria* (4)
Russet-winged Spadebill *Platyrinchus leucoryphus* (3)
Fork-tailed Pygmy-tyrant *Ceratotriccus furcatus*
Kaempfer's Tody-tyrant *Idioptilon kaempferi*
Sao Paulo Tyrannulet *Phylloscartes paulistus* (3)
Minas Gerais Tyrannulet *Phylloscartes roquettei*
Long-tailed Tyrannulet *Phylloscartes ceciliae*
Bearded Tachuri *Polystictus pectoralis* (9)
Grey-backed Tachuri *Polystictus superciliaris*
Sharp-tailed Tyrant *Culicivora caudacuta* (4)

Bananal Tyrannulet *Serpophaga araguayae*
Ochre-breasted Pipit *Anthus nattereri* (3)
Buffy-throated Seedeater *Sporophila frontalis* (3)
Temminck's Seedeater *Sporophila falcirostris*
Rufous-rumped Seedeater *Sporophila hypochroma* (3)
Marsh Seedeater *Sporophila palustris* (4)
Chestnut Seedeater *Sporophila cinnamomea* (3)
Blackish-blue Seedeater *Amaurospiza moesta* (3)
Black-masked Finch *Coryphaspiza melanotis* (4)
Yellow Cardinal *Gubernatrix cristata* (3)
Cone-billed Tanager *Conothraupis mesoleuca*
Cherry-throated Tanager *Nemosia rourei*
Green-throated Euphonia *Euphonia chalybea* (3)
Seven-coloured Tanager *Tangara fastuosa*
Black-backed Tanager *Tangara peruviana*
White-bellied Dacnis *Dacnis albiventris* (5)
Black-legged Dacnis *Dacnis nigripes*
Pearly-breasted Conebill *Conirostrum margaritae* (2)
Para Oropendola *Psarocolius bifasciatus*
Saffron-cowled Blackbird *Xanthopsar flavus* (5)
Pampas Meadowlark *Sturnella defilippi* (3)
Forbes's Blackbird *Curaeus forbesi*
Yellow-faced Siskin *Carduelis yarrellii* (2)
Azure Jay *Cyanocorax caeruleus* (2)

Bulgaria

Dalmatian Pelican *Pelecanus crispus* (13)
Pygmy Cormorant *Halietor pygmeus* (9)
Lesser White-fronted Goose *Anser erythropus* (15)
Red-breasted Goose *Branta ruficollis* (4)
White-tailed Eagle *Haliaeetus albicilla* (22)
Imperial Eagle *Aquila heliaca* (12)
Lesser Kestrel *Falco naumanni* (27)
Corncrake *Crex crex* (33)
Great Bustard *Otis tarda* (18)

Burma

White-bellied Heron *Ardea imperialis* (5)
Lesser Adjutant *Leptoptilos javanicus* (11)
Greater Adjutant *Leptoptilos dubius* (7)
White-shouldered Ibis *Pseudibis davisoni* (8)
White-winged Duck *Cairina scutulata* (7)
Baer's Pochard *Aythya baeri* (11)
Pallas's Fish Eagle *Haliaeetus leucoryphus* (8)
Wallace's Hawk-eagle *Spizaetus nanus* (4)
Blyth's Tragopan *Tragopan blythii* (4)

Sclater's Monal *Lophophorus sclateri* (3)
Crested Fireback *Lophura ignita* (4)
White Eared-pheasant *Crossoptilon crossoptilon* (3)
Hume's Pheasant *Syrmaticus humiae* (4)
Malaysian Peacock-pheasant *Polyplectron malacense* (4)
Green Peafowl *Pavo muticus* (8)
Black-necked Crane *Grus nigricollis* (5)
Masked Finfoot *Heliopais personata* (6)
Spotted Greenshank *Tringa guttifer* (11)
Asian Dowitcher *Limnodromus semipalmatus* (13)
Pale-capped Pigeon *Columba punicea* (7)
Large Green-pigeon *Treron capellei* (4)
White-fronted Scops Owl *Otus sagittatus* (4)
Blyth's Kingfisher *Alcedo hercules* (9)
Rufous-necked Hornbill *Aceros nipalensis* (8)
Plain-pouched Hornbill *Aceros subruficollis* (4)
Helmeted Hornbill *Rhinoplax vigil* (4)
Gurney's Pitta *Pitta gurneyi* (2)
Grey-sided Thrush *Turdus feae* (4)
Wedge-billed Wren-babbler *Sphenocichla humei* (2)
Jerdon's Babbler *Moupinia altirostris* (3)
Black-breasted Parrotbill *Paradoxornis flavirostris* (6)
Short-tailed Parrotbill *Paradoxornis davidianus* (5)
Greater Rufous-headed Parrotbill *Paradoxornis ruficeps* (6)
White-browed Nuthatch *Sitta victoriae*
Giant Nuthatch *Sitta magna* (3)
Beautiful Nuthatch *Sitta formosa* (7)
Hooded Treepie *Crypsirina cucullata*

Burundi

Itombwe Owl *Phodilus prigoginei* (2)
Grauer's Swamp Warbler *Bradypterus graueri* (4)
Papyrus Yellow Warbler *Chloropeta gracilirostris* (6)
Kungwe Apalis *Apalis argentea* (4)

Cameroon

Mount Cameroon Francolin *Francolinus camerunensis*
Damara Tern *Sterna balaenarum* (6)
Bannerman's Turaco *Tauraco bannermani*
Fernando Po Swift *Apus sladeniae* (4)
Yellow-footed Honeyguide *Melignomon eisentrauti* (3)
Mount Kupe Bush-shrike *Malaconotus kupeensis*
Green-breasted Bush-shrike *Malaconotus gladiator* (2)
Monteiro's Bush-shrike *Malaconotus monteiri* (2)
White-throated Mountain Babbler *Lioptilus gilberti* (2)
Grey-necked Picathartes *Picathartes oreas* (4)

Dja River Warbler *Bradypterus grandis* (2)
River Prinia *Prinia "fluviatilis"* (3)
Banded Wattle-eye *Platysteira laticincta*
Bannerman's Weaver *Ploceus bannermani* (2)
Bates's Weaver *Ploceus batesi*

Campbell Island (to New Zealand)
Yellow-eyed Penguin *Megadyptes antipodes* (3)
New Zealand Brown Teal *Anas aucklandica* (3)

Canada
Whooping Crane *Grus americana* (2)
Piping Plover *Charadrius melodus* (12)
Eskimo Curlew *Numenius borealis* (10)
Spotted Owl *Strix occidentalis* (3)
Kirtland's Warbler *Dendroica kirtlandii* (4)

Canary Islands (to Spain)
Houbara Bustard *Chlamydotis undulata* (23)
Canarian Black Oystercatcher *Haematopus meadewaldoi*
Dark-tailed Laurel Pigeon *Columba bollii*
White-tailed Laurel Pigeon *Columba junoniae*
Fuerteventura Stonechat *Saxicola dacotiae*
Blue Chaffinch *Fringilla teydea*

Cape Verde Islands
Gon-gon *Pterodroma feae* (2)
Raso Lark *Alauda razae*

Cayman Islands (to U.K.)
West Indian Whistling Duck *Dendrocygna arborea* (9)
Vitelline Warbler *Dendroica vitellina* (2)

Central African Republic
Shoebill *Balaeniceps rex* (8)

Chad
Marbled Teal *Marmaronetta angustirostris* (15)
River Prinia *Prinia "fluviatilis"* (3)

Chatham Islands (to New Zealand)
Magenta Petrel *Pterodroma magentae*
Chatham Island Petrel *Pterodroma axillaris*
New Zealand King Cormorant *Phalacrocorax carunculatus* (2)
Chatham Island Oystercatcher *Haematopus chathamensis*
New Zealand Snipe *Coenocorypha aucklandica* (4)

Chatham Island Black Robin *Petroica traversi*

Chile (see also Desventuradas Islands, Juan Fernandez Islands)
   Peruvian Penguin *Spheniscus humboldti* (2)
   Pink-footed Shearwater *Puffinus creatopus* (2)
   Markham's Storm-petrel *Oceanodroma markhami* (5)
   Ringed Storm-petrel *Oceanodroma hornbyi* (3)
   Peruvian Diving-petrel *Pelecanoides garnoti* (2)
   Andean Flamingo *Phoenicoparrus andinus* (4)
   Puna Flamingo *Phoenicoparrus jamesi* (4)
   Ruddy-headed Goose *Chloephaga rubidiceps* (3)
   Rufous-tailed Hawk *Buteo ventralis* (2)
   Austral Rail *Rallus antarcticus* (2)
   Horned Coot *Fulica cornuta* (3)
   Eskimo Curlew *Numenius borealis* (10)
   Chilean Woodstar *Eulidia yarrellii* (2)
   Austral Canastero *Asthenes anthoides* (2)
   White-tailed Shrike-tyrant *Agriornis albicauda* (5)
   Slender-billed Finch *Xenospingus concolor* (2)
   Tamarugo Conebill *Conirostrum tamarugense* (2)

China
   Dalmatian Pelican *Pelecanus crispus* (13)
   Japanese Night-heron *Gorsagius goisagi* (6)
   White-eared Night-heron *Gorsachius magnificus*
   Chinese Egret *Egretta eulophotes* (5)
   White-bellied Heron *Ardea imperialis* (5)
   Oriental White Stork *Ciconia boyciana* (4)
   White-shouldered Ibis *Pseudibis davisoni* (8)
   Crested Ibis *Nipponia nippon*
   Black-faced Spoonbill *Platalea minor* (7)
   Lesser White-fronted Goose *Anser erythropus* (15)
   Crested Shelduck *Tadorna cristata* (5)
   Baykal Teal *Anas formosa* (5)
   Baer's Pochard *Aythya baeri* (11)
   Scaly-sided Merganser *Mergus squamatus* (4)
   White-headed Duck *Oxyura leucocephala* (9)
   Pallas's Fish Eagle *Haliaeetus leucoryphus* (8)
   White-tailed Eagle *Haliaeetus albicilla* (22)
   Black Vulture *Aegypius monachus* (10)
   Imperial Eagle *Aquila heliaca* (12)
   Lesser Kestrel *Falco naumanni* (27)
   Sichuan Hill-partridge *Arborophila rufipectus*
   Rickett's Hill-partridge *Arborophila gingica*
   White-eared Hill-partridge *Arborophila ardens*
   Western Tragopan *Tragopan melanocephalus* (3)

Blyth's Tragopan *Tragopan blythii* (4)
Cabot's Tragopan *Tragopan caboti*
Sclater's Monal *Lophophorus sclateri* (3)
Chinese Monal *Lophophorus lhuysii*
White Eared-pheasant *Crossoptilon crossoptilon* (3)
Brown Eared-pheasant *Crossoptilon mantchuricum*
Elliot's Pheasant *Syrmaticus ellioti*
Hume's Pheasant *Syrmaticus humiae* (4)
Reeves's Pheasant *Syrmaticus reevesii* (2)
Green Peafowl *Pavo muticus* (8)
Black-necked Crane *Grus nigricollis* (5)
Hooded Crane *Grus monacha* (5)
Red-crowned Crane *Grus japonensis* (5)
White-naped Crane *Grus vipio* (6)
Siberian Crane *Grus leucogeranus* (5)
Corncrake *Crex crex* (33)
Asian Yellow Rail *Coturnicops exquisitus* (5)
Great Bustard *Otis tarda* (18)
Houbara Bustard *Chlamydotis undulata* (23)
Spotted Greenshank *Tringa guttifer* (11)
Wood Snipe *Gallinago nemoricola* (5)
Asian Dowitcher *Limnodromus semipalmatus* (13)
Spoon-billed Sandpiper *Eurynorhynchus pygmeus* (9)
Relict Gull *Larus relictus* (4)
Saunders's Gull *Larus saundersi* (7)
Chinese Crested Tern *Sterna bernsteini* (5)
Pale-capped Pigeon *Columba punicea* (7)
Blakiston's Fish Owl *Ketupa blakistoni* (3)
Vaurie's Nightjar *Caprimulgus centralasicus*
Blyth's Kingfisher *Alcedo hercules* (9)
Rufous-necked Hornbill *Aceros nipalensis* (8)
Red-collared Woodpecker *Picus rabieri* (3)
Fairy Pitta *Pitta nympha* (7)
Rusty-bellied Shortwing *Brachypteryx hyperythra* (2)
Rufous-headed Robin *Erithacus ruficeps* (2)
Black-throated Robin *Erithacus obscurus* (2)
Hodgson's Bushchat *Saxicola insignis* (5)
Grey-sided Thrush *Turdus feae* (4)
Sukatschev's Laughingthrush *Garrulax sukatschewi*
Biet's Laughingthrush *Garrulax bieti*
Emei Shan Liocichla *Liocichla omeiensis*
Gold-fronted Fulvetta *Alcippe variegaticeps*
Black-breasted Parrotbill *Paradoxornis flavirostris* (6)
Crested Parrotbill *Paradoxornis zappeyi*
Przevalski's Parrotbill *Paradoxornis przewalskii*
Short-tailed Parrotbill *Paradoxornis davidianus* (5)

Greater Rufous-headed Parrotbill *Paradoxornis ruficeps* (6)
Large-billed Bush-warbler *Bradypterus major* (4)
Speckled Reed Warbler *Acrocephalus sorghophilus* (2)
Japanese Marsh Warbler *Megalurus pryeri* (2)
Brown-chested Flycatcher *Rhinomyias brunneata* (3)
Yunnan Nuthatch *Sitta yunnanensis*
Giant Nuthatch *Sitta magna* (3)
Beautiful Nuthatch *Sitta formosa* (7)
Japanese Yellow Bunting *Emberiza sulphurata* (2)
Silver Oriole *Oriolus mellianus* (3)
Sichuan Grey Jay *Perisoreus internigrans*

Christmas Island (to Australia)

Abbott's Booby *Sula abbotti* (2)
Christmas Frigatebird *Fregata andrewsi* (4)
Christmas Imperial-pigeon *Ducula whartoni*

Clipperton Island (to France)

Markham's Storm-petrel *Oceanodroma markhami* (5)

Cocos Island (to Costa Rica)

Markham's Storm-petrel *Oceanodroma markhami* (5)
Cocos Cuckoo *Coccyzus ferrugineus*

Colombia

Black Tinamou *Tinamus osgoodi* (2)
Magdalena Tinamou *Crypturellus saltuarius*
Colombian Grebe *Podiceps andinus*
Zigzag Heron *Zebrilus undulatus* (9)
Northern Screamer *Chauna chavaria* (2)
Semicollared Sparrowhawk *Accipiter collaris* (4)
Grey-bellied Hawk *Accipiter poliogaster* (10)
Plumbeous Hawk *Leucopternis plumbea* (4)
Solitary Eagle *Harpyhaliaetus solitarius* (10)
Crested Eagle *Morphnus guianensis* (15)
Harpy Eagle *Harpia harpyja* (18)
Plumbeous Forest-falcon *Micrastur plumbeus* (2)
Orange-breasted Falcon *Falco deiroleucus* (17)
Cauca Guan *Penelope perspicax*
Northern Helmeted Curassow *Pauxi pauxi* (2)
Blue-billed Curassow *Crax alberti*
Wattled Curassow *Crax globulosa* (5)
Chestnut Wood-quail *Odontophorus hyperythrus*
Gorgeted Wood-quail *Odontophorus strophium*
Bogota Rail *Rallus semiplumbeus*
Tolima Dove *Leptotila conoveri*

Golden-plumed Conure *Leptosittaca branickii* (3)
Yellow-eared Conure *Ognorhynchus icterotis* (2)
Flame-winged Parakeet *Pyrrhura calliptera*
Rufous-fronted Parakeet *Bolborhynchus ferrugineifrons*
Spot-winged Parrotlet *Touit stictoptera* (3)
Rusty-faced Parrot *Hapalopsittaca amazonina* (3)
Banded Ground-cuckoo *Neomorphus radiolosus* (2)
Long-tailed Potoo *Nyctibius aethereus* (7)
Rufous Potoo *Nyctibius bracteatus* (5)
White-chested Swift *Cypseloides lemosi*
Sapphire-bellied Hummingbird *Lepidopyga lilliae*
Chestnut-bellied Hummingbird *Amazilia castaneiventris*
Black Inca *Coeligena prunellei*
Turquoise-throated Puffleg *Eriocnemis godini* (2)
Colourful Puffleg *Eriocnemis mirabilis*
Black-thighed Puffleg *Eriocnemis derbyi* (2)
Hoary Puffleg *Haplophaedia lugens* (2)
White-mantled Barbet *Capito hypoleucus*
Toucan Barbet *Semnornis ramphastinus* (2)
Recurve-billed Bushbird *Clytoctantes alixii* (2)
Speckled Antshrike *Xenornis setifrons* (2)
Argus Bare-eye *Phlegopsis barringeri*
Giant Antpitta *Grallaria gigantea* (2)
Moustached Antpitta *Grallaria alleni*
Bicoloured Antpitta *Grallaria rufocinerea*
Brown-banded Antpitta *Grallaria milleri*
Crescent-faced Antpitta *Grallaricula lineifrons* (2)
Hooded Antpitta *Grallaricula cucullata* (2)
Shrike-like Cotinga *Laniisoma elegans* (6)
Long-wattled Umbrellabird *Cephalopterus penduliger* (2)
Bearded Tachuri *Polystictus pectoralis* (9)
Apolinar's Wren *Cistothorus apolinari*
Niceforo's Wren *Thryothorus nicefori*
Tumaco Seedeater *Sporophila insulata*
Olive-headed Brush-finch *Atlapetes flaviceps*
Tanager-finch *Oreothraupis arremonops* (2)
Yellow-green Bush-tanager *Chlorospingus flavovirens* (2)
Sooty Ant-tanager *Habia gutturalis*
Black-and-gold Tanager *Buthraupis melanochlamys*
Gold-ringed Tanager *Buthraupis aureocincta*
Multicoloured Tanager *Chlorochrysa nitidissima*
White-bellied Dacnis *Dacnis albiventris* (5)
Turquoise Dacnis *Dacnis hartlaubi*
Scarlet-breasted Dacnis *Dacnis berlepschi* (2)
Grey-throated Warbler *Basileuterus cinereicollis* (2)
Chestnut-mantled Oropendola *Psarocolius cassini*

Red-bellied Grackle *Hypopyrrhus pyrohypogaster*
Bronze-brown Cowbird *Molothrus armenti*
Beautiful Jay *Cyanolyca pulchra* (2)

Comoro Islands

Madagascar Heron *Ardea humbloti* (3)
Grand Comoro Scops Owl *Otus pauliani*
Grand Comoro Flycatcher *Humblotia flavirostris*
Mount Karthala White-eye *Zosterops mouroniensis*
Grand Comoro Drongo *Dicrurus fuscipennis*

Congo

Black-chinned Weaver *Ploceus nigrimentum* (2)

Cook Islands (to New Zealand)

Blue Lorikeet *Vini peruviana* (3)
Atiu Swiftlet *Aerodramus sawtelli*
Mangaia Kingfisher *Halcyon ruficollaris*
Rarotonga Monarch *Pomarea dimidiata*
Rarotonga Starling *Aplonis cinerascens*

Costa Rica (see also Cocos Island)

Solitary Eagle *Harpyhaliaetus solitarius* (10)
Crested Eagle *Morphnus guianensis* (15)
Harpy Eagle *Harpia harpyja* (18)
Orange-breasted Falcon *Falco deiroleucus* (17)
Mangrove Hummingbird *Amazilia boucardi*
Resplendent Quetzal *Pharomachrus mocinno* (7)
Baird's Trogon *Trogon bairdii* (2)
Keel-billed Motmot *Electron carinatum* (6)
Turquoise Cotinga *Cotinga ridgwayi* (2)
Yellow-billed Cotinga *Carpodectes antoniae* (2)
Bare-necked Umbrellabird *Cephalopterus glabricollis* (2)
Black-cheeked Ant-tanager *Habia atrimaxillaris*

Crozet Islands (to France)

Kerguelen Tern *Sterna virgata* (3)

Cuba

Black-capped Petrel *Pterodroma hasitata* (3)
West Indian Whistling Duck *Dendrocygna arborea* (9)
Gundlach's Hawk *Accipiter gundlachii*
Zapata Rail *Cyanolimnas cerverai*
Piping Plover *Charadrius melodus* (12)
Grey-headed Quail-dove *Geotrygon caniceps* (2)
Blue-headed Quail-dove *Starnoenas cyanocephala*

Cuban Conure *Aratinga euops*
Bee Hummingbird *Calypte helenae*
Cuban Flicker *Colaptes fernandinae*
Ivory-billed Woodpecker *Campephilus principalis* (2)
Bahama Swallow *Tachycineta cyaneoviridis* (2)
Zapata Wren *Ferminia cerverai*
Cuban Gnatcatcher *Polioptila lembeyei*
Zapata Sparrow *Torreornis inexpectata*
Bachman's Warbler *Vermivora bachmanii* (2)
Red Siskin *Carduelis cucullata* (3)

Cyprus

Imperial Eagle *Aquila heliaca* (12)
Lesser Kestrel *Falco naumanni* (27)
Audouin's Gull *Larus audouinii* (10)

Czechoslovakia

Red Kite *Milvus milvus* (19)
White-tailed Eagle *Haliaeetus albicilla* (22)
Imperial Eagle *Aquila heliaca* (12)
Reeves's Pheasant *Syrmaticus reevesii* (2)
Corncrake *Crex crex* (33)
Great Bustard *Otis tarda* (18)

Denmark (see also Greenland)

Red Kite *Milvus milvus* (19)
Corncrake *Crex crex* (33)

Desventuradas Islands (to Chile)

Defilippe's Petrel *Pterodroma defilippiana* (2)

Djibouti

Djibouti Francolin *Francolinus ochropectus*

Dominica

Red-necked Amazon *Amazona arausiaca*
Imperial Amazon *Amazona imperialis*

Dominican Republic

Black-capped Petrel *Pterodroma hasitata* (3)
West Indian Whistling Duck *Dendrocygna arborea* (9)
Ridgway's Hawk *Buteo ridgwayi* (2)
Piping Plover *Charadrius melodus* (12)
Grey-headed Quail-dove *Geotrygon caniceps* (2)
White-winged Ground-warbler *Xenoligea montana* (2)

East Germany
    Red Kite *Milvus milvus* (19)
    White-tailed Eagle *Haliaeetus albicilla* (22)
    Corncrake *Crex crex* (33)
    Great Bustard *Otis tarda* (18)
    Aquatic Warbler *Acrocephalus paludicola* (5)

Ecuador (see also Galapagos Islands)
    Ringed Storm-petrel *Oceanodroma hornbyi* (3)
    Zigzag Heron *Zebrilus undulatus* (9)
    Semicollared Sparrowhawk *Accipiter collaris* (4)
    Grey-bellied Hawk *Accipiter poliogaster* (10)
    Plumbeous Hawk *Leucopternis plumbea* (4)
    Grey-backed Hawk *Leucopternis occidentalis* (2)
    Solitary Eagle *Harpyhaliaetus solitarius* (10)
    Crested Eagle *Morphnus guianensis* (15)
    Harpy Eagle *Harpia harpyja* (18)
    Plumbeous Forest-falcon *Micrastur plumbeus* (2)
    Traylor's Forest-falcon *Micrastur buckleyi* (2)
    Orange-breasted Falcon *Falco deiroleucus* (17)
    Rufous-headed Chachalaca *Ortalis erythroptera* (2)
    Bearded Guan *Penelope barbata* (2)
    Wattled Curassow *Crax globulosa* (5)
    Ochre-bellied Dove *Leptotila ochraceiventris* (2)
    Golden-plumed Conure *Leptosittaca branickii* (3)
    Yellow-eared Conure *Ognorhynchus icterotis* (2)
    White-necked Parakeet *Pyrrhura albipectus*
    Grey-cheeked Parakeet *Brotogeris pyrrhopterus* (2)
    Spot-winged Parrotlet *Touit stictoptera* (3)
    Rusty-faced Parrot *Hapalopsittaca amazonina* (3)
    Banded Ground-cuckoo *Neomorphus radiolosus* (2)
    Long-tailed Potoo *Nyctibius aethereus* (7)
    Rufous Potoo *Nyctibius bracteatus* (5)
    Black-breasted Puffleg *Eriocnemis nigrivestis*
    Turquoise-throated Puffleg *Eriocnemis godini* (2)
    Black-thighed Puffleg *Eriocnemis derbyi* (2)
    Hoary Puffleg *Haplophaedia lugens* (2)
    Violet-throated Metaltail *Metallura baroni*
    Little Woodstar *Acestrura bombus* (2)
    Esmeraldas Woodstar *Acestrura berlepschi*
    Toucan Barbet *Semnornis ramphastinus* (2)
    Chestnut-throated Spinetail *Synallaxis cherriei* (3)
    Rufous-necked Foliage-gleaner *Automolus ruficollis* (2)
    Henna-hooded Foliage-gleaner *Automolus erythrocephalus* (2)
    Cocha Antshrike *Thamnophilus praecox*
    Grey-headed Antbird *Myrmeciza griseiceps* (2)

Giant Antpitta *Grallaria gigantea* (2)
Crescent-faced Antpitta *Grallaricula lineifrons* (2)
Shrike-like Cotinga *Laniisoma elegans* (6)
Long-wattled Umbrellabird *Cephalopterus penduliger* (2)
White-tailed Shrike-tyrant *Agriornis albicauda* (5)
Grey-breasted Flycatcher *Empidonax griseipectus* (2)
Pale-headed Brush-finch *Atlapetes pallidiceps*
Tanager-finch *Oreothraupis arremonops* (2)
Yellow-green Bush-tanager *Chlorospingus flavovirens* (2)
White-bellied Dacnis *Dacnis albiventris* (5)
Scarlet-breasted Dacnis *Dacnis berlepschi* (2)
Saffron Siskin *Carduelis siemiradzkii*
Beautiful Jay *Cyanolyca pulchra* (2)

Egypt

Northern Bald Ibis *Geronticus eremita* (7)
Marbled Teal *Marmaronetta angustirostris* (15)
Lesser Kestrel *Falco naumanni* (27)
Houbara Bustard *Chlamydotis undulata* (23)
Sociable Plover *Chettusia gregaria* (10)
White-eyed Gull *Larus leucophthalmus* (3)

El Salvador

Highland Guan *Penelopina nigra* (5)
Resplendent Quetzal *Pharomachrus mocinno* (7)

Equatorial Guinea (see Bioko)

Ethiopia

Shoebill *Balaeniceps rex* (8)
Northern Bald Ibis *Geronticus eremita* (7)
Wattled Crane *Bugeranus carunculatus* (11)
White-winged Flufftail *Sarothrura ayresi* (4)
Sociable Plover *Chettusia gregaria* (10)
Prince Ruspoli's Turaco *Tauraco ruspolii*
Degodi Lark *Mirafra degodiensis*
Sidamo Long-clawed Lark *Heteromirafra sidamoensis*
White-tailed Swallow *Hirundo megaensis*
Red Sea Cliff Swallow *Hirundo perdita* (2)
Ankober Serin *Serinus ankoberensis*
Yellow-throated Serin *Serinus flavigula*
Ethiopian Bush-crow *Zavattariornis stresemanni*

Falkland Islands (to U.K.)

Ruddy-headed Goose *Chloephaga rubidiceps* (3)

Federated States of Micronesia (to U.S.A)
  Truk Monarch *Metabolus rugensis*
  Great Truk White-eye *Rukia ruki*
  Great Pohnpei White-eye *Rukia longirostra*
  Pohnpei Mountain Starling *Aplonis pelzelni*

Fiji
  Fiji Petrel *Pterodroma macgillivrayi*
  Barred-wing Rail *Nesoclopeus poeciloptera*
  Woodford's Rail *Nesoclopeus woodfordi* (3)
  Bristle-thighed Curlew *Numenius tahitiensis* (9)
  Long-legged Warbler *Trichocichla rufa*
  Pink-billed Parrotfinch *Erythrura kleinschmidti*

Finland
  Lesser White-fronted Goose *Anser erythropus* (15)
  White-tailed Eagle *Haliaeetus albicilla* (22)
  Corncrake *Crex crex* (33)

France (see also Amsterdam Island, Clipperton Island, Crozet Islands, Kerguelen Islands, Marquesas Islands, Martinique, Mayotte, New Caledonia, Reunion, Society Islands, Tuamotu Archipelago, Tubuai Islands)
  Red Kite *Milvus milvus* (19)
  Lesser Kestrel *Falco naumanni* (27)
  Corncrake *Crex crex* (33)
  Little Bustard *Tetrax tetrax* (8)
  Audouin's Gull *Larus audouinii* (10)

French Guiana
  Zigzag Heron *Zebrilus undulatus* (9)
  Solitary Eagle *Harpyhaliaetus solitarius* (10)
  Crested Eagle *Morphnus guianensis* (15)
  Harpy Eagle *Harpia harpyja* (18)
  Eskimo Curlew *Numenius borealis* (10)

Gabon
  Damara Tern *Sterna balaenarum* (6)
  Grey-necked Picathartes *Picathartes oreas* (4)
  Dja River Warbler *Bradypterus grandis* (2)
  Gabon Batis *Batis minima*
  Loango Slender-billed Weaver *Ploceus subpersonatus* (3)

Galapagos Islands (to Ecuador)
  Dark-rumped Petrel *Pterodroma phaeopygia* (2)
  Markham's Storm-petrel *Oceanodroma markhami* (5)
  Galapagos Flightless Cormorant *Nannopterum harrisi*

Galapagos Hawk *Buteo galapagoensis*
Floreana Tree-finch *Camarhynchus pauper*
Mangrove Finch *Camarhynchus heliobates*

Ghana

White-breasted Guineafowl *Agelastes meleagrides* (4)
Damara Tern *Sterna balaenarum* (6)
Rufous Fishing Owl *Scotopelia ussheri* (5)
Yellow-footed Honeyguide *Melignomon eisentrauti* (3)
Western Wattled Cuckoo-shrike *Campephaga lobata* (4)
Yellow-throated Olive Greenbul *Criniger olivaceus* (6)
White-necked Picathartes *Picathartes gymnocephalus* (5)

Gibraltar (to U.K.)

Lesser Kestrel *Falco naumanni* (27)

Greece

Dalmatian Pelican *Pelecanus crispus* (13)
Pygmy Cormorant *Halietor pygmeus* (9)
Lesser White-fronted Goose *Anser erythropus* (15)
White-tailed Eagle *Haliaeetus albicilla* (22)
Black Vulture *Aegypius monachus* (10)
Imperial Eagle *Aquila heliaca* (12)
Lesser Kestrel *Falco naumanni* (27)
Corncrake *Crex crex* (33)
Slender-billed Curlew *Numenius tenuirostris* (9)
Audouin's Gull *Larus audouinii* (10)

Greenland (to Denmark)

White-tailed Eagle *Haliaeetus albicilla* (22)

Grenada

Grenada Dove *Leptotila wellsi*

Guadalupe Islands (Mexico)

Guadalupe Storm-petrel *Oceanodroma macrodactyla*
Guadalupe Junco *Junco insularis*

Guam (to U.S.A.)

Guam Rail *Rallus owstoni*
Marianas Fruit-dove *Ptilinopus roseicapilla* (2)
Guam Flycatcher *Myiagra freycineti*
Marianas Crow *Corvus kubaryi* (2)

Guatemala

Atitlan Grebe *Podilymbus gigas*

Solitary Eagle *Harpyhaliaetus solitarius* (10)
Crested Eagle *Morphnus guianensis* (15)
Harpy Eagle *Harpia harpyja* (18)
Orange-breasted Falcon *Falco deiroleucus* (17)
Highland Guan *Penelopina nigra* (5)
Horned Guan *Oreophasis derbianus* (2)
Ocellated Turkey *Agriocharis ocellata* (3)
Resplendent Quetzal *Pharomachrus mocinno* (7)
Keel-billed Motmot *Electron carinatum* (6)
Azure-rumped Tanager *Tangara cabanisi* (2)
Golden-cheeked Warbler *Dendroica chrysoparia* (5)

Guinea

Rufous Fishing Owl *Scotopelia ussheri* (5)
Yellow-throated Olive Greenbul *Criniger olivaceus* (6)
White-necked Picathartes *Picathartes gymnocephalus* (5)

Guyana

Zigzag Heron *Zebrilus undulatus* (9)
Grey-bellied Hawk *Accipiter poliogaster* (10)
Crested Eagle *Morphnus guianensis* (15)
Harpy Eagle *Harpia harpyja* (18)
Orange-breasted Falcon *Falco deiroleucus* (17)
Eskimo Curlew *Numenius borealis* (10)
Long-tailed Potoo *Nyctibius aethereus* (7)
Rufous Potoo *Nyctibius bracteatus* (5)
Bearded Tachuri *Polystictus pectoralis* (9)

Haiti

Black-capped Petrel *Pterodroma hasitata* (3)
West Indian Whistling Duck *Dendrocygna arborea* (9)
Ridgway's Hawk *Buteo ridgwayi* (2)
Piping Plover *Charadrius melodus* (12)
White-winged Ground-warbler *Xenoligea montana* (2)

Hawaiian Islands (to U.S.A.)

Dark-rumped Petrel *Pterodroma phaeopygia* (2)
Newell's Shearwater *Puffinus newelli*
Townsend's Shearwater *Puffinus auricularis* (2)
Hawaiian Goose *Branta sandvicensis*
Hawaiian Duck *Anas wyvilliana*
Laysan Duck *Anas laysanensis*
Hawaiian Hawk *Buteo solitarius*
Bristle-thighed Curlew *Numenius tahitiensis* (9)
Kamao *Myadestes myadestinus*
Olomao *Myadestes lanaiensis*

Puaiohi *Myadestes palmeri*
Nihoa Reed Warbler (Millerbird) *Acrocephalus familiaris*
Kauai Oo *Moho braccatus*
Bishop's Oo *Moho bishopi*
Akepa *Loxops coccineus*
Akikiki *Oreomystis bairdi*
Kakawahie *Paroreomyza flammea*
Oahu Creeper *Paroreomyza maculata*
Akialoa *Hemignathus obscurus*
Nukupuu *Hemignathus lucidus*
Akiapolaau *Hemignathus munroi*
Maui Parrotbill *Pseudonestor xanthophrys*
Ou *Psittirostra psittacea*
Nihoa Finch *Telespyza ultima*
Laysan Finch *Telespyza cantans*
Palila *Loxioides bailleui*
Poo Uli *Melamprosops phaeosoma*
Crested Honeycreeper *Palmeria dolei*
Hawaiian Crow *Corvus hawaiiensis*

Honduras (see also Swan Islands)
Solitary Eagle *Harpyhaliaetus solitarius* (10)
Crested Eagle *Morphnus guianensis* (15)
Harpy Eagle *Harpia harpyja* (18)
Orange-breasted Falcon *Falco deiroleucus* (17)
Highland Guan *Penelopina nigra* (5)
Honduran Emerald *Amazilia luciae*
Resplendent Quetzal *Pharomachrus mocinno* (7)
Keel-billed Motmot *Electron carinatum* (6)
Golden-cheeked Warbler *Dendroica chrysoparia* (5)

Hong Kong (to U.K.)
Chinese Egret *Egretta eulophotes* (5)
Black-faced Spoonbill *Platalea minor* (7)
Spotted Greenshank *Tringa guttifer* (11)
Asian Dowitcher *Limnodromus semipalmatus* (13)
Spoon-billed Sandpiper *Eurynorhynchus pygmeus* (9)
Saunders's Gull *Larus saundersi* (7)

Hungary
Red Kite *Milvus milvus* (19)
White-tailed Eagle *Haliaeetus albicilla* (22)
Imperial Eagle *Aquila heliaca* (12)
Corncrake *Crex crex* (33)
Great Bustard *Otis tarda* (18)
Slender-billed Curlew *Numenius tenuirostris* (9)

Aquatic Warbler *Acrocephalus paludicola* (5)

Iceland

White-tailed Eagle *Haliaeetus albicilla* (22)

India (see also Andaman Islands, Nicobar Islands)

Spot-billed Pelican *Pelecanus philippensis* (2)
Dalmatian Pelican *Pelecanus crispus* (13)
White-bellied Heron *Ardea imperialis* (5)
Lesser Adjutant *Leptoptilos javanicus* (11)
Greater Adjutant *Leptoptilos dubius* (7)
Lesser White-fronted Goose *Anser erythropus* (15)
White-winged Duck *Cairina scutulata* (7)
Marbled Teal *Marmaronetta angustirostris* (15)
Pink-headed Duck *Rhodonessa caryophyllacea* (2)
Baer's Pochard *Aythya baeri* (11)
Pallas's Fish Eagle *Haliaeetus leucoryphus* (8)
Black Vulture *Aegypius monachus* (10)
Swamp Partridge *Francolinus gularis* (3)
Manipur Bush Quail *Perdicula manipurensis* (2)
Himalayan Quail *Ophrysia superciliosa*
Western Tragopan *Tragopan melanocephalus* (3)
Blyth's Tragopan *Tragopan blythii* (4)
Sclater's Monal *Lophophorus sclateri* (3)
White Eared-pheasant *Crossoptilon crossoptilon* (3)
Cheer Pheasant *Catreus wallichii* (3)
Hume's Pheasant *Syrmaticus humiae* (4)
Green Peafowl *Pavo muticus* (8)
Black-necked Crane *Grus nigricollis* (5)
Siberian Crane *Grus leucogeranus* (5)
Masked Finfoot *Heliopais personata* (6)
Great Indian Bustard *Ardeotis nigriceps*
Houbara Bustard *Chlamydotis undulata* (23)
Bengal Florican *Houbaropsis bengalensis* (4)
Lesser Florican *Sypheotides indica* (2)
Sociable Plover *Chettusia gregaria* (10)
Jerdon's Courser *Cursorius bitorquatus*
Wood Snipe *Gallinago nemoricola* (5)
Asian Dowitcher *Limnodromus semipalmatus* (13)
Spoon-billed Sandpiper *Eurynorhynchus pygmeus* (9)
Nilgiri Woodpigeon *Columba elphinstonii*
Pale-capped Pigeon *Columba punicea* (7)
Rothschild's Parakeet *Psittacula intermedia*
Red-faced Malkoha *Phaenicophaeus pyrrhocephalus* (2)
Forest Owlet *Athene blewitti*
Dark-rumped Swift *Apus acuticauda* (3)

Blyth's Kingfisher *Alcedo hercules* (9)
Rufous-necked Hornbill *Aceros nipalensis* (8)
Rusty-bellied Shortwing *Brachypteryx hyperythra* (2)
Stoliczka's Bushchat *Saxicola macrorhyncha* (3)
Hodgson's Bushchat *Saxicola insignis* (5)
Grey-sided Thrush *Turdus feae* (4)
Marsh Babbler *Pellorneum palustre* (2)
Rufous-throated Wren-babbler *Spelaeornis caudatus* (3)
Rusty-throated Wren-babbler *Spelaeornis badeigularis*
Tawny-breasted Wren-babbler *Spelaeornis longicaudatus*
Wedge-billed Wren-babbler *Sphenocichla humei* (2)
Snowy-throated Babbler *Stachyris oglei*
Jerdon's Babbler *Moupinia altirostris* (3)
Black-breasted Parrotbill *Paradoxornis flavirostris* (6)
Greater Rufous-headed Parrotbill *Paradoxornis ruficeps* (6)
Large-billed Bush-warbler *Bradypterus major* (4)
Long-tailed Prinia *Prinia burnesii* (2)
Bristled Grass-warbler *Chaetornis striatus* (4)
White-winged Tit *Parus nuchalis*
Beautiful Nuthatch *Sitta formosa* (7)
Green Munia *Estrilda formosa* (2)
Finn's Baya Weaver *Ploceus megarhynchus*

Indonesia
Abbott's Booby *Sula abbotti* (2)
Christmas Frigatebird *Fregata andrewsi* (4)
Milky Stork *Mycteria cinerea* (4)
Storm's Stork *Ciconia stormi* (3)
Lesser Adjutant *Leptoptilos javanicus* (11)
White-shouldered Ibis *Pseudibis davisoni* (8)
White-winged Duck *Cairina scutulata* (7)
Small Sparrowhawk *Accipiter nanus*
New Guinea Harpy-eagle *Harpyopsis novaeguineae* (2)
Javan Hawk-eagle *Spizaetus bartelsi*
Wallace's Hawk-eagle *Spizaetus nanus* (4)
Sula Scrubfowl *Megapodius bernsteinii*
Moluccan Scrubfowl *Megapodius wallacei*
Waigeo Brush-turkey *Aepypodius bruijnii*
Maleo *Macrocephalon maleo*
Chestnut-necklaced Partridge *Arborophila charltonii* (3)
Salvadori's Pheasant *Lophura inornata*
Crested Fireback *Lophura ignita* (4)
Bulwer's Pheasant *Lophura bulweri* (2)
Malaysian Peacock-pheasant *Polyplectron Malacense* (4)
Green Peafowl *Pavo muticus* (8)
Sumba Button-quail *Turnix everetti*

Snoring Rail *Aramidopsis plateni*
Bald-faced Rail *Gymnocrex rosenbergii*
Invisible Rail *Habroptila wallacii*
Masked Finfoot *Heliopais personata* (6)
Javanese Wattled Lapwing *Vanellus macropterus*
Sulawesi Woodcock *Scolopax celebensis*
Obi Woodcock *Scolopax rochussenii*
Asian Dowitcher *Limnodromus semipalmatus* (13)
Chinese Crested Tern *Sterna bernsteini* (5)
Grey Woodpigeon *Columba argentina* (2)
Nicobar Pigeon *Caloenas nicobarica* (7)
Wetar Ground-dove *Gallicolumba hoedtii*
Western Crowned-pigeon *Goura cristata*
Southern Crowned-pigeon *Goura scheepmakeri* (2)
Victoria Crowned-pigeon *Goura victoria* (2)
Sumba Green-pigeon *Treron teysmanni*
Timor Green-pigeon *Treron psittacea*
Large Green-pigeon *Treron capellei* (4)
Red-naped Fruit-dove *Ptilinopus dohertyi*
Carunculated Fruit-dove *Ptilinopus granulifrons*
Grey Imperial-pigeon *Ducula pickeringii* (3)
Biak Red Lory *Eos cyanogenia*
Blue-streaked Lory *Eos reticulata*
Red-and-blue Lory *Eos histrio*
Purple-naped Lory *Lorius domicellus*
Blue-fronted Lorikeet *Charmosyna toxopei*
Yellow-crested Cockatoo *Cacatua sulphurea*
Salmon-crested Cockatoo *Cacatua moluccensis*
White Cockatoo *Cacatua alba*
Tanimbar Corella *Cacatua goffini*
Salvadori's Fig-parrot *Psittaculirostris salvadorii*
Buru Racquet-tailed Parrot *Prioniturus mada*
Sangihe Hanging-parrot *Loriculus catamene*
Green-cheeked Bronze-cuckoo *Chrysococcyx rufomerus*
Sunda Ground-cuckoo *Carpococcyx radiceus* (2)
Short-toed Coucal *Centropus rectunguis* (2)
Javan Coucal *Centropus nigrorufus*
Taliabu Owl *Tyto nigrobrunnea*
Minahassa Owl *Tyto inexspectata*
Lesser Masked Owl *Tyto sororcula*
White-fronted Scops Owl *Otus sagittatus* (4)
Sumatran Scops Owl *Otus stresemanni*
Javan Scops Owl *Otus angelinae*
Flores Scops Owl *Otus alfredi*
Dulit Frogmouth *Batrachostomus harterti* (2)
Satanic Nightjar *Eurostopodus diabolicus*

Salvadori's Nightjar *Caprimulgus pulchellus*
Waterfall Swift *Hydrochous gigas* (2)
Cinnamon-banded Kingfisher *Halcyon australasia*
Biak Paradise Kingfisher *Tanysiptera riedelii*
Wrinkled Hornbill *Aceros corrugatus* (3)
Plain-pouched Hornbill *Aceros subruficollis* (4)
Sumba Hornbill *Rhyticeros everetti*
Helmeted Hornbill *Rhinoplax vigil* (4)
Black-banded Barbet *Megalaima javensis*
Schneider's Pitta *Pitta schneideri*
Fairy Pitta *Pitta nympha* (7)
Slaty Cuckoo-shrike *Coracina schistacea*
Sula Cuckoo-shrike *Coracina sula*
Wattled Bulbul *Pycnonotus nieuwenhuisii*
Sumatran Cochoa *Cochoa beccarii*
Javan Cochoa *Cochoa azurea*
Timor Bushchat *Saxicola gutturalis*
Slaty-backed Thrush *Zoothera schistacea*
Orange-banded Thrush *Zoothera peronii*
Fawn-breasted Thrush *Zoothera machiki*
Black-browed Babbler *Trichastoma perspicillatum*
Vanderbilt's Babbler *Trichastoma vanderbilti*
White-breasted Babbler *Stachyris grammiceps*
Biak Gerygone *Gerygone hypoxantha*
Henna-tailed Jungle-flycatcher *Rhinomyias colonus*
Damar Blue Flycatcher *Ficedula henrici*
Lompobattang Flycatcher *Ficedula bonthaina*
Sumba Flycatcher *Ficedula harterti*
Black-banded Flycatcher *Ficedula timorensis*
Matinan Flycatcher *Cyornis sandfordi*
Rueck's Blue Flycatcher *Cyornis ruecki*
Caerulean Paradise-flycatcher *Eutrichomyias rowleyi*
Black-chinned Monarch *Monarcha boanensis*
White-tipped Monarch *Monarcha everetti*
Biak Monarch *Monarcha brehmii*
Biak Black Flycatcher *Myiagra atra*
Vogelkop Whistler *Pachycephala meyeri*
Brown-backed Flowerpecker *Dicaeum everetti* (2)
Apricot-breasted Sunbird *Nectarinia buettikoferi*
Elegant Sunbird *Aethopyga duyvenbodei*
Javan White-eye *Zosterops flavus* (2)
Golden-bellied White-eye *Zosterops uropygialis*
Lemon-throated White-eye *Zosterops anomalus*
Ambon Yellow White-eye *Zosterops kuehni*
Rufous-throated White-eye *Madanga ruficollis*
Spot-breasted White-eye *Heleia muelleri*

Black-chested Honeyeater *Lichmera notabilis*
Crimson-hooded Honeyeater *Myzomela kuehni*
Brass's Friarbird *Philemon brassi*
Dusky Friarbird *Philemon fuscicapillus*
Bali Starling *Leucopsar rothschildi*
Helmeted Myna *Basilornis galeatus*
Bare-eyed Myna *Streptocitta albertinae*
Golden-fronted Bowerbird *Amblyornis flavifrons*
Long-tailed Paradigalla *Paradigalla carunculata*
Black Sicklebill *Epimachus fastuosus* (2)
Banggai Crow *Corvus unicolor*
Flores Crow *Corvus florensis*

Iran

Dalmatian Pelican *Pelecanus crispus* (13)
Pygmy Cormorant *Halietor pygmeus* (9)
Lesser White-fronted Goose *Anser erythropus* (15)
Marbled Teal *Marmaronetta angustirostris* (15)
White-headed Duck *Oxyura leucocephala* (9)
Pallas's Fish Eagle *Haliaeetus leucoryphus* (8)
White-tailed Eagle *Haliaeetus albicilla* (22)
Black Vulture *Aegypius monachus* (10)
Imperial Eagle *Aquila heliaca* (12)
Lesser Kestrel *Falco naumanni* (27)
Siberian Crane *Grus leucogeranus* (5)
Great Bustard *Otis tarda* (18)
Little Bustard *Tetrax tetrax* (8)
Houbara Bustard *Chlamydotis undulata* (23)

Iraq

Dalmatian Pelican *Pelecanus crispus* (13)
Pygmy Cormorant *Halietor pygmeus* (9)
Lesser White-fronted Goose *Anser erythropus* (15)
Marbled Teal *Marmaronetta angustirostris* (15)
Great Bustard *Otis tarda* (18)
Houbara Bustard *Chlamydotis undulata* (23)
Sociable Plover *Chettusia gregaria* (10)

Ireland

Corncrake *Crex crex* (33)

Israel

Marbled Teal *Marmaronetta angustirostris* (15)
Imperial Eagle *Aquila heliaca* (12)
Lesser Kestrel *Falco naumanni* (27)
Houbara Bustard *Chlamydotis undulata* (23)

Italy

Red Kite *Milvus milvus* (19)
Lesser Kestrel *Falco naumanni* (27)
Corncrake *Crex crex* (33)
Little Bustard *Tetrax tetrax* (8)
Slender-billed Curlew *Numenius tenuirostris* (9)
Audouin's Gull *Larus audouinii* (10)

Ivory Coast

White-breasted Guineafowl *Agelastes meleagrides* (4)
Rufous Fishing Owl *Scotopelia ussheri* (5)
Western Wattled Cuckoo-shrike *Campephaga lobata* (4)
Yellow-throated Olive Greenbul *Criniger olivaceus* (6)
White-necked Picathartes *Picathartes gymnocephalus* (5)
Nimba Flycatcher *Melaenornis annamarulae* (2)
Gola Malimbe *Malimbus ballmanni* (3)

Izu Islands (to Japan)

Japanese Murrelet *Synthliboramphus wumizusume* (5)

Jamaica

West Indian Whistling Duck *Dendrocygna arborea* (9)
Ring-tailed Pigeon *Columba caribaea*
Jamaican Pauraque *Siphonorhis americanus*

Japan (see also Bonin Islands, Izu Islands, Okinawa, Torishima, Volcano Islands)

Japanese Night-heron *Gorsagius goisagi* (6)
Black-faced Spoonbill *Platalea minor* (7)
Lesser White-fronted Goose *Anser erythropus* (15)
Crested Shelduck *Tadorna cristata* (5)
Baykal Teal *Anas formosa* (5)
Baer's Pochard *Aythya baeri* (11)
White-tailed Eagle *Haliaeetus albicilla* (22)
Steller's Sea Eagle *Haliaeetus pelagicus* (4)
Hooded Crane *Grus monacha* (5)
Red-crowned Crane *Grus japonensis* (5)
White-naped Crane *Grus vipio* (6)
Asian Yellow Rail *Coturnicops exquisitus* (5)
Spotted Greenshank *Tringa guttifer* (11)
Asian Dowitcher *Limnodromus semipalmatus* (13)
Spoon-billed Sandpiper *Eurynorhynchus pygmeus* (9)
Saunders's Gull *Larus saundersi* (7)
Japanese Murrelet *Synthliboramphus wumizusume* (5)
Blakiston's Fish Owl *Ketupa blakistoni* (3)
Fairy Pitta *Pitta nympha* (7)

Amami Thrush *Zoothera amami*
Japanese Marsh Warbler *Megalurus pryeri* (2)
Japanese Yellow Bunting *Emberiza sulphurata* (2)

Jordan
Houbara Bustard *Chlamydotis undulata* (23)

Juan Fernandez Islands (to Chile)
Defilippe's Petrel *Pterodroma defilippiana* (2)
Pink-footed Shearwater *Puffinus creatopus* (2)
Juan Fernandez Firecrown *Sephanoides fernandensis*
Masafuera Rayadito *Aphrastura masafuerae*

Kampuchea
Milky Stork *Mycteria cinerea* (4)
Lesser Adjutant *Leptoptilos javanicus* (11)
Greater Adjutant *Leptoptilos dubius* (7)
White-shouldered Ibis *Pseudibis davisoni* (8)
Giant Ibis *Pseudibis gigantea* (4)
White-winged Duck *Cairina scutulata* (7)
Chestnut-headed Partridge *Arborophila cambodiana* (2)
Siamese Fireback *Lophura diardi* (4)
Green Peafowl *Pavo muticus* (8)
Bengal Florican *Houbaropsis bengalensis* (4)
Rufous-necked Hornbill *Aceros nipalensis* (8)
Bar-bellied Pitta *Pitta ellioti* (3)
Silver Oriole *Oriolus mellianus* (3)

Kenya
Sokoke Scops Owl *Otus ireneae*
Sokoke Pipit *Anthus sokokensis* (2)
East Coast Akalat *Sheppardia gunningi* (4)
Spotted Ground-thrush *Turdus fischeri* (6)
Taita Thrush *Turdus helleri*
Hinde's Pied Babbler *Turdoides hindei*
Papyrus Yellow Warbler *Chloropeta gracilirostris* (6)
Tana River Cisticola *Cisticola restricta* (2)
White-winged Apalis *Apalis chariessa* (4)
Turner's Eremomela *Eremomela turneri* (3)
Chapin's Flycatcher *Muscicapa lendu* (3)
Amani Sunbird *Anthreptes pallidigaster* (2)
Clarke's Weaver *Ploceus golandi*
Abbott's Starling *Cinnyricinclus femoralis* (2)

Kerguelen Islands (to France)
Kerguelen Tern *Sterna virgata* (3)

Kiribati

Scarlet-breasted Lorikeet *Vini kuhlii* (2)

Kuwait

Houbara Bustard *Chlamydotis undulata* (23)

Laos

Lesser Adjutant *Leptoptilos javanicus* (11)
Greater Adjutant *Leptoptilos dubius* (7)
White-shouldered Ibis *Pseudibis davisoni* (8)
Giant Ibis *Pseudibis gigantea* (4)
Imperial Pheasant *Lophura imperialis* (2)
Siamese Fireback *Lophura diardi* (4)
Germain's Peacock-pheasant *Polyplectron germaini* (2)
Crested Argus *Rheinartia ocellata* (3)
Green Peafowl *Pavo muticus* (8)
Pale-capped Pigeon *Columba punicea* (7)
Blyth's Kingfisher *Alcedo hercules* (9)
Rufous-necked Hornbill *Aceros nipalensis* (8)
Red-collared Woodpecker *Picus rabieri* (3)
Bar-bellied Pitta *Pitta ellioti* (3)
Sooty Babbler *Stachyris herberti*
Short-tailed Parrotbill *Paradoxornis davidianus* (5)
Greater Rufous-headed Parrotbill *Paradoxornis ruficeps* (6)
Beautiful Nuthatch *Sitta formosa* (7)

Lebanon

Lesser Kestrel *Falco naumanni* (27)

Leeward Islands (to U.K.)

West Indian Whistling Duck *Dendrocygna arborea* (9)

Lesotho

Southern Bald Ibis *Geronticus calvus* (3)
Cape Vulture *Gyps coprotheres* (7)
South African Long-clawed Lark *Heteromirafra ruddi* (2)
Yellow-breasted Pipit *Anthus chloris* (2)

Liberia

White-breasted Guineafowl *Agelastes meleagrides* (4)
Rufous Fishing Owl *Scotopelia ussheri* (5)
Yellow-footed Honeyguide *Melignomon eisentrauti* (3)
Western Wattled Cuckoo-shrike *Campephaga lobata* (4)
Spot-winged Greenbul *Phyllastrephus leucolepis*
Yellow-throated Olive Greenbul *Criniger olivaceus* (6)
White-necked Picathartes *Picathartes gymnocephalus* (5)

Nimba Flycatcher *Melaenornis annamarulae* (2)
Gola Malimbe *Malimbus ballmanni* (3)

Libya

Houbara Bustard *Chlamydotis undulata* (23)
Audouin's Gull *Larus audouinii* (10)

Liechtenstein

Corncrake *Crex crex* (33)

Lord Howe Island (Australia)

Lord Howe Island Woodhen *Tricholimnas sylvestris*

Luxembourg

Red Kite *Milvus milvus* (19)
Corncrake *Crex crex* (33)

Madagascar

Madagascar Little Grebe *Tachybaptus pelzelnii*
Alaotra Grebe *Tachybaptus rufolavatus*
Madagascar Heron *Ardea humbloti* (3)
Madagascar Teal *Anas bernieri*
Madagascar Pochard *Aythya innotata*
Madagascar Fish Eagle *Haliaeetus vociferoides*
Madagascar Serpent-eagle *Eutriorchis astur*
White-breasted Mesite *Mesitornis variegata*
Brown Mesite *Mesitornis unicolor*
Subdesert Mesite *Monias benschi*
Slender-billed Flufftail *Sarothrura watersi*
Sakalava Rail *Amaurornis olivieri*
Madagascar Plover *Charadrius thoracicus*
Snail-eating Coua *Coua delalandei*
Madagascar Red Owl *Tyto soumagnei*
Short-legged Ground-roller *Brachypteracias leptosomus*
Scaly Ground-roller *Brachypteracias squamiger*
Rufous-headed Ground-roller *Atelornis crossleyi*
Long-tailed Ground-roller *Uratelornis chimaera*
Yellow-bellied Sunbird-asity *Neodrepanis hypoxantha*
Appert's Greenbul *Phyllastrephus apperti*
Dusky Greenbul *Phyllastrephus tenebrosus*
Grey-crowned Greenbul *Phyllastrephus cinereiceps*
Van Dam's Vanga *Xenopirostris damii*
Pollen's Vanga *Xenopirostris polleni*
Benson's Rockthrush *Monticola bensoni*
Madagascar Yellowbrow *Crossleyia xanthophrys*
Red-tailed Newtonia *Newtonia fanovanae*

Madeira (Portugal)
> Gon-gon *Pterodroma feae* (2)
> Freira *Pterodroma madeira*
> Madeira Laurel Pigeon *Columba trocaz*

Malawi
> Wattled Crane *Bugeranus carunculatus* (11)
> Corncrake *Crex crex* (33)
> East Coast Akalat *Sheppardia gunningi* (4)
> Thyolo Alethe *Alethe choloensis* (2)
> Spotted Ground-thrush *Turdus fischeri* (6)
> White-winged Apalis *Apalis chariessa* (4)

Malaysia
> Christmas Frigatebird *Fregata andrewsi* (4)
> Milky Stork *Mycteria cinerea* (4)
> Storm's Stork *Ciconia stormi* (3)
> Lesser Adjutant *Leptoptilos javanicus* (11)
> White-shouldered Ibis *Pseudibis davisoni* (8)
> White-winged Duck *Cairina scutulata* (7)
> Kinabalu Serpent-eagle *Spilornis kinabaluensis*
> Wallace's Hawk-eagle *Spizaetus nanus* (4)
> Chestnut-necklaced Partridge *Arborophila charltonii* (3)
> Crested Fireback *Lophura ignita* (4)
> Bulwer's Pheasant *Lophura bulweri* (2)
> Malaysian Peacock-pheasant *Polyplectron malacense* (4)
> Crested Argus *Rheinartia ocellata* (3)
> Masked Finfoot *Heliopais personata* (6)
> Spotted Greenshank *Tringa guttifer* (11)
> Asian Dowitcher *Limnodromus semipalmatus* (13)
> Chinese Crested Tern *Sterna bernsteini* (5)
> Grey Woodpigeon *Columba argentina* (2)
> Large Green-pigeon *Treron capellei* (4)
> Grey Imperial-pigeon *Ducula pickeringii* (3)
> Sunda Ground-cuckoo *Carpococcyx radiceus* (2)
> Short-toed Coucal *Centropus rectunguis* (2)
> White-fronted Scops Owl *Otus sagittatus* (4)
> Dulit Frogmouth *Batrachostomus harterti* (2)
> Waterfall Swift *Hydrochous gigas* (2)
> Wrinkled Hornbill *Aceros corrugatus* (3)
> Plain-pouched Hornbill *Aceros subruficollis* (4)
> Helmeted Hornbill *Rhinoplax vigil* (4)
> Fairy Pitta *Pitta nympha* (7)
> Rufous-headed Robin *Erithacus ruficeps* (2)
> Everett's Thrush *Zoothera everetti*
> Brown-chested Flycatcher *Rhinomyias brunneata* (3)

Brown-backed Flowerpecker *Dicaeum everetti* (2)
Javan White-eye *Zosterops flavus* (2)

Mali

Marbled Teal *Marmaronetta angustirostris* (15)

Marquesas Islands (to France)

Bristle-thighed Curlew *Numenius tahitiensis* (9)
Marquesas Ground-dove *Gallicolumba rubescens*
Marquesas Fruit-dove *Ptilinopus mercierii*
Marquesas Imperial-pigeon *Ducula galeata*
Ultramarine Lorikeet *Vini ultramarina*
Marquesas Kingfisher *Halcyon godeffroyi*
Marquesas Monarch *Pomarea mendozae*
Iphis Monarch *Pomarea iphis*
Fatu Iva Monarch *Pomarea whitneyi*

Marshall Islands (to U.S.A.)

Bristle-thighed Curlew *Numenius tahitiensis* (9)

Martinique (to France)

White-breasted Thrasher *Ramphocinclus brachyurus* (2)
Martinique Oriole *Icterus bonana*

Mauritius

Mauritius Kestrel *Falco punctatus*
Pink Pigeon *Nesoenas mayeri*
Mauritius Parakeet *Psittacula eques*
Mauritius Cuckoo-shrike *Coracina typica*
Mauritius Black Bulbul *Hypsipetes olivaceus*
Rodrigues Warbler *Acrocephalus rodericanus*
Mauritius Olive White-eye *Zosterops chloronothus*
Mauritius Fody *Foudia rubra*
Rodrigues Fody *Foudia flavicans*

Mayotte (to France)

Madagascar Heron *Ardea humbloti* (3)
Mayotte Drongo *Dicrurus waldeni*

Mexico (see also Guadalupe Islands, Revillagigedos Islands)

Solitary Eagle *Harpyhaliaetus solitarius* (10)
Harpy Eagle *Harpia harpyja* (18)
Orange-breasted Falcon *Falco deiroleucus* (17)
Highland Guan *Penelopina nigra* (5)
Horned Guan *Oreophasis derbianus* (2)
Bearded Wood-partridge *Dendrortyx barbatus*

Ocellated Turkey *Agriocharis ocellata* (3)
Piping Plover *Charadrius melodus* (12)
Thick-billed Parrot *Rhynchopsitta pachyrhyncha* (2)
Maroon-fronted Parrot *Rhynchopsitta terrisi*
Red-crowned Green-cheeked Amazon *Amazona viridigenalis* (3)
Spotted Owl *Strix occidentalis* (3)
White-tailed Hummingbird *Eupherusa poliocerca*
Oaxaca Hummingbird *Eupherusa cyanophrys*
Resplendent Quetzal *Pharomachrus mocinno* (7)
Eared Trogon *Euptilotis neoxenus* (2)
Keel-billed Motmot *Electron carinatum* (6)
Imperial Woodpecker *Campephilus imperialis*
Slender-billed Wren *Hylorchilus sumichrasti*
Sierra Madre Sparrow *Xenospiza baileyi*
Azure-rumped Tanager *Tangara cabanisi* (2)
Golden-cheeked Warbler *Dendroica chrysoparia* (5)
Altamira Yellowthroat *Geothlypis flavovelata*
Black-polled Yellowthroat *Geothlypis speciosa*
Black-capped Vireo *Vireo atricapillus* (2)
Dwarf Jay *Cyanolyca nana*
White-throated Jay *Cyanolyca mirabilis*

Mongolia

Dalmatian Pelican *Pelecanus crispus* (13)
Pallas's Fish Eagle *Haliaeetus leucoryphus* (8)
White-tailed Eagle *Haliaeetus albicilla* (22)
Black Vulture *Aegypius monachus* (10)
Lesser Kestrel *Falco naumanni* (27)
White-naped Crane *Grus vipio* (6)
Great Bustard *Otis tarda* (18)
Houbara Bustard *Chlamydotis undulata* (23)
Asian Dowitcher *Limnodromus semipalmatus* (13)
Relict Gull *Larus relictus* (4)
Hodgson's Bushchat *Saxicola insignis* (5)

Montserrat (to U.K.)

Montserrat Oriole *Icterus oberi*

Morocco

Northern Bald Ibis *Geronticus eremita* (7)
Marbled Teal *Marmaronetta angustirostris* (15)
Lesser Kestrel *Falco naumanni* (27)
Great Bustard *Otis tarda* (18)
Little Bustard *Tetrax tetrax* (8)
Houbara Bustard *Chlamydotis undulata* (23)
Slender-billed Curlew *Numenius tenuirostris* (9)

Audouin's Gull *Larus audouinii* (10)

Mozambique
Cape Vulture *Gyps coprotheres* (7)
Wattled Crane *Bugeranus carunculatus* (11)
Corncrake *Crex crex* (33)
Swynnerton's Forest Robin *Swynnertonia swynnertoni* (3)
East Coast Akalat *Sheppardia gunningi* (4)
Dappled Mountain Robin *Modulatrix orostruthus* (2)
Thyolo Alethe *Alethe choloensis* (2)
White-winged Apalis *Apalis chariessa* (4)
Long-billed Apalis *Apalis moreaui* (2)

Namibia
Jackass Penguin *Spheniscus demersus* (2)
Slaty Egret *Egretta vinaceigula* (3)
Cape Vulture *Gyps coprotheres* (7)
Lesser Kestrel *Falco naumanni* (27)
Wattled Crane *Bugeranus carunculatus* (11)
Damara Tern *Sterna balaenarum* (6)
Black-cheeked Lovebird *Agapornis nigrigenis* (3)

Nauru
Nauru Reed Warbler *Acrocephalus rehsei*

Nepal
Lesser Adjutant *Leptoptilos javanicus* (11)
Pink-headed Duck *Rhodonessa caryophyllacea* (2)
Baer's Pochard *Aythya baeri* (11)
Pallas's Fish Eagle *Haliaeetus leucoryphus* (8)
Swamp Partridge *Francolinus gularis* (3)
Cheer Pheasant *Catreus wallichii* (3)
Bengal Florican *Houbaropsis bengalensis* (4)
Lesser Florican *Sypheotides indica* (2)
Wood Snipe *Gallinago nemoricola* (5)
Dark-rumped Swift *Apus acuticauda* (3)
Blyth's Kingfisher *Alcedo hercules* (9)
Rufous-necked Hornbill *Aceros nipalensis* (8)
Hodgson's Bushchat *Saxicola insignis* (5)
Rufous-throated Wren-babbler *Spelaeornis caudatus* (3)
Black-breasted Parrotbill *Paradoxornis flavirostris* (6)
Bristled Grass-warbler *Chaetornis striatus* (4)

Netherlands (see also Netherlands Antilles)
Red Kite *Milvus milvus* (19)
Corncrake *Crex crex* (33)

Netherlands Antilles (to Netherlands)
   Yellow-shouldered Amazon *Amazona barbadensis* (2)

New Caledonia (to France)
   New Caledonian Rail *Tricholimnas lafresnayanus*
   Kagu *Rhynochetos jubatus*
   Cloven-feathered Dove *Drepanoptila holosericea*
   Giant Imperial-pigeon *Ducula goliath*
   New Caledonian Lorikeet *Charmosyna diadema*

New Zealand (see also Antipodes Islands, Auckland Islands,
   Campbell Island. Chatham Islands, Cook Islands, Shares Island)
   Little Spotted Kiwi *Apteryx owenii*
   Yellow-eyed Penguin *Megadyptes antipodes* (3)
   Cook's Petrel *Pterodroma cooki*
   Pycroft's Petrel *Pterodroma pycrofti*
   Black Petrel *Procellaria parkinsoni*
   Westland Black Petrel *Procellaria westlandica*
   New Zealand King Cormorant *Phalacrocorax carunculatus* (2)
   New Zealand Brown Teal *Anas aucklandica* (3)
   Takahe *Notomis mantelli*
   New Zealand Shore Plover *Thinornis novaeseelandiae*
   Black Stilt *Himantopus novaezealandiae*
   Black-fronted Tern *Sterna albostriata*
   Kakapo *Strigops habroptilus*
   Bush Wren *Xenicus longipes*
   Stitchbird *Notiomystis cincta*
   Kokako *Callaeas cinerea*
   Saddleback *Creadion carunculatus*

Nicaragua
   Harpy Eagle *Harpia harpyja* (18)
   Orange-breasted Falcon *Falco deiroleucus* (17)
   Highland Guan *Penelopina nigra* (5)
   Resplendent Quetzal *Pharomachrus mocinno* (7)
   Keel-billed Motmot *Electron carinatum* (6)
   Golden-cheeked Warbler *Dendroica chrysoparia* (5)

Nicobar Islands (to India)
   Nicobar Scrubfowl *Megapodius nicobariensis*
   Nicobar Pigeon *Caloenas nicobarica* (7)
   Nicobar Parakeet *Psittacula caniceps*

Niger
   River Prinia *Prinia "fluviatilis"* (3)

Nigeria

Damara Tern *Sterna balaenarum* (6)
Fernando Po Swift *Apus sladeniae* (4)
Green-breasted Bush-shrike *Malaconotus gladiator* (2)
White-throated Mountain Babbler *Lioptilus gilberti* (2)
Grey-necked Picathartes *Picathartes oreas* (4)
Anambra Waxbill *Estrilda poliopareia*
Bannerman's Weaver *Ploceus bannermani* (2)
Ibadan Malimbe *Malimbus ibadanensis*

Norfolk Island (to Australia)

White-breasted White-eye *Zosterops albogularis*

North Korea

Chinese Egret *Egretta eulophotes* (5)
Oriental White Stork *Ciconia boyciana* (4)
Black-faced Spoonbill *Platalea minor* (7)
Crested Shelduck *Tadorna cristata* (5)
Baykal Teal *Anas formosa* (5)
Baer's Pochard *Aythya baeri* (11)
Scaly-sided Merganser *Mergus squamatus* (4)
Steller's Sea Eagle *Haliaeetus pelagicus* (4)
Hooded Crane *Grus monacha* (5)
Red-crowned Crane *Grus japonensis* (5)
White-naped Crane *Grus vipio* (6)
Asian Yellow Rail *Coturnicops exquisitus* (5)
Spoon-billed Sandpiper *Eurynorhynchus pygmeus* (9)
Japanese Murrelet *Synthliboramphus wumizusume* (5)

North Yemen

Northern Bald Ibis *Geronticus eremita* (7)
Sociable Plover *Chettusia gregaria* (10)
White-eyed Gull *Larus leucophthalmus* (3)
Yemen Thrush *Turdus menachensis* (2)

Northern Marianas Islands (to U.S.A.)

Micronesian Megapode *Megapodius laperouse* (2)
Marianas Fruit-dove *Ptilinopus roseicapilla* (2)
Marianas Crow *Corvus kubaryi* (2)

Norway

Lesser White-fronted Goose *Anser erythropus* (15)
White-tailed Eagle *Haliaeetus albicilla* (22)
Corncrake *Crex crex* (33)

Okinawa (to Japan)
>Okinawa Rail *Rallus okinawae*
>Okinawa Woodpecker *Sapheopipo noguchii*

Oman
>Houbara Bustard *Chlamydotis undulata* (23)
>Sociable Plover *Chettusia gregaria* (10)

Pakistan
>Dalmatian Pelican *Pelecanus crispus* (13)
>Lesser White-fronted Goose *Anser erythropus* (15)
>Marbled Teal *Marmaronetta angustirostris* (15)
>White-headed Duck *Oxyura leucocephala* (9)
>Pallas's Fish Eagle *Haliaeetus leucoryphus* (8)
>Black Vulture *Aegypius monachus* (10)
>Western Tragopan *Tragopan melanocephalus* (3)
>Cheer Pheasant *Catreus wallichii* (3)
>Houbara Bustard *Chlamydotis undulata* (23)
>Sociable Plover *Chettusia gregaria* (10)
>Wood Snipe *Gallinago nemoricola* (5)
>Stoliczka's Bushchat *Saxicola macrorhyncha* (3)
>Jerdon's Babbler *Moupinia altirostris* (3)
>Large-billed Bush-warbler *Bradypterus major* (4)
>Long-tailed Prinia *Prinia burnesii* (2)
>Bristled Grass-warbler *Chaetornis striatus* (4)
>Green Munia *Estrilda formosa* (2)

Palau (to U.S.A.)
>Japanese Night-heron *Gorsagius goisagi* (6)
>Micronesian Megapode *Megapodius laperouse* (2)
>Nicobar Pigeon *Caloenas nicobarica* (7)

Panama
>Plumbeous Hawk *Leucopternis plumbea* (4)
>Solitary Eagle *Harpyhaliaetus solitarius* (10)
>Crested Eagle *Morphnus guianensis* (15)
>Harpy Eagle *Harpia harpyja* (18)
>Orange-breasted Falcon *Falco deiroleucus* (17)
>Glow-throated Hummingbird *Selasphorus ardens*
>Resplendent Quetzal *Pharomachrus mocinno* (7)
>Baird's Trogon *Trogon bairdii* (2)
>Speckled Antshrike *Xenornis setifrons* (2)
>Turquoise Cotinga *Cotinga ridgwayi* (2)
>Yellow-billed Cotinga *Carpodectes antoniae* (2)
>Bare-necked Umbrellabird *Cephalopterus glabricollis* (2)

Papua New Guinea

Beck's Petrel *Pterodroma becki* (2)
Heinroth's Shearwater *Puffinus heinrothi*
Black Honey-buzzard *Henicopernis infuscata*
New Britain Sparrowhawk *Accipiter brachyurus*
Imitator Sparrowhawk *Accipiter imitator* (2)
New Guinea Harpy-eagle *Harpyopsis novaeguineae* (2)
Woodford's Rail *Nesoclopeus woodfordi* (3)
Yellow-legged Pigeon *Columba pallidiceps* (2)
Nicobar Pigeon *Caloenas nicobarica* (7)
Southern Crowned-pigeon *Goura scheepmakeri* (2)
Victoria Crowned-pigeon *Goura victoria* (2)
Golden Owl *Tyto aurantia*
Moustached Kingfisher *Halcyon bougainvillei* (2)
Superb Pitta *Pitta superba*
Solomons Pittas *Pitta anerythra* (2)
Fly River Grassbird *Megalurus albolimbatus*
Sudest White-eye *Zosterops meeki*
Sudest Meliphaga *Meliphaga vicina*
Long-bearded Melidectes *Melidectes princeps*
Adelbert Bowerbird *Sericulus bakeri*
Black Sicklebill *Epimachus fastuosus* (2)
Ribbon-tailed Astrapia *Astrapia mayeri*
Wahnes's Parotia *Parotia wahnesi*
Goldie's Bird Of Paradise *Paradisaea decora*

Paraguay

Solitary Tinamou *Tinamus solitarius* (3)
Brazilian Merganser *Mergus octosetaceus* (3)
Grey-bellied Hawk *Accipiter poliogaster* (10)
Mantled Hawk *Leucopternis polionota* (3)
Crowned Eagle *Harpyhaliaetus coronatus* (4)
Crested Eagle *Morphnus guianensis* (15)
Harpy Eagle *Harpia harpyja* (18)
Orange-breasted Falcon *Falco deiroleucus* (17)
Black-fronted Piping Guan *Pipile jacutinga* (3)
Rufous-faced Crake *Laterallus xenopterus* (2)
Eskimo Curlew *Numenius borealis* (10)
Purple-winged Ground-dove *Claravis godefrida* (3)
Hyacinth Macaw *Anodorhynchus hyacinthinus* (3)
Glaucous Macaw *Anodorhynchus glaucus* (4)
Red-spectacled Amazon *Amazona pretrei* (4)
Vinaceous Amazon *Amazona vinacea* (3)
Long-tailed Potoo *Nyctibius aethereus* (7)

White-winged Nightjar *Caprimulgus candicans* (2)
Sickle-winged Nightjar *Eleothreptus anomalus* (4)
Helmeted Woodpecker *Dryocopus galeatus* (3)
Canebrake Groundcreeper *Clibanornis dendrocolaptoides* (3)
Black-and-white Monjita *Xolmis dominicana* (4)
Strange-tailed Tyrant *Yetapa risoria* (4)
Russet-winged Spadebill *Platyrinchus leucoryphus* (3)
Sao Paulo Tyrannulet *Phylloscartes paulistus* (3)
Bearded Tachuri *Polystictus pectoralis* (9)
Sharp-tailed Tyrant *Culicivora caudacuta* (4)
Chaco Pipit *Anthus chacoensis* (2)
Ochre-breasted Pipit *Anthus nattereri* (3)
Buffy-throated Seedeater *Sporophila frontalis* (3)
Marsh Seedeater *Sporophila palustris* (4)
Chestnut Seedeater *Sporophila cinnamomea* (3)
Blackish-blue Seedeater *Amaurospiza moesta* (3)
Black-masked Finch *Coryphaspiza melanotis* (4)
Green-throated Euphonia *Euphonia chalybea* (3)
Saffron-cowled Blackbird *Xanthopsar flavus* (5)

Peru

Black Tinamou *Tinamus osgoodi* (2)
Taczanowski's Tinamou *Nothoprocta taczanowskii*
Kalinowski's Tinamou *Nothoprocta kalinowskii*
Peruvian Penguin *Spheniscus humboldti* (2)
Junin Grebe *Podiceps taczanowskii*
Markham's Storm-petrel *Oceanodroma markhami* (5)
Ringed Storm-petrel *Oceanodroma hornbyi* (3)
Peruvian Diving-petrel *Pelecanoides garnoti* (2)
Zigzag Heron *Zebrilus undulatus* (9)
Andean Flamingo *Phoenicoparrus andinus* (4)
Puna Flamingo *Phoenicoparrus jamesi* (4)
Semicollared Sparrowhawk *Accipiter collaris* (4)
Grey-bellied Hawk *Accipiter poliogaster* (10)
Plumbeous Hawk *Leucopternis plumbea* (4)
Grey-backed Hawk *Leucopternis occidentalis* (2)
Solitary Eagle *Harpyhaliaetus solitarius* (10)
Crested Eagle *Morphnus guianensis* (15)
Harpy Eagle *Harpia harpyja* (18)
Traylor's Forest-falcon *Micrastur buckleyi* (2)
Orange-breasted Falcon *Falco deiroleucus* (17)
Rufous-headed Chachalaca *Ortalis erythroptera* (2)
Bearded Guan *Penelope barbata* (2)
White-winged Guan *Penelope albipennis*
Southern Helmeted Curassow *Pauxi unicornis* (2)

Wattled Curassow *Crax globulosa* (5)
Junin Rail *Laterallus tuerosi*
Ochre-bellied Dove *Leptotila ochraceiventris* (2)
Golden-plumed Conure *Leptosittaca branickii* (3)
Grey-cheeked Parakeet *Brotogeris pyrrhopterus* (2)
Spot-winged Parrotlet *Touit stictoptera* (3)
Long-tailed Potoo *Nyctibius aethereus* (7)
Rufous Potoo *Nyctibius bracteatus* (5)
Purple-backed Sunbeam *Aglaeactis aliciae*
Royal Sunangel *Heliangelus regalis*
Neblina Metaltail *Metallura odomae*
Grey-bellied Comet *Taphrolesbia griseiventris*
Marvellous Spatuletail *Loddigesia mirabilis*
Chilean Woodstar *Eulidia yarrellii* (2)
Little Woodstar *Acestrura bombus* (2)
Yellow-browed Toucanet *Aulacorhynchus huallagae*
White-bellied Cinclodes *Cinclodes palliatus*
Stout-billed Cinclodes *Cinclodes aricomae* (2)
White-browed Tit-spinetail *Leptasthenura xenothorax*
Apurimac Spinetail *Synallaxis courseni*
Chestnut-throated Spinetail *Synallaxis cherriei* (3)
Russet-bellied Spinetail *Synallaxis zimmeri*
White-tailed Asthenes *Asthenes usheri*
Line-fronted Canastero *Asthenes urubambensis* (2)
Rufous-necked Foliage-gleaner *Automolus ruficollis* (2)
Henna-hooded Foliage-gleaner *Automolus erythrocephalus* (2)
Ash-throated Antwren *Herpsilochmus parkeri*
Yellow-rumped Antwren *Terenura sharpei* (2)
Grey-headed Antbird *Myrmeciza griseiceps* (2)
Rufous-fronted Antthrush *Formicarius rufifrons*
Shrike-like Cotinga *Laniisoma elegans* (6)
White-cheeked Cotinga *Ampelion stresemanni*
White-tailed Shrike-tyrant *Agriornis albicauda* (5)
Grey-breasted Flycatcher *Empidonax griseipectus* (2)
Ash-breasted Tit-tyrant *Anairetes alpinus* (2)
Peruvian Plantcutter *Phytotoma raimondii*
Slender-billed Finch *Xenospingus concolor* (2)
Grey-winged Inca-finch *Incaspiza ortizi*
Plain-tailed Warbling-finch *Poospiza alticola*
Rufous-breasted Warbling-finch *Poospiza rubecula*
Golden-backed Mountain-tanager *Buthraupis aureodorsalis*
Green-capped Tanager *Tangara meyerdeschauenseei*
Sira Tanager *Tangara phillipsi*
White-bellied Dacnis *Dacnis albiventris* (5)
Pearly-breasted Conebill *Conirostrum margaritae* (2)

Tamarugo Conebill *Conirostrum tamarugense* (2)
Selva Cacique *Cacicus koepckeae*

Philippines

Japanese Night-heron *Gorsagius goisagi* (6)
Chinese Egret *Egretta eulophotes* (5)
Black-faced Spoonbill *Platalea minor* (7)
Philippine Eagle *Pithecophaga jefferyi*
Palawan Peacock-pheasant *Polyplectron emphanum*
Worcester's Button-quail *Turnix worcesteri*
Brown-banded Rail *Rallus mirificus*
Asian Dowitcher *Limnodromus semipalmatus* (13)
Chinese Crested Tern *Sterna bernsteini* (5)
Nicobar Pigeon *Caloenas nicobarica* (7)
Mindoro Bleeding-heart *Gallicolumba platenae*
Negros Bleeding-heart *Gallicolumba keayi*
Sulu Bleeding-heart *Gallicolumba menagei*
Negros Fruit-dove *Ptilinopus arcanus*
Mindoro Imperial-pigeon *Ducula mindorensis*
Grey Imperial-pigeon *Ducula pickeringii* (3)
Red-vented Cockatoo *Cacatua haematuropygia*
Green-headed Racquet-tailed Parrot *Prioniturus luconensis*
Black-hooded Coucal *Centropus steerii*
Mindoro Mountain Scops Owl *Otus mindorensis*
Blue-capped Wood Kingfisher *Halcyon hombroni*
Sulu Hornbill *Anthracoceros montani*
Whiskered Pitta *Pitta kochi*
Steere's Pitta *Pitta steerii*
Black Cuckoo-shrike *Coracina coerulescens*
White-winged Cuckoo-shrike *Coracina ostenta*
Mottle-breasted Bulbul *Hypsipetes siquijorensis*
Black Shama *Copsychus cebuensis*
Luzon Water-redstart *Rhyacornis bicolor*
Bagobo Babbler *Leonardina woodi*
Luzon Wren-babbler *Napothera rabori*
Flame-templed Babbler *Stachyris speciosa*
Negros Babbler *Stachyris nigrorum*
Speckled Reed Warbler *Acrocephalus sorghophilus* (2)
White-throated Jungle-flycatcher *Rhinomyias albigularis*
Blue-breasted Flycatcher *Cyornis herioti*
Short-crested Monarch *Hypothymis helenae*
Celestial Monarch *Hypothymis coelestis*
Long-billed Creeper *Rhabdornis grandis*
Green-faced Parrotfinch *Erythrura viridifacies*
Mindanao Parrotfinch *Erythrura coloria*
Isabella Oriole *Oriolus isabellae*

Pitcairn Islands (to U.K.)
>Henderson Rail *Nesophylax ater*
>Henderson Lorikeet *Vini stepheni*

Poland
>Red Kite *Milvus milvus* (19)
>White-tailed Eagle *Haliaeetus albicilla* (22)
>Corncrake *Crex crex* (33)
>Great Bustard *Otis tarda* (18)
>Aquatic Warbler *Acrocephalus paludicola* (5)

Portugal (see also Madeira)
>Red Kite *Milvus milvus* (19)
>Spanish Imperial Eagle *Aquila adalberti* (2)
>Lesser Kestrel *Falco naumanni* (27)
>Great Bustard *Otis tarda* (18)
>Little Bustard *Tetrax tetrax* (8)

Prince Edward Island (to South Africa)
>Kerguelen Tern *Sterna virgata* (3)

Puerto Rico (to U.S.A.)
>West Indian Whistling Duck *Dendrocygna arborea* (9)
>Piping Plover *Charadrius melodus* (12)
>Puerto Rican Amazon *Amazona vittata*
>Red-crowned Green-cheeked Amazon *Amazona viridigenalis* (3)
>Puerto Rican Whippoorwill *Caprimulgus noctitherus*
>Yellow-shouldered Blackbird *Agelaius xanthomus*
>Red Siskin *Carduelis cucullata* (3)

Qatar
>Houbara Bustard *Chlamydotis undulata* (23)

Reunion (to France)
>Mascarene Black Petrel *Pterodroma aterrima*
>Reunion Cuckoo-shrike *Coracina newtoni*

Revillagigedos Islands (to Mexico)
>Townsend's Shearwater *Puffinus auricularis* (2)
>Socorro Dove *Zenaida graysoni*
>Socorro Conure *Aratinga brevipes*
>Socorro Wren *Thryomanes sissonii*
>Clarion Wren *Troglodytes tanneri*
>Socorro Mockingbird *Mimodes graysoni*

Romania
>   Dalmatian Pelican *Pelecanus crispus* (13)
>   Pygmy Cormorant *Halietor pygmeus* (9)
>   Lesser White-fronted Goose *Anser erythropus* (15)
>   Red-breasted Goose *Branta ruficollis* (4)
>   White-headed Duck *Oxyura leucocephala* (9)
>   Red Kite *Milvus milvus* (19)
>   White-tailed Eagle *Haliaeetus albicilla* (22)
>   Imperial Eagle *Aquila heliaca* (12)
>   Lesser Kestrel *Falco naumanni* (27)
>   Corncrake *Crex crex* (33)
>   Great Bustard *Otis tarda* (18)
>   Slender-billed Curlew *Numenius tenuirostris* (9)

Rwanda
>   Shoebill *Balaeniceps rex* (8)
>   Albertine Owlet *Glaucidium passerinum* (2)
>   Grauer's Swamp Warbler *Bradypterus graueri* (4)
>   Papyrus Yellow Warbler *Chloropeta gracilirostris* (6)
>   Kungwe Apalis *Apalis argentea* (4)

Samoa (to U.S.A.)
>   Bristle-thighed Curlew *Numenius tahitiensis* (9)

Sao Tome e Principe
>   Dwarf Olive Ibis *Bostrychia bocagei*
>   Maroon Pigeon *Columba thomensis*
>   Sao Tome Scops Owl *Otus hartlaubi*
>   Sao Tome Fiscal Shrike *Lanius newtoni*
>   Sao Tome Short-tail *Amaurocichla bocagii*
>   Giant Sunbird *Dreptes thomensis*
>   Sao Tome White-eye *Zosterops ficedulinus*
>   Principe Speirops *Speirops leucophaeus*
>   Sao Tome Grosbeak *Neospiza concolor*

Saudi Arabia
>   Houbara Bustard *Chlamydotis undulata* (23)
>   Sociable Plover *Chettusia gregaria* (10)
>   White-eyed Gull *Larus leucophthalmus* (3)
>   Yemen Thrush *Turdus menachensis* (2)

Senegal
>   Northern Bald Ibis *Geronticus eremita* (7)
>   Marbled Teal *Marmaronetta angustirostris* (15)
>   Yellow-throated Olive Greenbul *Criniger olivaceus* (6)

Seychelles
Seychelles Scops Owl *Otus insularis*
Seychelles Swiftlet *Collocalia elaphra*
Seychelles Magpie-robin *Copsychus sechellarum*
Seychelles Warbler *Acrocephalus sechellensis*
Aldabra Warbler *Nesillas aldabranus*
Seychelles Paradise-flycatcher *Terpsiphone corvina*
Seychelles White-eye *Zosterops modestus*
Seychelles Fody *Foudia sechellarum*

Sierra Leone
White-breasted Guineafowl *Agelastes meleagrides* (4)
Rufous Fishing Owl *Scotopelia ussheri* (5)
Western Wattled Cuckoo-shrike *Campephaga lobata* (4)
Yellow-throated Olive Greenbul *Criniger olivaceus* (6)
White-necked Picathartes *Picathartes gymnocephalus* (5)
Gola Malimbe *Malimbus ballmanni* (3)

Singapore
Spotted Greenshank *Tringa guttifer* (11)
Asian Dowitcher *Limnodromus semipalmatus* (13)
Spoon-billed Sandpiper *Eurynorhynchus pygmeus* (9)

Snares Island (New Zealand)
New Zealand Snipe *Coenocorypha aucklandica* (4)

Society Islands (to France)
Society Islands Ground-dove *Gallicolumba erythroptera* (2)
Society Islands Imperial-pigeon *Ducula aurorae* (2)
Blue Lorikeet *Vini peruviana* (3)
Tahiti Swiftlet *Aerodramus leucophaeus*
Tahiti Monarch *Pomarea nigra*

Socotra (South Yemen)
Socotra Cisticola *Cisticola haesitata*

Solomon Islands
Beck's Petrel *Pterodroma becki* (2)
Solomons Sea Eagle *Haliaeetus sanfordi*
Imitator Sparrowhawk *Accipiter imitator* (2)
Woodford's Rail *Nesoclopeus woodfordi* (3)
San Cristobal Mountain Rail *Gallinula sylvestris*
Yellow-legged Pigeon *Columba pallidiceps* (2)
Nicobar Pigeon *Caloenas nicobarica* (7)
Santa Cruz Ground-dove *Gallicolumba sanctaecrucis* (2)
Thick-billed Ground-dove *Gallicolumba salamonis*

Solomon Island Crowned-pigeon *Microgoura meeki*
Moustached Kingfisher *Halcyon bougainvillei* (2)
Solomons Pitta *Pitta anerythra* (2)
Kolombangara Warbler *Phylloscopus amoenus*
Rennell Shrikebill *Clytorhynchus hamlini*
Malaita Fantail *Rhipidura malaitae*
Gizo White-eye *Zosterops luteirostris*
Nendo White-eye *Zosterops sanctaecrucis*
Sanford's White-eye *Woodfordia lacertosa*

Somalia

Somali Pigeon *Columba oliviae*
Ash's Lark *Mirafra ashi*
Somali Long-clawed Lark *Heteromirafra archeri*
Tana River Cisticola *Cisticola restricta* (2)
Warsangli Linnet *Acanthis johannis*

South Africa (see also Prince Edward Island)

Jackass Penguin *Spheniscus demersus* (2)
Southern Bald Ibis *Geronticus calvus* (3)
Cape Vulture *Gyps coprotheres* (7)
Lesser Kestrel *Falco naumanni* (27)
Wattled Crane *Bugeranus carunculatus* (11)
Corncrake *Crex crex* (33)
White-winged Flufftail *Sarothrura ayresi* (4)
Damara Tern *Sterna balaenarum* (6)
South African Long-clawed Lark *Heteromirafra ruddi* (2)
Botha's Lark *Spizocorys fringillaris*
Yellow-breasted Pipit *Anthus chloris* (2)
Spotted Ground-thrush *Turdus fischeri* (6)

South Korea

Oriental White Stork *Ciconia boyciana* (4)
Crested Shelduck *Tadorna cristata* (5)
Baykal Teal *Anas formosa* (5)
Baer's Pochard *Aythys baeri* (11)
Steller's Sea Eagle *Haliaeetus pelagicus* (4)
Hooded Crane *Grus monacha* (5)
Red-crowned Crane *Grus japonensis* (5)
White-naped Crane *Grus vipio* (6)
Asian Yellow Rail *Coturnicops exquisitus* (5)
Spotted Greenshank *Tringa guttifer* (11)
Spoon-billed Sandpiper *Eurynorhynchus pygmeus* (9)
Japanese Murrelet *Synthliboramphus wumizusume* (5)
Saunders's Gull *Larus saundersi* (7)
Fairy Pitta *Pitta nympha* (7)

South Yemen (see Socotra)

Spain (see also Canary Islands)
Marbled Teal *Marmaronetta angustirostris* (15)
White-headed Duck *Oxyura leucocephala* (9)
Red Kite *Milvus milvus* (19)
Black Vulture *Aegypius monachus* (10)
Spanish Imperial Eagle *Aquila adalberti* (2)
Lesser Kestrel *Falco naumanni* (27)
Great Bustard *Otis tarda* (18)
Little Bustard *Tetrax tetrax* (8)
Audouin's Gull *Larus audouinii* (10)

Sri Lanka
Spot-billed Pelican *Pelecanus philippensis* (2)
Lesser Adjutant *Leptoptilos javanicus* (11)
Sri Lanka Woodpigeon *Columba torringtoni*
Red-faced Malkoha *Phaenicophaeus pyrrhocephalus* (2)
Green-billed Coucal *Centropus chlororhynchus*
Sri Lanka Whistling Thrush *Myiophoneus blighi*
Ashy-headed Laughingthrush *Garrulax cinereifrons*
Sri Lanka Magpie *Urocissa ornata*

St Helena (to U.K.)
St Helena Plover *Charadrius sanctaehelenae*

St Lucia
St Lucia Amazon *Amazona versicolor*
White-breasted Thrasher *Ramphocinclus brachyurus* (2)
St Lucia Black Finch *Melanospiza richardsoni*
Semper's Warbler *Leucopeza semperi*

St Vincent
St Vincent Amazon *Amazona guildingii*
Whistling Warbler *Catharopeza bishopi*

Sudan
Shoebill *Balaeniceps rex* (8)
Sociable Plover *Chettusia gregaria* (10)
Red Sea Cliff Swallow *Hirundo perdita* (2)
Spotted Ground-thrush *Turdus fischeri* (6)

Suriname
Zigzag Heron *Zebrilus undulatus* (9)
Grey-bellied Hawk *Accipiter poliogaster* (10)
Crested Eagle *Morphnus guianensis* (15)

Harpy Eagle *Harpia harpyja* (18)
Orange-breasted Falcon *Falco deiroleucus* (17)
Eskimo Curlew *Numenius borealis* (10)
Bearded Tachuri *Polystictus pectoralis* (9)

Swan Islands (Honduras)
Vitelline Warbler *Dendroica vitellina* (2)

Swaziland
Southern Bald Ibis *Geronticus calvus* (3)
Cape Vulture *Gyps coprotheres* (7)

Sweden
Lesser White-fronted Goose *Anser erythropus* (15)
Red Kite *Milvus milvus* (19)
White-tailed Eagle *Haliaeetus albicilla* (22)
Corncrake *Crex crex* (33)

Switzerland
Red Kite *Milvus milvus* (19)
Corncrake *Crex crex* (33)

Syria
Lesser Kestrel *Falco naumanni* (27)
Great Bustard *Otis tarda* (18)
Houbara Bustard *Chlamydotis undulata* (23)

Taiwan
Japanese Night-heron *Gorsagius goisagi* (6)
Chinese Egret *Egretta eulophotes* (5)
Black-faced Spoonbill *Platalea minor* (7)
Swinhoe's Pheasant *Lophura swinhoii*
Mikado Pheasant *Syrmaticus mikado*
Spotted Greenshank *Tringa guttifer* (11)
Saunders's Gull *Larus saundersi* (7)
Fairy Pitta *Pitta nympha* (7)
Yellow Tit *Parus holsti*

Tanzania
Shoebill *Balaeniceps rex* (8)
Wattled Crane *Bugeranus carunculatus* (11)
Corncrake *Crex crex* (33)
Usambara Eagle Owl *Bubo vosseleri*
Sokoke Pipit *Anthus sokokensis* (2)
Uluguru Bush-shrike *Malaconotus alius*
Swynnerton's Forest Robin *Swynnertonia swynnertoni* (3)

East Coast Akalat *Sheppardia gunningi* (4)
Dappled Mountain Robin *Modulatrix orostruthus* (2)
Usambara Ground Robin *Dryocichloides montanus*
Iringa Ground Robin *Dryocichloides lowei*
Spotted Ground-thrush *Turdus fischeri* (6)
White-winged Apalis *Apalis chariessa* (4)
Karamoja Apalis *Apalis karamojae* (2)
Kungwe Apalis *Apalis argentea* (4)
Long-billed Apalis *Apalis moreaui* (2)
Mrs Moreau's Warbler *Bathmocercus winifredae*
Amani Sunbird *Anthreptes pallidigaster* (2)
Banded Green Sunbird *Anthreptes rubritorques*
Rufous-winged Sunbird *Nectarinia rufipennis*
Tanzanian Mountain Weaver *Ploceus nicolli*
Abbott's Starling *Cinnyricinclus femoralis* (2)

Thailand

Christmas Frigatebird *Fregata andrewsi* (4)
Storm's Stork *Ciconia stormi* (3)
Lesser Adjutant *Leptoptilos javanicus* (11)
Greater Adjutant *Leptoptilos dubius* (7)
White-shouldered Ibis *Pseudibis davisoni* (8)
Giant Ibis *Pseudibis gigantea* (4)
White-winged Duck *Cairina scutulata* (7)
Baer's Pochard *Aythya baeri* (11)
Wallace's Hawk-eagle *Spizaetus nanus* (4)
Chestnut-headed Partridge *Arborophila cambodiana* (2)
Chestnut-necklaced Partridge *Arborophila charltonii* (3)
Crested Fireback *Lophura ignita* (4)
Siamese Fireback *Lophura diardi* (4)
Hume's Pheasant *Syrmaticus humiae* (4)
Malaysian Peacock-pheasant *Polyplectron malacense* (4)
Green Peafowl *Pavo muticus* (8)
Masked Finfoot *Heliopais personata* (6)
Spotted Greenshank *Tringa guttifer* (11)
Asian Dowitcher *Limnodromus semipalmatus* (13)
Spoon-billed Sandpiper *Eurynorhynchus pygmeus* (9)
Chinese Crested Tern *Sterna bernsteini* (5)
Pale-capped Pigeon *Columba punicea* (7)
Large Green-pigeon *Treron capellei* (4)
White-fronted Scops Owl *Otus sagittatus* (4)
Dark-rumped Swift *Apus acuticauda* (3)
Blyth's Kingfisher *Alcedo hercules* (9)
Rufous-necked Hornbill *Aceros nipalensis* (8)
Wrinkled Hornbill *Aceros corrugatus* (3)
Plain-pouched Hornbill *Aceros subruficollis* (4)

Helmeted Hornbill *Rhinoplax vigil* (4)
Gurney's Pitta *Pitta gurneyi* (2)
White-eyed River-martin *Pseudochelidon sirintarae*
Black-throated Robin *Erithacus obscurus* (2)
Grey-sided Thrush *Turdus feae* (4)
Deignan's Babbler *Stachyris rodolphei*
Short-tailed Parrotbill *Paradoxornis davidianus* (5)
Giant Nuthatch *Sitta magna* (3)
Beautiful Nuthatch *Sitta formosa* (7)
Silver Oriole *Oriolus mellianus* (3)

Tonga
Niuafo'ou Megapode *Megapodius pritchardii*
Bristle-thighed Curlew *Numenius tahitiensis* (9)

Torishima (to Japan)
Short-tailed Albatross *Diomedea albatrus*

Trinidad and Tobago
Orange-breasted Falcon *Falco deiroleucus* (17)
White-tailed Sabrewing *Campylopterus ensipennis* (2)

Tristan da Cunha group (to U.K.)
Inaccessible Rail *Atlantisia rogersi*
Gough Moorhen *Gallinula comeri*
Gough Bunting *Rowettia goughensis*
Tristan Bunting *Nesospiza acunhae*
Grosbeak Bunting *Nesospiza wilkinsi*

Tuamotu Archipelago (to France)
Bristle-thighed Curlew *Numenius tahitiensis* (9)
Tuamotu Sandpiper *Prosobonia cancellatus*
Society Islands Ground-dove *Gallicolumba erythroptera* (2)
Society Islands Imperial-pigeon *Ducula aurorae* (2)
Blue Lorikeet *Vini peruviana* (3)
Tuamotu Kingfisher *Halcyon gambieri*

Tubuai Islands (to France)
Rapa Fruit-dove *Ptilinopus huttoni*
Scarlet-breasted Lorikeet *Vini kuhlii* (2)

Tunisia
Marbled Teal *Marmaronetta angustirostris* (15)
White-headed Duck *Oxyura leucocephala* (9)
Lesser Kestrel *Falco naumanni* (27)
Houbara Bustard *Chlamydotis undulata* (23)

Slender-billed Curlew *Numenius tenuirostris* (9)
Audouin's Gull *Larus audouinii* (10)

Turkey
Dalmatian Pelican *Pelecanus crispus* (13)
Pygmy Cormorant *Halietor pygmeus* (9)
Northern Bald Ibis *Geronticus eremita* (7)
Lesser White-fronted Goose *Anser erythropus* (15)
Red-breasted Goose *Branta ruficollis* (4)
Marbled Teal *Marmaronetta angustirostris* (15)
White-headed Duck *Oxyura leucocephala* (9)
White-tailed Eagle *Haliaeetus albicilla* (22)
Black Vulture *Aegypius monachus* (10)
Imperial Eagle *Aquila heliaca* (12)
Lesser Kestrel *Falco naumanni* (27)
Great Bustard *Otis tarda* (18)
Little Bustard *Tetrax tetrax* (8)
Slender-billed Curlew *Numenius tenuirostris* (9)
Audouin's Gull *Larus audouinii* (10)

Turks and Caicos Islands (to U.K.)
Kirtland's Warbler *Dendroica kirtlandii* (4)

U.K. (see also Ascension Island, Bermuda, Cayman Islands, Falkland Islands, Gibralter, Hong Kong, Leeward Islands, Montserrat, Pitcairn Islands, St Helena, Tristan da Cunha, Virgin Islands)
Red Kite *Milvus milvus* (19)
White-tailed Eagle *Haliaeetus albicilla* (22)
Corncrake *Crex crex* (33)

U.S.A. (see also Alaska, Federated States of Micronesia, Guam, Hawaiian Islands, Marshall Islands, Northern Marianas Islands, Palau, Puerto Rico, Samoa, Virgin Islands)
California Condor *Gymnogyps californianus*
Whooping Crane *Grus americana* (2)
Piping Plover *Charadrius melodus* (12)
Thick-billed Parrot *Rhynchopsitta pachyrhyncha* (2)
Red-crowned Green-cheeked Amazon *Amazona viridigenalis* (3)
Spotted Owl *Strix occidentalis* (3)
Eared Trogon *Euptilotis neoxenus* (2)
Red-cockaded Woodpecker *Picoides borealis*
Ivory-billed Woodpecker *Campephilus principalis* (2)
Bachman's Warbler *Vermivora bachmanii* (2)
Golden-cheeked Warbler *Dendroica chrysoparia* (5)
Kirtland's Warbler *Dendroica kirtlandii* (4)
Black-capped Vireo *Vireo atricapillus* (2)

U.S.S.R.

Dalmatian Pelican *Pelecanus crispus* (13)
Pygmy Cormorant *Halietor pygmeus* (9)
Oriental White Stork *Ciconia boyciana* (4)
Lesser White-fronted Goose *Anser erythropus* (15)
Red-breasted Goose *Branta ruficollis* (4)
Crested Shelduck *Tadorna cristata* (5)
Baykal Teal *Anas formosa* (5)
Marbled Teal *Marmaronetta angustirostris* (15)
Baer's Pochard *Aythya baeri* (11)
Scaly-sided Merganser *Mergus squamatus* (4)
White-headed Duck *Oxyura leucocephala* (9)
Red Kite *Milvus milvus* (19)
Pallas's Fish Eagle *Haliaeetus leucoryphus* (8)
White-tailed Eagle *Haliaeetus albicilla* (22)
Steller's Sea Eagle *Haliaeetus pelagicus* (4)
Black Vulture *Aegypius monachus* (10)
Imperial Eagle *Aquila heliaca* (12)
Lesser Kestrel *Falco naumanni* (27)
Hooded Crane *Grus monacha* (5)
Red-crowned Crane *Grus japonensis* (5)
White-naped Crane *Grus vipio* (6)
Siberian Crane *Grus leucogeranus* (5)
Corncrake *Crex crex* (33)
Asian Yellow Rail *Coturnicops exquisitus* (5)
Great Bustard *Otis tarda* (18)
Little Bustard *Tetrax tetrax* (8)
Houbara Bustard *Chlamydotis undulata* (23)
Sociable Plover *Chettusia gregaria* (10)
Slender-billed Curlew *Numenius tenuirostris* (9)
Spotted Greenshank *Tringa guttifer* (11)
Asian Dowitcher *Limnodromus semipalmatus* (13)
Spoon-billed Sandpiper *Eurynorhynchus pygmeus* (9)
Relict Gull *Larus relictus* (4)
Saunders's Gull *Larus saundersi* (7)
Japanese Murrelet *Synthliboramphus wumizusume* (5)
Blakiston's Fish Owl *Ketupa blakistoni* (3)
Large-billed Bush-warbler *Bradypterus major* (4)
Aquatic Warbler *Acrocephalus paludicola* (5)

Uganda

Shoebill *Balaeniceps rex* (8)
Nahan's Francolin *Francolinus nahani* (2)
African Green Broadbill *Pseudocalyptomena graueri* (2)
Forest Ground-thrush *Turdus oberlaenderi* (2)
Kibale Ground-thrush *Turdus kibalensis*

Grauer's Swamp Warbler *Bradypterus graueri* (4)
Papyrus Yellow Warbler *Chloropeta gracilirostris* (6)
Karamoja Apalis *Apalis karamojae* (2)
Turner's Eremomela *Eremomela turneri* (3)
Chapin's Flycatcher *Muscicapa lendu* (3)
Entebbe Weaver *Ploceus victoriae*

United Arab Emirates
Houbara Bustard *Chlamydotis undulata* (23)

Uruguay
Dot-winged Crake *Porzana spiloptera* (2)
Eskimo Curlew *Numenius borealis* (10)
Glaucous Macaw *Anodorhynchus glaucus* (4)
Red-spectacled Amazon *Amazona pretrei* (4)
Sickle-winged Nightjar *Eleothreptus anomalus* (4)
Black-and-white Monjita *Xolmis dominicana* (4)
Strange-tailed Tyrant *Yetapa risoria* (4)
Bearded Tachuri *Polystictus pectoralis* (9)
Marsh Seedeater *Sporophila palustris* (4)
Yellow Cardinal *Gubernatrix cristata* (3)
Saffron-cowled Blackbird *Xanthopsar flavus* (5)
Pampas Meadowlark *Sturnella defilippi* (3)

Vanuatu
Santa Cruz Ground-dove *Gallicolumba sanctaecrucis* (2)
Santo Mountain Starling *Aplonis santovestris*

Venezuela
Zigzag Heron *Zebrilus undulatus* (9)
Northern Screamer *Chauna chavaria* (2)
Semicollared Sparrowhawk *Accipiter collaris* (4)
Grey-bellied Hawk *Accipiter poliogaster* (10)
Solitary Eagle *Harpyhaliaetus solitarius* (10)
Crested Eagle *Morphnus guianensis* (15)
Harpy Eagle *Harpia harpyja* (18)
Orange-breasted Falcon *Falco deiroleucus* (17)
Northern Helmeted Curassow *Pauxi pauxi* (2)
Plain-flanked Rail *Rallus wetmorei*
Rusty-flanked Crake *Laterallus levraudi*
Rusty-faced Parrot *Hapalopsittaca amazonina* (3)
Yellow-shouldered Amazon *Amazona barbadensis* (2)
Long-tailed Potoo *Nyctibius aethereus* (7)
White-tailed Sabrewing *Campylopterus ensipennis* (2)
Tachira Emerald *Amazilia distans*
Scissor-tailed Hummingbird *Hylonympha macrocerca*

Orinoco Softtail *Thripophaga cherriei*
White-throated Barbtail *Margaromis tatei*
Recurve-billed Bushbird *Clytoctantes alixii* (2)
Tachira Antpitta *Grallaria chthonia*
Hooded Antpitta *Grallaricula cucullata* (2)
Shrike-like Cotinga *Laniisoma elegans* (6)
Short-tailed Tody-flycatcher *Todirostrum viridanum*
Bearded Tachuri *Polystictus pectoralis* (9)
White-bellied Dacnis *Dacnis albiventris* (5)
Venezuelan Flowerpiercer *Diglossa venezuelensis*
Yellow-faced Redstart *Myioborus pariae*
Grey-headed Warbler *Basileuterus griseiceps*
Grey-throated Warbler *Basileuterus cinereicollis* (2)
Yellow-faced Siskin *Carduelis yarrellii* (2)
Red Siskin *Carduelis cucullata* (3)

Viet Nam

Milky Stork *Mycteria cinerea* (4)
Lesser Adjutant *Leptoptilos javanicus* (11)
Greater Adjutant *Leptoptilos dubius* (7)
White-shouldered Ibis *Pseudibis davisoni* (8)
Giant Ibis *Pseudibis gigantea* (4)
Black-faced Spoonbill *Platalea minor* (7)
Baer's Pochard *Aythya baeri* (11)
Scaly-sided Merganser *Mergus squamatus* (4)
Orange-necked Partridge *Arborophila davidi*
Imperial Pheasant *Lophura imperialis* (2)
Vo Quy's Pheasant *Lophura hatinhensis*
Edwards's Pheasant *Lophura edwardsi*
Siamese Fireback *Lophura diardi* (4)
Germain's Peacock-pheasant *Polyplectron germaini* (2)
Crested Argus *Rheinartia ocellata* (3)
Green Peafowl *Pavo muticus* (8)
Black-necked Crane *Grus nigricollis* (5)
Bengal Florican *Houbaropsis bengalensis* (4)
Relict Gull *Larus relictus* (4)
Saunders's Gull *Larus saundersi* (7)
Pale-capped Pigeon *Columba punicea* (7)
Blyth's Kingfisher *Alcedo hercules* (9)
Rufous-necked Hornbill *Aceros nipalensis* (8)
Red-collared Woodpecker *Picus rabieri* (3)
Bar-bellied Pitta *Pitta ellioti* (3)
Fairy Pitta *Pitta nympha* (7)
Short-tailed Scimitar-babbler *Jabouilleia danjoui*
Black-hooded Laughingthrush *Garrulax milleti*
Collared Laughingthrush *Garrulax yersini*

Grey-crowned Crocias *Crocias langbianis*
Short-tailed Parrotbill *Paradoxornis davidianus* (5)
Greater Rufous-headed Parrotbill *Paradoxornis ruficeps* (6)
Yellow-billed Nuthatch *Sitta solangiae*
Beautiful Nuthatch *Sitta formosa* (7)

Virgin Islands (to U.K.)
Piping Plover *Charadrius melodus* (12)

Virgin Islands (to U.S.A.)
West Indian Whistling Duck *Dendrocygna arborea* (9)
Piping Plover *Charadrius melodus* (12)

Volcano Islands (to Japan)
Japanese Night-heron *Gorsagius goisagi* (6)

West Germany
Red Kite *Milvus milvus* (19)
White-tailed Eagle *Haliaeetus albicilla* (22)
Corncrake *Crex crex* (33)

Western Samoa
Bristle-thighed Curlew *Numenius tahitiensis* (9)
Tooth-billed Pigeon *Didunculus strigirostris*

Yugoslavia
Dalmatian Pelican *Pelecanus crispus* (13)
Pygmy Cormorant *Halietor pygmeus* (9)
Lesser White-fronted Goose *Anser erythropus* (15)
Red Kite *Milvus milvus* (19)
White-tailed Eagle *Haliaeetus albicilla* (22)
Imperial Eagle *Aquila heliaca* (12)
Lesser Kestrel *Falco naumanni* (27)
Corncrake *Crex crex* (33)
Great Bustard *Otis tarda* (18)
Slender-billed Curlew *Numenius tenuirostris* (9)

Zaire
Shoebill *Balaeniceps rex* (8)
Nahan's Francolin *Francolinus nahani* (2)
Congo Peacock *Afropavo congensis*
Wattled Crane *Bugeranus carunculatus* (11)
Corncrake *Crex crex* (33)
Itombwe Owl *Phodilus prigoginei* (2)
Albertine Owlet *Glaucidium passerinum* (2)

Schouteden's Swift *Schoutedenapus schoutedeni*
African Green Broadbill *Pseudocalyptomena graueri* (2)
Prigogine's Greenbul *Chlorocichla prigoginei*
White-headed Robin-chat *Cossypha heinrichi* (2)
Forest Ground-thrush *Turdus oberlaenderi* (2)
Spotted Ground-thrush *Turdus fischeri* (6)
Grauer's Swamp Warbler *Bradypterus graueri* (4)
Papyrus Yellow Warbler *Chloropeta gracilirostris* (6)
Kungwe Apalis *Apalis argentea* (4)
Kabobo Apalis *Apalis kaboboensis*
Turner's Eremomela *Eremomela turneri* (3)
Chapin's Flycatcher *Muscicapa lendu* (3)
Marungu Sunbird *Nectarinia prigoginei*
Rockefeller's Sunbird *Nectarinia rockefelleri*
Black-lored Waxbill *Estrilda nigriloris*
Loango Slender-billed Weaver *Ploceus subpersonatus* (3)
Lake Lufira Weaver *Ploceus ruweti*
Golden-naped Weaver *Ploceus aureonucha*
Yellow-legged Weaver *Ploceus flavipes*

Zambia

Slaty Egret *Egretta vinaceigula* (3)
Shoebill *Balaeniceps rex* (8)
Wattled Crane *Bugeranus carunculatus* (11)
Corncrake *Crex crex* (33)
White-winged Flufftail *Sarothrura ayresi* (4)
Black-cheeked Lovebird *Agapornis nigrigenis* (3)
White-chested Tinkerbird *Pogoniulus makawai*
Papyrus Yellow Warbler *Chloropeta gracilirostris* (6)

Zimbabwe

Cape Vulture *Gyps coprotheres* (7)
Wattled Crane *Bugeranus carunculatus* (11)
Corncrake *Crex crex* (33)
White-winged Flufftail *Sarothrura ayresi* (4)
Swynnerton's Forest Robin *Swynnertonia swynnertoni* (3)

Appendix 2
Near-threatened species throughout the world

The rationale for this list is given in the Introduction.

Rheidae
Greater Rhea *Rhea americana* Argentina, Bolivia, Brazil, Paraguay, Uruguay
Puna Rhea *Pterocnemia pennata* Argentina, Bolivia, Chile, Peru

Tinamidae
Pale-browed Tinamou *Crypturellus transfasciatus* Ecuador, Peru
Colombian Tinamou *Crypturellus (erythropus) columbianus* Colombia

Spheniscidae
Fiordland Crested Penguin *Eudyptes pachyrhynchus* New Zealand
Galapagos Penguin *Spheniscus mendiculus* Ecuador

Podicipedidae
Titicaca Flightless Grebe *Rollandia micropterum* Bolivia, Peru

Diomedeidae
Galapagos Albatross *Diomedea irrorata* Ecuador

Procellariidae
Providence Petrel *Pterodroma solandri* Lord Howe Island (Australia)
Murphy's Petrel *Pterodroma ultima* Pacific
Barau's Petrel *Pterodroma baraui* Mauritius, Reunion, Rodrigues
Jouanin's Petrel *Bulweria fallax* Indian Ocean
Black-vented Shearwater *Puffinus opisthomelas* Mexico

Hydrobatidae
Sooty Storm-petrel *Oceanodroma tristrami* Hawaiian Islands, Izu and Bonin
    Islands (Japan)

Phalacrocoracidae
Socotra Cormorant *Phalacrocorax nigrogularis* Persian Gulf, Red Sea
Bank Cormorant *Phalacrocorax neglectus* Namibia, South Africa
Crowned Cormorant *Phalacrocorax coronatus* Namibia, South Africa
Red-legged Cormorant *Phalacrocorax gaimardi* Chile, Peru

Ardeidae
Schrenck's Bittern *Ixobrychus eurhythmus* East Asia
Fasciated Tiger-heron *Tigrisoma fasciatum* South America
Malayan Night-heron *Gorsachius melanophus* South-East Asia

Madagascar Pond-heron *Ardeola idae* Madagascar; Central/East Africa
Sumatran Heron *Ardea sumatrana* South-East Asia, Australiasia
Agami Heron *Agamia agami* Central and South America

Ciconiidae
White Stork *Ciconia ciconia* Palearctic, Africa
Jabiru *Jabiru mycteria* Central and South America

Threskiornithidae
Madagascar Crested Ibis *Lophotibis cristata* Madagascar

Anatidae
Swan Goose *Anser cygnoides* East Asia
Bar-headed Goose *Anser indicus* eastern Palearctic; Indian subcontinent
Orinoco Goose *Neochen jubatus* South America
(American) Comb Duck *Sarkidiornis (melanotos) sylvicola* South America
Mandarin Duck *Aix galericulata* China, Japan, Korea, U.S.S.R.
Blue Duck *Hymenolaimus malacorhynchos* New Zealand

Accipitridae
Madagascar Cuckoo-falcon *Aviceda madagascariensis* Madagascar
Lammergeier *Gypaetus barbatus* Palearctic (including Himalayas); Africa, Arabia
Southern Banded Snake Eagle *Circaetus fasciolatus* East Africa to South Africa
Reunion Harrier *Circus maillardi* Comoros, Madagascar, Reunion
Black Harrier *Circus maurus* South Africa
Henst's Goshawk *Accipter henstii* Madagascar
Madagascar Sparrowhawk *Accipiter madagascariensis* Madagascar
New Britain Goshawk *Accipiter princeps* New Britain (Papua New Guinea)
White-browed Hawk *Leucopternis kuhli* Brazil, Peru
Black-and-white Hawk-eagle *Spizastur melanoleucus* Central and South America
Sulawesi Hawk-eagle *Spizaetus lanceolatus* Sulawesi (Indonesia)
Philippine Hawk-eagle *Spizaetus philippensis* Philippines
Black-and-chestnut Eagle *Oroaetus isidori* Andes to 25 degrees south

Falconidae
Striated Caracara *Phalcoboenus australis* Argentina, Chile, Falklands/Malvinas
White-fronted Falconet *Microhierax latifrons* Borneo
Pied Falconet *Microhierax melanoleucus* Indochina
Banded Kestrel *Falco zoniventris* Madagascar
New Zealand Falcon *Falco novaeseelandiae* New Zealand
Saker Falcon *Falco cherrug* Palearctic
Gyr Falcon *Falco rusticolus* Arctic
Taita Falcon *Falco fasciinucha* East and Central Africa

Megapodiidae
Philippine Scrub-fowl *Megapodius cumingii*   Indonesia, Philippines

Cracidae
Baudo Guan *Penelope ortoni*   Colombia, Ecuador
White-crested Guan *Penelope pileata*   Brazil
Black Guan *Chamaepetes unicolor*   Costa Rica, Panama

Tetraonidae
Siberian Spruce Grouse *Dendragapus falcipennis*   U.S.S.R.
Caucasian Black Grouse *Tetrao mlokosiewiczi*   Iran, Turkey, U.S.S.R.
Severtzov's Grouse *Bonasa sewerzowi*   China

Phasianidae
Black-fronted Wood-quail *Odontophorus atrifrons*   Colombia, Venezuela
Dark-backed Wood-quail *Odontophorus melanonotus*   Colombia, Ecuador
Chestnut Wood-quail *Odontophorus hyperythrus*   Colombia
Tacarcuna Wood-quail *Odontophorus dialeucos*   Colombia, Panama
Venezuelan Wood-quail *Odontophorus columbianus*   Venezuela
Black-breasted Wood-quail *Odontophorus leucolaemus*   Costa Rica, Panama
Salle's Quail *Cyrtonyx sallei*   Mexico
Verreaux's Pheasant-partridge *Tetraophasis obscurus*   China
Szechenyi's Pheasant-partridge *Tetraophasis szechenyii*   China
Przevalski's Partridge *Alectoris magna*   China
Snow Mountain Quail *Anurophasis monorthonyx*   Irian Jaya (Indonesia)
Harwood's Francolin *Francolinus harwoodi*   Ethiopia
Finsch's Francolin *Francolinus finschi*   Angola, Congo, Zaire
Grey-striped Francolin *Francolinus griseostriatus*   Angola
Black Wood Partridge *Melanoperdix nigra*   Borneo, Sumatra, West Malaysia
White-cheeked Partridge *Arborophila atrogularis*   Burma, India
Red-breasted Partridge *Arborophila mandellii*   Bhutan, India, Tibet
Crimson-headed Partridge *Haematoryx sanguiniceps*   Borneo
Satyr Tragopan *Tragopan satyra*   Himalayas
Temminck's Tragopan *Tragopan temminckii*   Burma, China, India, Tibet, Viet
    Nam
Crestless Fireback *Lophura erythropthalma*   Borneo, Malaysia, Sumatra
Blue Eared-pheasant *Crossoptilon auritum*   China
Copper Pheasant *Syrmaticus soemmerringi*   Japan
Golden Pheasant *Chrysolophus pictus*   China
Lady Amherst's Pheasant *Chrysolophus amherstiae*   Burma, China, Tibet
Bronze-tailed Peacock-pheasant *Polyplectron chalcurum*   Sumatra (Indonesia)
Mountain Peacock-pheasant *Polyplectron inopinatum*   Malaysia

Turnicidae
Chestnut-backed Button-quail *Turnix castanota*   Australia

Gruidae
Demoiselle Crane *Anthropoides virgo* Palearctic; Indian subcontinent, Sudan

Rallidae
Lesser Rail *Rallus limicola* Mexico, South America, U.S.A.
Andaman Banded Crake *Rallina canningi* Andamans (India)
White-striped Forest Rail *Rallicula leucospila* Irian Jaya (Indonesia)
Brown-backed Wood-rail *Aramides wolfi* Colombia, Ecuador
Black Rail *Laterallus jamaicensis* Central America, Cuba, U.S.A.
Galapagos Crake *Laterallus spilonotus* Galapagos Islands
Ocellated Crake *Micropygia schomburgki* Costa Rica, northern South America
Speckled Crake *Coturnicops notatus* South America
Colombian Crake *Neocrex colombianus* Colombia, Ecuador, Panama

Otididae
Nubian Bustard *Neotis nuba* Sahel
Little Brown Bustard *Eupodotis humilis* Ethiopia, Somalia

Haematopodidae
African Black Oystercatcher *Haematopus moquini* Namibia, South Africa

Charadriidae
Long-billed Plover *Charadrius placidus* Palearctic; Asia
Malaysian Plover *Charadrius peronii* Indonesia, West Malaysia
Sandpiper-plover *Phegornis mitchellii* Argentina, Bolivia, Chile, Peru
Magellanic Plover *Pluvianellus socialis* Argentina, Chile

Scolopacidae
Hudsonian Godwit *Limosa haemastica* North and South America
Little Curlew *Numenius minutus* Palearctic; Asia, Australasia
Latham's Snipe *Gallinago hardwickii* Japan; Australia
Great Snipe *Gallinago media* Palearctic; Africa
Strickland's Snipe *Gallinago stricklandii* Argentina, Chile, Falklands/Malvinas

Laridae
Pacific Gull *Larus pacificus* Australia
Lava Gull *Larus fuliginosus* Galapagos Islands
Roseate Tern *Sterna dougallii* Pan-oceanic
Fairy Tern *Sterna nereis* Australia, New Caledonia, New Zealand

Alcidae
Marbled Murrelet *Brachyramphus marmoratus* Japan, North America
Xantus's Murrelet *Brachyramphus hypoleuca* Mexico, U.S.A.
Craveri's Murrelet *Brachyramphus craveri* Mexico

Columbidae
Eastern Stock Dove *Columba eversmanni* central-southern Asia
White-naped Pigeon *Columba albinucha* Cameroon, Uganda, Zaire
Andaman Woodpigeon *Columba palumboides* Andaman and Nicobar Islands
Japanese Woodpigeon *Columba janthina* islands off Japan
Chilean Pigeon *Columba araucana* Argentina, Chile
Peruvian Pigeon *Columba oenops* Peru
Plain Pigeon *Columba inornata* Cuba, Hispaniola, Jamaica, Puerto Rico
White-winged Dove *Streptopelia reichenowi* Ethiopia, Kenya, Somalia
Andaman Cuckoo-dove *Macropygia rufipennis* Andaman and Nicobar Islands
   (India)
New Britain Bronzewing *Henicophaps foersteri* New Britain (Papua New
   Guinea)
Russet-crowned Quail-dove *Geotrygon goldmani* Panama
Southern Brown Fruit-dove *Phapiteron cinereiceps* Philippines
Crested Quail-dove *Geotrygon versicolor* Jamaica
Flores Green-pigeon *Treron flores* Lesser Sundas (Indonesia)
Yellow-bellied Pigeon *Treron oxyura* Java, Sumatra (Indonesia)
Yellow-vented Pigeon *Treron seimundi* Malaysia, Viet Nam
Marche's Fruit-dove *Ptilinopus marchei* Luzon (Philippines)
Merrill's Fruit-dove *Ptilinopus merrilli* Luzon (Philippines)
Maroon-chinned Fruit-dove *Ptilinopus subgularis* Sulawesi (Indonesia)
Spotted Imperial Pigeon *Ducula carola* Philippines
Blue-tailed Imperial Pigeon *Ducula concinna* Indonesia
Dark-backed Imperial Pigeon *Ducula lacernulata* Bali, Java (Indonesia)
Sombre Pigeon *Cryptophaps poecilorrhoa* Sulawesi (Indonesia)
Long-tailed Mountain Pigeon *Gymnophaps mada* Buru, Seram (Indonesia)

Psittacidae
Red Lory *Eos borneo* Moluccas (Indonesia)
Olive-headed Lorikeet *Trichoglossus euteles* Lesser Sundas (Indonesia)
Mindanao Lorikeet *Trichoglossus johnstoniae* Mindanao (Philippines)
Iris Lorikeet *Psitteuteles iris* Timor, Wetar (Indonesia)
White-naped Lory *Lorius albidinuchus* New Ireland (Papua New Guinea)
Chattering Lory *Lorius garrulus* Moluccas (Indonesia)
Streaked Lorikeet *Charmosyna multistriata* Irian Jaya (Indonesia)
Kaka *Nestor meridionalis* New Zealand
Blue-headed Racquet-tail Parrot *Prioniturus discurus* Philippines
Red-spotted Racquet-tail Parrot *Prioniturus flavicans* Sulawesi (Indonesia)
Black-lored Parrot *Tanygnathus gramineus* Buru (Indonesia)
Pesquet's Parrot *Psittrichas fulgidus* Indonesia, Papua New Guinea
Scarlet-chested Parrot *Neophema splendida* Australia
Wallace's Hanging-parrot *Loriculus flosculus* Indonesia
Javan Hanging-parrot *Loriculus pusillus* Bali, Java (Indonesia)
Blue-winged Macaw *Ara maacana* Argentina, Brazil, Paraguay
Hispaniolan Conure *Aratinga chloroptera* Dominican Republic, Haiti

Sun Conure *Aratinga solstitialis*   northern South America
Santa Marta Parakeet *Pyrrhura viridicata*   Colombia
Rose-crowned Parakeet *Pyrrhura rhodocephala*   Venezuela
Slender-billed Conure *Enicognathus leptorhynchus*   Chile
Barred Parakeet *Bolborhynchus lineola*   Central America, Colombia, Peru,
   Venezuela
Red-fronted Parrotlet *Touit costaricensis*   Costa Rica
Pileated Parrot *Pionopsitta pileata*   Argentina, Brazil, Paraguay
Vulturine Parrot *Gypopsitta vulturina*   Brazil
Yellow-billed Amazon *Amazona collaria*   Jamaica
Cuban Amazon *Amazona leucocephala*   Bahamas, Caymans, Cuba
Hispaniola Parrot *Amazona ventralis*   Dominican Republic, Haiti
Black-billed Amazon *Amazona agilis*   Jamaica

Cuculidae
Sulawesi Hawk-cuckoo *Cuculus crassirostris*   Sulawesi (Indonesia)
Moluccan Cuckoo *Cuculus heinrichi*   Moluccas (Indonesia)
Long-billed Cuckoo *Rhamphomantis megarhynchus*   New Guinea
Scaly Ground-cuckoo *Neomorphus squamiger*   Brazil
Coral-billed Ground-cuckoo *Carpococcyx renauldi*   South-East Asia
Verreaux's Coua *Coua verreauxi*   Madagascar
Kai Coucal *Centropus spilopterus*   Kai Islands (Indonesia)
Rufous Coucal *Centropus unirufus*   Luzon and Polillo Islands (Philippines)

Strigidae
Luzon Slender-billed Scops Owl *Otus longicornis*   Luzon (Philippines)
Rajah's Scops Owl *Otus brookii*   Borneo, Java, Sumatra (Indonesia)
Biak Scops Owl *Otus beccarii*   Biak Island (Indonesia)
Palau Owl *Otus podarginus*   Palau
Giant Scops Owl *Mimizuku gurneyi*   Mindanaao (Philippines)
White-chinned Owl *Pulsatrix koeniswaldiana*   Argentina, Brazil, Paraguay
Javan Owlet *Glaucidium castanopterum*   Java (Indonesia)
Long-whiskered Owlet *Xenoglaux loweryi*   Peru
Andaman Hawk-owl *Ninox affinis*   Andaman and Nicobar Islands (India)
Ochre-bellied Hawk-owl *Ninox ochracea*   Sulawesi (Indonesia)
Fearful Owl *Nesasio solomensis*   Solomon Islands
Unspotted Saw-whet Owl *Aegolius ridgwayi*   Central America
Buff-fronted Owl *Aegolius harrisii*   South America
Philippine Eagle-Owl *Bubo philippensis*   Philippines

Steatornithidae
Oilbird *Steatornis caripensis*   northern South America, Panama, Trinidad

Podargidae
Large Frogmouth *Batrachostomus auritus*   Borneo, Malaysia, Sumatra (Indonesia)

Sri Lanka Frogmouth *Batrachostomus moniliger*   India, Sri Lanka

Caprimulgidae
Hispaniolan Least Pauraque *Siphonorhis brewsteri*   Dominican Republic, Haiti
Eared Poorwill *Otophanes mcleodii*   Mexico
Yucatan Poorwill *Otophanes yucatanicus*   Guatemala, Mexico
St Lucia Nightjar *Caprimulgus otiosus*   St Lucia, Venezuela
Roraiman Nightjar *Caprimulgus whitelyi*   Venezuela
Pygmy Nightjar *Caprimulgus hirundinaceus*   Brazil
Red-necked Nightjar *Caprimulgus ruficollis*   Europe, north Africa; Sahel
Bonaparte's Nightjar *Caprimulgus concretus*   Borneo, Sumatra (Indonesia)

Apodidae
Great Dusky Swift *Aeromis senex*   Argentina, Brazil, Paraguay
Mascarene Swiftlet *Collocalia francica*   Mauritius, Reunion

Trochilidae
Saw-billed Hermit *Ramphodon naevius*   Brazil
Koepcke's Hermit *Phaethornis koepckeae*   Peru
Long-tailed Sabrewing *Campylopterus excellens*   Mexico
Santa Marta Sabrewing *Campylopterus phainopeplus*   Colombia
Napo Sabrewing *Campylopterus villaviscensio*   Ecuador
Fiery-tailed Awlbill *Avocettula recurvirostris*   north-east South America
Spangled Coquette *Lophornis stictolopha*   Colombia, Ecuador, Peru, Venezuela
Pirre Hummingbird *Goethalsia bella*   Panama, Colombia
Blossomcrown *Anthocephala floriceps*   Ecuador
Ecuadorian Piedtail *Phlogophilus hemileucurus*   Ecuador
Peruvian Piedtail *Phlogophilus harterti*   Peru
Pink-throated Brilliant *Heliodoxa gularis*   Ecuador, Peru
Wedge-tailed Hillstar *Oreotrochilus adela*   Bolivia
Rainbow Starfrontlet *Coeligena iris*   Ecuador, Peru
Gorgeted Sunangel *Heliangelus strophianus*   Colombia, Ecuador
Purple-throated Sunangel *Heliangelus viola*   Ecuador, Peru
Bronze-tailed Comet *Polyonymus caroli*   Peru
Perija Metaltail *Metallura iracunda*   Colombia, Venezuela
Hooded Visorbearer *Augastes lumachellus*   Brazil
Stripe-breasted Starthroat *Heliomaster squamosus*   Brazil
Magenta-throated Woodstar *Philodice bryantae*   Costa Rica, Panama

Trogonidae
Hispaniolan Trogon *Temnotrogon roseigaster*   Dominican Republic, Haiti
Ward's Trogon *Harpactes wardi*   Burma, India

Alcedinidae
Philippine Forest Kingfisher *Ceyx melanurus*   Philippines

Brown-winged Kingfisher *Pelargopsis amauroptera* South-East Asia
Javan Kingfisher *Halcyon cyanoventris* Bali, Java (Indonesia)
Winchell's Kingfisher *Halcyon winchelli* Philippines
Lazuli Kingfisher *Halcyon lazuli* Seram (Indonesia)
New Britain Kingfisher *Halcyon albonotata* New Britain (Papua New Guinea)
Sombre Kingfisher *Halcyon funebris* Halmahera (Indonesia)
Obscure Kingfisher *Halcyon enigma* Talaud Islands (Indonesia)
Spotted Wood Kingfisher *Halcyon lindsayi* Philippines

Todidae
Narrow-billed Tody *Todus angustirostris* Dominican Republic, Haiti

Momotidae
Tody Motmot *Hylomanes momotula* Central America, Colombia
Blue-throated Motmot *Aspatha gularis* El Salvador, Guatemala, Honduras, Mexico

Coraciidae
Pitta-like Ground-roller *Atelornis pittoides* Madagascar

Galbulidae
Copper-chested Jacamar *Galbula pastazae* Brazil, Colombia, Ecuador

Bucconidae
Sooty-capped Puffbird *Bucco noanamae* Colombia
Lanceolated Monklet *Micromonacha lanceolata* Brazil, Colombia, Costa Rica, Panama, Peru
Chestnut-headed Nunlet *Nonnula amaurocephala* Brazil

Capitonidae
Five-coloured Barbet *Capito quinticolor* Colombia
Red-vented Barbet *Megalaima lagrandieri* Kampuchea, Laos, Viet Nam
Black-throated Barbet *Megalaima eximia* Borneo
Red-faced Barbet *Lybius rubrifacies* Rwanda, Tanzania, Uganda
Chaplin's Barbet *Lybius chaplini* Zambia

Indicatoridae
Pygmy Honeyguide *Indicator pumilio* Kenya, Rwanda, Uganda, Zaire
Orange-rumped Honeyguide *Indicator xanthonotus* Himalayas
Malaysian Honeyguide *Indicator archipelagicus* Borneo, Malaysia, Sumatra, Thailand

Ramphastidae
Saffron Toucanet *Baillonius bailloni* Argentina, Brazil

Grey-breasted Mountain-toucan *Andigena hypoglauca* Colombia, Ecuador, Peru
Plate-billed Mountain-toucan *Andigena laminirostris* Colombia, Ecuador
Black-billed Mountain-toucan *Andigena nigrirostris* Colombia, Ecuador
Red-breasted Toucan *Ramphastos dicolorus* Argentina, Brazil, Paraguay

Picidae
Tawny Piculet *Picumnus fulvescens* Brazil
Mottled Piculet *Picumnus nebulosus* Argentina, Brazil, Paraguay, Uruguay
Spot-crowned Piculet *Picumnus subtilis* Peru
Speckle-chested Piculet *Picumnus steindachneri* Peru
Hispaniolan Piculet *Nesoctites micromegas* Dominican Republic, Haiti
Stierling's Woodpecker *Dendropicos stierlingi* Malawi, Mozambique, Tanzania
Arabian Woodpecker *Picoides dorae* Saudi Arabia, North Yemen, South Yemen
White-browed Woodpecker *Piculus aurulentus* Argentina, Brazil, Paraguay
Black-bodied Woodpecker *Dryocopus schulzi* Argentina, Paraguay
Robust Woodpecker *Campephilus robustus* Argentina, Brazil, Paraguay

Eurylaimidae
Wattled Broadbill *Eurylaimus steeri* Philippines
Hose's Broadbill *Calyptomena hosei* Borneo

Furnariidae
Tawny Tit-spinetail *Synallaxis yanacensis* Bolivia, Peru
Araucaria Tit-spinetail *Leptasthenura setaria* Argentina, Brazil
Hoary-throated Spinetail *Synallaxis kollari* Brazil
Russet-mantled Canastero *Thripophaga berlepschi* Peru
Red-eyed Thornbird *Phacellodomus erythrophthalmus* Brazil
Chestnut-backed Thornbird *Phacellodomus dorsalis* Peru
Bay-capped Wren-spinetail *Spartonoica maluroides* Argentina, Brazil, Uruguay
Curve-billed Reedhaunter *Limnornis curvirostris* Argentina, Brazil, Uruguay
Equatorial Greytail *Xenerpestes singularis* Ecuador, Peru
White-browed Foliage-gleaner *Philydor amaurotis* Argentina, Brazil
Ochre-breasted Foliage-gleaner *Philydor lichtensteini* Argentina, Brazil, Paraguay
Black-capped Foliage-gleaner *Philydor atricapillus* Argentina, Brazil
Russet-mantled Foliage-gleaner *Philydor dimidiatus* Brazil, Paraguay
White-collared Foliage-gleaner *Philydor fuscus* Brazil
Peruvian Recurvebill *Philydor ucalayae* Peru
Chestnut-capped Foliage-gleaner *Automolus rectirostris* Brazil
Rufous-breasted Leafscraper *Sclerurus scansor* Argentina, Brazil, Paraguay

Formicariidae
Spot-backed Antshrike *Hypoedaleus guttatus* Argentina, Brazil, Paraguay

Large-tailed Antshrike *Mackenziaena severa* Argentina, Brazil, Paraguay
Silvery-cheeked Antshrike *Sakesphorus cristatus* Brazil
Upland Antshrike *Thamnophilus aroyae* Bolivia, Peru
Spot-breasted Antvireo *Dysithamnus stictothorax* Argentina, Brazil
Klages's Antwren *Myrmotherula klagesi* Brazil
Unicoloured Antwren *Myrmotherula unicolor* Brazil
Band-tailed Antwren *Myrmotherula urosticta* Brazil
Serra Antwren *Formicivora serrana* Brazil
Rufous-tailed Antbird *Drymophila genei* Brazil
Ochre-rumped Antbird *Drymophila ochropygia* Brazil, Paraguay
Streak-capped Antwren *Terenura maculata* Argentina, Brazil, Paraguay
Yapacana Antbird *Myrmeciza disjuncta* Venezuela
Bare-eyed Antbird *Rhegmatorhina gymnops* Brazil
Buff-banded Antpitta *Myrmornis stictoptera* Colombia, Nicaragua, Panama
Great Antpitta *Grallaria excelsa* Venezuela
Elusive Antpitta *Grallaria eludens* Peru
Scallop-breasted Antpitta *Grallaricula loricata* Venezuela
Peruvian Antpitta *Grallaricula peruviana* Peru
Ochre-fronted Antpitta *Grallaricula ochraceifrons* Peru

Conopophagidae
Black-cheeked Gnateater *Conopophaga melanops* Brazil

Rhinocryptidae
Slaty Bristlefront *Merulaxis ater* Brazil
White-breasted Tapaculo *Scytalopus indigoticus* Brazil

Cotingidae
Black-and-gold Cotinga *Tijuca atra* Brazil
Hooded Berryeater *Carpornis cucullatus* Brazil
Scarlet-breasted Fruiteater *Pipreola frontalis* Bolivia, Ecuador, Peru
Fiery-throated Fruiteater *Pipreola chlorolepidota* Ecuador, Peru
Scaled Fruiteater *Ampelioides tschudii* Colombia, Ecuador, Peru, Venezuela
Purple-throated Cotinga *Porphyrolaema porphyrolaema* Brazil, Colombia,
     Ecuador, Peru
Crimson Fruitcrow *Haematoderus militaris* Brazil, Guianas, Suriname
Red-ruffed Fruitcrow *Pyroderus scutatus* South America
White Cotinga *Carpodectes hopkei* Colombia, Ecuador, Panama
Three-wattled Bellbird *Procnias tricarunculata* Costa Rica, Nicaragua, Panama
Bare-throated Bellbird *Procnias nudicollis* Argentina, Brazil, Paraguay

Pipridae
Orange-crowned Manakin *Heterocercus aurantiivertex* Ecuador, Peru

Tyrannidae
Cinnamon-bellied Ground-tyrant *Muscisaxicola capistrata* southern South America
Santa Marta Bush-tyrant *Myiotheretes pernix* Colombia
Rufous-bellied Bush-tyrant *Myiotheretes fuscorufus* Bolivia, Peru
D'Orbigny's Chat-tyrant *Ochthoeca oenanthoides* Argentina, Bolivia, Chile, Peru
Piura Chat-tyrant *Ochthoeca piurae* Peru
Cock-tailed Tyrant *Alectrurus tricolor* Argentina, Bolivia, Brazil, Paraguay
Velvety Black-tyrant *Knipolegus nigerrimus* Argentina, Bolivia, Chile, Peru
Shear-tailed Grey-tyrant *Muscipipra vetula* Argentina, Brazil, Paraguay
Tumbes Tyrant *Tumbezia salvini* Peru
Ochraceous Pewee *Contopus ochraceus* Costa Rica, Panama
Belted Flycatcher *Xenotriccus callizonus* Guatemala, Mexico
Pileated Flycatcher *Aechmolophus mexicanus* Mexico
Tawny-chested Flycatcher *Aphanotriccus capitalis* Costa Rica, Nicaragua
Black-billed Flycatcher *Aphanotriccus audax* Colombia, Panama
Orange-banded Flycatcher *Myiophobus lintoni* Ecuador
White-cheeked Tody-flycatcher *Todirostrum albifacies* Peru
Hangnest Tody-tyrant *Idioptilon nidipendulum* Brazil
Zimmer's Tody-tyrant *Idioptilon aenigma* Brazil
Eye-ringed Tody-tyrant *Idioptilon orbitatum* Brazil
Boat-billed Tody-tyrant *Microcochlearius josephinae* Brazil, Guyana, Suriname
White-breasted Pygmy-tyrant *Myiornis albiventris* Peru
Buff-throated Tody-tyrant *Hemitriccus rufigularis* Bolivia, Peru
Cinnamon-breasted Tody-tyrant *Hemitriccus cinnamomeipectus* Peru
Southern Bristle-tyrant *Pogonotriccus eximius* Argentina, Brazil, Paraguay
Venezuelan Bristle-tyrant *Pogonotriccus venezuelanus* Venezuela
Bay-ringed Tyrannulet *Leptotriccus sylviolus* Argentina, Brazil, Paraguay
Oustalet's Tyrannulet *Phylloscartes oustaleti* Brazil
Serra do Mar Tyrannulet *Phylloscartes difficilis* Brazil
Reiser's Tyrannulet *Xanthomyias reiseri* Brazil, Paraguay
Grey-capped Tyrannulet *Oreotriccus griseocapillus* Brazil

Pittidae
Mangrove Pitta *Pitta megarhyncha* Bangladesh south-east to Sumatra
Blue-naped Pitta *Pitta nipalensis* Bhutan, Burma, India, Nepal, Viet Nam
Elegant Pitta *Pitta elegans* Moluccas, Lesser Sundas (Indonesia)
Giant Pitta *Pitta caerulea* Burma, Borneo, Sumatra, Thailand, West Malaysia
Blue-headed Pitta *Pitta baudi* Borneo
Garnet Pitta *Pitta granatina* Borneo, Malaysia, Sumatra

Alaudidae
Williams's Bush Lark *Mirafra williamsi* Kenya
Friedmann's Bush Lark *Mirafra pulpa* Ethiopia, Kenya

Short-clawed Lark *Mirafra chuana* Botswana, South Africa
Red Lark *Mirafra burra* South Africa
Sclater's Lark *Spizocorys sclateri* Namibia, South Africa
Obbia Lark *Calandrella obbiensis* Somalia

Hirundinidae
Golden Swallow *Tachycineta euchrysea* Dominican Republic, Haiti, Jamaica
Blue Swallow *Hirundo atrocaerulea* East, Central and southern Africa
Cameroon Mountain Roughwing *Psalidoprocne fuliginosa* Cameroon, Fernando Po

Motacillidae
South Georgia Pipit *Anthus antarcticus* South Georgia

Campephagidae
Buru Cuckoo-shrike *Coracina fortis* Buru (Indonesia)
Kai Cuckoo-shrike *Coracina dispar* east Banda Sea islands (Indonesia)
Pied Cuckoo-shrike *Coracina bicolor* Sulawesi (Indonesia)
Sumba Cuckoo-shrike *Coracina dohertyi* Sumba and Flores (Indonesia)
Sharp-tailed Cuckoo-shrike *Coracina mcgregori* Mindanao (Philippines)
Black-breasted Triller *Chlamydochaera jefferyi* Borneo
Little Minivet *Pericrocotus lansbergei* Sumbawa and Flores (Indonesia)
White-bellied Minivet *Pericrocotus erythropygius* India

Pycnonotidae
Straw-headed Bulbul *Pycnonotus zeylanicus* Thailand, Greater Sundas, West Malaysia
Grey-headed Bulbul *Pycnonotus priocephalus* India
Yellow-throated Bulbul *Pycnonotus xantholaemus* India
Yellow-eared Bulbul *Pycnonotus penicillatus* Sri Lanka
Cameroon Mountain Greenbul *Andropadus montanus* Cameroon, Nigeria
Grey-headed Greenbul *Phyllastrephus poliocephalus* Cameroon, Nigeria
Sassi's Olive Greenbul *Phyllastrephus lorenzi* Uganda, Zaire
Nicobar Bulbul *Hypsipetes nicobariensis* Nicobar Islands (India)

Irenidae
Yellow-quilled Leafbird *Chloropsis flavipennis* Mindanao, Cebu, Leyte (Philippines)
Blue-masked Leafbird *Chloropsis venusta* Sumatra

Laniidae
Grey-crested Helmet-shrike *Prionops poliolopha* Kenya, Tanzania
Turati's Boubou *Laniarius turatii* Guinea, Guinea-Bissau, Sierra Leone
Mfumbiri Bush-shrike *Laniarius mufumbiri* Burundi, Kenya, Rwanda, Uganda, Zaire
Bornean Bristlehead *Pityriasis gymnocephala* Borneo

Vangidae
Bernier's Vanga *Oriolia bernieri* Madagascar

Troglodytidae
Bar-winged Wood-wren *Henicorhina leucoptera* Peru

Mimidae
Galapagos Mockingbird *Nesomimus transfasciatus* Galapagos Islands

Muscicapidae
Turdinae
Gould's Shortwing *Brachypteryx stellata* Himalayas to China, Viet Nam
White-bellied Shortwing *Brachypteryx major* India
Herero Chat *Namibornis herero* Angola, Namibia
Angola Cave-chat *Xenocopsychus ansorgei* Angola
Ryukyu Robin *Erithacus komadori* Nansei Shoto (Japan)
Przevalski's Redstart *Phoenicurus alaschanicus* China
Blue-fronted Robin *Cinclidium frontale* Nepal east to Laos, Viet Nam
Purple Cochoa *Cochoa purpurea* Himalayas to China, Viet Nam
Green Cochoa *Cochoa viridis* Himalayas to China, Viet Nam
Rufous-brown Solitaire *Myadestes leucogenys* Brazil, Ecuador, Guyana, Peru, Venezuela
White-tailed Bushchat *Saxicola leucura* Burma, Indian subcontinent
Jerdon's Bushchat *Saxicola jerdoni* India east to Laos
Malayan Whistling-thrush *Myiophoneus robinsoni* Malaysia
Red-backed Thrush *Zoothera erythronota* Sulawesi and Banggai Islands (Indonesia)
Pied Thrush *Zoothera wardii* Bhutan, India, Nepal, Sri Lanka
Ashy Thrush *Zoothera cinerea* Luzon, Mindoro (Philippines)
Spot-winged Thrush *Zoothera spiloptera* Sri Lanka
Long-billed Thrush *Zoothera monticola* Himalayas east to Viet Nam
Kivu Ground-thrush *Turdus tanganjicae* Rwanda, Uganda, Zaire
Sao Tome Thrush *Turdus olivaceofuscus* Sao Tome e Principe
Unicoloured Thrush *Turdus haplochrous* Bolivia
La Selle Thrush *Turdus swalesi* Dominican Republic, Haiti

Orthonychinae
Papuan Whipbird *Androphobus viridis* Irian Jaya (Indonesia)
Greater Melampitta *Melampitta gigantea* New Guinea

Timaliinae
Rufous-winged Illadopsis *Trichastoma rufescens* West Africa
Grey-breasted Babbler *Malacopteron albogulare* Borneo, Sumatra, West Malaysia
Bornean Wren-babbler *Ptilocichla leucogrammica* Borneo

Streaked Ground-babbler *Ptilocichla mindanensis* Philippines
Marbled Wren-babbler *Napothera marmorata* Sumatra, West Malaysia
Spotted Wren-babbler *Spelaeornis formosus* Bangladesh, Burma, India
Wedge-tailed Jery *Hartertula flavoviridis* Madagascar
Chestnut-eared Babbler *Stachyris whiteheadi* Luzon (Philippines)
Striped Babbler *Stachyris striata* Luzon (Philippines)
Grey-faced Tit-babbler *Macronous kelleyi* Laos, Viet Nam
Miniature Tit-babbler *Micromacronus leytensis* Philippines
Rufous-tailed Moupinia *Moupinia poecilotis* China
Slender-billed Babbler *Turdoides longirostris* Burma, India, Nepal
Giant Babax *Babax waddelli* China
Grey Laughingthrush *Garrulax maesi* China, Viet Nam
Chestnut-backed Laughingthrush *Garrulax nuchalis* Burma, India
White-cheeked Laughingthrush *Garrulax vassali* Laos, Viet Nam
Yellow-throated Laughingthrush *Garrulax galbanus* Bangladesh, China, India
Barred Laughingthrush *Garrulax lunulatus* China
Spot-breasted Laughingthrush *Garrulax merulinus* India east to Viet Nam
Nilgiri Laughingthrush *Garrulax cacchinans* India
White-breasted Laughingthrush *Garrulax jerdoni* India
Striped Laughingthrush *Garrulax virgatus* India
Brown-capped Laughingthrush *Garrulax austeni* Burma, India
Streaked Barwing *Actinodura souliei* China, Viet Nam
Yellow-throated Fulvetta *Alcippe cinerea* Bangladesh, India, Nepal
Spectacled Fulvetta *Alcippe ruficapilla* China
Rufous-throated Fulvetta *Alcippe rufogularis* India east to Viet Nam
Red-collared Flycatcher-babbler *Lioptilus rufocinctus* Rwanda, Zaire
Chapin's Flycatcher-babbler *Lioptilus chapini* Zaire
Spotted Crocias *Crocias albonotatus* Java (Indonesia)

Panurinae
Spot-breasted Parrotbill *Paradoxornis guttaticollis* India east to China
Spectacled Parrotbill *Paradoxornis conspicillatus* China
Brown-winged Parrotbill *Paradoxornis brunneus* China
Chinese Parrotbill *Paradoxornis heudei* China, U.S.S.R.

Polioptilinae
Cream-bellied Gnatcatcher *Polioptila lactea* Argentina, Brazil, Paraguay

Sylviinae
White-winged Warbler *Bradypterus carpalis* East and Central Africa
Bamboo Warbler *Bradypterus alfredi* East and Central Africa
Long-tailed Bush-warbler *Bradypterus caudatus* Luzon and Mindanao (Philippines)
Friendly Bush-warbler *Bradypterus accentor* Sabah (Malaysia)
Sri Lanka Bush-warbler *Bradypterus palliseri* Sri Lanka

Mrs Benson's Warbler *Nesillas mariae*   Comoros
Broad-billed Flycatcher-warbler *Abroscopus hodgsoni*   Bhutan, Burma, India, Nepal
White-eyed Prinia *Prinia leontica*   Guinea, Ivory Coast, Sierra Leone
Forest Prinia *Prinia robertsi*   Mozambique, Zimbabwe
Rudd's Apalis *Apalis ruddi*   Malawi, Mozambique, South Africa
Chirinda Apalis *Apalis chirindensis*   Mozambique, Zimbabwe
Pearson's Warbler *Apalis melanura*   Angola, Zaire
Brown Emu-tail *Dromaeocercus brunneus*   Madagascar
Black-headed Stream Warbler *Bathmocercus cerviniventris*   West Africa
Somali Short-billed Crombec *Sylvietta philippae*   Ethiopia, Somalia
Yemen Warbler *Parisoma buryi*   Saudi Arabia, North Yemen
Rand's Warbler *Randia pseudozosterops*   Madagascar
Whitney's Thicket-warbler *Cichlornis whitneyi*   Solomons, Vanuatu
Bougainville Thicket-warbler *Cichlornis llaneae*   Bougainville (Papua New Guinea)
New Britain Thicket-warbler *Cichlornis grosvenori*   New Britain (Papua New Guinea)
Rufous-faced Thicket-warbler *Ortygocichla rubiginosa*   New Britain (Papua New Guinea)
Shade Warbler *Vitia parens*   San Cristobal (Solomons)

Malurinae
White-throated Grasswren *Amytornis woodwardi*   Australia
Black Grasswren *Amytornis housei*   Australia
Yellowhead *Mohoua ochrocephala*   New Zealand
Yellow Chat *Epthianura crocea*   Australia

Muscicapinae
Streaky-breasted Jungle-flycatcher *Rhinomyias addita*   Buru (Indonesia)
Russet-backed Jungle-flycatcher *Rhinomyias oscillans*   Flores, Sumba (Indonesia)
Luzon Jungle-flycatcher *Rhinomyias insignis*   Luzon (Philippines)
Goodfellow's Jungle-flycatcher *Rhinomyias goodfellowi*   Mindanao (Philippines)
Kashmir Red-breasted Flycatcher *Ficedula subrubra*   India, Pakistan, Sri Lanka
Rufous-throated Flycatcher *Ficedula rufigula*   Sulawesi (Indonesia)
Cryptic Flycatcher *Ficedula crypta*   Luzon, Mindanao (Philippines)
Black-and-orange Flycatcher *Ficedula nigrorufa*   India
White-bellied Blue Flycatcher *Niltava pallipes*   India
Sunda Blue Flycatcher *Niltava caerulata*   Borneo, Sumatra (Indonesia)
Dusky Blue Flycatcher *Muscicapa sordida*   Sri Lanka
Nilgiri Flycatcher *Muscicapa albicaudata*   India
Kimberley Flycatcher *Microeca tormenti*   Australia

Platysteirinae
Ward's Flycatcher *Pseudobias wardi*   Madagascar
Margaret's Batis *Batis margaritae*   Angola, Zaire, Zambia
Woodward's Batis *Batis fratrum*   Malawi, Mozambique, South Africa, Zimbabwe
White-fronted Wattle-eye *Platysteira albifrons*   Angola

Monarchinae
Sao Tome Paradise-flycatcher *Terpsiphone atrochalybea*   Sao Tome
Bedford's Paradise-flycatcher *Terpsiphone bedfordi*   Zaire
Rufous Paradise-flycatcher *Terpsiphone cinnamomea*   Philippines
Versicolour Flycatcher *Mayrornis versicolor*   Fiji
Flores Monarch *Monarcha sacerdotum*   Flores (Indonesia)
White-tailed Monarch *Monarcha leucurus*   Kai Islands (Indonesia)
Black-tipped Monarch *Monarcha loricatus*   Buru (Indonesia)

Rhipidurinae
Blue Fantail *Rhipidura superciliaris*   Philippines
Black-and-cinnamon Fantail *Rhipidura nigrocinnamomea*   Mindanao (Philippines)
Tawny-backed Fantail *Rhipidura superflua*   Buru (Indonesia)
St Matthias Fantail *Rhipidura matthiae*   St Matthias Islands (Indonesia)

Aegithalidae
Pygmy Tit *Psaltria exilis*   Java (Indonesia)

Paridae
White-fronted Tit *Parus semilarvatus*   Luzon, Mindanao (Philippines)

Sittidae
Corsican Nuthatch *Sitta whiteheadi*   Corsica

Dicaeidae
Legge's Flowerpecker *Dicaeum everetti*   Sri Lanka
Mindoro Flowerpecker *Dicaeum retrocinctum*   Mindoro (Philippines)

Nectariniidae
Plain-backed Sunbird *Anthreptes reichenowi*   Central and East Africa
Uluguru Violet-backed Sunbird *Anthreptes neglectus*   Kenya, Mozambique, Tanzania
Ursula'a Mouse-coloured Sunbird *Nectarinia ursulae*   Cameroon
Moreau's Sunbird *Nectarinia moreaui*   Tanzania
Neergaard's Sunbird *Nectarinia neergaardi*   Mozambique, South Africa
Loveridge's Sunbird *Nectarinia loveridgei*   Tanzania

Zosteropidae
Pale-bellied White-eye *Zosterops consobrinorum* Sulawesi (Indonesia)
Pearl-bellied White-eye *Zosterops grayi* Kai Besar (Indonesia)
Buru Yellow White-eye *Zosterops buruensis* Buru (Indonesia)
Pagalu White-eye *Zosterops griseovirescens* Pagalu Island (Equatorial Guinea)
Crested White-eye *Lophozosterops dohertyi* Flores, Sumbawa (Indonesia)
Pygmy White-eye *Oculocincta squamifrons* Borneo
Thick-billed White-eye *Heleia crassirostris* Flores, Sumbawa (Indonesia)

Meliphagidae
White-tufted Honeywater *Lichmera squamata* Lesser Sundas, Tanimbars
   (Indonesia)
Buru Honeyeater *Lichmera deningeri* Buru (Indonesia)
White-chinned Myzomela *Myzomela albigula* East Papuan Islands (Indonesia)
Eungella Honeyeater *Meliphaga (Lichenostomus) hindwoodi* Australia
Orange-cheeked Honeyeater *Oreornis chrysogenys* Irian Jaya (Indonesia)
Black-faced Friarbird *Philemon moluccensis* Buru, Kai, Tanimbar Islands
   (Indonesia)
Short-bearded Melidectes *Melidectes nouhuysi* Irian Jaya (Indonesia)
Vogelkop Melidectes *Melidectes leucostephes* Irian Jaya (Indonesia)
Grey Honeyeater *Conopophila whitei* Australia
Gurney's Sugarbird *Promerops gurneyi* Mozambique, South Africa, Zimbabwe

Emberizidae
Emberizinae
Fukien Slaty Bunting *Latoucheornis siemsseni* China
Jankowski's Bunting *Emberiza jankowskii* China, North Korea, U.S.S.R.
Henslow's Sparrow *Ammodramus henslowii* Canada, U.S.A.
Oaxaca Sparrow *Aimophila notosticta* Mexico
White-throated Sierra-finch *Phrygilus erythronotus* Bolivia, Peru
Peg-billed Finch *Acanthidops bairdii* Costa Rica
Black-throated Finch *Melanodera melanodera* southern South America
Little Inca-finch *Incaspiza watkinsi* Peru
Citron-headed Yellow Finch *Sicalis luteocephala* Bolivia
Buff-throated Pampa-finch *Embernagra longicauda* Brazil
Dubois's Seedeater *Sporophila ardesiaca* Brazil
White-throated Seedeater *Sporophila albogularis* Brazil
Tawny-bellied Seedeater *Sporophila hypoxantha* central South America
Dark-throated Seedeater *Sporophila ruficollis* central South America
Black-bellied Seedeater *Sporophila melanogaster* Brazil
Greater Large-billed Seed-finch *Oryzoborus maximiliani* Latin America
Lesser Large-billed Seed-finch *Oryzoborus crassirostris* northern South Amer-
   ica
Slate-blue Seedeater *Amaurospiza relicta* Mexico
Santa Marta Seedeater *Catamenia oreophila* Colombia

White-rimmed Brush-finch *Atlapetes leucopis*   Colombia, Ecuador
Dusky-headed Brush-finch *Atlapetes fuscoolivaceus*   Colombia
Rufous-eared Brush-finch *Atlapetes rufigenis*   Peru

Cardinalinae
Thick-billed Saltator *Saltator maxillosus*   Argentina, Brazil, Paraguay
Black-cowled Saltator *Saltator nigriceps*   Ecuador, Peru
Masked Saltator *Saltator cinctus*   Ecuador

Thraupinae
Brown Tanager *Orchesticus abeillei*   Brazil
Tacarcuna Bush-tanager *Chlorospingus tacarcunae*   Panama
Pirre Bush-tanager *Chlorospingus inornatus*   Panama
Slaty-backed Hemispingus *Hemispingus goeringi*   Venezuela
Rufous-browed Hemispingus *Hemispingus rufosuperciliaris*   Peru
Chat-tanager *Calyptophilus frugivorus*   Dominican Republic, Haiti
Azure-shouldered Tanager *Thraupis cyanoptera*   Brazil, Paraguay
Blue-and-gold Tanager *Buthraupis arcaei*   Costa Rica, Panama
Orange-throated Tanager *Wetmorethraupis sterrhopteron*   Peru
Gilt-edged Tanager *Tangara cyanoventris*   Brazil
Blue-whiskered Tanager *Tangara johannae*   Colombia, Ecuador
Dotted Tanager *Tangara varia*   Brazil, French Guiana, Suriname, Venezuela
Green-naped Tanager *Tangara fucosa*   Panama
Viridian Dacnis *Dacnis viguieri*   Colombia, Panama
Tit-like Dacnis *Xenodacnis parina*   Ecuador, Peru
Giant Conebill *Oreomanes fraseri*   Bolivia, Colombia, Ecuador, Peru

Parulidae
Colima Warbler *Vermivora crissalis*   Mexico, U.S.A.
Pirre Warbler *Basileuterus ignotus*   Panama
White-striped Warbler *Basileuterus leucophrys*   Brazil

Drepanididae
Hawaii Creeper *Oreomystis mana*   Hawaiian Islands
Maui Creeper *Paroreomyza montana*   Hawaiian Islands

Vireonidae
Chestnut-sided Shrike-vireo *Vireolanius melitophrys*   Guatemala, Mexico
Slaty Vireo *Vireo brevipennis*   Mexico
San Andres Vireo *Vireo caribeus*   Isla San Andres (Colombia)
Dwarf Vireo *Vireo nelsoni*   Mexico
Blue Mountain Vireo *Vireo osburni*   Jamaica

Icteridae
St Lucia Oriole *Icterus laudabilis*   St Lucia

Jamaican Blackbird *Nesopsar nigerrimus* Jamaica
Mountain Grackle *Macroagelaius subalaris* Colombia
Nicaraguan Grackle *Quiscalus nicaraguensis* Nicaragua

Fringillidae
Tristram's Serin *Serinus syriacus* Middle East
Papyrus Canary *Serinus koliensis* Burundi, Kenya, Rwanda, Uganda, Zaire
Salvadori's Serin *Serinus xantholaema* Ethiopia
Lemon-breasted Canary *Serinus citrinipectus* Central and South Africa
Protea Serin *Serinus leucopterus* South Africa
Drakensberg Siskin *Serinus symonsi* Lesotho, South Africa
Roborovski's Rosefinch *Kozlowia roborowskii* China
Scottish Crossbill *Loxia scotica* Scotland

Estrildidae
Shelley's Crimson-wing *Cryptospiza shelleyi* Burundi, Rwanda, Uganda, Zaire
Pink-throated Twinspot *Hypargos margaritatus* Mozambique, South Africa
Neumann's Waxbill *Estrilda thomensis* Angola
Five-coloured Munia *Lonchura quinticolor* Lesser Sundas (Indonesia)
Yellow-rumped Mannikin *Lonchura flaviprymna* Australia
Timor Sparrow *Padda fuscata* Timor (Indonesia)

Ploceidae
Passerinae
Sind Sparrow *Passer pyrrhonotus* Pakistan

Ploceinae
Fox's Weaver *Ploceus spekeoides* Uganda
Black-throated Weaver *Ploceus benghalensis* India

Sturnidae
Copper-tailed Glossy Starling *Lamprotornis cupreocauda* West Africa
Spot-winged Starling *Saroglossa spiloptera* Bhutan, Burma, India, Nepal
Sri Lanka White-headed Starling *Sturnus senex* Sri Lanka
White-headed Starling *Sturnus erythropygius* Andamans and Nicobars (India)
Mount Apo Myna *Basilornis miranda* Mindanao (Philippines)

Dicruridae
Principe Drongo *Dicrurus modestus* Principe
Aldabra Drongo *Dicrurus aldabranus* Aldabra
Andaman Drongo *Dicrurus andamanensis* Andamans (India)

Cracticidae
Tagula Butcherbird *Cracticus louisiadensis* Tagula Island (Papua New Guinea)

Paradisaeidae
Macgregor's Bird-of-paradise *Macgregoria pulchra*   Indonesia, Papua New Guinea
Paradise Crow *Lycocorax phrrhopterus*   Moluccas (Indonesia)
Wallace's Standard-wing *Semioptera wallacei*   Moluccas (Indonesia)
Pale-billed Sicklebill *Drepanornis bruijnii*   New Guinea
Brown Sicklebill *Epimachus meyeri*   New Guinea
King Bird-of-paradise *Diphyllodes respublica*   West Papuan Islands
Red Bird-of-paradise *Paradisaea rubra*   West Papuan Islands
Emperor Bird-of-paradise *Paradisaea guilielmi*   Papua New Guinea
Blue Bird-of-paradise *Paradisaea rudolphi*   Papua New Guinea

Corvidae
Tufted Jay *Cyanocorax dickeyi*   Mexico
Lidth's Jay *Garrulus lidthi*   Amami-oshima, Tokunoshima (Japan)
White-winged Magpie *Urocissa whiteheadi*   China, Laos, Viet Nam
White-bellied Treepie *Dendrocitta leucogastra*   India
Black-browed Treepie *Dendrocitta frontalis*   India east to Viet Nam
Andaman Treepie *Dendrocitta bayleyi*   Andamans (India)
Ratchet-tailed Treepie *Temnurus temnurus*   Hainan (China), Viet Nam
Pleske's Ground Chough *Podoces pleskei*   Iran
Palm Crow *Corvus palmarum*   Cuba, Dominican Republic, Haiti
White-necked Crow *Corvus leucognaphalus*   Caribbean

INDEXES

This index covers species mentioned in the Checklist and those in Appendix 1, but not Appendix 2. Entries for English names are in almost all cases restricted to the last word of the name: when the name consists of a single word, it is included in the index. Page numbers are for the first occurrence of each name in the Checklist; subsequent occurrences are not included.

This index covers species mentioned in the Checklist and those in Appendix 1, but not Appendix 2. Genera are listed with their starting page number. Species are listed in the form *olivei, Turnix.*

Hylorchilus 118
hyperythra, Brachypteryx 119
hyperythrus, Odontophorus 35
hypochroma, Sporophila 150
hypoleucos, Falco 30
hypoleucus, Capito 95
Hypopyrrhus 160
Hypothymis 138
hypoxantha, Gerygone 134
hypoxantha, Neodrepanis 111
hypoxantha, Pyrrhura 75
Hypsipetes 116

ibadanensis, Malimbus 164
icterotis, Ognorhynchus 74
Icterus 159
Idioptilon 108
ignita, Lophura 38
iheringi, Formicivora 101
imitator, Accipiter 26
imperialis, Amazona 78
imperialis, Ardea 14
imperialis, Campephilus 96
imperialis, Lophura 38
Incaspiza 148
indica, Sypheotides 51
inexpectata, Torreornis 148
inexspectata, Tyto 81
infuscata, Henicopernis 23
infuscata, Synallaxis 98
innotata, Aythya 21
inornata, Lophura 38
insignis, Saxicola 122
insularis, Junco 148
insularis, Otus 82
insulata, Sporophila 150
intermedia, Psittacula 72
internigrans, Perisoreus 169
Iodopleura 106
iphis, Pomarea 138
ireneae, Otus 82
isabellae, Oriolus 166

Jabouilleia 125
Jacamaralcyon 94

jacucaca, Penelope 33
jacutinga, Pipile 33
jamesi, Phoenicoparrus 17
japonensis, Grus 44
javanicus, Leptoptilos 15
javensis, Megalaima 95
jefferyi, Pithecophaga 28
johannis, Acanthis 161
jubatus, Rhynochetos 50
Junco 148
junoniae, Columba 60

kaboboensis, Apalis 132
kaempferi, Idioptilon 108
kalinowskii, Nothoprocta 4
karamojae, Apalis 131
keayi, Gallicolumba 62
Ketupa 83
kibalensis, Turdus 123
kinabaluensis, Spilornis 25
kirtlandii, Dendroica 155
kleinschmidti, Erythrura 162
kochi, Pitta 110
koepckeae, Cacicus 159
kubaryi, Corvus 169
kuehni, Myzomela 146
kuehni, Zosterops 144
kuhlii, Vini 68
kupeensis, Malaconotus 117

lacernulata, Leucopternis 26
lacertosa, Woodfordia 145
lafresnayanus, Tricholimnas 46
lanaiensis, Myadestes 122
langbianis, Crocias 127
Laniisoma 105
lanioides, Lipaugus 106
Lanius 117
laperouse, Megapodius 31
Larus 57
Laterallus 48
laticincta, Platysteira 137
laysanensis, Anas 20
leari, Anodorhynchus 73
ledanti, Sitta 141

ICBP Study Reports

1. Turkish Bustard Survey 1981
2. Bengal Florican Survey 1982
7. Bird Conservation in the Pacific Islands 1986
8. The Fuerteventura Stonechat Project 1985
9. Waterbirds in South-East Sumatra 1984
10. Survey of Houbara Bustards in Fuerteventura 1984/85
11. Bird Conservation Priorities in Nigeria 1985
12. Ornithological Survey of Lake Tota 1982
13. Assessment of Illegal Shooting & Catching of Birds in Malta 1985
14. Results of Census of Milky Stork in West Java 1984
15. Conservation of Oku Mountain Forest, Cameroon 1986
17. Eradication of Feral Goats from Small Islands 1986
18. Bottleneck Areas for Migratory Birds in the Mediterranean Region 1987
19. Cambridge Conservation Study: Taita Hills, Kenya 1985
20. Zahamena Forest (Madagascar) Expedition 1985
21. An Account of the Illegal Catching and Shooting of Birds in Cyprus during 1986
22. A Review of the Problems affecting Palearctic Migratory Birds in Africa 1987
23. Report of the University of East Anglia Martinique Oriole Expedition 1986
24. A Survey of the Avifauna of Sao Tome and Principe 1987
25. A Survey of the Endemic Avifauna of the Comoro Islands 1985
26. The Coastal Wetlands of Liberia: Their Importance for Wintering Waterbirds 1986
27. The Conservation Status of Imperial and Red-necked Parrots on Dominica 1987

£4 each from ICBP

Other ICBP Publications

Threatened Birds of Africa and related Islands – The ICBP/IUCN Red Data Book 1985. Fully revised 3rd edition (Part I) Authors: N. J. Collar and S. N. Stuart. 795 pp. (£24.00 incl. of p & p).
Birds of Lebanon and the Jordan Area (English text) 1970. S. Vere Benson. 218 pp. (£4.50 incl. of p & p).
Birds of Lebanon, Syria and Jordan and for use in neighbouring Arab states (Arabic text) 1984. S. Vere Benson. 127 pp. (£5.00 incl. of p & p).
A Guide to Birds of South America 1982. Rodolphe Meyer de Schauensee. 498 pp. (£23.50 incl. of p & p).